Music vs The Man

Music vs The Man

Peter Rowe

Music vs The Man

Copyright © 2020 by Peter Rowe

All rights reserved under the Pan-American and International Copyright Conventions. This book may not be reproduced in whole or in part, except for brief quotations embodied in critical articles or reviews, in any form or by any means, electronic or mechanical, including photocopying, recording, or by any information storage and retrieval system now known or hereinafter invented, without written permission of the publisher, Armin Lear Press.

Cover Design: C.S. Fritz
Line Drawings and Mugshots Montage: Peter Rowe

For further information, contact:

Armin Lear Press
825 Wildlife
Estes Park, CO 80517

ISBN 978-1-7354650-7-4

*When asked by an interviewer
if he considered jazz to be serious music,
trumpeter Dizzy Gillespie replied,
"People have died for this music.
It doesn't get much more serious than that."*

Publisher's Note: To support the focus on storytelling in this book, we have deliberately broken with conventions related to citations. All source material for quoted passages is noted in the Bibliography, regardless of whether or not Endnotes are associated with them.

Contents

1. **The Clash** **1**
   - The Roots of the Conflict. 2
2. **You Say You Want a Revolution** **25**
   - John Lennon. 26
   - Victor Jara 40
   - The Rolling Stones 44
   - The Plastic People and the
   - Velvet Revolution 79
   - Dead on Arrival 85
3. **Up from Slavery** **99**
   - Josephine Baker. 100
   - Paul Robeson. 120
   - Leadbelly. 130
   - Billie Holiday. 142
   - Chuck Berry. 159
   - Nina Simone. 176
4. **Music and Power.** **183**
   - Music vs The Kremlin. 184
   - Wagner, Strauss and Hitler. 210
   - Miriam Makeba 218
   - Singing for a Cause 228
   - Narcocorridos: Mexico's Deadly Music Business ... 243
   - Music vs Donald Trump 254
5. **Only in America** **265**
   - Frank Sinatra. 266
   - Rock and Roll. 292
   - Louie Louie and the FBI 326
   - Van Halen 337
   - Michael Jackson. 353
6. **But Wait! There's More!** **368**
   - Sir Paul McCartney. 369
   - Fans, Groupies and the Death of a Blues Brother. . 386
   - Charlie Manson. 403
   - The Twenty-Seven Club 418
   - Songs About The Man. 439

Endnotes **456**
Bibliography **474**
Acknowledgments **482**
Index **484**
The Author **495**

1. The Clash

The Roots of the Conflict

The Urban Dictionary defines "The Man" as: *Noun (derogatory, semi-proper) A term used to describe any class of people who wield power and are seen as oppressive.*

The Man usually wears a uniform. A cop, a jailer, a border guard. For Keith Richards and Jimi Hendrix, The Man wore the uniforms of Canadian customs guards and Mounties. For Jim Morrison, the uniform of the Miami Police. But The Man isn't always uniformed. He can be an oppressive father, as it was for Elton John, Brian Wilson and Lou Reed. The Man can be a powerful political figure. For Pussy Riot it was Vladimir Putin. For German composer Richard Strauss it was Adolf Hitler. For John Lennon it was J. Edgar Hoover. For Billie Holiday it was Harry Anslinger, the first commissioner of the United States Treasury Department's Federal Bureau of Narcotics. For Frank Sinatra it was…complicated. We'll get to Frank later.

Since time immemorial fierce battles have raged between singers, musicians, bands, fans, and The Man—the authorities. The battle has raged since the days of the Greek and Roman empires. In ancient Greece, Apollo represented order, harmony and civilization while Dionysus was the chaotic, frenzied god of wine, women and song—in modern parlance, "sex, drugs and rock and roll." Dionysus even had his own groupies, the Maenads, the "raving ones", intoxicated by music and drink. When King Pentheus of Thebes banned the worship of Dionysus, the Maenads lured him into the woods and tore him apart.

The battle between *Music* and *The Man* heated to fever pitch in the twentieth century. The Man won most battles, but music ultimately won most wars. The passionate embattled response of young Russians to the Beatles turned out to be a far more potent force in winning the Cold War and ending the USSR than all of America's missiles and rhetoric. On the other hand, many musicians, including the Beatles, were victims of the War on Drugs—a war, I argue, that was specifically created in the 1920s to battle the insidious force of jazz.

Many singers have been incarcerated for their music. Others have died for it, like Chilean folksinger Victor Jara, baritone Paul Robeson, DJ Alan Freed, protest singer Phil Ochs and Rolling Stone Brian Jones. Young readers in the twenty-first century may be astonished to learn of the fear that the authorities had of jazz and rock and roll in the twentieth century and the lengths they went to control and destroy the music and the musicians.

Before diving into the particular tales of the many musicians, singers and bands who have butted heads with the authorities over the years, let's consider what it is about music of all the arts that makes it so uniquely vulnerable to run-ins with the law. Dozens of musicians from ancient times to the present have found themselves in conflict with the authorities. One would be hard pressed to make a similar list of other kinds of artists. Painters lead lives every bit as bohemian as musicians, yet few of them have ended up in prison. It is true that Renaissance painter Michelangelo Caravaggio was charged with murder. Alcoholic action painter Jackson Pollock killed himself (and a passenger) in a car accident. His wife, Lee Krasner, also an acclaimed painter, was arrested for her political activism and claimed that she had "seen the insides of most of New York's best jails". But the short list of painters interacting with The Man virtually ends there. Novelists and dramatists have far more opportunity to create subversive criticism of authority than musicians do yet few of them are in active conflict with the authorities. So, what is it about musicians that puts them so frequently in the crosshairs of The Man?

For starters, perhaps it is the nature of musicians' lives. Writers and painters, and even filmmakers and architects, largely toil away in the quiet privacy of their studios. Musicians by contrast work in public—usually at night, in alcohol-fueled bars, nightclubs, and if they are lucky, arenas—creating rambunctious reactions from large numbers of people. Musicians often come from the wrong side of the tracks, and often, almost by necessity, flaunt flamboyance in lifestyle, hairstyle, and dress. There is also something similar about the star and the politician that perhaps naturally brings the two into conflict. Both, with their big egos, commanding personalities and bravura, must get on stage and engage an audience. The meek and shy need not apply. It certainly seems in the careers of people as diverse as Frank Sinatra, the Rolling Stones, and Paul Robeson that the *elected* authorities were offended by the attention that these *unelected* performers were getting, and wanted to use their authority to knock them off their perch. There does seem to be something about the typical personalities of musicians and the typical personalities of political officials that so often brings them into conflict with each other. It is much more than just "hip vs straight". It is a culture war between the two.

Perhaps it is the music they make, which seems to inflame passions and engage energy in a way few other things on earth can do. This is plainly witnessed at a midnight mid-summer rave on a beach in Ibiza, with Electronic Dance Music being pumped through massive speakers, splitting the eardrums of sweating dancers. Crazily it also can be the case when simply the quality or genre of music is being questioned. In 1979, at the infamous Disco Demolition Night at Comisky Park in Chicago, 50,000 people showed up to watch the explosion of a huge crate of disco records. This sacrificial ritual, honoring their faintly ridiculous mantra "Disco Sucks" got the giant crowd so aroused that they stormed the baseball field and had to be dispersed by riot police.

This writer was part of a riot at the 1966 Newport Folk Festival, battling police and tearing down fences to try to gain entry to the festival. What revolutionary superstar were we risking life and limb to hear? Bob Dylan? Joan Baez? No – the goofy minor league folk sextet Jim Kweskin's Jug Band, who sang their quaint old-tyme tunes to the accompaniment of washboards, cider-jugs, combs and kazoos.

Even when music itself does not incite passion and violence, it seems to attract it. In November 2015, an attack on a concert by the Eagles of Death in the Bataclan Theatre in Paris left ninety dead and two hundred wounded. Six months later a shooter killed fifty people inside the Pulse nightclub in Orlando and wounded fifty-three more, many of whom later reported that they thought the gunshots were part of the music blasting through the nightclub's speakers. A 2017 attack on Ariana Grande's concert in Manchester, England killed twenty-two and wounded one hundred and twenty. In October of that same year, the deadliest mass shooting in American history took place at the Harvest Music Festival, when a gunman fired one thousand rounds at the audience, killing sixty and wounding more than eight hundred.

Perhaps we should back up and ask a more basic question—why do people sing songs? Why do we make music? The answers may reveal something ancient and profound about the battle between Music and The Man and the links between music, sex and violence.

Charles Darwin has something to say about it. During and following his epic five-year sailing trip around the world on the *Beagle* the acclaimed British scientist made many startling and world-altering observations, not least of which was the concept of evolution.

Darwin described an utterly new way of looking at man's place in nature, one that would shake the religious view of creation to its core.

One of Darwin's proposals was that humans developed music in imitation of the way that birds used music, first as a way of finding, courting and wooing sexual partners (and thus continuing the species), and second as tool for organizing society for hunting and battle. "Musical tones and rhythms," said Darwin, "were used by our half-human ancestors, during the season of courtship, when animals of all kinds are excited not only by love, but by the strong passions of jealousy, rivalry and triumph."

What Darwin did not know but anthropologists have discovered in recent years is that music likely predated speech. We made music before we could speak—and not only our crowd of *Homo Sapiens*, but the Neanderthals as well. Scientists are virtually unanimous in thinking that Neanderthals did not have speech—but apparently had music, because in recent years, a carved flute found in a Neanderthal graveyard in Slovenia was carbon-dated back to 30,000 BCE.

Birds use their songs to announce *Here I am! I'm full of energy! I can make a pretty song, and I can do other things too! I'm feeling horny! Where are you? Are you interested in getting together?* They also use songs to say, *Watch out—there's danger! This is my territory! This is my mate! We're going to build a nest here, so this tree is for me – for us.* Humans, unlike birds, could not fly away from danger, but they could make noises that would say all the same things. They could communicate, *Let's band together and maybe make a big enough noise that we can scare away those lions and tigers and bears that are threatening us.* Perhaps they could even use their new musical voices and sounds to stealthily communicate with each other saying, *Let's go and kill one of them, and eat it.* Then, as the human population began to grow, and one group of people was in competition with another for the resources and the food, they could use the drums and horns to make a big noise to stoke up their courage up so they could, *Go kill those other people who want to eat all those wild animals, and then go and kill and eat them ourselves.*

So developed the two predominant strains of music—music in the service of love and sex, and music in the service of hunting, violence and warfare. Both strains are very much alive today. Way back in the mid-nineteenth century, as he analyzed the early origins of music, Darwin observed that "love is still the commonest theme of our songs," and it is of course just as true today. A recent study of *Billboard* Magazine's Top 100 songs over the last decade found that eighty percent of them referenced sex and lovemaking. Unquestionably, in our contemporary society, and in a commercial, popular sense, love songs are most important to us. In ancient societies, though, songs of love and courtship were perceived as inferior "female" songs, whereas songs of bravery, of the hunt, of warfare were thought of as "male" songs.

The first instruments—horns, ripped from the skulls of recently killed rams—were likely still dripping with blood when they were first used. They are of course themselves a symbol of power, sex and virility—hence the expression, "horny".

Since music releases the hormone oxytocin, which makes us more trusting of other people, it can serve both romance and the tribal, aggressive requirements of communal hunting and warfare. But since males ran the society, it was the male songs invoking action and aggression that were thought important and that were honored and preserved. Female songs, often frankly quite bold in their descriptions and yearnings about love-making—and often drifting into ecstatic and mystical territory that women were more comfortable in than men, were often dismissed, scorned or even banned by the frequently misogynistic men who ruled ancient, and, let's face it, modern societies. It is little wonder considering some of the lyrics. *Plow My Vulva*, one of the very few female songs that survives from the ancient society of Mesopotamia, goes like this, first in the imagined words of Inanna, the goddess of love and fertility, then in the words of the king of Mesopotamia, Dumuzi. (WARNING: Parental guidance recommended.)

(Inanna)

I, the maiden—who will plow it?

My nakedness, the wet and well-watered ground—

I, the young lady—who will station there an ox?

(King Dumuzi)

Young lady, may the king plow it for you.

May Dumuzi, the king, plow it for you.

(Inanna)

The lord of all things, fill my holy churn!

Plow my vulva, man of my heart!

Try and get that one into rotation on Top 40 radio without getting the station closed down. It is perhaps little wonder that this "female" music was scorned and often destroyed, whereas the "male" music, often overtly militaristic, has survived. "Male" music is not used much in hunting anymore, but it is certainly used to pump up adrenalin and team spirit in sports. Skiers give themselves courage by blasting down mountains with AC/DC playing in their earbuds. In the empty wilderness, hikers and climbers bellow out old Beatles tunes like *Twist and Shout*, exuberantly off-key. Football fans howl the ubiquitous Queen anthem, *We Are the Champions* in arenas around the world. Though it seems unlikely one would be able to imagine Henry David Thoreau drunkenly belting out Queen songs in Wembley Stadium, he attested that "When I hear music, I fear no danger. I am invulnerable. I see no foe. I am related to the earliest times, and to the latest."

In a world where warfare is now dominated by drones, smart bombs and intercontinental missiles (and soon, space forces!) military music no longer has quite the role that it once did. It is not gone, though. The United States supports 130 military bands, spending three times as much on military music as on the National Endowment for the Arts—making military music the largest commitment to the arts of the entire US government.

Curiously both strains (music in the service of love and sex, and music in the service of hunting, violence and warfare) developed from the very fringes of society—often in fact, from slaves. The long history of music is one of creation by outsiders, by the underclass, by the young and powerless, with this outsider music being shunned, scorned and shut down by the authorities, then, after years or even decades, being co-opted, accepted and eventually even celebrated by the people in power.

Slaves played a very important role in the development of music in the ancient world. This should not come as any surprise to us, since almost all the important idioms of modern popular music were created by black American slaves—or their very recent descendants. This strange tradition began in Egypt, continued to Greece and Rome, and was extensively practiced by the Arabs, who bought their female slave singers, the *quiyan*, with them as they successfully invaded Spain and Portugal in the Eighth Century.

In societies like ancient Egypt or Greece, or nineteenth century America, where slaves did much of the singing, and indeed the songwriting, we can easily understand how the charged relationship between musicians coming from the very margins of society and the authorities who ran and policed society could easily be strained.

The Arabs chose their slaves according to their perceptions and stereotypes. Berbers were praised for their "fidelity and energy", while Nubians were thought to be "self-indulgent and delicate".

Abyssinians were condemned as being "useless for singing". The *qiyan* were sexual slaves, women kept both for their sexual prowess and their skills as singers. Some were bold and outrageous. One, known as Inan, sang about a drunken male lover's uselessness in a similar tone to Shakespeare's famous description of liquor as a drink that "increases the passion but decreases the performance." Inan sang:

There is no pleasure in a lover that is unattainable
O host of lovers, how execrable is love
If there is flabbiness in the lover's prick

Once The Man, her owner, sobered up, one can only imagine there might have been hell to pay for such a provocative lyric.

Male singing slaves in the ancient Arabic world were known as mukhammathum, which translates as "effeminate men". One of the most famous of them, Abū Nuwās, is described in classical Arabic literature as the great master of wine songs. His reputation did not prevent The Man from destroying his music. Centuries later, the Egyptian Ministry of Culture in 2001 burned 6000 copies of his rhymes because of what they felt were homoerotic themes in his work.

The culture wars over music extended to Greece as well. Socrates described extensively his distinction between what he called "popular music" (dēmōdēs mousikē) and "great music" (megistē mousikē). Once again, popular music was slagged as being only suitable for women to hear. A flute known as an aulos, usually played by women, was particularly scorned, just as 2000 years later the Soviet Union would damn—and ban—the saxophone. Aristotle joined in the battles over music. "The flute is not an instrument which is expressive of moral character," he declared in his tome Politics'. "It is too exciting."

Plato, in The Laws, distinguished between "songs fitting for females and those fitting for males." The manly songs included those that "incline towards courage," and "lean towards the orderly and the moderate." Female songs were seen as immoderate and dangerous. The most infamous female songs of the Greek era were those sung by the (female, harp-playing) Sirens. As described by Homer in the Odyssey, those songs so enchanted the sailors on King Odysseus' ships that they drew in too near and crashed onto the rocks of their island.

The Greeks recognized two strains in their culture—the Apollonian, emphasizing rule-making and restraint, and the Dionysian, embracing rule-breaking and excess. Two instruments were emblematic—the lyre, an elegant stringed instrument promoting harmony and order, and the flute, demanding human breath to operate, and thus considered a dangerous instigator of Dionysian passion. It's not hard to guess which one the authorities approved of, and which one they condemned.

The wild Dionysian cults of Greece morphed into the even wilder Bacchanalian sects of Rome. These cults, honoring the god Bacchus, held orgiastic festivals mostly but not entirely run by women that featured loud music created by drums and cymbals, rivers of wine, and violent sexual promiscuity. The Bacchanalian revels lasted for many years, but when a prostitute named Hispala Faecenia spilled the beans on the goings-on, the Roman Senate suppressed the cults, and according to the historian Livy the authorities arrested 7000 members of the cult and executed many of them.

It is easy to draw parallels between the response of the authorities to the Bacchanalian festivals of ancient Rome and the response of the authorities to the rock festivals of the late 1960s and early 1970s. Like the establishment and authorities in the hippie era, the Romans got exercised about hair as well as music. Seneca the Elder beefed about how the "revolting pursuits of singing and dancing" were corrupting the youth so much so that they were "braiding their hair and thinning their voices to a feminine lilt."

Almost no accounts exist of Roman popular music, since the pantomimes where it was performed were feared and smeared by the Roman authorities. Roman senators were forbidden to attend these popular pantomimes, and soldiers forbidden to participate in them.

The most famous story of music in ancient Rome is the one about how Emperor Nero "fiddled while Rome burned." Rome certainly did burn in AD 64, and (to the consternation of more conservative Roman authorities) Nero did play an instrument known as the kithara. Whether he really was plucking away on it as the city went up in flames is not accurately known, but the story does tell us about the general disapproving attitude of the Roman authorities toward music.

There was an Altamont-like event in ancient Rome that several historians of the day refer to as the "Pantomime riots", when frenzied music fans revolted after a star performer cancelled his performance over a pay dispute. Within a few years Tiberius banished the pantomimes, claiming they were "frequently the fomenters of sedition against the state and of debauchery."

At about the same time, the Chinese authorities were even more adamantly opposed to music. The Chinese thinker Mozi wrote a very hostile diatribe titled Against Music that elaborated on his simple premise that "Making music is wrong!"

Through Europe's Dark Ages there are many examples of the authorities' condemnation of music. Pope Eutychius commanded, "Do not allow women's song and ring-dances and playful games and songs in the churchyard." St. Augustine complained that "all night long abominations have been sung and danced to with songs." Bishop Caesarius of Arles whined about people "who come to the feasts of saints only to get drunk, sing songs with lewd words, lead ring-dances and twirl like the devil." Frequently, the church fathers would get back to the familiar theme of blaming women for music. Caesarius complained about the women "who know by heart and recite out loud the Devil's songs, erotic and obscene," and Bishop Haymo in the ninth century managed to get lawmakers to pass statutes outlawing the "whorish wantonness" of the "songs of prostitutes."

The Middle Ages give us one of the strangest and perhaps most shocking stories of Music vs The Man. According to the tale, the German village of Hamelin had become so infested by rats that the desperate Town Fathers hired a Pied Piper to try to solve the problem. A "pied" piper was an itinerant musician who dressed in "pied" or multi-colored clothing and played what were thought to be "magic pipes". The mayor of the village offered the piper one thousand guilders to get rid of the rats, which the musician promptly did by using his magic flute to lure the rats into the Weser River, where they all drowned. The mayor, like countless officials since, then proceeded to welch on the deal, and offered to pay only fifty guilders for the de-ratting. The piper extracted a horrifying revenge. He returned to the town on a Sunday when all the adults were in church and used his magical musical skills to lure all the town's children to the same river to suffer the same fate as the rats.

Various analysts have tried to parse the violent tale. The most lurid, perhaps, is from historian William Manchester, (most famous for his definitive book about the killing of John F. Kennedy), who proposed a theory that the Pied Piper was a psychopathic pedophile. Others have debunked his claim and proposed alternate stories of what might have happened to the musically bewitched kids. Regardless, the story passed down at bedtime to generations of children certainly indicates the fear and awe in which musicians—especially itinerant, travelling ones—were held a thousand years ago. It isn't that different today. When a busload of scruffy heavy metal rockers or rap singers show up in town dressed in their version of "pied" garb, the local establishment and authorities still get worried.

The musical stars of our age are generally fairly tame by comparison to those of the Renaissance. With the exception of Howlin' Wolf, Leadbelly and Phil Spector, few have been accused of murder. Benvenuto Cellini confessed to several murders, and numerous other crimes, including sodomy and embezzlement. He was the ultimate Renaissance Man, working as a musician, a poet, a goldsmith, a sculptor and a writer. He is immortalized today by the Rolex Cellini brand of watches. His criminal lifestyle and many interactions with The Man ultimately resulted in almost no time behind bars. He was protected by both the Medicis and the Church. When one of the Pope's advisors suggested that Cellini ought to be punished for committing a murder, the pontiff demurred, saying "You don't understand the matter as well as I do. You should know that men like Benvenuto, unique in their profession, need not be subject to the law."

Other Renaissance musicians managed to escape punishment for violent crimes. Bartolomeo Tromboncino, one of the leading musicians of his day, murdered his wife in a jealous rage, but he too seems to have had a Sinatra-like immunity to prosecution, and went unpunished for the crime. Carlo Gesualdo, a celebrated composer of madrigals, went even further, murdering both his wife and her lover, the Duke of Andria, and mutilating their bodies. The crime only seems to have increased the interest in him by music lovers, and so even though historians describe him as a psychopath and a sadist, and music critic Alex Ross calls him "irrefutably badass", he was never charged or had to suffer for his crime.

While the church and the authorities of the Renaissance seemed to treat the extraordinary transgressions of musicians with silk gloves, they got wildly exercised about some of the technicalities of the music. Again, it seems to have been a result of the long-standing hatred and fear of women by the Roman Catholic Church.

Vocal polyphony (multiple voices, twin melodies, or, in essence, the use of harmony) was first created in the Renaissance period, used both by secular and religious singers. It was considered frivolous, impious and lascivious by the Church, and was banned by Pope John XXII in 1322. He railed against "disciples of the new school, concerned with dividing the beat." The Church saw polyphony as an incitement to sin, with John Wycliffe believing that the new kind of music would "stir vain men to dancing". Dominican Giovanni Caroli was more pointed in his critique of the new style of music. "I rather hate and detest those things," he declared, "since they most truly seem to pertain more to the levity of women than to the dignity of leading men." Once again, The Man was blaming women for the perceived sinfulness of music.

Eventually the Church gave up the fight, and accepted and co-opted the new music, indeed almost canonizing the very polyphonous Gregorian chants sung by monks and named after Pope Gregory I. Six hundred years later, in the 1970s and 80s, the Church would repeat the process, abandoning their fight against the electric guitar and instead creating what only a few years earlier would have been thought to be oxymoronic genres of Christian Heavy Metal music and Christian Rap.

Back in the day when Kings and Queens really knew how to throw their weight around, they sometimes just banned music altogether. England's King Henry V issued a royal decree that "no ditties shall be made or sung by minstrels or others." One hundred years after that, another royal decree banned the printing of song sheets, since they could "subtilly and craftily instruct the kings' people and especially the youth of the nation."

It wasn't only in Europe where music was slagged, but in China as well. Sinologist Kuang Yu Chen describes the music of the Middle Ages as "composed by licentious or promiscuous young women." Confucian philosopher Zhu Xi (1130-1200) stirred up a huge controversy about the music he condemned as "coming from the streets and alleys as folk songs, that youth, male and female, sang to each other, expressing their love and feelings."

No one, though, could come up with grotesque solutions to imaginary problems like the Church of Rome. Since the Church did not want and did not allow women in their religious choirs, young boys were enlisted to sing the high notes. But their voices changed when they hit puberty just as they had mastered the art. The Church came up with the idea of castrating the boys to delay or avoid puberty, so they could continue to hit those high soprano notes. So that evil female temptresses would not sully the hallowed choir lofts, boys were turned, with a surgeon's scalpel, into what became known as *castrati*. The tradition—surely the most aggressive and disgusting attempt by The Man to influence music, continued from the Renaissance right into the twentieth century. The castrato Alessandro Moreschi sang in the Sistine Chapel in 1913, and some believe that soprano Domenico Mancini, singing in the papal choir as late as 1959, was a *castrati*. In 2001, the Italian newspaper *Corriere della Sera* urged the Vatican to make a formal apology for the practice, but to date it has not done so.

For the record, the Bee Gees, skilled as they were in the upper octaves, were not castrati.

Today, there is nothing considered more high-brow, dignified, and establishment than the work of classical composers like Bach, Haydn or Beethoven, or opera librettists and composers like Rossini, Mozart and Verdi. Little do many of the elegantly dressed patrons of the world's opera houses and concert halls know that the composers of the respectable music they are nodding off to were the Axl Roses and Ozzy Osbournes of their day, acting up and creating music that was frequently condemned by the authorities.

J.S. Bach, today considered by many to be the most respected of all Baroque composers, was in his own lifetime branded as "incorrigible" by his employers, the city councilors of Leipzig. Early in his life, he was a truant, missing 258 days in his first three years at school. He was a major drinker, and once billed his church for *eight gallons* of beer for a two-week trip. He was accused of ignoring assigned duties without explanation, and also of consorting in the organ loft with an unmarried woman. He had twenty known children—a fact that led to the jape that "Bach's organ has no stops."

Bach once pulled a knife on a fellow musician in a street fight. From November 6 to December 2, 1717 he was imprisoned for comments and activities found offensive by the local *grand-fromage*, Duke William II. He danced to the usual tune of Sex, Drugs and Rock and Roll, but in his case, it was more Sex, Booze and Harpsichord Concertos. Bach mellowed with age and became one of the greatest composers of all time. By the end of his career, he was considered stodgy by most contemporary composers, including his illustrious sons.

Mozart composed what is likely the most famous work of high-brow culture about one-night stands and easy hook-ups—his opera *Don Giovanni*, written with librettist Lorenzo Da Ponte. Both men were contemporaries of the notorious rake, Giacomo Casanova, from whom they both learned seduction strategies. Casanova, himself a musician (amongst many other skills), was arrested and imprisoned in a Venetian jail for "affront to common decency" (from which, like a character in a Mozart opera, he brazenly escaped.) Mozart largely managed to avoid this sort of drama, but only just—his published erotic love letters to Baroness Martha Elisabeth von Waldstätten almost got him into a cell beside his pal Casanova.

The other candidate for Greatest Classical Composer, Ludwig van Beethoven, also managed to get himself thrown into prison. Wandering the streets of Baden in 1820, somewhat the worse for wear, he was mistaken for a tramp and tossed in jail. He was never threatened with three years in a Florida prison, as Jim Morrison was, or twenty years in an Ontario penitentiary, as Keith Richards and Jimi Hendrix both were, but like them he did have a record. A jail record, not a LP.

Like Bach and Mozart, Beethoven's music received stiff criticism in his own day. One critic wrote that his *Eroica Symphony* was "too difficult, too long and (its composer) too impolite." At the premiere, one patron rose up in the middle of the performance and shouted: "I'll give another *kreutzer* if this thing will stop!"

His appearance was much derided. Pianist Frau von Bernhard, described him as being "short and insignificant with an ugly red face full of pockmarks. His hair was very dark and hung tousled about his face. His attire was very ordinary and not remotely of the choiseness [sic] that was customary...in our circles. He spoke in a pronounced dialect and had a rather common way of expressing himself, indeed his entire deportment showed no signs of exterior polish; on the contrary, he was unmannerly both in demeanor and behavior, and very proud." Translated into more contemporary language, it sounds like a description one might hear of Nirvana, the Sex Pistols or the Ramones.

Beethoven did work hard to gain acceptance by The Man. His first two sonatas for cello were dedicated to Friedrich Wilhelm II, the King of Prussia. His *Septet in E-flat major, Opus 20*, is dedicated to Empress Maria Theresa, and in 1802 he dedicated three sonatas for piano and violin to Russian Tsar Alexander 1. Twelve years later he dedicated another piece to England's George IV, and in 1827 he dedicated the last work he completed before dying, his *String Quartet No.13 in B-flat Major*, to Russian Prince Nikolai Golitsyn. However he didn't always come through with his planned dedications. His third symphony was written to honor Napoleon, but when Bonaparte egotistically declared himself Emperor, the composer was so dismayed that he removed the dedication and renamed it the *Eroica Symphony*.

To this day Beethoven is held up as the height of respectability and power by both the establishment and the anti-establishment. Chuck Berry ushered in a musical revolution with his anthem *Roll Over Beethoven*. In *A Clockwork Orange* Anthony Burgess (and later Stanley Kubrick) had a Beethoven-loving young thug receiving aversion therapy from The Man that made him violently vomit every time he heard Ludwig's *Ninth Symphony*. The *Ode to Joy* from this masterpiece was selected as the official anthem of the European Union, and in 2017 when Vladimir Putin and Donald Trump consummated their cozy relationship at the G-20 conference in Germany, Angela Merkel made sure that it was played before the Russian and American leaders.

As wealth began to spread more widely through society through the nineteenth century, music became an even more important part of culture and society. Strictures began to loosen. Music became more salacious, and thus more interesting to more people. Just for instance, rape became a central theme in the operas of the eighteenth and nineteenth centuries. *The Beggars Opera, Il Rapimento di Cefalo,* Bizet's *Carmen*, Rossini's *Guillaume Tell*, and Mozart's *Don Giovanni, The Marriage of Figaro,* and *The Abduction* from the Seraglio are just a few of these rape-themed operas. The Man sometimes interfered with censorship of these racy plots about clearly illicit and lawless activity, and sometimes not.

As music performances began to be heard by a larger and larger number of people, the notion of celebrity and star power began to develop. One of biggest stars of the 19th Century was Niccolò Paganini, the most celebrated violinist of his time, and a guitarist, composer, partier, gambler and womanizer. The hirsute musician who began performing publicly at age 11 was beset with rumors and controversy for his entire life. Stories swirled that his mother had sold his soul to the devil so that he could become the greatest virtuoso in history. Another had it that he had murdered a woman, used her intestines as violin strings and imprisoned her soul inside the instrument. Women's screams were said to come from inside his fiddle when he performed onstage.

Like Johnny Cash, he dressed all in black, and with his shoulder-length flowing locks of hair, long, thin fingers, hollow cheeks and pale demeanor, he struck a powerful, almost macabre image on the concert stages of Europe. Unlike other classical musicians (but in the style of all modern pop stars) he did not play from sheet music, but instead memorized the long complex scores and thus could flail himself across the stage as he sawed on his fiddle, earning the nickname "Rubber Man". If he'd been born a hundred years later he likely would have been a world-famous rock virtuoso like Jeff Beck or Carlos Santana, but for a musician living in an era when the only means of promotion was word of mouth and handbills, he did not do at all badly, becoming the acclaimed (and feared) bad-boy of European concert halls.

In one concert in Vienna an audience member became convinced he had seen the Devil helping Paganini play. In another, it was claimed that the Devil made lightning strike the end of his bow. It is not known whether it was the Devil or one of his many female acolytes who gave him syphilis, but a combination of it, tuberculosis and larynx cancer killed him at age 54 in 1840. His devilish reputation meant the Church refused to bury him on consecrated ground, and so the body of the very appropriately named musician remained unburied for four years until Pope Gregory XVI finally allowed it to be transported to Parma, Italy and laid to rest there.

Just as it would seventy years later with bluesman Robert Johnson, the Church and the public assumed Paganini must have sold his soul to the Devil in return for his unearthly skills. However the power of the Church was beginning to wane, and it had trouble fighting the new forms of secular music that developed towards the end of the nineteenth century. New, irreverent music was being performed in the cabarets that sprang up across Europe, and then in the vaudeville houses of London and the theaters on New York's Broadway. It was attacked but not stopped by the authorities. The French Minister of Public Education called the new cabaret music a "depraved orgy of songs", and another public official described it as "a disgraceful invention that is spreading across our country like leprosy."

In the early 20th Century, many assumed that cabaret would be the genre that would continue as the favorite force of popular music. Few saw that, just as it had in Mesopotamia, Egypt, and medieval Europe, slaves, and their immediate descendants would instead create the music that would dominate the pop culture of the twentieth and (so far) the twenty-first centuries. Virtually every new genre of music, with one notable exception, was created by slaves, or their recent descendants. Gospel, Jazz, Ragtime, Bebop, Rhythm and Blues, Boogie-woogie, Soul, Rock and Roll, Reggae, Pop, Hip-hop and Rap—all created by black musicians. Although they had to fight a long and difficult battle to get their music heard, they became the predominant force in music. Today, with the exception of the Beatles, Elvis and Madonna (all of whom would confess to owing a huge debt to the heritage of black music), all the artists with the most Number One hits are black—Mariah Carey with eighteen, Michael Jackson with thirteen, Whitney Houston with eleven, and Janet Jackson and Stevie Wonder, each with ten.

The history of musical creativity springing from slavery even pre-dates the arrival of blacks in America, as slave-music was encouraged on the ships crossing from Africa to the New World. At times the ships would have been driven at high speeds by the northwest trade winds towards Georgia and the Carolinas, but at other times they would have been caught for days or weeks in the windless Doldrums. Since the mortality rates were high in the hot, fetid holds where they were chained, the ships' captains frequently brought the slaves on deck in these still conditions to sing and dance as a way of trying to improve their health so the cargo would stay alive. British doctor Alexander Falconbridge, who travelled on four slave-trading voyages in the 1780s, described the singing and drumming of the slaves as the "melancholy lamentation of their exile from their native country", yet said the music was kept lively because, "if they go about it reluctantly or do not move with agility, they are flogged."

The tradition continued once the slaves arrived in the Americas. Gradually they changed the words of the songs from their native languages of West Africa to English, and added Christian imagery, thus creating the beginnings of gospel music. The slaves were also widely used to provide musical entertainment for the white slave-owners of the American south, and later through the north. As early as the 1690s slave fiddlers were enlisted to accompany white dancers in Virginia. By the 1700s, black musicians began calling out steps and movements to white dancers. By the 1800s there were even black musical stars in northern cities like the freed slave Frank Johnson who performed across Philadelphia. The familiar trope that the blues and jazz were born in New Orleans and travelled up the Mississippi to Memphis and Chicago was actually true about black music long before the birth of jazz or the blues. Black musicians provided most of the entertainment aboard Mississippi and Ohio River steamboats in the early 19th Century, before the Civil War and the abolition of slavery. Jazz and ragtime were created at almost the exact same time as the creation of the automobile, the airplane and radio, so by the early twentieth century the steamboat was no longer required. There were many other ways of getting black music from the south out to a larger audience, whether The Man approved or not. But of course one could now add systemic racism to the other many reasons for the battle between Music and The Man.

The establishment was deeply concerned about the effects they perceived that jazz was having on society. A 1921 article in the *Ladies Home Journal* headed "Does Jazz Put The Sin in Syncopation? breathlessly reported, "Jazz disorganizes all regular laws and orders; it stimulates to extreme deeds, to a breaking away from all rules and conventions; it is harmful and dangerous, and its influence is wholly bad." Even if the text did not mention it, the illustrations certainly reminded readers that the creators of this "wholly bad" new music were black.

The one exception to the rule that blacks created the new idioms of music was the very white genre of Country, or as it was once called "Country and Western", or "Hillbilly Music." Created by the serfs of the west (first cowboys, later truck drivers) it would be melded (against its better judgement) with black rhythm and blues (aka "race music") to create the most revolutionary new musical genre ever. Perhaps the most prescient man in the musical history of the twentieth century and the man who helped turn music from a relatively modest business into an economic juggernaut was Sam

Phillips, owner of Sun Records, a small recording studio in Memphis, Tennessee. Phillips used to muse to his secretary and associates that "if I could just find a white boy who could sing and dance like a Negro, I'd make a million." In 1953, just such a specimen nervously shambled into his studio—a hick Southern truck driver with a repertoire of hillbilly tunes and covers of black rhythm and blues songs. His name was Elvis Presley, and with Sam Phillips' help he would change the world. The first record they cut cost Elvis two dollars, and he sent it home to his mama in Tupelo, Mississippi. Within a year, though, he was recording and performing songs that were sending both young women and men into delirium, played on radio and later (with his gyrating pelvis framed out) on television.

The Man, and the press responded to Elvis with an astounding amount of venom. Shocked by Presley's joyously uninhibited singing and dancing, and by the overwhelming reaction of teenage fans to it, police chiefs and magistrates were sent to matinee shows to determine whether they should shut down his evening performances. In Oklahoma City, Baptist minister Rupert Naney watched over the show to determine if Elvis was getting too lewd for his tastes. In Jacksonville, a juvenile court judge, Marion Gooding, along with a committee of citizens sat in the back row of the matinee. He ordered Presley to tone down his act for the evening show, and made out arrests for his arrest should he disobey. The head of the music department in Bryant High School was quoted in the Charlotte, NC newspaper saying, "The guest performer Elvis Presley presented a demonstration which was in execrable taste bordering on obscenity. The gyrations of this young man were such an assault to the senses as to repel even the most tolerant observer."

Louisville Police Chief Carl Huestis declared and enforced a ban on what he called "lewd movements and onstage wiggles" from the entertainer. After Presley's show, Tom Davis, the manager of the Corpus Christi Coloseum claimed it was "a contributing factor in juvenile delinquency" and banned all future rock and roll shows from his venue. In La Crosse, Wisconsin, an FBI agent reported to his boss J.Edgar Hoover that the Presley show was, "the filthiest and most harmful production ever to come to La Crosse for exhibition to teenagers...sexual gratification on stage...a strip-tease with clothes on...may possibly be a drug addict and sexual pervert."

There was frequently the undertone in the press reports reminding readers of the black origins of the new music. The San Antonio *News* claimed, "it is an appalling commentary on the taste of his audiences that he performs in such bad taste, for his act as presented in San Antonio was the essence of vulgarity...an unholy roller. He got more body English into his songs that a Ubangi witch doctor trying to cure a pestilence."

Recognizing that while Presley himself was white, the music he was singing was mostly black, The Man retaliated by shutting him down. They conscripted him into the lowest rank of the army, shaved his ducktail hair off, and shipped him off to Germany. Elvis, however, survived, returned in triumph and, although both his music and persona were somewhat gutted, from then on lived a fairly charmed life as "The King"—unlike the often tortured singers, bands and musicians described in the following pages.

2. You Say You Want a Revolution

John Lennon

It almost seems The Man was on the hunt for John Lennon before he was even born. On the night of October 9, 1940, as his mother went into labor in the Oxford Street Maternity Hospital in Liverpool, a giant fleet of Luftwaffe bombers prepared to make one of the largest ever bombing raids on the city.

As the bombs came raining down, killing dozens of people, destroying houses, factories and shipyards, 26-year-old Julia Lennon gave birth to the baby she named John Winston Lennon—the middle name after the Prime Minister who was leading Britain through its darkest hour. After a brief lull in the bombing as the German fleet re-grouped over the Irish Sea, the newborn's cries were met with the renewed wailing of the air-raid sirens, and the nurses tucked the baby on the floor under Julia's hospital bed for safety.

It was only the first of many attacks on Lennon by The Man. Between his birth and his death from an assassin's bullet 40 years later, he would go up against childhood bullies, school masters, British police, mobs of angry evangelicals, immigration authorities, and J. Edgar Hoover's FBI.

Considering his rough-and-tumble childhood and teenage years, he was lucky to have avoided even more scrutiny from the authorities than he did. His father, born an orphan, had shipped to sea at fifteen, and, against her family's wishes, married Julia in 1938. On North Atlantic convoys throughout the war, he barely saw his son. When John was eighteen months old, his father was caught stealing liquor from the cargo of a ship and thrown in jail. Julia began seeing another man and became pregnant by him. Her family forced her to give the baby up for adoption.

Following that she met yet another man, and moved into his tiny apartment with baby John, but her sister Mimi, shocked by the cramped and squalid conditions, took the boy away from her to live at her house.

Just as the kid was getting used to this change, his father, released from jail, arrived at Mimi's, and in effect kidnapped him, taking him off to Blackpool. Today, of course, there would be an AMBER alert and all-points bulletin for such an event. Not so back then. However, Julia did discover the pair in the seaside resort town, and there was a massive scene in which the five-year old boy was given the decision of who he wanted to live with. Twice he chose his father, but when his mother left in tears, he ran from his father and went chasing after her. Mother and son escaped by train, managing to avoid the involvement of the authorities, and John was returned to her sister's home near Penny Lane.

A poor student and a troublemaker, Lennon was frequently "caned" for his behavior at the Quarry Bank school. Leader of a gang of boys who careened around Liverpool making mischief, he was lucky not to have more attention from the police. "The sort of gang I led went for things like shoplifting and pulling girls' knickers down," he later confessed (or is it crowed?).

His life was changed by Radio Luxembourg, the pirate radio station that sent the first sounds of Elvis, Chuck Berry, Fats Domino and Bill Haley through the static-filled airwaves to British teenagers.

His record at school was lousy: "Still lazy", according to the French teacher. "On the road to failure," said the math prof. But the records on Radio Luxembourg pointed him down a new and very different path.

Scraping together enough money to buy a cheap Gallotone Champion guitar ("Guaranteed not to split"), he formed and led a group originally named The Quarrymen. Their first big gig was the annual St. Peter's Parish Garden Summer Fete, where they were second on the bill only to the obedience trials of the German Shepherd dogs of the Liverpool City Police Department. A 14-year-old rode his bike to the garden fete to hear the group, and by the end of the night had been asked to join it. His name was Paul McCartney.

John and Paul became inseparable. They bonded together not just by their love of rock and roll and their rapidly increasing skills as singers and songwriters, but also by the twin tragedies of both of them losing their mothers when they were in their teens. Paul's died from cancer, John's mother Julia was killed by a drunken, off-duty policeman who was charged but acquitted for reckless driving.

John took out his anger on his guitar and his girlfriend (and future wife), Cynthia Powell. "I was in a sort of blind rage for two years", he later said. "I was either drunk or fighting. There was something wrong with me."

John and Paul decided to re-name their band after an obscure line from the Marlon Brando film *The Wild One*, and so became The Beatles. They also acquired a new guitarist, George Harrison. Their first gig using the new name was an illegal strip club, where the strippers would take off some of their clothes facing the audience but only go for the full monte with their back to the audience, the charms visible only to the young band on stage with them.

The owner of the strip club heard of the opportunities for bands in Hamburg, Germany, and offered to drive them over. En route, they stopped at a Dutch music store, where Lennon shoplifted a harmonica to use in the German gig. Their manager was shocked that John would jeopardize their gig with such a risky move, but once again, Lucky Lennon got away with it.

The Beatles went crazy ("benakked", the locals called them) in the rough bars of Hamburg. Lennon would scream at the crowd that they were all Nazis and Hitlerites. In return, the drunken sailors and prostitutes would send up rounds of beer and "prellies" (Preludin uppers) for the band. On several occasions John rolled drunken sailors in the dark Hamburg alleys. Once, a sailor, after being attacked by Lennon and Pete Best, fired at them with a tear gas gun. Another time, John beat a man so badly he feared he had left him dead. It seems unlikely, since there is no record of such a thing in the Hamburg press, but Lennon was consumed with guilt about the event, and years later told his friend the guitarist Jesse Ed Davis that he believed he would one day die a violent death, because it was his "karmic destiny."

When the band moved from the Kaiserkeller bar to the larger Top Ten club, the furious Kaiserkeller owner reported to the police that George was only 17, thus underage to perform in the bars. He was deported back to England. A few weeks later the police charged Paul and Pete Best under provisions of the local fire code. They were briefly jailed, then they too were deported.

Back in Liverpool, the band re-united to play the first of their gigs at the Cavern Club. They got an explosive, extraordinary reaction. Girls went crazy with adoration. Guys, in particular the "Teddy-boy" hooligans, went crazy with envy and anger at the girls' response to the band, and so beat them up. In one gig John, Paul George and their drummer Pete Best were beaten. John got a broken finger. Their bandmate Stuart Sutcliff was kicked so viciously that John and Paul had to pull him from the melee. Bloodied and battered, he suffered a fractured skull. Sutcliff soon decided to leave the group and ditch rock and roll forever. He suffered from extreme headaches ever after and died a year later of a brain aneurysm.

The next years brought the incredible whirlwind of Beatlemania. By 1963 they had acquired the final three major pillars of The Beatles—their new drummer, Ringo Starr, new manager, Brian Epstein, and new producer, George Martin. By August 1963 they had their first album, *Please Please Me* and first Number One song, *From Me to You*. They were touring almost continually across England. The police, on hand to control the delirious crowds, had never seen anything like it. Urine dripped down the aisles from the out-of-control teenage girls, and nurses and cops dealt as best they could as the swooning, screaming fans rushed the stage in an orgy of adulation.

In September 1963 the band was invited to play a Royal Command Performance at London's Albert Hall. Lennon, ever the anti-establishment rebel, was conflicted. Ultimately, they did play the gig, but with John, in his introduction to *Twist and Shout* demanding that "you people in the cheaper seats clap your hands; and the rest of you—just rattle your jewelry." Many in the crowd were mortified that Lennon would make such a cheeky remark to British royalty, but he pulled it off, and the show went on. Certainly, one can imagine that in an only-slightly earlier time, the reaction would have been "off with his head!"

Instead, two years later, the Queen awarded The Beatles the title of Members of the Order of the British Empire (MBE). John had begun feeling his life was spinning out of control. "It just happens bit by bit, until this complete craziness surrounds you," he said, "and you're doing exactly what you don't want to do with people you can't stand—the people you hated when you were ten." He wanted to turn the honor down, but Epstein and the other Beatles convinced him they all had to accept it. He claims to have smoked a joint in the palace washroom before the ceremony. Numerous past holders of the MBE angrily objected to the Beatles receiving the honor. Lennon responded by saying that "many of the previous recipients got theirs by killing people in wars. We got ours by entertaining people—I think we deserve ours more."

Lennon gave his to his aunt Mimi, who proudly placed it in a frame above her TV—but three years later Lennon had his chauffeur pick up the medal, and he sent it back to the palace, with the following note:

> *Your Majesty,*
>
> *I am returning this MBE in protest against Britain's involvement in the Nigeria-Biafra thing, against our support of America in Vietnam, and against Cold Turkey slipping down the charts.*
>
> *With love,*
> *John Lennon*

The Beatles were turned on to marijuana by Bob Dylan and a year later to LSD by, of all people, George Harrison's dentist. It became Lennon's new fixation, and a huge influence on the music they made throughout the late 1960s. It also put him in the crosshairs of the vice squad of Scotland Yard and the British police.

In the summer of 1965, he was embroiled in yet another giant controversy. Interviewed by the *London Evening Standard*, he commented that he had been reading extensively about religions and had decided that "Christianity will go. It will vanish and shrink." He then added a comment that would reverberate around the world, stating "We're more popular than Jesus now."

America, which takes its religion very seriously, went crazy. As the Beatles started another North American tour, there were death threats, record burnings, banned radio play, and Ku Klux Klan marches outside their concerts. Lennon made a mild attempt at an apology for having offended people with the Jesus comparison; but then created a new firestorm by stating his opposition to the rapidly escalating war in Southeast Asia.

By the final stop on the tour in San Francisco, the Beatles decided they had had enough of America, and enough of hotels, road-food and screaming tennyboppers getting manhandled by paid-duty policemen. They stopped touring forever and returned to England. John cut off his hair to play a WW1 soldier in Richard Lester's anti-war film, *How I Won the War.*

In 1968 Lennon met a unique Japanese performance artist named Yoko Ono. Within months his marriage to Cynthia was over, and he was spending twenty-four hours of every day, smitten with the avant garde artist. Those twenty-four hours included the time the Beatles were recording their final, brilliant albums, the *White Album*, and *Abbey Road.* It was too much for the other members of the band—particularly for Paul McCartney. By the end of the tumultuous decade he had left the band, and the Beatles were finished.

John's life began to spiral into a chaotic whirl. The police showed up at his apartment, found a small amount of marijuana and charged him with possession of cannabis. With his new passion for peace, he tried to change his name, wanting to lose the old moniker of imperialist Winston Churchill, and replace it with Yoko's surname Ono. The authorities told him he could add Ono but could not legally remove Winston.

In 1969, Lennon became involved in three major quasi-political events, all of them in Canada. In May, he and Yoko moved into the Fairmont Queen Elizabeth Hotel in Montreal to hold what they called a "Bed-In for Peace". They had developed the Bed-In idea first in Amsterdam, then wanted to carry on with their grand plans for world peace in New York. Arriving at the Southampton docks with plans to sail on the *Queen Elizabeth II*, with an entourage of five, and twenty-six pieces of luggage, they were shocked to learn that due to Lennon's cannabis conviction, American Immigration officials would refuse them entry. Undeterred, they jumped on a plane, first to

Jamaica (which they found too isolated), Nassau (which they thought too hot), Toronto, and finally Montreal.

Decked out in white pajamas, and lying in a king-size bed, John and Yoko were visited by celebrities such as LSD guru Timothy Leary, comedians Tommy Smothers and Dick Gregory, right-wing cartoonist Al Capp, the self-appointed "fifth Beatle" Murray the K, and beat poet Allan Ginsberg. They also spoke with an average of over one hundred reporters a day, and called more than three hundred and fifty radio stations, preaching their message of world peace. The timing was appropriate: There were major wars, battles and protests being fought in Asia, Africa, South America, Europe and across North America that year. When Lennon called a radio station in San Francisco, a pitched battle was going on between anti-war demonstrators and police. When the famous ex-Beatle was asked for his recommendation for protest tactics, he was ambivalent. Just as the uncertain words of his song *Revolution* indicate, when it came to destruction, we were never sure whether we could count him in or out.

What he did know was that he wanted to compose an anthem for the Peace Movement that could replace the aging chestnut *We Shall Overcome*, and in Montreal, he did—writing and recording in the hotel room, with a chorus of celebrities, fans and newsmen the new classic *Give Peace A Chance.*

Four months later, he was invited to return to Canada to participate in an outdoor festival called the *Toronto Rock and Roll Revival*. The opportunity to help revive the careers of all his teenage role models—Chuck Berry, Little Richard, Fats Domino, Jerry Lee Lewis, and others—appealed, and so Lennon threw together what became *The Plastic Ono Band,* and flew to Toronto. It was a shaky flight, with Lennon and Eric Clapton, both at the time addicted to heroin, trying to fly cold turkey, and The Man, naturally, giving them grief as they tried to enter the country—this time over Yoko Ono's lack of a vaccination certificate. They were then greeted by limousines flanked by eighty members of the Vagabonds motorcycle club, who led them on Harley-Davidsons from the airport through the city to the downtown stadium.

After battling with both Little Richard and Jim Morrison over who would close the show (The Doors eventually won), Lennon's new band took to the stage, with two old classics, *Blue Suede Shoes* and *Dizzy Miss Lizzy*, followed by two of Lennon's new solo efforts, *Yer Blues* and the very appropriate *Cold Turkey*. This was followed by Yoko climbing into a bag and yodeling and wailing for twenty minutes while Clapton, the man widely thought to be the world's greatest guitarist, merely created feedback by rubbing his instrument against an amplifier. Finally, the sound of the restless, booing crowd ended the ordeal and the band left the stage to let Morrison and gang light their fire.

John and Yoko returned to Toronto in December, with a much grander plan. This time he was announcing the *Music and Peace Conference of the World*—a planned festival of two million people ("bigger than Woodstock", it was promised) to be held at Mosport Park, a picturesque auto-racing track forty miles east of the city, in the summer of 1970.

Except that it would no longer be called 1970—Lennon proposed that the calendar be re-named and the new year would be called Year One AP (After Peace).

To announce it he and Yoko had huge billboards reading "War is Over (If You Want It)" mounted across the city. They followed it with a similar billboard campaign in eleven other cities around the world. Impressario John Brower, who had also created the Rock Revival event, put the famous pair up in Ronnie Hawkins' country mansion outside of Toronto, where they proceeded to run amok, letting their bathtub overflow all night, and thus causing the kitchen ceiling below it to collapse, exposing Hawkins' young children to Lennon's erotic lithographs, crashing a snowmobile and running up $5000 worth of phone calls trying to get Elvis and others to join in on the summer festivities.

Lennon then moved on to meet the erudite master of pop mumbo-jumbo, Marshall McLuhan, in his offices at the University of Toronto. "Language", said the man to whom the media was the message, "is a form of organized stutter. Literally, you chop your sounds up into bits in order to talk. Now, when you sing, you don't stutter, so singing is a way of stretching language into long harmonious patterns and cycles."

"How do you think about language in songs?" he asked Lennon.

Instead of simply answering "You are the eggman/you are the eggman/I am the walrus," Lennon responded to McLuhan with a typically 1969 stream of babblespeak: "Language and song to me, apart from being pure vibrations, is like trying to describe a dream. And because we don't have telepathy, we try and describe the dream to each other, to verify to each other what we know, what we believe to be inside each other. And the stuttering is right, because we *can't* say it. No matter how you say it, it's never how you want to say it."

Take that, Mr. McLuhan. From there it was off to meet the big kahuna—the Prime Minister of Canada, Pierre Trudeau. The previous summer John and Yoko had mailed acorns to thirty world leaders, asking them to plant them "for peace". They did not get a single reply. Now, however, Lennon had found a major politician curious enough about the musician's plans for world peace that he was willing to meet with him. The ex-Beatle and his new bride piled into a Volkswagen Beetle driven by Allan Rock, then a student leader, years later to become Justice Minister of Canada, and he drove them to Ottawa.

It was a successful meeting. Trudeau said that John and Yoko had given him a positive feeling about the future of youth and its efforts to bring peace to the world. As for Lennon, he announced, "If there were more leaders like Mr. Trudeau, the world would have peace."

Unfortunately, the Peace Festival itself, planned for the following summer, was not as successful. It derailed into a chaotic mess and was abandoned.

While Lennon was talking peace in Canada, others were protesting war in the United States. In the winter of 1970, Lennon was pleased—and amazed—to hear hundreds of thousands of people singing his new anthem *Give Peace a Chance* at a massive anti-war rally in Washington. He wasn't the only person who took note. J. Edgar Hoover opened an FBI file on the British singer—a file that would eventually grow to hundreds of pages.

Revolution was in the air, and Lennon joined in, writing, recording and performing new provocative songs. Some, like "Power to the People", were aggressively political. Perhaps his greatest song, "Imagine" is disguised as a syrupy ballad, but contained in the beautiful melody are truly bold and radical lyrics. In recent years it has been sung in many venues where it might not be expected (such as the opening ceremonies of the 2018 Olympics) but it has also got lots of reactionary authorities hot under the collar. Just for instance, the 1972 graduating class at Denmark High School in Green Bay, Wisconsin, who voted to make "Imagine" the official song of their graduation. The principal of the school forbade them from doing this, thus causing an unsuccessful student protest, saying the song was "anti-religious and anti-American with communist overtones." Of course, it is. Lennon imagines a world where there is "no religion, no countries", instead only "a brotherhood of man". Fighting words, not just to Wisconsin high school principals, but to Hoover's FBI. Numerous agents were assigned to keep tabs on the ex-mop-top singer.

John and Yoko also got into a spat with the authorities that was almost a carbon copy of the one he himself had been involved in as a child. Yoko had a child, Kyoko, with her previous husband, Tony Cox. In 1971 the girl was living with her father in Majorca, Spain. Yoko enlisted John to help retrieve her. The pair flew to the island, found Kyoko at a school playground, and whisked her off to their hotel. Cox immediately called the police, who got to the famous pair before they could leave. For fourteen hours they were detained on suspicion of kidnapping. Yoko was outraged that she could be charged with kidnapping her own daughter. The case went before a Spanish judge, who, just as Lennon's parents had done when he was five, left the decision up to the girl, who chose to stay with her father. This time, unlike the incident in 1946, the child did not come running to her mother. The rock and roll couple left the country, Lennon furious, Ono in tears.

Sick of the hassles associated with England and the breakup of The Beatles, John and Yoko moved to New York City, where he became enmeshed in the radical politics of the early seventies. He performed at a benefit concert for singer John Sinclair, busted for ten years for possession of two joints, and another for the prisoners killed at Attica State Prison in upstate New York. He also appeared at the trial of the "Harlem Six", six black men charged with murder and held without bail or trial.

Strom Thurmond, the longstanding Dixiecrat senator from South Carolina, sent a secret memo to Nixon's Attorney General John Mitchell, recommending that John Lennon, "a member of the former musical group known as 'The Beatles'" have his visa terminated as a "strategic counter-measure". Mitchell, leery about alienating the "youth vote" in the upcoming election with such a draconian move, first just had the FBI "tailgate" Lennon—blatantly harass and follow him wherever he went. While it certainly unnerved Lennon, it didn't stop him. When he continued to speak and sing at anti-war rallies, Mitchell dropped the hammer on him. Lennon was told by the Immigration Department that his US visa was revoked, and he had ten days to get out of the country.

He hired a high-profile immigration lawyer, Leon Wildes, to try to fight the deportation order, and continued to record and demonstrate. At the same time Lennon was in the studio, G. Gordon Liddy was in Washington working for CREEP, the Committee to Re-elect the President, coming up with ideas to try to destroy the leaders of the New Left's Youth Voting Registration movement, such as Jerry

Rubin, Abbie Hoffman, and Lennon. Abductions and assassinations were considered. Ultimately, he began to focus on a break-in of the Democratic Party committee headquarters in the Watergate Hotel—the burglary that would lead to the downfall of Richard Nixon and the first ever resignation of an American president.

Meanwhile, Lennon was behind a new cause, recording *Woman is the Nigger of the World*, which he considered "the first Women's Liberation song".

The Immigration department continued to hound John and Yoko, and their lawyer continued to work to keep them in the United States. His work on their behalf was not necessarily aided by their antics. In April 1973 they declared that they were now founding the country of Nutopia, a country with no boundaries and no passports, and as ambassadors of Nutopia, they were asking for diplomatic immunity.

Crazed by all the immigration hassles and by his very messy divorce from Paul McCartney and the Beatles, Lennon left again, this time without Yoko, for Los Angeles. He spent a year in the sun, in the company (encouraged by Ono) of a new lover, their 22-year old assistant May Pang, along with John's son Julian, fellow songwriter Harry Nilsson, singers Anne Murray and Alice Cooper, and the wildest man in rock and roll, Phil Spector.

After a year of California debauchery, he returned to New York, returned to Yoko Ono, had a new son, Sean, and settled into a somewhat more stable life. He even began to patch up his differences with Paul McCartney and his lawyers began to clear up the feud with the immigration department.

By 1980, he was confident enough in the status of his passport and visa that he chartered a sailboat, the *Megan Jaye,* and sailed for Bermuda. He later credited the intense experience, especially single-handedly helming the boat for six hours through a mid-Atlantic gale, with helping him get his head, and his songwriting back on track. On December of that year, he was back in New York, recording new music, and returned on the evening of the 8th to his home in the Dakota Apartments, to be accosted at the entrance and shot dead by a deranged fan, Mark David Chapman.

There was an outpouring of grief around the world. One hundred thousand people poured into New York's Central Park the following Sunday to honor him and mourn his death. There were thirty thousand in the streets of Liverpool, a candlelight vigil of thirty five thousand on a snowy night in Toronto, and many thousands more in cities across Europe and North America. There were tributes from around the world. Chuck Berrry said, "I feel as if I lost a little part of myself when John died." Norman Mailer simply said, "We have lost a genius of the spirit."

Many wondered whether Chapman was truly a lone killer, or whether he was somehow programmed by rogue forces in the United States or British governments to get rid of Lennon. The FBI files on Lennon, though, were quickly sealed by the Reagan administration on grounds of "national security". It took years of effort, mostly by California professor Jon Wiener and the American Civil Liberties Union, to use the Freedom of Information Act to get the Lennon files released. When they finally were, in 1996, they were so heavily redacted as to reveal very little.

The files certainly do describe great motive and desire to muzzle Lennon. Was Chapman alone, or was he somehow unwittingly manipulated by the authorities, possibly by the CIA's *Manchurian Candidate*-like Project MKULTRA? It is a mystery that will likely never be solved, and today is left to conspiracy theorists.

Mark David Chapman received a sentence of twenty years to life and began serving it in the same Attica Prison that Lennon had campaigned against. As of this writing he has been turned down for parole ten times, and remains in the US prison system.

Victor Jara

Many singers have been harassed by the Man, but few have actually been tortured to death because of their music, as Chilean singer-songwriter, poet and political activist Victor Jara was on September 16, 1973.

Called "a cross between Bob Dylan and Martin Luther King", Chilean authorities fumed, "One song by Victor Jara is more dangerous than one hundred machine guns."

Born into extreme poverty in 1932 to peasant farmers, he was already working on the land at age six. After stabs at accountancy, the seminary, and the army, he was able to enter the University of Chile, where he began singing and directing theater. By the 1960s, he began recording. Early in his career, his music began antagonizing conservative Chileans. Even before he began writing political songs, his recording of a comic song about a religious woman with a crush on the priest she visits for confession was banned for sale or radio airplay.

As the political situation in Chile deteriorated, he began to write about police attacks on rural peasants and was beaten up for it on several occasions by right-wing thugs.

In 1970, he actively supported Salvadore Allende, the Popular Unity coalition candidate for president, composing the Marxist leader's election theme song *Venceremos (We Will Triumph)* and playing free concerts for the campaign.

His popular success exploded during the cultural renaissance of the Allende years. American folk artists sang his songs, and he toured internationally, as far as Moscow. The Russian propaganda machine latched on to his popularity in the USSR and beyond, claiming that his vocal prowess was the result of Russian throat surgery.

Jara was the most prominent of the many artists and singers who participated in Allende's Popular Unity movement. His music was considered essential not just to Allende's election victory but also his presidency. Allende spoke in front of giant banners reading *No Hay Revolución Sin Canciones* ("There is no revolution without songs").

His presidency, though, did not last long. Backed by Richard Nixon, Henry Kissinger and the CIA, the Chilean right wing and army staged a coup d'état on September 11, 1973. Jets attacked the presidential palace, Allende was killed, and General Augusto Pinochet was installed as dictator.

The next day, September 12, thousands of people believed to be supporters of Allende were rounded up and herded into the Chile Stadium. One of them was Victor Jara. He was recognized by the soldiers and quickly picked out for special treatment.

When one of the army officers discovered that Victor Jara was among the prisoners, he went into what stadium survivor Erica Osorio calls a "furious rage".

"You're that motherfucker son of a bitch, Victor Jara, singer of communist songs. I'll teach you, asshole, how to sing!" The soldier raised his machine gun and struck Victor hard on the back, then another soldier hit him again, forcing him to fall to his knees. Victor tried to protect his face with his hands, but when he opened up his hands, the officer kicked him, almost taking out his eye.

"Then", said Osorio, "an air force officer approached, smoking, and flicked his cigarette near Victor and told him, "smoke it, asshole!" Jara told him he didn't smoke, but as the officer violently insisted, the singer, with a hesitant and trembling hand, reached for the cigarette butt. The guard smashed Jara's wrists, saying "Try playing the guitar now, with hands like that, you son of a bitch."

Augusto Samaniego Mesias, one of the political prisoners held in the stadium, saw Victor, "beaten and destroyed inside", trying to stand up, but always falling down. Ultimately Jara was tortured to death. His battered, bloody body was displayed at the entrance to the stadium for other prisoners to see. It was later discarded outside the stadium and was found and taken to the city's morgue. His wife Joan identified it there and gave him a quick and clandestine burial in a general cemetery. She then fled the country and would spend the much of the rest of her life in exile, trying to bring his killers to justice. She herself was not killed in 1973, but in effect her life was destroyed by forty years of relentless attempts to find justice for her husband's death.

Pinochet, with the enthusiastic support of the Nixon administration, became President and ruled Chile for the next seventeen years. Considered by the world to be one of the most brutal dictators of Latin America, his junta killed over 3,000 people and tortured more than 27,000 between 1973 and 1990.

Only after Pinochet left office and was arrested in London on October 16, 1998 did a Chilean judge re-open the case of the murder of Victor Jara. Slowly, some of the conscripted soldiers who had participated in the stadium murders began identifying the officers who had led the operation. One of them fingered Lieutenant Pedro Barientos as the one who had killed Victor Jara.

Many Chileans associated with the Pinochet regime, following the arrest of Pinochet and the realization that their protection might be coming to an end, emmigrated to the United States. Barrientos fled in 1989 and settled in Deltona, Florida.

In 2009 a Chilean police investigation identified Barrientos as the man who had killed the singer. It was revealed that following Jara's torture and the insults about his guitar-playing and folksinging, Barrientos played Russian Roulette with him by placing a bullet in his revolver, spinning the cylinder, placing the gun at Jara's ear, and pulling the trigger. He repeated this a few times until finally killing the singer. He then ordered two conscripts to finish the job by firing into Jara's body.

In 2012, after nearly thirty years of advocacy work by Jara's widow, a Chilean judge ordered the arrest of eight officers for involvement in the murder, and an international arrest warrant for Barrientos. Finally, in 2015, a Florida court found Barrientos guilty. He was ordered to pay $28 million to Jara's family. At this writing he has not paid the fine, and the US government has refused to extradite him to Chile.

In his home country, Jara's music and recordings were banned for many years. A distributor of his early non-political songs was jailed for six months for "violating an internal security law."

Outside of Chile, there were attempts to honor the martyred musician. In 1974, folksinger Phil Ochs organized a tribute concert to Jara and Allende, featuring Bob Dylan, Arlo Guthrie and Pete Seeger. Both U2 and Bruce Springsteen performed covers of Jara's songs in his memory.

Within Chile, things finally began to change following the fall of Pinochet's regime. In 2004, the Chile Stadium where Jara was killed was renamed the Victor Jara Stadium. In 2009, his body was reburied in a massive public ceremony in the Galpón Victor Jara Cultural Centre, across from Santiago's Plaza Brasil. The slain singer was also honored with an asteroid named the 2644 Victor Jara, and now, every year, the Festival of 1000 Guitars for Victor Jara is held in Santiago to celebrate his life and his music.

The Rolling Stones

There has never been, and likely never again will be a group of musicians that has seen such fame and success, and has battled with power, with the authorities and with the police, as the Rolling Stones. However, unlike the Beatles, the band in whose shadow they grew up, they were not born as outsiders. The Beatles were. The Beatles were from Liverpool, a town that much of the rest of England looked down on, they came from rough working class backgrounds, and their leader, John Lennon, came from a broken family. The Rolling Stones were not. They grew up in the suburbs of London in vaguely middle-class circumstances. While there was little that was very pleasant growing up either in the "crossfire hurricane" of World War II, or in the ten dreary years that followed it in England, the young Stones' were not really any more deprived than thousands of others in that grey period.

Mick Jagger, in particular, had a relatively decent childhood. He was a model student, a good athlete, the teacher's pet, the tallest kid in his class, and captain of the school basketball team. Early in his teens, he began to rebel against the hidebound class-driven strictures of 1950s Britain, and fell in with Keith Richards, self-described angry runt and budding hooligan. The pair bonded over love of what in 1955 Britain was an extremely arcane passion—the American blues of John Lee Hooker, Muddy Waters, Howlin' Wolf and Chuck Berry. They would transform their obsession into a wildly powerful force that would circle the globe for decades to come, but not without a great deal of resistance from The Man.

After a few years of self-imposed abject bohemian poverty putting their band together and incessantly honing their musical skills, the group met the Svengali who would create an image for the Stones that they would follow for many years. Andrew Loog Oldham, was a young active participant in the new "Swinging London" scene of the mid-60s. He had worked as a publicist for both dress designer Mary Quant and Beatles manager Brian Epstein, and was described by Keith Richards as "a fantastic bullshitter and an incredible hustler." Writer Victor Bockris called him "a twenty-four-hour-a-day bag of nerves who saw himself as a Phil Spector, the British version of the 'teenage tycoon shit.'"

Oldham, as their new manager, made some dumb decisions—kicking pianist Ian Stewart out of the band because "he didn't look right for the part" (Stewart valiantly stayed on as their road manager, and continued to play piano on the band's recordings), and demanding that the scruffy band, in imitation of the Liverpool groups, wear matching skimpy 'bumfreezer' houndstooth jackets. He quickly realized the error of trying to turn the Stones into an only slightly scruffier version of the squeaky-clean Beatles. Instead, he urged the band to create an image that was the opposite—dirty, rude, sullen, chain-smoking, and generally obnoxious—the anti-Beatles. He dreamed up the provocative line, "Would you let your daughter marry a Rolling Stone?" and the press, the police and the authorities fell for it, hook, line and sinker. "By the time I was finished," crowed Oldham, "every parent in England was disgusted by the Rolling Stones."

In a period where everything hated by the establishment was embraced by their children, young Britain (and soon, the rest of the world) went crazy for the Stones. Why wouldn't they? The British tabloid papers were filled with stories about ambulance men carrying out hysterical teenage girls in straightjackets, the police stopping the performances after ten minutes because of rioting teenagers, knocking down rioting fans with batons, and hurling tear-gas. West German papers luridly described the European premiere of the Stones as "hell broken loose" and a "witches' cauldron."

Richards, who was almost crushed to death, knocked unconscious or electrocuted on at least six occasions, said, "I needed an army to protect me. It was like they had the Battle of Crimea going on, people gasping, tits hanging out, chicks choking, nurses running around with ambulances. You took your life in your hands just to walk out there. I was strangled twice. It was living *A Hard Day's Night*—climbing over rooftops with chief constables who don't know their way, getaways down fire escapes, through laundry chutes, into bakery vans. It was all mad."

People remember Beatlemania, but in many ways the mania for the Stones was even more intense and primordial. Nick Kent, who travelled with the band in the early years, says, "You could see the whole audience change when the Rolling Stones came on. These young girls became wild and violent and made this weird, bestial noise. It was an electrifying experience. I had front-row seats and this girl from the third row threatened me with a stiletto so I immediately sat in the third row." Keith Richards remembers the energy building night after night until it exploded in "a sort of hysterical wail, a weird sound that hundreds of chicks make when they're coming... They sounded like hundreds of orgasms at once. They couldn't even hear the music, and we couldn't hear the music we were playing."

Continental Europe was even wilder than Great Britain. In Warsaw, about 3,000 fans pushed past police barricades and stormed the theater where they were performing. The army rolled in with tanks, tear gas and water cannons to subdue the crowd. Once the shows were finished (or aborted), the band usually escaped as fast as they could, but on one occasion were trapped inside long after the completion of the concert and evacuation of the audience. "Great show tonight," an elderly custodian told the band. "Wasn't a dry seat in the house."

Urination was also the issue in the Stones' first brush with the law. On March 18, 1965, returning from a London concert, the band stopped at a gas station so that bassist Bill Wyman could relieve himself. The uptight attendant, a 41-year-old named Charles Keeley, took offense that Wyman used the phrase, "Where can I take a leak?" and so refused him admission to the station's washroom. When Wyman reported back to his musical compatriots, Jagger took over, re-opened the argument with the attendant, who then "began screaming at them." Jagger, Wyman, Richards and a roadie named Joey Page all decided that if they couldn't use the washroom they would use the outside wall of the station. Before they were finished (Richards claims Wyman has "one of the biggest bladders in human existance") the police were on the scene, charging them with various high crimes and misdemeanors. The British tabloid press had a field day, re-hashing the lurid story for several months, until in July they appeared before Chairman of the Magistrates Mr. A.C.Morey, who found them guilty of using insulting language, told them in no uncertain terms that they were guilty of "behaviour not becoming of a young gentleman" and that "just because you have reached the exalted heights of your profession does not mean you have the right to act like this," then fined them each £5. They could afford it. The same day, their new release *Satisfaction* hit Number One on the British charts.

The trivial gas station incident was the first of the Stones' many busts, and the only one that did not center around drugs. Since the others, including the three biggest ones—at Keith Richards' home Redlands, in Toronto, and in Arkansas were all drug-related, it is informative to hear the expert's take on the matter. This is what Richards, a man who has likely taken more illicit drugs than anyone on the planet, has to say. "Usually drug taking in music starts off on a very, very mundane level—just keeping going to make the next gig. They're nothing I'd recommend to anybody, drugs, but it's a musician's life—it's very difficult to get anyone to understand. It's an underworld life, anyway. Musicians start to work when everybody else stops working and wants some entertainment. If you get enough work, you're working 350 days a year because you want to fill up every gig. And you reach a point very early on when you're sitting around in the dressing room with some other acts in the show and you say, 'I've got to drive 500 miles tomorrow and do two shows tomorrow and I can't make it,' And so you look around at the other guys and say, 'How the hell having you been making it for all these years?" And they say, 'Well, baby, take one of these.' Musicians don't start off thinking, 'We're rich and famous, let's get high.' It's a matter of making the next gig. Like the bomber pilots–if you've got to bomb Dresden tomorrow, you get, like, four or five bennies to make the trip and keep yourself together. 'Do you want me to crash this sucker, or do you want me to stay awake?' 'Here, squadron leader, open your mouth and I'll pop a couple of these blighters in.' I'm sure it was really good speed those fuckers got as well. Government issue. That's how it starts out, and it's usually speed. And once you've got past that, the next question is an escalation."

  Richards also famously once said, apropos of his many busts, "I don't have a drug problem. I have a police problem."

  Their first major battle with The Man took place in February of 1967. LSD had exploded the scene in 1966, and the Stones and Beatles were merely the more visible of the thousands of people around the world exploring the drug. Lysergic Acid Diethylamide was first synthesized by Swiss chemist Albert Hoffman in 1938. In the 1950s the CIA purchased the entire world's supply of the drug, and began testing the use of it as a truth serum, primarily in secret labs and in psychiatric wards, most of them in Montreal and Saskatchewan. By the mid 60s it had seeped into the counter culture and the arts world, popularized by British writer Aldous Huxley, who described it in his book *The Doors of Perception* (from which The Doors get their name) and by Harvard professors Timothy Leary and Richard Alpert (aka Baba Ram Dass).

With acid out of the exclusive control of the CIA and now being used by people swinging to Leary's mantra of "Turn on, tune in, drop out", the British parliament made LSD illegal in 1966. It was a hard drug to control, though, since it was normally distributed on everyday items like sugar cubes or small pieces of blotting paper, not by drug cartels but by individuals. The most famous of these was San Francisco-based Augustus Owsley Stanley (aka Bear). Another was David Sneiderman (aka The Acid King), purveyor of LSD to certain members of the British aristocracy, and...to the Rolling Stones. "He was a sort of upmarket flower child," according to Stones associate Christopher Gibbs. "He knew more about drugs than anyone the Stones had ever met. 'What?' he'd say, 'You mean you've never heard of dimethyl tryptomine?'"

Sniderman, tripping around Europe on a hippie acid distribution mission, was busted trying to enter Britain through Heathrow airport. The authorities gave him two choices—they could arrest him and send him to jail, or they could connect him to "some heavy people" who they hinted were part of Britain's MI5 secret intelligence service, who might have a new mission for him. Sneiderman, who fancied himself as a sort of counter-culture James Bond, naturally took the latter alternative, and learned that MI5, working in concert with the FBI, were most interested in busting The Rolling Stones. J. Edgar Hoover, Director of the FBI, had been obsessed with the Stones, in particular with Mick Jagger, for several years. Hoover, widely thought to be himself homosexual and a secret cross-dresser, was offended by Jagger's openly androgynous style and his sway over American youth, so opened a file on him and assigned a number of agents in his COINTELPRO unit to tail him.

MI5, the FBI and the tabloid *News of the World* conspired together to get Sniderman to alert them to an appropriate time and place for a Stones bust. It wasn't a difficult task. The abstemious Jagger had resisted taking LSD, but Richards and band mate Brian Jones were keen to get him turned on, as they were sure this new wonder drug would open new psychedelic windows of creativity through which the Stones could catch up not only to their rivals The Beatles but also with the new music coming from California bands like the Jefferson Airplane and the Grateful Dead.

Richards invited Jagger to a weekend party at his country estate Redlands, along with Jagger's girlfriend Marianne Faithful, George and Patti Harrison, Pop Art dealer Robert Frazer, and Acid King David Sneiderman. "The only reason he was there is he had the stuff," says Richards. "Otherwise I never would have put up with him. In my profession there are people who are hangers-on who you have to tolerate."

After a day of acid-tripping in the sunshine, the party moved inside. In the early evening, they were listening to Dylan's new album *Blonde on Blonde*, when, remembers Richards, "There's a knock on the door, I look through the window and there's this whole lots of dwarves outside, but they're all wearing the same clothes! They were policemen, but I didn't know it. They just looked like very small people wearing dark blue with shiny bits and helmets. 'Wonderful attire! Am I expecting you? Anyway, come on in, it's a bit chilly out.' They were trying to read a warrant to me. 'Oh, that's very nice, but it's a bit cold ouside, so come on in and read it to me by the fireplace.'"

Marianne Faithful ended up being the star of the bust, as she had just climbed from a bath and was simply wearing a big fur rug, which she let fall from time to time. The fuzz were quoted in all the London newspapers with front page headlines like NAKED GIRL AT STONES PARTY. The rags included in their stories a never-to-be-forgotten tidbit involving a Mars chocolate bar that has become part of the Stones legend. The salacious tale was probably invented by the senior police officer who was overheard joshing with sniggering crime reporters "She even had a Mars bar in her fanny and Mick Jagger was eating it." Richards dismisses it: "The Mars bar as a dildo? That's rather a large leap. The weird thing about these myths is that they stick when thet're so obviously false. Perhaps the idea is that it's so outlandish or crude or prurient that it can't have been invented." The salacious claims about the Redlands bust and the Stones in general were typical of the journalism of the *News of the World* from its beginnings in 1843 until the Robert Murdoch-owned tabloid was finally shut down in scandal and law suits in 2011.

The cops found four amphetamine tablets on Jagger (legal in Italy, where they'd been purchased) and some heroin on Robert Frazer. They told Richards that since it was his house, he would be the one who would be facing the music.

These were serious charges that could have resulted in significant jail time. Richards' regular dealer, "Spanish Tony" Sanchez claimed that he had learned through his contacts with the underworld and the police that the charges could be dropped with a £6,000 bribe to the cops. He was immediately dispatched with the money. At first it seemed to work, then suddenly it didn't. A court date was set for June 27.

Waiting for the trial, the band went out on another European tour. Because of the Redlands raid, they were continually harassed by The Man. In Sweden, customs officials strip-searched the entire band, and spent hours going through all of their luggage. In Paris, a customs officer aggresively grabbed Richards by his jacket, shook his fist in his face and then punched him. "They seem to think we are working for Che Guevera," said Keith.

Back in England, Mick continued to hob-nob with the cream of the British aristocracy. He became connected with Sir David Ormsby-Gore, the one-time British ambassador to the United States (and likely more interesting to Jagger, the ambassador's 16-year-old daughter, Lady Victoria Ormsby-Gore). He also partied with Tom Driberg, a

Member of Parliament who would soon be made a member of the peerage by the Queen. Driberg, who after his death was revealed to have been a spy for the KGB, was openly gay, and once made a very audacious pass at Jagger that apparently was not rebuffed. Jagger later confessed to having spent a night in bed with Driberg and American poet Allan Ginsberg, even though homosexuality was still illegal in England at the time. Jagger's connection with Driberg would soon prove extremely helpful regarding their battles with The Man.

Even more intriguing than his connections with Ormsby-Gore or Driberg was his involvement with Queen Elizabeth's vivacious sister, Princess Margaret. According to one royal courtier, the Princess and Mick "spoke on the phone constantly, and she invited him to social events. Like many other women she found him sexy and exciting. If you saw them laughing together, dancing, the way she'd put her hand on his knee and giggle at his stories like a schoolgirl, you'd have thought there was something going on."

The Queen was not amused. According to Harold Brooks-Baker, the publisher of *Burke's Peerage*, "The Queen could tolerate the Beatles because they were clean cut and sort of sweet—at least that was their reputation at the time, but the Stones were quite another matter. Princess Margaret caused more than her share of scandal. The last thing the Queen wanted was her sister running off with Mick Jagger."

In June, at the very moment that Jagger and Richards were filing into a courtroom in Chichester for the Redlands trial, the police, and their friends in the tabloid press, released a new piece of front page news: Brian Jones was busted too on new drug charges. "They had it timed to the minute," said Richards. "When we were in the fucking courtroom, up in London, an hour and a half drive away, they were going into Brian's house to do him so that the papers would come out with 'Rolling Stones Keith Richards and Mick Jagger on trial for this, meanwhile Brian Jones has just been found with this.' So they could lay that on—'Well, they must be guilty.' I suddenly realized,

They really want to nail us. They seem to be trying to lock us all in jail where we can't pose a threat to them anymore.'"

"They bloody well know they haven't got enough evidence to do us," added Mick, "so they have gone out and nicked Brian so that every member of the jury we get will think of drugs and the Stones as being synonymous. It's hard to believe that even cops can be so evil. We are actually in there in court asking for bail, and they are out there tearing Brian's flat apart."

Mick's trial went first, all over four—count 'em—uppers. Mick told the court, as he had told the police, that he had bought the pills, quite legally, in an Italian drugstore, and had phoned his doctor on his return to confirm that he was okay to use them. His lawyer, Michael Havers, then brought his doctor, Dixon Firth, to the stand, who confirmed this and stated that in his mind it was the equivalant of a prescription. The judge soon flipped this on its head, and told the jury that "these remarks cannot be regarded as a perscription by a duly authorized medical practitioner, and it therefore follows that the defense open to Mr. Jagger is not available...I therefore direct you that there is no defense to this charge." It was obvious to all that he was being caught on a technicality, but the jury understood what the judge wanted them to do. It took them only a few minutes to find Jagger guilty. Knowing he was facing a maximum of two years imprisonment, Jagger, in shock, was taken by paddy wagon to Lewes Prison.

The next day it was the court's turn to deal with Richards. It was his lawyer's intent to try to prove that the raid had been orchestrated by the *News of the World*, the police and their informer, David "Acid King" Schneiderman. However Schneiderman had been whisked out of the country only days after the bust, and the police stated they had no knowledge of his whereabouts. Indeed, he did seem to drop off the face of the earth, until thirty years later, when, under the new name of "David Jove", living in Los Angeles, he confessed to his role in the drug bust.

Without him, Richards' counsel was unable to mount a successful defense with a judge who, it was obvious from the start, was out to get them. The bewigged judge told Richards, "The offense of which you have been properly convicted by the jury carries with it a maximum sentence of as much as ten years, which is a view of the seriousness of this offence which is taken by Parliament." There were gasps in the crowded courthouse and cries of "Oh, no!" from several girls in the audience. Judge Block, calling him "scum" and "filth", sentenced Richards to a year in prison and £500 in court costs. The court room reeled at the sentence, with two teen girls sobbing hysterically and one of them wailing, probably accurately, "He's going to prison because they hate his long hair."

Tony Sanchez reported from the courtroom that Judge Block "wore the smug, bourgeois smile of a man who had done what had to be done." Later in the summer the judge would jest at an agricultural society dinner that, "We did our best, your fellow countrymen, I and my fellow magistrates, to cut these Stones down to size, but alas, it was not to be."

Richards was sent to the fearsome and medieval Wormwood Scrubs prison, where he was promptly demeaned, deloused, stripped of his Carnaby Street finery, given prison duds, and bizarrely given lessons in his new task as a prisoner—making miniature Christmas trees to put on cakes. The other prisoners went wild for their new inmate, but Richards found the ordeal unnerving and unpleasant. "The food's awful, the wine list is terribly limited, and the library is abysmal."

Within a few days, though, there was a powerful reaction from the public, politicians and the press. M.P. Tom Driberg rose in the House of Commons to express "revulsion" at the way the two Stones were being punished "as if they were murderers." Many British newspapers denounced the sentence as "another case of British hypocrisy" (London *Evening News*) or "monstrously out of proportion" (the *Sunday Express*). Most importantly, the world's most prestigious newspaper, the London *Times* wrote a long editorial condemning the sentence under the title, taken from a line from 18th Century poet Alexander Pope, WHO BREAKS A BUTTERFLY ON A WHEEL?

Within days the pair were released, with the warden shouting after Richards as he was driven away in a Bentley, "You'll be back, you bastard!" He never has. England's Lord Chief Justice, Lord Parker reversed both their convictions.

Free again, the two were able to again gambol in the famous "Summer of Love" of 1967. Jagger and his sexy hippie girlfriend Marianne Faithful were invited to a very chic, upper crusty party at the home of his friend Christopher Gibbs that had once belonged to the painter James McNeill Whistler. Along with the rock star were five cabinet members, the uber wealthy Paul Getty II and his elegant wife Talitha, a smattering of Cambridge and Oxford intellectuals, and numerous members of Britain's titled aristocracy, led by Jagger's friend Princess Margaret. The butler began passing around a silver platter of hash brownies, made with twice the appropriate proportions of the Afghan drug. Soon the lords and ladies were freaking out, being rushed off by chauffeur-driven cars to have their stomachs pumped. Around midnight, the Queen was awakened at Buckingham Palace to be told that her sister had been rushed to hospital with what was described as "acute food poisoning." Somehow, the Fleet Street press missed the story, or they would have turned it into a scandal that could have escalated to unimaginable proportions for the British government and the Royal Family.

With his ever-increasing fame/notoriety, Jagger was approached with a proposal from the Labour Party that he himself run for Parliament. He seriously considered it, then realized he could have a lot more fun, make a lot more money, and have a lot more power continuing to be a rock star. Instead he began acting in movies—playing the nineteenth century Australian gangster in *Ned Kelly*, and playing a rock star interacting with contemporary London gangsters in *Performance*. He also managed to get busted again, after a police raid on his house yielded the cops a quarter ounce of marijuana.

The now rather hapless Brian Jones was harassed even more. He kept moving, but wherever he moved he would be found again by a London detective who demanded £1000 to avoid prosecution. "The third time I didn't even have any dope in the place," said Jones, "so he just pulled some out of his pocket and told me he'd plant it on me if I didn't pay over the money." On the next raid a group of policemen crashed through a window with a warrant in hand, ripped his place apart and "found" a chunk of hashish in a ball of wool. This bust Jones had to take seriously. "They'd have just asked for the usual pay-off if they were doing it for fun", he said. "This time they really want to nail me. They want to see me locked up for a very long time."

"I have never had a ball of wool in my life," Jones told the court."I don't darn socks. I don't have a girlfriend who darns socks." This time the case turned out a little differently than the Jagger/Richards bust. The judge did not buy any of the evidence presented by the prosecution or police, and made that clear to the jury. However they ignored him, went ahead on their own and declared him guilty. Jagger, a spectator at his bandmate's trial, glared at the jury in a rage. "Even when the courts are just, the dummies who make up the older generation still seem to be out to destroy us." The judge appeared to agree, fining Jones only £50 and 100 guineas court costs. However, with the guilty verdict hanging over his head, Jones was unable to now get a US work visa, and so no longer able to join the upcoming Stones' American tour. That, along with his dissolute lifestyle and flagging musicianship, meant that he received a visit at his home from Jagger, Richards and Watts, who told him he was fired from the band. Three weeks later he was found dead in his swimming pool, possibly killed by a disgruntled carpenter named Frank Thorogood, with the police investigation allegedly covering up the case.

The four remaining Stones, with Mick Taylor added to replace Jones, then went on what rock critic Robert Christgau would call, "history's first mythic rock and roll tour" across America, which would climax with possibly the worst event ever in the history of music. Giant outdoor rock festivals are exceedingly complicated and difficult events to organize and manage, and in 1969, no-one really had a clue how to make them work. The much ballyhooed Woodstock Festival had come to within a whisker of disaster. John Lennon's Peace Festival was probably lucky it fell apart before it even started. The event it morphed into, the Peace Train across Canada, was mostly a drunken mess. The two Isle of Wight festivals of 1969 and 1970 also proved to be largely disastrous events mitigated by some memorable performances. Fifty years later, it seemed no-one had learned anything, as the Fyre Festival in the Bahamas descended into bankruptcy and a prison term for the organizer. None of these, though, compare with the utterly dreadful orgy of violence and mayhem that was the Altamont Speedway Free Festival.

The idea of a free concert grew out of the resistance from the music community, the revolutionaries and hippies who held sway in the era that "the music should be free," and that the ticket prices for the Stones tour were too high. Laughably, from today's perspective, the ticket prices ranged from $3 to $8. Nonetheless the Stones were felt to be gouging their audience, and so, badgered by journalists, Jagger announced that at the end of the tour they would headline a free music concert. He then left all the details of organizing it to others, and from the very start of the planning, everything about it proved to be, not to put too fine a point on it, a fuck-up.

Originally the plan was to do it in Los Angeles, but as no-one could find an appropriate venue there, it was moved to the San Francisco Bay area, and the Stones management team got involved with the people who knew how to do concerts there—The Grateful Dead, Emmett Grogan and his hippie co-op The Diggers, and concert promoter Bill Graham. All three knew the San Francisco scene well, and knew how to deal with the mayor and city authorities, who were antagonistic towards the counter culture and more or less sick of seeing Golden Gate Park used as a venue for concerts, demonstrations and love-ins, but could have approved it for this big event if approached the right way.

Unfortunately the Stones' team ignored their advice and went off half-cocked on their own, and were soon turned down by the city. Graham, with hundreds of past shows under his belt, backed away from this one, deciding that this cockamamie event looked like it would become a disaster, largely because he had decided that Jagger was a "selfish prick" who would sacrifice all else for his own ends, including the safety of the audience. Others, of course, had a similar view of Graham himself.

The cracks were already starting to show, but the Stones' team, along with the Dead's management, did find an alternate venue—the Sears Point Raceway, 35 miles north of San Francisco. Physically it was a fairly attractive location. Had it been used most or perhaps all of the problems that arose at Altamont would not have occured. However after booking the racetrack, Stones tour manager Ronnie Schneider discovered that it had recently been bought by Filmways, a Hollywood company that produced lowbrow TV like *Mister Ed* and *The Beverly Hillbillies*. Filmways learned that Jagger & Co's plan was not just to headline a peace-and-love free festival, but also to make a commercial film of the event similar to the very successful, recently released doc *Monterey Pop,* and so they now demanded a $100,000 site rental fee for the racetrack, and distribution rights to the film. Jagger, sick of bad deals with record companies and promoters like Decca and Allan Klein, went apoplectic and pulled out of the deal, even though construction was underway and the event was less than a week away.

Schneider brought in two more chefs to stir the broth, both with impressive resumés. Melvin Belli was a high profile, high priced and colorful San Francisco attorney with a string of celebrity clients, including Jack Ruby, the killer of Lee Harvey Oswald. Michael Lang was the hippie promoter who had pulled off both the Monterey Pop

Festival *and* the Woodstock Festival. Both ultimately proved unable to control the swirling mess of Altamont. However they were responsible for helping find the new venue. They jumped into high-priced helicopters (chalking up bills that would never be paid) and flew about the state, looking for an alternative spot for the alternative-lifestyle set to groove out the following Saturday night. They discovered the Altamont Race Track, a beat up venue at the end of a single dirt road, where a onetime, so-so race driver named Dick Carter ran occasional unsanctioned races, drag events and demolition derbies. It was littered with broken down race cars, used tires, broken glass and tumberweed, but it was available and the price was right—Carter was willing to give it to them for nothing.

A band of volunteer carpenters got to work dismantling the Sears Point stage and relocating it to Altamont. Unfortunately, the flimsy four foot stage that might have worked on top of a hill at Sears Point was going to sit at the bottom of a valley at the new venue, giving no protection to the musicians from the giant crowd around them. A pathetic piece of twine was erected as the sole barrier between performers and audience. There were almost no food facilities and only 100 toilets for a crowd that would swell to about 300,000. Jagger insisted that there should be no police on the site, so, in what would be the biggest mistake of the event, The Grateful Dead enlisted the Hells Angels motorcycle gang to provide security. There was confusion over this as well. The Stones' organization agreed to pay the bikers by providing them with $500 of cold beer, but it was unclear what services the violent gang was supposed to provide. "We ain't no cops," they told the organizers, but were reassured they would only have to protect the generators and the stage from being messed with by the crowd. The move from Golden Gate Park to Sears Point to Altamont meant that the violent but not quite psychotic Sonny Barger would no longer have control over the Angels, and instead three different "chapters" of the gang would be vying for power. Jagger was more interested in the filmmakers than the security detail. He brought in the team of Albert and David Maysles, two documentarians skilled in the new genre of *cinema verité* filming, if not in the complex organization needed to capture big rock concerts.

Once the Saturday of the concert dawned, it was clear that in terms of numbers it was a huge success, but in terms of vibes a total failure. Astrologers—very big in those days, predicted doom (Scorpio was rising) and for once they were absolutely right. The few police who patrolled the county took one look at the impending insanity and decided to keep their distance, retreating to a distant hilltop in their squad cars to let the hippies, hooligans, musicians and bikers work things out on their own. The huge crowd began mixing large quantities of Red Mountain wine with bad acid. The diggers and volunteer medics were soon overwhelmed by freaked out, paranoid and sometimes violent people on bad LSD trips. Many of the camera and sound people employed by the filmmakers such as cinematographer Joan Churchill found themselves accidently dosed with acid and unable to shoot. Another, George Lucas, retreated to a distant vantage point to try to shoot the event with an ridiculously inappropriate 1000 mm lens. Only one of his shots ended up in the film.

The Jefferson Airplane were the first band to take to the stage, and had barely begun when the Angels began fighting with people in the front rows of the audience. When the bikers began beating up a black man, Jefferson Airplane singer Marty Balin threw his tambourine at them, and began yelling at the bikers to stop. Paul Hibbits, an Angel wearing a fearsome cougar headdress and known as "Animal", walked up to the singer and smashed him in the face. Balin went down in front of the band's drum kit.

Grace Slick ran to the mike and began trying to sooth the crowd. "Easy. Please be kind. Please be kind." As the band attempted to continue to play, an unconscious Balin was dragged backstage to an impromptu dressing room, and sprawled over the body of a girl trying to recover from an overdose. Meanwhile Animal was admonished for slugging the lead singer of San Francisco's most beloved band, and so went backstage to apologize to him. The fearsome looking biker, looking like a medieval Viking with his dead animal on his head, slurred out some intoxicated concession, then concluded, "You just can't say 'Fuck you' to an Angel."

The dazed Balin stood up and replied, "Oh yeah? Fuck you!"

The enraged Animal reacted immediately, slugging him again as hard as he could. Balin again collapsed to the floor.

The band somehow finished their set. Balin was hustled on to a helicopter, and returned to San Francisco. The rest of the band stayed behind. Even though they recognized that things were getting crazy, they, like almost everyone else, wanted to see the Stones.

Not the Grateful Dead. Even though they were central to the organization of the event, they realized the ridiculous concert was getting montrously out of hand, and left, giving up their spot in the lineup. The violence continued. An enormous fat guy took all his clothes off, then was beaten to a pulp by some Angels. The Stones arrived by helicopter in mid-afternoon, and within two minutes of landing Jagger had been accosted by a young fan who screamed "I hate you" at him, then punched him in the face. Medivac helicopters lifted injured people from the field as if it was a war zone. Santana, The Flying Burrito Brothers, and Crosby, Stills, Nash and Young all played. More Angels showed up, driving their choppers right through the densely packed crowd. Finally, with darkness fallen, the Stones took the stage. They tried to rip into one of their all-too-appropriate signature hits, *Sympathy for the Devil*, but the shear violent insanity of the California crowd being beaten up by the satanic bikers meant for the first time in his long career Jagger lost control of his audience. He signaled to Richards and Watts to stop playing, and pleaded with the crowd.

"Uh, people—I mean, who's fighting, what for? Why are we fighting? Be cool. We don't want to fight. Come on. Do you want—who wants to fight?"

Gamely the band tried to start up the song again, and remarkably continued with a musically tight set of their top tunes. As they began their bluntly misogynistic *Under My Thumb*, a black man named Meredith Hunter, a would-be gangster in a lime green suit with his young white girlfriend Patti Bredehoft in tow, pushed his way forward toward the stage. Apparently upset that the black man was with a white girl, four or five Angels jumped on him. As he crashed to the ground, he pulled a revolver from his waistband. As the Maysles' cameras rolled and the Stones' powerful rhythms continued to throb, biker Al Passaro leapt from the stage, pulled a knife from an ankle sheath, and began plunging it into Hunter's neck and back.

The Stones were not sure if they could believe their eyes. Someone, though, was certain they had just witnessed a murder, and called police, who radioed the call to the cops observing from the hill high above. Reluctantly, the pair of Alameda County Sheriffs drove toward the stage. Medics pulled Hunter backstage. They immediately realized he would have to get to a hospital fast, so tried to put him on the helicopter, but were told it was exclusively for the use of the Stones. As the police showed up, the medic declared Hunter dead. He was the fourth fatality of the day. The Stones' set continued—*Brown Sugar*, then *Midnight Rambler*, then *Gimme Shelter*, *Satisfaction*, *Honky Tonk Women* and finally *Street Fighting Man*. The irony of lines like *Rape, murder—it's just a shot away* were likely not lost on any of them. They finally ran from the stage to the waiting helicopter to whisk them to the tiny local airport. With seventeen people clambering aboard a chopper designed for eight, it was like a scene from the fall of Saigon, though that was still, at that point, six years in the future.

As they regrouped in the tiny airfield waiting for the plane to return them to San Francisco, they slumped on wooden benches, overwhelmed by the sordid events. Richards cursed the Hells Angels. "They're sick, man," he said. "They're worse than cops. I'm never going to have anything to do with them again." A bit later he would call them, "homicidal maniacs...who should be thrown in jail."

A dazed Jagger concurred. "How could anybody think they're people you should have around?" he asked. "I'd rather have cops."

The catastrophic debacle which many ultimately blamed on the Rolling Stones was certainly the worst night in the long career of the Stones, but it was not the last bad one.

Bill Wyman and Charlie Watts were nominally Rolling Stones, but in sense were just talented but bland session players providing background rhythm for Richards, Jagger and (until his death) Jones. The person who really seemed much more of a Stone than either of them was the beautiful, decadent Eurotrash scene-maker, Anita Pallenberg. She had been a lover of all three of the Stones front men. She had acted with Jagger in the extraordinary film *Performance*, and had sung back up vocals on some of their hits. By the 1970s she was living with Richards, both of them outdoing the other in consumption of heroin and cocaine and creation of constant dissolute melodrama. There were car crashes, fires, drug busts, voodoo black magic and breakups through the early 70s. Pallenberg and Richards exiled themselves to France and later Jamaica and both those refuges ended in disaster. In the south of France, they were hounded by the *flics* due to Pallenberg's outrageous activities. In Jamaica, her flirtations with Rastafarians led to a drug bust and a horrific gang rape of her in a jail cell.

The 1972 North American tour was the first of the giant, crazy summer rock tours of the 70s. It began in Vancouver, where 2000 ticketless fans battled with Mounties, and 30 ended up in hospital. In San Diego, fans lit police barricades on fire, and the street battles ended with fifteen in the hospital and sixty in jail. In Tucson, 300 were jailed by police. In Montreal, F.L.Q. separatists blew up their equipment truck, destroying their equipment, while an overflow crowd of 2,000 battled with police.

Three years later, was North America ready for another assault by the band? It seemed unlikely either the United States or Canada would let them in, since Richards now had several new French heroin convictions hanging over his head. Fortunately his well-connected partner Mick Jagger was able to get one of his new powerful friends to help. He went to Walter Annenberg, the United States Ambassador to Britain, to ask what it would take to get work visas for all of the band. Annenberg was impressed with the humanitarian work Jagger had done earlier in the year following the earthquake in Managua, Nicaragua. Jagger, along with his wife du jour Bianca had chartered a plane to fly down with medical supplies, then made a $787,500 disaster relief donation to the Pan-American Development Fund. Annenberg looked around Washington for a solution, and came back with good news—the only issue was Richards, but if he could get a London doctor to certify with a blood test that he was free of heroin, he too would get a visa.

Richards' blood was of course *not* free of heroin, so, adding another wild chapter to the wild history of the band, the guitarist found a doctor at a clinic called Le Pec Varp in Villars-sun-Ollon, Switzerland who would drain the blood out of his body, somehow magically cleanse it, then put it back in. It did seem just a little bit radical, so an apprehensive Keith took along his entourage—Anita, his young son Marlon, his dealer "Spanish Tony" Sanchez, and Marshall Chess, the President of Chicago's Chess Records, to give him courage. All four of the adults were wired on heroin at the time, but only Richards and Chess had the nerve to go through with the scary-sounding operation. Apparently, though, it worked. Richards got his Harley Street doctor's letter, and the tour was on. Twenty-seven dates were booked across the United States and Canada. Ronnie Woods, replacing Mick Taylor, would trade licks with Richards, the famous lips logo was emblazoned on a 747, The Eagles booked as their opening act, General Motors as the sponsor and an enormous phallus constructed to inflate over the stage during the second act (something new for The Man to hassle them about).

Before the tour began a pair of heavies showed up to meet Richards. With General Motors involved, they didn't want any scandals. They told him they would provide him with whatever drugs he needed. He wasn't to buy or accept any from anyone else, nor travel anywhere except by the tour jet. They were taking no chances—no chance of an overdose, a police set up or a bust to embarrass the auto maker.

Nice offer if you can get it, but Richards, always the rule-bender, couldn't resist the chance to break free and see a little of the "real America." After playing Memphis, he decided he was "planed out", so instead of flying to the next gig in Dallas, he grabbed one of the sponsor's bright yellow Chevy Impalas, shanghaied Ronnie Woods and a couple of guys from the security crew, a bag full of pharmaceuticals and thirst-quenchers, and set off on a Hunter Thompson-like journey through the American South.

Stopping at a roadhouse called the 4-Dice Restaurant in Fordyce, Arkansas, (get it?) the pair of longhaired British rock and rollers retreated to the joint's washroom to indulge in the pure Merck blow provided by GM. Fortified by the cocaine, grits and hush puppies, they squealed out of the parking lot and took to the road again, and were almost immediately pulled over by a local cop, who'd been doubtless alerted by one of the local crackers in the restaurant.

The cop arrested them and escorted them, as they tried to toss various drugs out the window, back to the small town station, where they were presented to the police chief, an archetypical Southern redneck appropriately named Bill Gober. Chief Gober thought he had died and gone to cop heaven when Keith Richards was escorted into his police station. Indeed, had things gone differently and he found and identified all the cocaine, peyote, grass, hashish and mescaline that was stuffed into the door panels of the Impala, and successfully led the prosecution of the world's most infamous rock star, he could likely gone on to become...maybe Governor of Arkansas! After that, who knows: A Governor of Arkansas had never become President of the United States up to that point, but surely it wasn't impossible.

It was not to be. Richards and Woods faced serious jail time with the absurd amount of dope they had in the car. At the very least, a bust would unquestionably mean the loss of their work visas, and thus the cancellation of the biggest, most profitable tour in music history. But they had an ace up their sleeve, and they pulled it out.

The Stones had hired a top Washington lawyer from the beginning to run interference for them for the huge tour. Bill Carter had been in the USAF in Korea. He'd been a member of the Secret Service during the Kennedy era. He was an investigator on the Warren Commission. He then moved back to his home state of…, guess what? Arkansas, where he was now based in Little Rock. He had warned the Stones about driving in Arkansas, had told them the state was at that very moment trying to draw up legislation to *ban* rock and roll, had told them if they ever did have cross the state to do so in their big plane the *Starship*, not to drive in Arkansas, certainly never to get off the Interstate, certainly never to stop in rinky dink joints like the 4-Dice in podunk towns well off the beaten path like Fordyce.

They didn't listen to him, but he did listen to them, when they finally found him. That summer Saturday afternoon, he was out playing golf, with, conveniently, a judge, in Little Rock. Carter immediately recognized the serious nature of what was happening. He chartered a jet, and with his golf partner in tow flew up to Fordyce. He wasn't alone. A Dallas TV station also chartered a jet to get a reporter and crew up to Arkansas to cover the shenanigans. The news hit the radio and hundreds of rock fans from around the South—Mississippi, Tennessee, Texas—started flooding into the tiny town to take in the spectacle. Why not? This might be their last time to ever see one of the notorious Stones in 'Murica. The cops had to set up roadblocks to prevent more people from flooding their town.

What followed was a crazy Saturday night court, with the Little Rock judge, still in his golfing duds and by now well inebriated, presiding. In the midst of it he had to take a call from the BBC to do a radio interview. Police Chief Gober was still frothing to throw the book at Richards, but everyone else was keen to have the problem just go away, and they were getting slightly anxious about the giant crowd of Stones fans outside the tiny courtroom. Eventually, like a cat with nine lives, Keith once again dodged the bullet. He had to pay $162.50 for the reckless driving charge, lose his beloved hunting knife (he claims it is still on display in the Fordyce courtroom), and do a photo-op press conference with the judge (with Richards now decked out, for some reason, in a fireman's hat). But he was free! He and his pals were sent on their way.

The next time wouldn't be so easy.

By 1977, the Stones felt their turf was being threatened by new punk rock bands like the Ramones and the Sex Pistols, who were loudly accusing them of being dinosaurs. Sex Pistols lead singer Johnny Rotten called the Stones "revolting", and Sid Vicious chimed in that he "wouldn't piss on Keith Richards if he was on fire." Clearly something had to be done to put these whippersnappers in their place, so Jagger came up with the idea that he should find a small, funky, perhaps even *grotty* bar, and make a live recording in it.

The El Mocambo fit the bill. Housed in a Toronto building that was once part of the Underground Railway, a haven for escaped American slaves, it had been a music venue since 1850. With a garish green and yellow neon palm tree sprouting above the marquee, the joint had been slinging beer and hosting local R&B and rock bands, and some internationally known artists like Charles Mingus and Bo Diddly, since acquiring one of Toronto's first liquor licenses in 1948. A little bit like the Stones themselves, no matter how much money you might throw at it, it could never be gentrified. It was the perfect venue, but was almost the end of the Rolling Stones.

The band and entourage convened at Toronto's swanky Harbour Castle Hilton hotel on February 20, 1977, with their lead guitar player missing. The band hadn't played together in some time and badly needed to rehearse. A telegram was fired to the heavily strung out Richards, still in England, reading WE WANT TO PLAY. YOU WANT TO PLAY. WHERE ARE YOU? MICK. Finally, on February 24, Keith, Anita, Marlon and twenty-eight pieces of luggage departed on a British Airways flight from LHR to YYZ. Midway across the Atlantic, Richards retired to the airplane toilet for three hours, shooting up. When he returned he tossed the spoon he had used to cook up the heroin into Pallenberg's bag.

At Customs, the border agents discovered the spoon, and with it a chunk of hash. They confiscated both for examination, let the pair enter the country, but apparently alerted the Mounties. Within twenty-four hours Richards had acquired an ounce of heroin and five grams of cocaine, either purchased locally—perhaps from Cathy Evelyn Smith, who will be featured in an upcoming chapter—or possibly sent by mail from England. Three days later fifteen Mounties crashed into the Richards/Pallenberg suite at the Harbour Castle. It took them little time to find the drugs, but a long time to wake Keith from a deep dopey sleep. They spent so long slapping his cheeks to try to waken him that, he says, "his cheeks were rosy." Finally, they let him know he was under arrest. "What disapointed me was that none of them was wearing a proper Mountie uniform when they burst into my hotel room. They were all in anoraks with droopy mustaches and bald heads. Real weeds, the whole lot of them, all just after their picture in the paper. Fifteen of 'em around my bed, trying to wake me up. I'd have woken a lot quicker if I'd seen the red tunic and Smokey the Bear hat."

They booked him at the RCMP downtown headquarters, took away his passport (and of course his drugs) and released him on bail. The new bust made headlines around the world. The *New York Times* and *Rolling Stone* sent reporters north to cover the story. Back at the Harbour Castle, Richards expounded to Chet Flippo of *Rolling Stone*, "They are out to make rock and roll illegal. That's the basic drive behind the whole thing. They are just scared of that rhythm. Every sound has an effect on the body and the effects of a good backbeat makes these people shiver in their boots. So you are fighting some primeval fear that you can't rationalize."

Notwithstanding his pontifications on the subject of Music vs The Man, Richards and the band and the Stones management team took this bust very seriously. The ounce of heroin discovered was enough to warrant a charge of possession with intent to traffic. He faced the possibility of a lifetime jail sentence that would likely be a deathblow to the world's greatest rock and roll band. Richards took it in stride, though, heading from the Mountie lockup to the El Mocambo, where, said Mick, "He played his fucking heart out—better than I'd heard in years."

At this point in the tale, two even bigger figures than the Stones injected themselves into the story. Pierre Elliot Trudeau, later to be declared the "Canadian Newsmaker of the Twentieth Century", ran for Prime Minister in 1968. The crazed response to this hip, relatively young, dashing, single, unorthodox politician was dubbed "Trudeaumania." Just as Paul McCartney, Brian Jones and Keith Richards had been, Trudeau, on his campaign trail, was mobbed by young women smitten with him. He lived up to the image, sliding down Parliamentary bannister rails, showing his pecs off by doing risky flips into swimming pools, cheekily pirouetting behind the Queen's back, scuba diving with Fidel Castro and dating singers, musicians and actresses such as Barbra Streisand, Liona Boyd and Margot Kidder. In 1971 he dated and married a 23 year old flower child named Margaret Sinclair. On Christmas Day of that year, they would have their first son, Justin, who in 2015 followed in his father's footsteps and became Prime Minister of Canada.

It was not a happy marriage. By 1977, Margaret Trudeau was chafing at the constrictions of life as a Prime Minister's wife, and falling out of love with Pierre. He lived by the motto *Raison de Passion* (Reason over Passion); she lived by its opposite.

When she discovered along with everyone else that the Stones were in Toronto, she abandoned her husband and three kids and flew down from Ottawa to take a suite on the Stones' floor of the Harbour Castle. Why? "She was a groupie, that's all she was, pure and simple," says Keith Richards. "Nothing wrong with that. But you shouldn't be a Prime Minister's wife if you want to be a groupie."

She wandered the halls of the hotel in her bathrobe. Mick accompanied her to the El Mocambo for the two gigs, and according to some accounts had an assignation with her in a backstage dressing room. He denied he ever had an affair with her. "I wouldn't touch her with a barge pole," he claimed. "She was just a very sick girl in search of something. She found it—but not with me." She instead found it with Ronnie Wood, who later confessed that he and Margaret had "shared something very special for that short time." She also tried to ingratiate herself with Richards and Pallenberg with promises that she would use her political influence to make sure he didn't have to go to jail, and an offer to take care of Marlon if he did. Junior, who would have been about the same age as her five year old Justin at the time, snapped at her to "Fuck off!"

Once the concerts were completed, the band, less Richards, left for New York. Margaret followed and hung out with them there, and was famously photographed, dishevelled and quite obviously pantyless, sitting spreadlegged on the sidewalk in front of the dissolute Studio 54 nightclub, her feet in the gutter. The picture, unfortunately, got back to her husband. When she finally decided to fly home, she was met by a furious Prime Minister, who according to later disclosures by his Mountie security team, slugged, or at least slapped her, and the pair got into a physical fight on the tarmac. Soon after, Pierre filed for divorce.

Richards, unable to leave Toronto, passed the time playing a giant slot racing car game in his hotel room with Marlon, and recording a solo blues album at the *Sounds Interchange* studio. His Toronto lawyer eventually got the court to allow him to fly to Philadelphia to enter a rehab clinic and suffer through under a new radical shock therapy addiction cure. He was also allowed to tour with the band on their 1978 US tour. He flew back to Toronto on October 22, 1978, checked in to the Four Seasons Hotel and prepared for his trial. Sid Vicious of the Sex Pistols was on trial in New York at the same time for the murder in the Chelsea Hotel of his girlfriend Nancy Spungen. Keith thought it ironic that if convicted Vicious might get a lighter sentence for murder than he could for drug possession.

"I don't think it's gonna be as bad as *that*," jeered Jagger. "You've got to say if the worst happens and Keith gets put in an open prison with Mrs. Trudeau for life, that I am still gonna go on the road. Maybe we could play a tour of Canadian prisons. Ha, ha, ha."

Richards felt the involvement of Margaret Trudeau in the events the previous year was going to work to his benefit. "The Mounties and their allies were thinking, 'Oh, great! Wonderful job! We delivered him to the Canadian government with a hook in his mouth.' And the Trudeaus were thinking, 'Uh-uh, pal, this is the last thing we need.'" The prosecution's case had also become somewhat derailed by the death (in a traffic accident) of their star witness, RCMP arresting officer William Seward.

Keith and his legal team led by Toronto lawyer Austin Cooper arrived in court each morning through a phalanx of 500 to 600 fans shouting "Free Keith! Free Keith!" Cooper argued successfully that while Richards was certainly an addict, and while the amount he was caught with was certainly large, the Mounties and the prosecution had overstepped the charges. There was no way that multi-millionaire musician Richards was a drug dealer or would ever have to resort to crime to pay for his habit.

Cooper asked Judge Lloyd Grayburn to understand that Richards was "a tortured creative person—a major contributor to an art form, who was wracked with emotional pain," and compared him to Sylvia Plath, Vincent Van Gogh, Aldous Huxley, Judy Garland, Billie Holiday and F. Scott Fitzgerald. Cooper quoted Baudelaire, who had once declared that art is created by "pieces of the shattered self". Comedian Dan Ackroyd and *Saturday Night Live* producer Lorne Michaels, both Canadians, spoke on behalf of Richards, as did local music journalist and lawyer Jack Batten.

The defense worked. Judge Grayburn, noting that "this is a matter of great importance to Keith Richards and to Canada", said that he would give his judgement at ten the next morning. Later that afternoon he had a short meeting with an unusal petitioner. A nineteen-year-old Quebeçoise blind woman named Rita Bèdard found the judge's house, knocked on the door, and told him her story. She was a Rolling Stones fan who somehow hitchiked to cities where the band was playing, and once had been lucky enough to meet Keith Richards in person following a concert in Fort Worth, Texas. He had been a perfect gentleman, she told the judge, and actually organized opportunities for her to travel with the band's equipment trucks, rather than have to depend on her thumb for lifts. The judge was moved by her story, as of course Richards had been. Keith described her as being "absolutely fearless", later called her his "blind angel" and said that "the love and devotion of people like Rita is something that still amazes me."

The next day Judge Grayburn pronounced his judgement on Richards, saying that he "would not incarcerate him for addiction and wealth", and instead gave him one year's probation, no fine, no jail, with the caveats being that he keep his parole officer updated on his treatments at the Turning Point Clinic in Philadelphia, and that the Rolling Stones perform a benefit concert within six months for the Canadian Institute for the Blind.

What an incredible relief! What a Solomon-like sentence! The Toronto bust and trial had a tremendous affect on both Richards and Pallenberg. Anita called the Toronto bust a "lightening bolt of logic." "The bust was reality," she admitted. "I had already lost a baby. I am sure that the drugs had something to do with it. I had lost my daughter. But I couldn't stop, basically. But now we had to do something about it, because otherwise we could go to jail. That was made clear to us."

Richards concurred. "Toronto made me realize this was it. If I could get off the court thing I would quit. I finally realized it wasn't just me, it was everybody I cared about. I was jeopardizing my children, the guys in the band. So in a way they did me a favor. God bless the Mounties."

Not everyone agreed with the verdict, of course. Ex-Prime Minister John Diefenbaker, now a Conservative M.P., spoke out in the House of Commons against what he called the "preposterous and more than lenient" sentence, to the groans of the governing Liberals. One of the arresting Mounties, Constable A.J. Hachinski alleged that the RCMP had received a call from the Justice Department asking that the trafficking charge be reduced to simple possession—thus stoking speculation that either Pierre or Margaret Trudeau had directly influenced the case, a charge the PMO vehemently denied.

On April 22, 1979, the Stones played two shows at the Oshawa Civic Auditorium just east of Toronto, co-hosted by John Belushi and a local blind deejay, Cliff Lorimer, with Rita Bèdard in the audience. The proceeds—$50,000—went to the Canadian National Institute for the Blind. The charity acted a bit sniffy about the event. They did not keep the money, but instead passed it on to the Toronto Hospital for Sick Children, and they did not distribute the programs the band had specially printed in Braille for the concert, claiming they found the offer "patronizing".

The Crown did appeal Graburn's sentence, but ultimately the Ontario Court of Appeal dismissed their motion.

Richards, true to his word, gave up all drugs and became totally clean. [Editor's note—Not true.] Richards continued with heroin until finally giving it up in the mid 80s. He continued with cocaine until falling out of a palm tree in an accident in Fiji in 2006 convinced him it was finally time to throw in the towel on it as well.

The Stones made a serious connection with Toronto because of the events in the 1970s. All their big North American tours of the 80s and 90s were run from Toronto, with the band spending months rehearsing in the city before going out on the road. In 2003, when Toronto was the main site (along with Hong Kong) of the SARS epidemic, the band volunteered to headline a major outdoor concert to help the city get back on its feet. They have played bigger concerts since, in South America, but at that point it was the biggest event, with about 600,000 in attendence, that the Stones had ever played.

"Toronto is obviously a special place for me, for many reasons," said Keith. "It's always important to come back, because of what I went through there. I think people in Toronto have a special affection for me because they know I was red in the palm then. Yeah, I was guilty as shit, but there was obviously so much more involved. Toronto and me have been mixed up and embroiled in loads of stuff over the years, and so in a way I just feel privileged to come back. Hell, they could have said, you screwed up here, just go away."

The Toronto arrest was also, strangely, the event that somehow brought Keith and Mick back together. "I have to say that during the bust in Toronto, in fact all busts, Mick looked after me with great sweetness, never complaining," noted Richards. "He ran things, he did the work and marshalled the forces that saved me. Mick looked after me like a brother."

Years later, though, Richards was considerably less supportive of his partner when Jagger enthusiastically accepted the British government's offer that he receive the highest honor The Man had to offer.

In 2003, Jagger called his longtime mate, with some news.

"Keef," he told him, "I've got to tell you this now: Tony Blair is insisting that I accept a knighthood."

"Oh, come on, man," moaned Richards. "Just fucking ridiculous. A knighthood? What the fuck would you want with *that?* That's not you, is it? That's not what we're about."

Jagger went on the defensive. "I mean, Paul has one, and Elton. It's not really the kind of thing you turn down, is it?"

Yes, it is, thought Richards. What had happened to the iconoclastic, convention-smashing anarchist rebel he had met fifty years earlier and had been touring, recording and partying with ever since?

"You can turn down anything you like, pal. Tell them to stick it up their arse."

Richards wasn't the only one offended by the notion. Queen Elizabeth was horrified by it. The Prime Minister, a keen rock fan, had first submitted Jagger's name in 1997. Although the Queen seldom interferes with the government's proposals for the twice-annual honors list, she did strenuously object to this one. Jagger, she told Blair, was "not suitable." She had been willing to make both Paul McCartney and Elton John knights, but both of them, despite their questionable profession and their various peccadillos, were at least loyal British taxpayers and generous charitable donors. Jagger appeared to be neither. He had been a tax exile since the 70s, and despite a wealth of over £250 million, was not known to have embraced many charitable causes.

There was far more to it than that. Jagger was the personification of everything despised by British royalty and the British establishment. He was not just scruffy, loud, blatantly sexual, wildly offensive to public order, but he had over the years declared his political views to be anarchism and his spiritual ones satanism. He had openly called for revolution and repeatedly mocked the royal family, often referring to the Queen as England's "Chief Witch."

Worst of all, from the Queen's point of view, was Jagger's forty-year friendship with her sister, Princess Margaret. Elizabeth had known, from her childhood, that her sister was a loose cannon, a chain-smoking, hard-drinking firecracker that could easily be set off by the wrong kind of influences. The Queen viewed Mick Jagger as the very worst kind of influence—"mad, bad, and dangerous to know," as Byron was famously described by his lover Lady Caroline Lamb. Over the years the Queen and the Palace had had to cover up numerous scandals involving Mick and Margaret, including the sex and drugs party in the 60s that could have taken the government and the royalty down had Fleet Street ever learned the full details of it.

Even though the Queen's objections were well known, Tony Blair kept proposing Jagger's name, and finally, in 2003, she acquiesed, providing she didn't have to perform the deed herself. Learning that the investiture was to be on Friday, December 12, she decided that day would the perfect one to get some elective surgery done on her knee and face, and handed the responsibility to her son Prince Charles. When one of her attending physicians told her he was sorry she had to go under his scalpel, she replied to him, "I would much rather be here than at Buckingham Palace knighting a certain party."

Charles had his own issues with Jagger. Although he is exactly of the baby boom cohort that largely embraced the Brit pop of the 60s, his conservative tastes run much more along traditional, classical lines. He also had a personal ax to grind with Jagger. In 1991, at a Prince's Trust dinner at Windsor Castle, Jagger was photographed shaking hands with the Prince while keeping his other hand in his pocket—a faux pas the Prince apparently considered a flagrant breach of royal etiquette. Princess Diana later said, "Charles was really appalled by that. It's the kind of silly thing they never forget."

Diana, shortly after marrying Charles in 1981, had wanted to invite Jagger to tea at Kensington Palace. Knowing Jagger's reputation as a womanizer and his wife's as a flirt, Charles hit the roof, and the Prince and Princess got into a nasty row over the matter, the outcome being that she was not allowed Jagger but instead permitted an audience with the chubby, happily married, prematurely balding Phil Collins. The Jagger affair was yet another of the many rifts between the royal couple.

While Charles could not turn down the task, he was not keen on it. "It's really quite difficult to believe. Mick Jagger. A *knighthood*. Just incredible," he kvetched to the Queen's Chief Usher. "My mother didn't have the stomach for it."

It was also uncertain when or if Jagger would deign to accept the high award. He had postponed the date ten times, most recently two days earlier when he heard he would have to share the investiture with rugby star Jonny "Wilko" Wilkinson, who had just led England to victory in the World Cup. He wasn't about to share the spotlight with a rugby player. However he did arrive at the palace on the 12th, wearing a suit along with a pair of Adidas sneakers. Each honoree was allowed three guests, so Jagger brought his father, Joe, then 92, and two of his seven children, 33 year old Karis and 19 year old Elizabeth.

Jagger was the only knighthood of the day; the rest were receiving the much lower orders of an MBE (Member of the Most Excellent Order of the British Empire), an OBE (an Officer of same) or a CBE (Commander of same). The world famous rock star was in line between a priest and an elderly man honored for his services to the sheep industry.

"Sir Michael Philip Jagger", announced Master of the Royal Household Vice Admiral Tom Blackburn, "for services to popular music."

Jagger stepped up to the Prince, knelt before him and bowed his head.

"I dub thee," said Charles, tapping each of Jagger's shoulders with a sword, "Sir Michael Jagger."

Some of Jagger's compatriots were not surprised to learn that he had finally been offered, and had accepted the honor. "He's always wanted a knighthood," said Charlie Watts. Marianne Faithful concurred. "Mick's a tremendous snob," she opined. "He always wanted that so much. That's why I'm sort of compassionate about it."

Not so Keith Richards. "I went fucking berserk when I heard. I thought it was ludicrous to take one of those gongs from the establishment when they did their very best to throw us in jail and kill us one time. It's not not what the Stones is about, is it? I don't want to step onstage with someone wearing a fucking coronet and sporting the old ermine."

If anyone hadn't got the message, he added, when asked whether he would accept a knighthood himself, if it were ever offered, "I would tell them where to put it. I wouldn't let that family near me with a sharp stick, much less a sword."

The Plastic People and the Velvet Revolution

Many musicians see themselves as revolutionaries, but very few can say they have been a part of bringing down a government. The Plastic People of the Universe, formed following the Soviet invasion of Czechoslovakia in 1968, played a part, some claim a major part, in ending, twenty-one years later, the one-party communist dictatorship of Milos Jakes and replacing it with a parliamentary democracy led by the band's muse and sometime songwriter, Václav Havel.

In the mid-60s, Czechoslovakia, although deeply imbedded behind the Iron Curtain, was feeling the influence of the musical winds of change blowing out of places like Liverpool and San Francisco. Underground clubs began opening in Prague. Dozens of rock groups began to form. Radio stations switched from the outmoded music of the past to new western rock and roll. The hardline Communist leader of the country, Antonin Novotny, reacted with a vengeance, fighting back against anything that smacked of "western influence", purging his cabinet of reformers, and increasing censorship laws. This, though, resulted in a counter-revolt. Feeling he had gone too far, the Communist Party ousted him, and replaced him with a liberal reformer, Alexander Dubcek, who instituted a brief flowering of freedom known as the Prague Spring.

The Soviets, fearing that the Prague Spring could spread to all their Eastern European satellite states, invaded Czechoslovakia with tanks and 650,000 soldiers on August 21, 1968. There was little resistance other than students and hippies mixing up street signs to try to confuse the tank commanders. Within three days it was over, with the Soviets in total control, a new hardliner, Gustav Husak replacing Dubcek as leader, and all the reforms wiped away.

Less than a month after the invasion, bassist Milan Hlavsa formed The Plastic People of the Universe, partially in political protest, partially as a tribute to the revolutionary American bands The Fugs, the Mothers of Invention, and the Velvet Underground. He brought in guitarist Josef Janicek and viola-player Jiri Kabes. They allied with art critic Ivan Jirous, who served as artistic director and manager of the band in a similar way that Andy Warhol had done with the Velvet Underground.

The Plastics were considered the leading psychedelic band in the country until January of 1970, when the government shut them down by revoking their professional license. They could no longer receive fees for their performances and they no longer had access to either instruments or rehearsal space, both of which were controlled by the state. The band had to scrounge old instruments, and Janicek, an auto mechanic by trade, had to build amplifiers from old radio sets. It was safer to sing songs in English than Czech, so Jirous brought Paul Wilson, a young Canadian living in Prague, to teach the band lyrics to songs by Zappa and the Velvet Underground, and to sing and play guitar with the group.

In order to get around the government's increasingly tough rules, the only way the band could perform was to bill the concerts as "lectures", with art critic Jirous pontificating about Andy Warhol for ten minutes, then bringing the band on stage to play a two hour set of Velvet Underground tunes. The secret police soon caught on to this ploy, shut it down, and banned the group from playing in Prague.

In 1972 an accomplished jazz saxophonist named Vratislav Brabanec joined the group, convincing the band they should shift gears, perform only original material, in Czech, and reapply for a performance permit. It seemed at first to work—the band was given the license, but two weeks later the government revoked it. Czechoslovakia is, after all, the home of Franz Kafka: Czechs are used to mind-numbing incomprehensible bureaucracy. The authorities claimed the music of the Plastics was "morbid" and would have a "negative social impact," and they were totally banned from playing in public.

The band abandoned Prague and took up residence in distant small villages in Bohemia, where an underground culture grew up around the Plastics and other artists, *Samiizdat* writers and hippies (Bohemia being, of course, the origin of the word *Bohemian*.) Through the 70s the band was only able to play at secret concerts, the location only revealed at the last minute, fans clandestinely promoting it by word of mouth, usually having to walk long distances to remote farms to attend. The secret police often learned of these events from informers. At one in 1974, known as the "Ceske Budovice Massacre", the police led over 1000 fans through a dark tunnel, where they beat them with clubs, forced them back on to a train and sent them back to Prague with the concert cancelled.

In response the band went deeper underground, taking fake names but continuing to search for opportunities to be heard. On February 21, 1976 they created a "happening" called the Musical Festival of the Second Culture in the village of Bojanovice. Once again, they were busted by the Secret Police, who arrested 100 fans and twenty-seven musicians, including all the members of the Plastic People, and seized all their equipment, tapes, films and notebooks of lyrics. Paul Wilson was deported back to Canada. The Czech members of the band were put on trial, found guilty of "organized disturbance of the peace, extreme vulgarity with an anti-socialist and an anti-social impact, extolling nihilism, decadence and clericalism." Four of them were given jail sentences of between eight and 18 months. A group of dissident Catholics, former and excluded communists and university intellectuals, at the risk of their own safety, protested the sentences given to the rockers. They were led by playwright and future President Vaclav Havel, who was not just a fan but a sometime songwriter for the avant-guard band. Havel and his group of political dissidents, calling themselves Charter 77, coalesced around the underground movement created by the Plastic People of the Universe.

Once released from prison, the band held another of their "happenings" at Havel's country house, where they later recorded their album *Leading Horses*. The police watched over the events but did not break them up. However, in April of 1981 the band performed at another friend's house near Česká Lípa and two weeks later the house mysteriously burned to the ground. Vratislav Brabenec was picked up for questioning, and the police all but admitted to torching the house. Brabenec, beaten and interrogated by the police numerous times, finally decided to escape the country, going to live in exile in Canada. He took with him the master tapes of *Leading Horses* and was able to get them to his old bandmate Paul Wilson, who released the album under his tiny indy label Bozi Myln Records. Brabenec settled in the Toronto suburb of Scarborough, where he found work as a landscape gardener. He wasn't the only exiled Eastern European rock star in the working-class east end of Toronto. The two leaders of the Zlatni Struni, (the Golden Strings), considered the biggest rock band of Bulgaria in the 1970s, defected and ended up living close to Brabenec, running a used car lot.

Some glimmers of hope and signs of liberalization appeared in Czechoslovakia in 1986, and in 1987 the remaining members of the Plastic People were told they could get their performing license back, but only if they would change their name. It caused a rift in the group, with some including drummer Jan Brabec abandoning the group over the government-forced name change. However, leader Milan Hlavsa did agree to it, re-named what was left of his band Pulnoc (Midnight) and began performing once again. Their manager was not so lucky. Ivan Jirous (now going by the underground name Magor, meaning "Shithead") was sentenced to sixteen months in prison for reading protest poems in public. Brabenec left his exile in Toronto to join poet Allan Ginsberg and Ed Sanders, leader of The Fugs at a benefit in New York City for Jirous, who by now had spent eight of the last fifteen years in prison.

In 1989 things began to happen fast in Eastern Europe. In June, Solidarity defeated communism in Poland, and Hungary began dismantling the physical Iron Curtain with the west. In November, the Berlin Wall came down and the Velvet Revolution began in Czechoslovakia. It is debated whether the word "Velvet" was just a synonym for gentle, or whether the revolution was named after the Velvet Underground, but it is certain that one of the first visitors to President Havel after he took office was Lou Reed, founder of the underground rock group. Both rock and classical musicians played an important part in the short, twenty-four-day revolution, with both the members of Pulnoc and the entire Czech Philharmonic Orchestra leading the battle for freedom.

Vaclav Havel became the new President of Czechoslovakia on December 29, 1989. A few days later, Frank Zappa, at the invitation of Havel, flew to Prague, where 5,000 fans were at the airport to greet him. The American Ambassador, Shirley Temple Black, happened to cross paths with the eccentric rocker at the airport, where she getting ready to leave the country. She of course had herself been a singer and performer long before becoming a Republican-appointed ambassador—her songs *The Good Ship Lollipop* and *Animal Crackers in my Soup* were two of the biggest hits of the 1930s. The Czechs, who mistakenly thought Frank Zappa was beloved across American society, could not understand the frosty, horrified response of Mrs. Black to the goateed, ponytailed rocker.

Zappa, though, got a very warm reception from Havel, who offered the hirsute musician the exalted post of "Special Ambassador to the West on Trade, Culture and Tourism." That proposed extraordinary mash up of Music and The Man did not last long, after the US Secretary of State James Baker III heard about it. Baker already had history with Zappa. Baker's wife, Susan Baker, was one of the leading lights of the Parents Music Resource Center, the rock and rap censorship group run from Washington by Tipper Gore. Zappa was a leading opponent of the PMRC, speaking out against it at congressional hearings, where he had once dismissed Susan Baker as a "bored housewife."

Vaclav Havel got some sort of a lesson in *realpolitik* during Secretary Baker's official visit to Prague to meet the new President. The upshot was a statement from Havel's press secretary Michael Zantovsky saying, "We like Frank Zappa, but he is not authorized to arrange any trade agreements with our government." Zappa was demoted to the role of "Unofficial Cultural Attaché."

In 1997, on the twentieth anniversary of his Charter 77 movement, President Havel pleaded with the Plastic People to come out of retirement and perform what was meant to be a one-off concert at Prague Castle. The band agreed and played a short set. They performed in the very building where their persecutors had plotted against them years earlier, with cabinet ministers in the new government and their wives enthusiastically dancing to their music.

No other rock band has had to put up with the abuse and obstruction that the Plastics did during their lifetime. Now that the struggle was over and the country's new president had brought them back together, they came to the conclusion that they still liked making their eccentric brand of music. Following the Prague Castle concert, the band officially re-united, went out on the road, and are still touring and performing today.

Dead on Arrival

They played like shit. They looked like shit. And they didn't give a shit. That was their reputation. The truth was often exactly the opposite. They were creating a new music—punk rock. On the west coast of North America, a sub-set of punk emerged, calling itself Hardcore. One of the most prominent, longest-lasting and hardest-working of these west coast bands was Vancouver-based D.O.A, led by Joe Keithley, *aka* Joey Shithead.

The usual life expectancy of punk bands was very short. The Sex Pistols lasted for all of two and a half years. D.O.A., by contrast, began in 1978 and is still with us today. It has, of course, gone through many changes since the '70s, and in fact Keithley is the only member of the group who was there at the beginning and is still standing today. While rockers and rappers were flying in Lear jets and driving Ferraris, D.O.A endured forty years of brutal touring, criss-crossing North America and Europe in clapped-out vans, playing in some of the roughest venues in the world, billeted in squats and harassed by The Man not just for their music but also for their in-your-face politics. Frequently, they were playing for free, shouting out their lyrics about racism, globalism, poverty and environmentalism at benefits for leftwing, controversial causes.

The extraordinary thing about Keithley is that he graduated from fighting for change as a punk-rocker with an electric guitar around his neck to fighting on the political stage, now with a tie around his neck. He unsuccessfully ran three times as a candidate of the Green Party in the British Columbia provincial elections of 1996, 2001, and 2017. Then in 2018, again under the banner of the Green Party, he won a seat on the City Council of Burnaby, the third largest city in British Columbia. His motto is Talk-Action=Zero. Throughout his life, there has been no shortage of either talk or action, nor was there with the only other three prominent musicians who transformed themselves into politicians.

Sonny Bono began in the music business as a gofer for infamous producer Phil Spector, then joined forces with his wife to create the folk-rock duo Sonny and Cher. After a long and successful music career Bono entered politics, first becoming mayor of Palm Springs, California from 1988 to 1992, then Member of the US House of Representatives for California's 44th District, serving from 1995 to 1998. He died in a skiing accident, hitting a tree at Heavenly Mountain resort in 1998.

Peter Garrett was the lead singer and frenetic, mesmerizing dancer for the Australian rock group Midnight Oil. After years of recording and touring, he disbanded the group to run for political office. He was the Australian Labor Party member of the House of Representatives from 2004 to 2013. In 2007, he was appointed Minister for the Environment, Heritage and the Arts, and after the 2010 he took the portfolio of Minister for School Education, Early Childhood and Youth.

Ignacy Jan Paderewski was both one of the most celebrated pianists of the twentieth century and composer of over seventy symphonies, operas, and other orchestral and vocal pieces, and also—the Prime Minister of Poland. Born in a tiny village in what then was Poland but is now Ukraine, Paderewski eventually settled in California, touring relentlessly around the world. He made thirty tours of the United States alone, and was the first person ever to give a solo performance in Carnegie Hall.

At the onset of World War 1, he returned to Europe to work as a diplomat in London on behalf of Poland. At the end of the war he became Prime Minister of the re-organized state of Poland and signed the Treaty of Versailles on behalf of the country. Even in the international turmoil following the war, his term as a political leader was remarkably successful. He led the country in ending ethnic and social strife, creating a public education system, tackling the outbreak of epidemics and solving border disputes with Poland's many neighbors. He also represented Poland at the newly formed League of Nations, where he was the only delegate not to require a translator, since he spoke seven languages fluently.

In 1922 he retired from politics and returned to music, touring the United States in a private railway car, and filling 20,000 seats in a concert in Madison Square Gardens. When the Second World War broke out, he returned to political life to become head of the National Polish Council, a Polish parliament in exile in London while the Nazis occupied Poland. He died in 1941, leaving an almost unique legacy of someone who made a huge contribution to both worlds of Music and The Man.

Joey "Shithead" Keithley, though, made a bigger leap from anarchist musician to mainstream, suit-wearing politician than either Bono, Garrett or Paderewski. As a punk-rocker, he never asked for or expected to get any help from the straight world for his efforts. As a west coast Canuck hoser, his style was to just to open the throttle and *give 'er*. For his first gig, he rented the Legion Hall in the hick town of Port Moody and travelled by public transit to paper the blue-collar burg with hand-drawn posters promoting the event. This caught the attention of the local fuzz who came to visit before the show. Two undercover police demanded to know, "Who's in charge of this shindig?" Keithley fessed up. The cop held up one of the posters, ripped from a telephone pole, and asked, "What's this? 'Piss on You Productions'. 'Joey Shithead' That's sick!" Keithley replied he had a democratic right to print whatever he wanted. The cops snarled that they would be back later, "to keep an eye on things." It was only the first of many interactions between Keithley's band and men in uniform.

D.O.A. became the house band at the Smilin' Buddha, a seedy bar in Vancouver's Lower East Side—the poorest neighborhood in Canada. The bar was only a block from the local police station, so the cops were able to keep a close eye on what was happening. They sent undercover cops in, who reported back that D.O.A. was filling the club to well over its fire-code capacity and were singing songs like *Royal Police,* with very provocative, damning lyrics about Canada's famous Mounties.

One night, ten policemen burst into the club and it became a battle royale between cops and punks. Keithley was put in a chokehold and with the cops kicking him in the groin and stomach, dragged out the front door. He remembers regaining consciousness in the back of a paddy wagon filled with ten others, and says, "The cops were having fun with us," by driving on a bumpy road beside the railroad tracks running alongside Vancouver's waterfront, with the driver of the van speeding up to 50 mph, then slamming on the brakes, sending the punks flying around in the back of the paddy wagon. Once at Police Headquarters, they were put in an elevator that was infamous for the beatings that would be administered in it as it rose to the booking floor. Keithley and his cohorts managed to survive the trip, the elevator, and a night in the drunk tank in which there were more beatings. In an article about the incident in Vancouver's underground paper the *Georgia Straight,* he was quoted saying "We're not looking for a riot, but we are going to continue playing music and saying what we believe."

On July 1, 1978, the band was booked to play an outdoor Canada Day concert in Stanley Park. Without a permit. "The bulls were having none of it," recalls Keithley. "They blocked us from playing until we borrowed a permit from a picnicking church group. Right Christian of them, I would say. The cops were not crazy about this and they spent the afternoon haranguing the 400 people that showed up."

After two years of heavy-duty touring across North America, the band was invited to perform at a "Rock Against Reagan" concert at the Republican National Convention in Detroit. Keithley recalls that in that baking hot Detroit summer there was a garbage strike going on, so "there were so many rats running around you needed name tags to be able to tell them from the Republicans." While D.O.A. was performing on the outdoor stage, a group of what he calls "the pea-brained Americans-for-Reagan chapter" descended on the event and tried to break it up. A phalanx of Detroit police then appeared and tried to get between the punk audience and the young Republican troublemakers. To create a soundtrack for the melee, Keithley and band broke into their tune *Fucked Up Ronnie:*

> *You're fucked up, Ronnie. You're not going to last*
> *You're gonna die too, from a neutron blast.*
> *I'm lyin' in a pool of blood leave me alone*
> *I don't want your help anyway*
> *When you march us off to war*
> *Will you be there to save the day*
> *You're fucked up Ronnie, leave me alone.*

Three months later they were involved in an even bigger riot while playing at the famous Whisky À Go Go in Los Angeles. A street disturbance outside the club led to a scene with forty cop cars, each with three or four officers inside, racing to the club, and two police helicopters hovering overhead. "They jumped out of their patrol cars with shields and batons, swinging at anything and everything," remembers Keithley. "The street was instant carnage. Blood, chaos and people running, trying to find a way out."

Keithley also recalls one of their next interactions with The Man, in which they were mistaken for agents of Pablo Escobar. "Right after a show in Long Beach, CA, we left for our next gig in Las Vegas, just so we could get an early start on losing our dough in Sin City. About three AM we were way east of L.A., just getting deep into the desert in San Berdoo [San Bernadino County]. We were partying as we raced along when all of a sudden, the Five-O was flashing their lights behind us. A solo cop came near the van and then darted back to his cruiser. Next thing we knew there were six cop cars, lights a blazin' in the desert night. They pulled out their guns, cuffed all six of us and threw us in the back of their cruisers. It turned out that the cop that first pulled us over looked at our British Columbia license plate and figured that we had a mobile meth lab fresh up from South America. Yeah, right! When they finally cut us loose, the only African-American cop of the six asked us what our band's name was. When I told him D.O.A. he said, 'I know you guys, can I get your autograph?' The white cops shot him a dirty look."

With Reagan in power, America was becoming more reactionary every day. D.O.A. responded with new songs confronting mainstream American life, and then got a backlash to that from the more conservative elements of society. "I hate it when people say you shouldn't mix politics with music," responded Keithley. "How the hell can you not? If an actor can become the president of the United States, why can't a musician become an activist?"

One of their pals, Gerry Hannah (*aka* Gerry Useless), a founding member of the Vancouver punk scene with his band The Subhumans, crossed the line from music into activism in a very radical way. While D.O.A. was performing in the US, Keithley got a call from their manager in Vancouver, telling them that their good friend had been arrested near the town of Squamish along with four others and charged with the bombings of Litton Industries in Toronto, three Red Hot Adult Video stores in Vancouver, and a BC Hydro substation on Vancouver Island. The anarchist bombings were considered the biggest "underground" action in Canada since the FLQ crisis of 1970. Litton Industries was an electronics company building the guidance system for US cruise missiles. Ten people had been injured in that bombing. The five arrested, two women and three men, were soon dubbed the "Squamish Five." Their goals were anti-war (hence the Litton bombing), environmental (hence the BC Hydro bombing) and feminist (hence the bombing of the porn shops).

Joey Shithead and D.O.A. sprang into action. "We believed that injustice and inequality could be dealt with through words, ideas, and people power, not through violence and bombs," says Keithley, "but one of our best friends was now in bad trouble. We knew right away that we wanted to help him and the others." Feeling that the Five would need some money to try to get a fair trial, D.O.A. produced a benefit record and performed benefit concerts for the activists' defense fund. The Squamish Five were all found guilty and got sentences ranging from six years to life. All are now long out of prison.

With the rightwing Bill Bennett in power as premier, a series of what Keithley calls "harsh economic measures" were instituted that affected the poor, the unemployed, and most of the middle class. There was a strong likelihood of a province-wide general strike, so Keithley wrote and recorded a song with that name, and, now considered B.C.'s premier protest band, prepared to perform *General Strike* at a massive rally for the event, only called off when the province's biggest union, the International Woodworkers' Union struck a last-minute deal with the government.

The band had a worldwide reputation, unfortunately one that was much more impressive than its income—they were now down to eating peanut butter sandwiches on soup lines. When the opportunity arose, they jumped at the chance to make a European tour. It was not, though, done in the grandiose manner of an Elton John or Rod Stewart. Instead, the band travelled by third class rail to play in dingy halls to drunken audiences in the far corners of Eastern Europe, often with The Man hot on their trail.

Returning from what was then Yugoslavia into Italy, the band got into a wrangle over their train tickets. The train lurched to a stop, and five policemen stormed aboard. The cops backhanded two of the band members, seized their passports and threw the entire gang off the train. Eventually the police let them re-board but alerted the Italian police to search the band for drugs once they hit the border. The plainclothes Italian cop that showed up to demand their passports was dressed for the part in a stylin' black leather coat in the manner of the then-popular TV cop "Beretta". He was okay with the Canadian passports and just threw them back in their faces, but he took one look at drummer Greg James' American passport, spat on it and hurled it to the floor of the railway car.

For their tour of East Germany, they managed to get an old van that they named "Gertie". When they crossed back into West Germany, Keithley remembers, "We were promptly ordered out of Gertie. The guards yelled *'Mach schnell! Mach shnell!* [Make it snappy!]. Apparently German border guards and cops were on alert for anarchist and leftist troublemakers and I guess we fit the description. The guards ripped the van apart from top to bottom, looking for weapons, propaganda, and drugs. They even sent in a drug dog. Of course, they found nothing."

With all the unwanted attention from the police and European border guards, touring a band like D.O.A. is very different to the coddled lives of the superstars of music. The giant stadium tours have teams of travel and logistics experts making sure the pampered rock stars don't have to worry their little heads about getting to the next gig on time. Whatever the demands, they look after them. Well, almost. Elton John recalls that at the height of his cocaine-fueled craziness in the 1990s, he once called up his management team and berated them for 15 minutes about the wind outside his hotel room window and demanded they do something about it.

D.O.A. didn't have anyone they could call about turning off the wind. Nor did they have any multilingual advance men to look after all the potential grief of crossing the many borders of Eastern Europe. One of the most onerous tools The Man uses to hassle touring musicians (and doc filmmakers and TV journalists) is the *carnet*. A carnet is a fancy French word for a bond that has to be purchased in advance listing every piece of the travelling kit, every cymbal, every microphone stand, every cable that guarantees that the group isn't going to sell any of those beaten up old mike stands or cymbals while on the road. Carnets are ridiculous, long obsolete pieces of bureaucratic paperwork that are the bane of travelling musicians. If ever the group's gear gets split between two vehicles travelling separately, or if a piece of gear gets broken and has to be replaced, clearing carnets can become a nightmare, something that happened many times on D.O.A.'s long touring career. Keithley remembers one incident, dealing with what he calls the "fascists" controlling entry into Italy:

"It took six different border guards before one of them finally understood. Even then, he had to take me and the carnet to the "big bossio" of the frontier. The big jerk blew his top. He got up from his desk and screamed first at me and then individually at each of his six subordinates who were standing there. He pounded his fist on the table and repeatedly slammed down the carnet. He acted like we had been pissing all over the Sistine Chapel. After about an hour of this, they fined us some lira and let us go."

There was no time to spare. The band frequently played five or more gigs a week, each one in a different town, often in a different country. The band's "Endless Tour" finally ended, after 132 shows in 105 different cities in thirteen countries on three different continents. "We'd covered 63,000 miles, about two-and-a-half times the circumference of the earth," remembers Keithley. "We'd gotten our asses kicked a few times, but we'd done most of the ass-kicking."

They returned to Vancouver to find the city embroiled in a controversial debate over the large number of people evicted from their apartments to make way for the upcoming Expo 86 World's Fair. D.O.A. recorded and released another of their "crisis EP's", this one titled *Expo Hurts Everyone.* They also performed at a benefit concert for the evicted tenants, opening for legendary protest singer Pete Seeger and singer/songwriter Arlo Guthrie, son of the even more legendary Woody Guthrie.

They continued to perform for benefits, and for causes they believed in, such as the release of Nelson Mandela who had been held in jail in South Africa for 27 years, and was finally released in 1990. Keithley also organized a benefit for the defense fund of Jello Biafra. Biafra, songwriter and lead singer for the San Francisco punk band the Dead Kennedys, had been charged with "distributing harmful material to minors" following a complaint made by Tipper Gore's group, the Parents Music Resource Center. D.O.A.'s benefit concert managed to raise about $5000 to help with Biafra's legal defense. Biafra's trial ended with a hung jury. He was acquitted although not totally vindicated.

D.O.A. also played in a big concert fighting against the new free trade agreement between Canada and the US that was being promoted by the Canadian Prime Minister and American President. Keithley referred to the pair as "Bullshittin' Brian Mulroney and his pal Ronnie Raygun." This deal, which expanded into NAFTA, the North American Free Trade Agreement, says Keithley, "allowed the US to exploit both Canada's natural resources *and* Mexico's cheap labor pool." It was the first time Keithley began to move from music into politics—the first time he was speaking, not singing about NAFTA at colleges in British Columbia.

The band continued to play benefits and at offbeat venues. The most hardcore of these was probably the Prince Albert, Saskatchewan maximum-security prison. Keithley sang Johnny Cash's standard *San Quentin*, changing the lyrics to *Saskatchewan Pen, I hate every inch of you. You've tortured me since 1972.* He then fired up a chainsaw, a traditional highlight of the band's stage performances, and one that certainly got the attention of the overseeing prison guards. The warden later told the MuchMusic host of the event Terry David Mulligan that the next year they'd be sticking to country and western music.

D.O.A. performed as part of the Resist in Concert! event at the New York Palladium along with other bands and entertainers such as Sinéad O'Connor and Susan Sarandon. They also played a Peace Concert in Parksville on Vancouver Island to protest the US nuclear submarines that were re-fueling there. More and more, the band, and the world, were getting into environmental issues. Keithley helped organize and perform (with headliners Terry Jacks and Bryan Adams) at a major concert protesting against what he called, "the damage caused by B.C.'s pulp and paper industry as it pumped crap into the air and dumped toxic effluent into the waterways."

He also organized a "Rock Against Radiation" show in Vancouver. He remembers, "the city was totally opposed to it and tried to stop the show, but it went ahead anyway. The very next year, the mayor was leading the Stop the Arms Race parade in Vancouver. It takes people a while to catch up, sometimes."

Keithley's involvement in all these political, protest, and benefit concerts led to his own remarkable transformation from punk rocker to politician. "I got involved trying to save a second-growth forest in our neighborhood," he recalls. "A bunch of fuckheads from a few high-tech companies wanted to cut down the trees so their employees could work in a "park-like" setting. Then, the Green Party asked me to be a candidate for them in the upcoming provincial election in British Columbia."

Thinking it was way too much of a stretch for Joey Shithead to be running for a position as an M.L.A. (Member of the Legislative

Assembly), Keithley initially declined the offer but then changed his mind and went for it. "I never thought I could get elected but I believed I could make people think. I knew I could operate in my usual maverick fashion. The press would ask me what kind of record I had to stand on. I'd say 'I've got lots of good records to stand on'." Keithley ran in two provincial elections but "In the end I quit the Green Party and stopped running for office, because people will always vote for shitheads, just not necessarily Joe Shithead."

It was not, though, the end of his political career. In 2000, he got a Vancouver radio talk show, talking politics and talking to politicians from downtown storefront window studio. "Folks, the other media outlets give you a bunch of crap," he would shout into the mike with his distinctive junkyard dog growl, "but here at MyCityRadio, we look under every rock. We comb the wire services. We peruse the check-out aisles of the grocery stores and we look at the National Enquirer. We cut through the crap and give you the real shit."

At a concert celebrating the fiftieth anniversary of the famous 1952 Paul Robeson concert at the Peace Arch on the BC/Washington border (described in the Paul Robeson chapter), Joey was asked to sing Robeson's most famous song, *Ol' Man River*, which he did, *a cappella*, and then the full band did a set.

D.O.A. took on a new cause, touring under the banner of the *Festival of Atheists,* spamming right-wing Christian evangelical organizations, and urging them to join their nightly onstage rituals of atheism. Some evangelicals took the bait, holding prayer meetings outside the concert halls, splashing holy water on the arena doors and trying to stop the audience from entering.

In 2002, Vancouver mayor Larry Campbell's first (!) official act was to officially declare December 21 as "D.O.A. Day" in the city. The elaborate printed proclamation full of lines such as "And Whereas D.O.A. burst out of Vancouver's underground to become one of the most influential bands on the punk circuit", was read by City Council Jim Green at an acoustic performance at the Railway Club. In typical anarchic punk fashion, by the time Green got to the fifth line, "And whereas D.O.A.'s exceptional longevity as a band in a milieu known for the early demise of musical groups is to be highly commended," the audience was getting restless so Keithley yanked the proclamation from Green's hands and laughingly finished reading it himself, with a lot of abbreviations and "blah-blah-blah's". For all that, he very much appreciated the city's gesture, and began thinking of running again for political office.

He must have gotten an ego-boost when in December 2010, the Vancouver Sun created an online poll asking readers for the most influential British Columbian of all time. Joey ended up as Number One, which shows at very least he has a very loyal and enthusiastic fan base. Vote early! Vote often!

In the somewhat more legitimate election of 2012 he decided again to try to run, this time for the New Democratic Party, but he failed to win the nomination. He was back with the Green Party for a 2016 by-election, and again for a general election in 2017. Both times he failed to garner enough votes. That changed with his electoral success on October 20, 2018 when he won a council seat in the City of Burnaby. Many people were shocked, including *Burnaby Now* magazine, which reported the story under the headline, WHAT THE HELL HAPPENED TO JOEY SH*THEAD?

"The legendary punk seems transformed since becoming a municipal politician. Did he sell out or just grow up? Joey Shithead has been possessed. A politician has taken control of the punk rocker, stuffed him into a suit and given him a new name: Councillor Joe Keithley. The man who sang 'Smash the State' is now a cog in the political machine he spent decades raging against. The guy who pilloried developers for their heartless greed now calls them 'nice people'. And the punk who penned anti-police anthems now boasts of a 'good relationship' with the local detachment. What the hell happened?"

On his victory night, still surprised he had won, Keithley decided, "I'm elected now, so I'm going to make the best of it."

He did don a suit and tie and begin his new work as a councilor. One of the steepest learning curves he faced was realizing change in big city politics doesn't happen overnight.

"As an activist and a would-be politician before I got elected, I thought, 'Damn, why doesn't council do stuff faster?' And people would always say to me, "Joe, you can't fight city hall.' I always hated that expression and thought, 'Of course you can fight city hall.'" After a few months on the council, Keithley began realizing there are many hidden complexities to city politics. "The activists would have us build 50,000 housing units and have them operating in six months. It's not going to happen. You can't build stuff that fast. You can't set aside the land that quickly. Now I realize there are a lot of competing interests."

The transformation from punker Joey Shithead to Councillor Joe Keithley may seem remarkable to outsiders, but this is how the man in question sees it: "I kind of was an unofficial politician for 40 years, and I guess on October 20th I became an official politician." His legacy, of course, is still 40 years of wild touring, and dozens of albums, books, and punk posters full of images of skulls, marauding soldiers, sexy vixens and burning cop cars, and lyrics like these:

> *Your neighbor down the street is a little crazy*
>
> *Nothin too bad, just a little off*
>
> *The cops bust in, they take a stance*
>
> *They gun him down, never had a chance.*
>
> *Some local kids, pull some minor shit*
>
> *The cops react an' have a fit*
>
> *The people are mad, seen this before,*
>
> *They fight back, it's like a war.*

3. Up from Slavery

Josephine Baker

Nothing symbolizes the *Années Foules* (crazy years) of the Roaring 20s like the image of Josephine Baker, dancing and singing in *La Revue Nègre,* dressed only in a shell necklace and a string of bananas around her waist. Her performance electrified Paris, and the city continued its infatuation with her for the next 50 years. "*Quel cel elle a!*" said her friend and occasional lover Maurice Bataille. "It gave all of Paris a hard-on."

She returned the affections of the city and of France. Bataille was only one of her hundreds of French lovers—a list going right up, according to journalist and writer Marcel Sauvage, to President Charles De Gaulle. In 1961 De Gaulle would award her the *Legion d'Honneur,* for her work as a Secret Agent fighting the Nazis for the French Resistance. "France is the country that adopted me without reservation," she told the commandant who recruited her for the Resistance. "I am willing to give my life for her."

While she was rewarded and revered for fighting The Man in World War II, she was also hounded by him throughout the rest of her life. Her arrival on the French stage was almost shut down by the authorities. Nudity was common on Parisian stages like the Moulin Rouge and the Folies-Bergère, but that was white nudity, not black. The Prefect of Police tried to shut down her performance at the *Revue Nègre,* harrumphing that "The color black alone does not dress one." She continued to have battles with the authorities throughout her long, complicated life, especially in the USA. She renounced her US citizenship in 1937 but would return to her native country to perform, to participate in the civil rights movement, and to engage in feuds and battles with The Man.

She was born Freda J. McDonald on June 3, 1906 in the Social Evil Hospital, originally built to service prostitutes suffering from venereal disease. She died on April 12, 1975, in the Salpêtrière Hospital in Paris, which also had been built to care for prostitutes, beggars and female criminals. What an extraordinary life she packed in between the two.

Her mother Carrie McDonald was twenty when Josephine was born. Her father, unknown, was simply named as "Edw" on her birth certificate and is thought to have been white. Josephine was brought up in part by her grandmother, Elvira, an ex-slave who told her with stories of slave days, including one, repeated many times, about a pregnant woman put in a hole, belly down, and beaten. Elvira also introduced Josephine to music. "The songs she sang as she rocked me to sleep," she said, "told of the freedom that would someday come." By the age of ten, Josephine was already herself a musical performer, dancing and singing on the streets of St. Louis for nickels thrown at her feet by passers-by. She played hooky more than she went to school, showing up in class only sixty-seven days in 1916. She claims her mother "gave her" to a local family jazz band, for whom she carried instruments from gig to gig (a twelve-year-old roadie), and eventually learned the trombone, an instrument she said "was bigger than I was."

It was a rough time in America. Josephine witnessed one of the worst race riots in American history, in which a huge white mob in East St. Louis killed between forty and two hundred and fifty African Americans and burned down entire neighborhoods, leaving six thousand homeless. World War I was raging across Europe, revolution was in the air, lynchings were commonplace, and the flu epidemic killed over half a million in the US alone, forty to one hundred million worldwide, the worst pandemic in human history (at least, so far). In St. Louis, Josephine's family decided she was trouble and they should marry her off. At thirteen, she was married to a thirty-eight-year-old steelworker named Willie Wells. It was totally against the law, since the age of consent in Missouri was fifteen, but it was done. The marriage didn't last long, and was replaced with another, to one Willie Baker. Josephine took his surname, but they too were divorced, and she was off touring with a vaudeville troupe in a revue called *Shuffle Along.*

The young Ms. Baker was not just stagestruck, but full of ambition and talent. "She was very adventurous," remembers fellow-performer Maude Russell. "She was like a black Chaplin, and she would step on anybody's shoulders to get where she wanted to get. She didn't give a damn about me, you, or anybody else." The rough-and-tumble theatres of the so-called "chitlin circuit" were organized by an outfit known as the Theatre Owners' Booking Association (T.O.B.A.) which the vaudevillians joked stood for Tough on Black Asses. The audiences were naively participatory in their responses to the plays and skits, often shouting out warnings to ingenue heroines like Baker that stage villains were hiding behind doors, or even pulling knives and razors out and charging the stage to protect the young performers.

Baker saw the country from New Orleans to Rochester while touring with the vaudeville troupe. The highlight of the season was the number one tourist town of the day, Atlantic City, New Jersey, but even in that relatively cosmopolitan town, there were issues. "Like everywhere," recalls Russell, "there was a white beach and a colored beach, and the fancy hotels posted signs saying NO DOGS, NO JEWS. They didn't have to put up NO NIGGERS, because we knew it."

They finally made it to the Big Apple and performed at the Colonial Theatre. New York was the big time, but in the 1920s, Paris was even bigger. The city was crazy for jazz, which black American soldiers had introduced during WWI. On the hunt for the latest and greatest, a Parisian impresario named Rolf de Maré sent an agent, Caroline Dudley Reagan to New York to find a singing, dancing star and a troupe of jazzmen and dancers to support her. Reagan discovered and signed Baker for the gig in Paris that would change the singer's life, and transform her into one of the superstars of the Twentieth Century.

The Man twice almost ended the trip before she got there. First, she couldn't get a passport. She was only nineteen, but her life was already so complicated the passport office didn't know what to make of her. She didn't have a birth certificate, and when one was finally found it listed only the cryptic inscription "Edw" for a father. She had two husbands already but knew the whereabouts of neither. Finally, with only days to spare before her transport, the *S.S. Berengaria* was to depart, she came up with a little white lie—her husbands were both dead, she claimed. Satisfying the office that that if she was a widow, she wouldn't need her husbands' approval to get a passport, she was given the document and sailed for Europe.

In mid-ocean, the ship was unexpectedly warned that there was a German mine floating in the area. All passengers were called to the deck and put in life-jackets. Josephine recalled that she could hear the first class passengers on the deck above her shouting, their children crying, while she and the other members of the jazz troupe "began to sing the same songs our ancestors had sung on the slave ships that carried them to America." The spirituals worked; the ship did not hit the German mine.

Josephine was amazed by the freedom of Paris. "Men and women kissing in the streets! In America, you were sent to prison for that!" Most extraordinary for her was that, "for the first time in my life, I was invited to sit at a table and eat with white people."

Baker had all kinds of famous admirers—the British Prince of Wales, Hemingway, Gertrude Stein, Picasso, Jean Cocteau and a string of very wealthy lovers, one of whom built a giant apartment with an interior swimming pool for her on the Champs-Élysées. "People so crazy for you, you forgot you were black." Not everyone forgot, though. There were forty-three thousand American expatriates in Paris during the 20s and four hundred thousand more visiting every summer, many of them ready to start a fight when they saw inter-racial couples walking on the streets.

Jazzman Johnny Hudgins remembered the French police's impatience with the racial strife. "The *gendarmes* got tired of it. They thought Americans were crazy to have fights because of color." However, the battles continued. After one concert ended, a group of white Americans launched into *The Star-Spangled Banner*, while their black compatriots stood silent. One of the whites exhorted the blacks to join in singing "your national anthem." Just as in the famous scene from *Casablanca*, the blacks conferred, then began to sing, not *The Star-Spangled Banner*, but the *Marseillaise*. The French orchestra, and the rest of the audience, joined in, drowning out the American anthem with the French.

Baker conquered the heart of France, with her wild performances both onstage and in the streets. She often walked the Parisian boulevards with a cheetah on a leash. On other occasions she would drive in a cart pulled by an ostrich—prompting a wit to observe that ostriches had been often kind to Josephine, with so many feathers plucked from their tails to decorate hers. "My God," said fellow performer Leslie Gaines, "there was nobody in France the people loved more than Josephine. She was the Frenchmen's mistress."

Baker moved on to conquer Europe, though her conquest was not without difficulties. In Vienna, a petition was circulated attempting to ban her "brazen-faced heathen dances," that triggered a debate in Parliament over whether people should be paying "100,000 shillings to see nudity when one hundred thousand workmen are walking the streets of Vienna searching for employment and food." Catholic priests preached against her, the Russian prima-ballerina Anna Pavlova attacked her in the press, and the city council refused to give her a work permit.

Eventually (though with church bells loudly ringing around the theatre to try to drown her out) she did perform and set the city ablaze with a month of sold-out performances. Still, there was trouble. The local rag, *Der Tag*, compared her to Jezebel. A young Austrian ran up to her and shot himself, falling dead at her feet.

In Prague, there were more mobs gathering to see her, stampeding, smashing windows, stranding her on top of a limousine. She claimed she never feared a crowd, saying "It is a duel between them and me...my heart becomes as hard as my fist, it's a matter of winning," but the crowds of Eastern Europe unnerved her. In Budapest, "they tore my dress apart, they wanted to see me naked." In the Hungarian capitol, she provoked an actual duel. The attentions of a cavalry officer, Andrew Czlovoydi provoked her lover and manager, Count Guiseppe Pepito to challenge him to a duel. With Josephine screaming on the sidelines, Pepito was nicked by a bullet in the shoulder, which apparently brought the shooting match to a satisfactory conclusion.

Vanity Fair Magazine reported that dictator Mussolini "out of Fascist racial fanaticism," had banned her from singing in Italy, but then relented, "whereupon the entire royal family turned out to applaud her."

In Sweden there was another passport incident, though this time, not about Josephine's passport, but about one for her dogs. Baker, like many black touring musicians in the 20s and 30s, always travelled with dogs. As many have suggested, it was possibly a reaction to their collective memory of the bloodhounds that chased runaway slaves and later blacks running from lynch mobs in the American South. Regardless of the hidden motivation for why she kept the animals, the Swedish authorities caused her weeks of grief when she tried to enter their country without canine passports.

In Berlin, the problems were more acute. Hitler was now in power; when Josephine performed in her girdle of bananas, singing *J'ai Deux Amours*, and performing her *Danse Sauvage*, the Germans responded both with what was described as "the collective lust that raged as in a menagerie when the meat is thrown into the cage," but also with Nazi hoots and catcalls. After three weeks of what was planned to be a six-month run, Josephine was banned from Germany, escaped back to the sanity of France, and began performing at the *Folies Bergere*.

From there, she left for a tour of South America that proved just as contentious. In Buenos Aires, she was denounced by Argentine President Yrigoyen, and the theatre (2500 sold-out seats, 200 performances) was filled with Josephine supporters fighting Josephine detractors. She became angry about being used "as a banner waved by some in the name of free expression and by others in defence of public morality...What did I care about Argentine politics?"

She moved on to Chile and Brazil, and then returned north to New York. Playing at the Lafayette Theatre on 7th Avenue, she again attracted huge crowds, including the mayor, James J. Walker—"The first time," said one of the New York papers, "that such a high official of this city ever decided to enter one of the local playhouses." However her reception in Manhattan was unpleasant. Even though she was starring in one of Broadway's biggest theatres, none of the city's major hotels would accept her because of her color. Her high-falutin' white European husband was able to stay at the St. Moritz, but Baker had to stay with friends and later at a small two-star actor and artist's hotel called the Bedford, on East 44th Street.

She also got poor reviews. *Time* magazine, as was its misguided norm in that era, called her "a slightly buck-toothed Negro wench whose singing and dancing could be topped practically anywhere outside France." Sensibly, Baker, calling herself "heartbroken over the hostile attitudes" of Americans, decided she would return to Paris, become a legal citizen of France, and renounce her American citizenship. If she wanted to hang out with Americans, it would be with people like Ernest Hemingway, who spent hours talking to her in Parisian cafes, calling her "the most sensational woman anyone ever saw." She also got much better reviews in Europe than in America. Singer Shirley Bassey exclaimed, "I swear in all my life I have never seen, and probably shall never see again, such a spectacular singer and performer."

Her love life was also much more exciting across the pond. She was not quite as promiscuous as one of her lovers, the author George Simenon (creator of the character Inspector Maigret) but she came close. He claimed to have bedded ten thousand women in his lifetime (along with writing nearly five hundred novels!) Many called her an almost insatiable lover. Maurice Bataille once bragged that he and Josephine "had sex nine times" in a single day. She was generous in many ways. It is believed that her fourth husband, Jean Lion, spent five million francs of Josephine's money—in a single year.

When WW II arrived, Baker's generosity certainly extended to her adopted country and all those suffering from the fighting. After the Nazis invaded Belgium and Holland in May of 1940, Paris began to fill with refugees. Every evening after her performance at the *Casino de Paris*, she ran a homeless shelter on the Rue du Chevaleret, feeding, bathing and comforting the refugees.

France was a shambles—financially and militarily ruined. It was also filled not just with Nazis but with collaborators and fifth columnists. The Deuxième Bureau, the French military intelligence service, had no budget to fight an undercover war, so one of their commandants, Jacques Abtey was assigned the task of trying to find patriots he wouldn't have to pay to work as secret agents for the French Resistance, working only for *la gloire et la patrie*, not le cash. One of the first and most important he found was Josephine Baker. When he proposed the unusual offer to her, she readily agreed. "France made me what I am," she told him. "The Parisians gave me their hearts, and I am ready to give them my life."

Through her past showbiz life, she had good connections at both the Japanese and Italian embassies. She would attend social events, pick up information and write it along her arms. Abtey told her this was dangerous, but she would just laugh at his concerns, telling him, "Nobody would think I'm a spy."

She became Abtey's student in the secret arts of military surveillance, and also his lover. He would reject the claims that she was insatiable. "She was not a crazy sex-obsessed person," he later said. "Sometimes we could go one or two weeks without having sex."

With the fall of France, Baker and Abtey, like so many others, became separated. General Charles de Gaulle, then undersecretary of war, fled to England to head up a government in exile. Convinced that he should try to join de Gaulle in London, Abtey concocted a plan to try to escape Vichy France, using Baker as cover. "Nobody would suspect an officer of the Deuxième Bureau to be associated with Josephine Baker." He managed to reconnect with her at her chateau in Southern France and presented her with the audacious plan. "I told her if she came with me, there would be no secrets between us, no flirtations with foreigners who might be spies. She pledged herself to the cause, I never saw anyone with such fire."

Her singing career was ended, as in August 1940 the Nazis had banned blacks and Jews from the French theatre. Baker witnessed many of her stage compatriots capitulating to the Germans. French superstar Maurice Chevalier was now singing on German-controlled Radio-Paris; Jacques Copeau, the head of the Comédie Française, demanded that his male actors display their non-circumcision to him. Baker, though, unlike the male actors, could not hide behind clothes. As a black person, she would have been sent to a concentration camp had she got in any trouble with the occupying Germans.

Baker enthusiastically agreed to help smuggle all the information the Deuxiéme Bureau had about the German army positions in France out to England. Agents sewed photographs of the German positions into her dresses and transcribed all the written information using invisible ink onto her sheet music. The tough intelligence officer Abtey was given a new passport and a new identity, amusingly, as Baker's *maître de ballet.* Josephine convinced the Spanish consul in Toulouse to grant the pair a transit visa. They successfully crossed the Pyrenees and on to Madrid by train, then caught the last two tickets of a final plane leaving for Lisbon.

"You see what good cover I am?" laughed Baker.

"Let me try to explain the importance of what she had just done," said her French spymaster. "If the Spanish or German authorities had discovered my true identity and arrested me, if they found the information on the music sheets, they would have realized that the French Secret Service had covertly reorganized and was working against them, that we were not respecting the terms of the armistice, and as to the fate that would have been meted out to Josephine and myself, I would rather not dwell on it."

"This woman had undertaken, of her own volition, to cover me to the very end, closing the door behind her and binding her fate to mine. I call that courage."

Lisbon during the war was seething with spies, German agents, intrigue, exotic mysterious women, war profiteers and desperate people offering jewels, paintings and gold to get exit visas and berths on ships leaving for North and South America. Abtey and Baker connected with the head of British Intelligence. They gave him all of the photos and information hidden in her dress and sheet music. He transmitted the secrets to London. Within a week word came back that the British were pleased with the clandestine information and wanted the pair of agents not to come to London but instead return to France, then set up a secret liaison centre in Casablanca.

The two made their way back to Marseilles, where Josephine briefly mounted a revival of the revue *La Créole*, but then, with the predicted imminent fall of the port city to the Germans, she abruptly closed the play and the pair boarded a ship, the *Governor General Guyedon*, for Morocco. She insisted on taking her full menagerie, which Aptey described as "Bonzo, a Great Dane, Glug Glug, a malicious female monkey, Mica, a suave lion-monkey, Gugusse, a tiny monkey, nasty as the plague, and Curler and Question Mark, two white mice. As soon as she freed them from their cages, it was madness in the cabin, Josephine laughing, trying to catch one or another."

"Poor darlings," said the diva/secret agent. "For them, too, it is a great adventure. *Allez*, we all go together." Then, according to André Rivollet, "She moved from her Creole yelling to singing the *Marseillaise*, then bravely to the songs of the Resistance."

Once in Africa the intrigues continued. Baker developed yet another affair, this time with Ahmed Ben Bachir, the court chamberlain to the caliph of Spanish Morocco. She managed to pass messages from the Americans, who were about to enter the African theatre of war under the command of General Patton, through Ben Bachir to Spanish dictator Francisco Franco. The Americans hoped to be able to persuade Franco to let them use the Spanish Sahara as a base for Patton's upcoming battles with Rommel, who had just invaded Libya.

Josephine then returned to Lisbon, performing to sold-out crowds, and receiving secret information from other Resistance agents that she then smuggled, pinned inside her bra, back to their new clandestine headquarters in Casablanca. "Who," she asked, "would dare search Josephine Baker?"

She also developed a network securing Spanish Moroccan passports for Eastern European and French Jews (one of them a Rothschild) so they could leave the dangers of Europe and Morocco for the safety of Latin America. Josephine fell very sick in Tangiers, but apparently did not lose her sense of humor. Doctors operated on her so many times that she once asked them, "Why don't you just put a zipper in? It would be so much easier." The hospital sickroom proved to be ideal cover for her to meet American diplomats and Moroccan leaders she could pass secrets to about the German intentions in Morocco, North Africa and Syria. Her long stay in the African hospital resulted in wild rumours in both Paris and America. The occupying Germans told the French press she had syphilis; the American press reported she was dead.

She was still alive, but she was weakened by the African climate and her intense wartime activity. When she was introduced to General George Patton, she fainted into his arms.

Once the battle for North Africa heated up Josephine shifted gears back into performing for the British, French and American troops as an entertainer, ranging 15,000 kilometres across Tunisia, Libya, Egypt and Lebanon. Abtey remembered that "Josephine had a good black orchestra backing her up, and at the end of every show, she would sing three anthems, the *Marseillaise, God Save the King,* and *The Star-Spangled Banner*, in which she would be joined by the audience."

"This one night, German planes flew over and started shooting. There was a crackling and sputtering, and the theatre—it was just a stage set up outside—was plunged into darkness. Josephine used the unexpected intermission to help herself to the supper the American Army had set out in a tent. The sky was lighted by fire, everyone flat on the ground, and finally, things became so violent she was obliged to throw herself down like everyone else."

Later, recounting the air raid, she laughed. "Me, belly down, among soldiers from Texas, Missouri and Ohio in my 1900 Paris dress, must have been an irresistibly funny sight. Mostly because I kept on eating my ice cream."

In Algiers, de Gaulle and Baker combined forces for a massive parade and a gala at L'Opéra d'Alger. De Gaulle was obviously the more important attendee, but Baker was the bigger draw. Hours before the event, Baker had the idea to create a giant tricolour flag that would descend from above the stage during the playing of the *Marseillaise*. Somehow, in the mayhem of the war, deep in the casbah of Algiers she found the vast swaths of red, white and blue muslin needed to create the giant flag, and enlisted a convent of nuns to sew it together for her. During the powerful ceremonies, after Baker sang against the backdrop of the enormous flag, de Gaulle presented her with a tiny gold Cross of Lorraine, the symbol of the Free French movement and the first of many honors she would get for her contribution to the Resistance.

She was soon back on the road, travelling in a convoy of two jeeps as far east as Jerusalem and Beirut, entertaining the troops. Wrapped in her Army great coat and wearing a helmet, she took her solo turn guarding their little convoy. When parked at night, they were often threatened by packs of wild dogs that were eating the hundreds of corpses on the desert floor. They would also attack the living if given the opportunity.

On June 6, 1944, as the British, American and Canadian troops invaded the beaches of Normandy to begin the liberation of Europe, Josephine was on another mission, heading with Abtey by plane from Africa to Corsica to sing in the service of the Free French. Their plane crash-landed in the waters off the Corsican coast. Baker's theatrical costumes were ruined, but there were no injuries. She, Abtey and the pilots made it to shore, where they were welcomed by local Police Commandant Victor Gianviti, whom she knew from the Parisian shelter for refugees she had run at the beginning of the war. Gianviti showed his visitors two anti-aircraft guns named *Josephine* and *J'ai Deux Amours*. He told them had been already used to shoot down six German planes.

In October, after the liberation of France, she made a triumphant return to Paris. According to Buddy Smith, a black American soldier and musician who witnessed her arrival, there were "a million people up and down the Champs to see her when she came in, throwing flowers at her." Once in Paris she pawned her jewels and mortgaged her apartment in order to buy food and coal for needy old people of the war-torn city.

Paris was free but the war was not yet over. Baker went on tour through the newly-liberated countries, dressed in her full uniform, singing for the Free French troops. She even made it into Germany, performing at Buchenwald, the notorious concentration camp turned at the end of the war into a camp for refugees and displaced persons.

In March of 1945 she was back in Paris, appearing at a massive "Festival of French Song and Dance" at the same theatre her *Revue Nègre* had opened twenty years earlier. Two months later Churchill personally invited her to participate in a victory celebration in London.

With her extremely complex and lavish lifestyle, Josephine could not afford to rest on her laurels, so within months of the end of the war, she was back singing in cabarets, recording and touring. Very quickly she was involved in a new war—the battle for racial equality and civil rights. Having promised black American servicemen in Europe and Africa that she would help support their struggles for desegregation once the war ended, she was back touring the United States by 1951.

Her first American booking was a nightclub in Miami, but when she learned the club did not allow blacks, she refused to go onstage. The battle became a *cause célèbre* that Josephine eventually won. The club date proved a success, and she began a national tour. However, when she got to New York she was turned away from 36 hotels because of racial discrimination.

She spent her nights singing —making $10,000 a week—and her days fighting for the civil rights movement. She took on the cause of the falsely accused "Trenton Six", fought to get black stage hands and musicians working in the theatre, made a citizen's arrest of a salesman who made racial insults to her in Dallas, challenged segregation in the hotels of Las Vegas, and battled the city of San Francisco over their policy of not hiring black bus drivers.

Her most contentious fight started with New York's famous nightspot The Stork Club and grew into a long-running feud with the most influential newspaper columnist of the day, Walter Winchell. Baker believed she had been the subject of discrimination at the club. While movie star Grace Kelly had come to her aid in the brouhaha, Winchell, also present in the club, had not. Baker turned the incident into a major battle. Prizefighter Sugar Ray Robinson warned her not to get into a feud with Winchell. He described him as "too powerful. He can kill your career," but she persisted, involving the NAACP and hiring a New York lawyer to sue the powerful columnist and snappy fast-talking radio personality. Even though he was widely thought of as being cruel and ruthless, his syndicated column was read by fifty million people a day, and his staccato-voiced radio reports were heard by another twenty million. If he wasn't himself "The Man", he certainly knew Him.

He described himself as being "just a son-of-a-bitch." He fought back against Baker, accusing her of being a Communist, and slipping information about her to his friends J. Edgar Hoover and Senator Joe McCarthy. The FBI, CIA and State Department began assembling files on Baker's activities. She soon lost her work visa, had to leave the U.S., and it was nearly a decade before American authorities would allow her back into the country.

She headed north to perform in Montreal, where she told *Le Petit Journal,* "You know I have a tough skin. To discourage me, they are nasty, they dig up my past, they falsify it...I'm convinced that millions of people are thinking like me, even if they can't say it out loud for fear of being martyred. I will keep on being a missionary of peace, I will keep on fighting for Americans because I don't want them separated by prejudice."

Baker left Canada for a South American tour, performing in Brazil, Uruguay and Argentina, where she hung out with the highly controversial President Juan Perón. There she learned that the American Department of Justice was studying ways to bar her from the United States. "I shall consider it an honor to be barred," she sniffed.

In Cuba, an audience with the dictator President Batista went badly. He refused to second her tirades against America, and the next day, she was arrested. Military Intelligence officers seized belongings from her hotel room, took her to their headquarters and interrogated her about her Communist leanings. She denied she had any. She was fingerprinted and photographed with a number across her chest.

It was not her only arrest—she would be charged a few years later in Quebec. Back in Europe, though, she continued to perform and tour. As part of her crusade to try to fight racial prejudice, she adopted a group of multi-racial orphans from around the world who she would raise as a "Rainbow Tribe" in her French chateau. There were Japanese babies, black babies, South American Indian babies, Arab babies, even white babies—fifteen in all. She brought them up (between singing engagements) and paid for the extraordinary exercise in peace and brotherhood by turning the chateau into a tourist destination, where visitors, for a fee, could watch the "Rainbow Tribe" play together. Not surprisingly, the grand social experiment was not without problems, especially as the cute babies grew into often surly, rebellious teenagers, unappreciative of their role as guinea pigs in their famous adoptive mother's cause of world brotherhood.

On August 18, 1961, a pair of helicopters landed at her chateau with WWII Free French generals aboard to present Josephine with the Légion d'Honneur, the highest honor of France, for her secret work during the war. Two years later, she would wear the medal, along with the Croix de Guerre, the Médaille de la Resistance and the Médaille de la France Libre on her uniform to attend, with Dr. Martin Luther King, the famous March on Washington. The March ended up being peaceful, but there was a lot of fear in the air that the marchers might be beaten up. It took a lot of courage for Josephine, or indeed for anyone to attend. No wonder she wore her military uniform.

"You are here on the eve of a complete victory," she told the huge crowd. "You can't go wrong. The world is behind you. I've been following this movement for thirty years. Now the fruit is ripe, I want to be here. You can't put liberty at the tip of the lips and expect people not to drink it. This is the happiest day of my life."

Three months later she received a letter from the United States that read:

> *Dear Miss Baker,*
> *This is just a brief note to express my deep gratitude to you for all of your kind expressions of support. We were all inspired by your presence at the March on Washington. I am deeply moved by the fact that you would fly such a long distance to participate in that momentous event. We were further inspired that you returned to the States to do a benefit concert for the civil rights organizations. I only regret that a long standing previous commitment made it impossible for me to come to New York to witness the Carnegie Hall affair. I was pleased to learn that it was a great success.*
> *You are certainly doing a most dedicated service for mankind. Your genuine good will, your humanitarian concern, and your unswerving devotion to the cause of freedom and human dignity will remain an inspiration to generations yet unborn.*
> *Martin Luther King Jr.*

A few days later, she, and the rest of the world, heard that President Kennedy had been shot. Again, she flew to Washington, for his funeral.

Three years later she was invited by Fidel Castro to the first Tricontinental Conference celebrating "the solidarity of the peoples of Africa, Asia and Latin America and Cuba." Josephine wanted "to see the Cuban Revolution with my own eyes," and so she headed for Havana to sing and dance for the delegates. The FBI duly noted her presence in their file on her, which had grown to over a thousand pages.

In January 1968, she again applied to the America consulate in Paris for a visa, but was refused. She believed it was because she had joined King on the March on Washington and had visited Cuba. She wrote Robert Kennedy and he called the State Department, which put the papers through. Kennedy sent her a telegram saying I AM HAPPY TO INFORM YOU THAT YOUR REQUEST FOR A VISA HAS BEEN GRANTED AND YOU WILL HAVE IT ON MONDAY. His office also told her that the delay had nothing to do with Cuba, or civil rights. It was just that she had not filled in the forms correctly. The Man sometimes really has his patience tried by scatterbrained, sensitive artistes. Or...perhaps his office was prevaricating, and it really was about her political activities.

Within six months King and then Kennedy would both be dead, and Paris on fire with the Student Revolution. Josephine donned her uniform again to march with the Gaullists. The unrest closed her show at the Olympia. She spent the last of her money on airline tickets so that she and five of her "Rainbow Tribe" could attend Bobby Kennedy's funeral. When she returned to France, she discovered that her creditors had taken possession of her chateau.

Even though she was evicted from her castle and her vast collection of jewels, carpets, furniture and clothes auctioned off to pay off the creditors, she refused to give in. She broke a window to get back into the house and barricaded herself in the kitchen with her maid and a little cat. Journalists, thrilled by this new act of the Josephine Baker drama, camped outside, trading quotes for food. Meanwhile the new owner and his gang of men showed up. Just as Ronald Reagan would do a few years later to force strongman Manuel Noriega from his refuge in Panama City, they blared loud music at her nonstop so she could not sleep. (One presumes it was not Josephine Baker music.) They also turned off the water and when she went out to turn on an auxiliary tank, grabbed her and wrestled her away from the chateau. According to the press, the thugs handled her, "like a bundle of dirty laundry." She was photographed sitting forlorn and bedraggled on the steps of the chateau—an image of her that would unfortunately become almost as iconic as the happier ones of her at nineteen dressed in only a string of bananas.

Josephine managed to survive this catastrophe, and make yet another comeback, this time helped by her new best friend Princess Grace Kelly and her husband Prince Rainier of Monaco. She had to move to a smaller house, but nonetheless one in Monte Carlo, with her Rainbow Tribe. The kids were no longer cute pliant toddlers, but now a rambunctious herd of teenagers, wanting to wear long hair, flowered shirts and bellbottoms, which she claimed were "for homosexuals."

It was hard for her to enforce rules and become The Man when she herself had been such a rule-breaker, especially when they found images of her on a Canadian TV show, dancing the Charleston half-naked and telling the interviewer, "Cocteau, Paul Colin, Fujita, we were young together…I posed at the Beaux-Arts, they wanted to see me naked, so they saw me. What is wrong with admiring what nature and God have created."

"So, if you could do it, Mama, why can't we?" After she caught one of her boys in a bathtub fondling a (male) friend, she banished him from the Tribe. The Musician had become The Man. Now she claimed to be disgusted by "the artificial life of the theatre." and said, "if one of my children one day wants to go on the stage, I will strangle him with these two hands, I swear it."

Amazingly, she had one last show in her. On April 8th 1975 she performed a grand show in Paris, bankrolled by Princess Grace, Prince Rainier and Jackie Onassis to celebrate the fifty years since she arrived with the *Revue Nègre*. Mick Jagger, Sophia Loren, Diana

Ross and Liza Minnelli attended. The full house gave her a 30-minute standing ovation, followed by the reading of a telegram from French President Giscard d'Estaing wishes her fond wishes IN THE NAME OF A GRATEFUL FRANCE WHOSE HEART HAS BEATEN SO OFTEN WITH YOURS.

After three more performances, she was discovered in her bed in a coma after suffering a cerebral haemorrhage. She died in hospital on April 12, 1975. Three thousand people attended her funeral, but even in death she had to battle The Man. The Catholic Church, in typical form, resisted burying her, because "of her past." It took some greasing, with a hefty payment by theatrical impresario Jean Bodson before they relented. Even then, the Canon in his homily carried on about how Josephine "had been a great sinner." He then softened the blow by adding, "but aren't we all." Probably especially you, you hypocrite.

Josephine Baker was certainly no hypocrite. She was one of the most original, and at times courageous show business personalities of the Twentieth Century. For the French, it is said there are only two Josephines—Napoleon's Josephine Bonaparte, and Josephine Baker.

Paul Robeson

Few singers, few celebrities of any stripe, have been as revered and reviled, loved and hated, idolized and persecuted as Paul Robeson. No others have received law degrees from Columbia while playing football in the NFL while singing with a rich baritone. None have performed starring roles on Broadway and London's West End, personally petitioned a US President, been vilified by the House on Un-American Activities Committee, been hung in effigy by the Ku Klux Klan, had their concert attacked by New York State Troopers, had their passport revoked by the U.S. State Department. How many celebrities have been poisoned by the CIA, as some sources report Robeson was?

He was born in 1898 to a Quaker mother who died when he was six, and a father who was born a slave and became a Presbyterian minister. Robeson's excellence in athletics, academics and music in his Princeton, New Jersey high school won him a scholarship to Rutgers University.

Only the third black to attend Rutgers, and the only one there at the time, he overcame numerous racial barriers to make it on to the university football team. He was twice selected for the All-American team. Walter Camp, the so-called "Father of American Football" described him as the greatest tight end ever.

After graduating as valedictorian with numerous athletics letters, Robeson studied law at the New York University School of Law and at Columbia University, while simultaneously playing for the Akron Pros and the Milwaukee Badgers in the National Football League and singing off-Broadway and in England. Yikes! Slow down, Paul!

After graduation, he was accepted at a New York City law firm, but when secretaries there refused to take dictation from him because of his color, he left law for show business, appearing on Broadway in the plays of Eugene O'Neill—with one of them, *The Emperor Jones* scaring the hell out of him but wowing the audience with a 90-minute soliloquy required by his part as the title character.

As Robeson's star ascended, so did his involvement with The Man, and his increased political activities. He was a supporter of both the Chinese in the Sino-Japanese War and the Republican anti-Fascist movement in Spain, where he visited the battlefront of the Spanish Civil War and sang benefits for both causes. One of the biggest of these, in Washington, D.C., was blocked by the Daughters of the American Revolution due to Robeson's race. During his Chinese concerts, Robeson popularized a song by progressive activist Liu Liangmo to such an extent that in 1949 it was adopted as the new Chinese national anthem.

He also modified his signature song, *Old Man River*, changing the stereotypical dialect to standard English, removing the word "niggers" used in the original song as written by Oscar Hammerstein, and changing lines to transform it from a song of resignation to what has been called "a battle hymn of unwavering defiance."

"The artist must take sides," said Robson. "He must elect to fight for freedom or slavery. I have made my choice. I had no alternative." Through the 1930's Robeson lived in England, where he performed on behalf of striking Welsh coal miners and African political movements seeking to shake their colonial shackles. In 1940 he returned to America and began touring billed as "America's No. One Entertainer", though, like Josephine Baker, he was frequently unable to find hotel accommodation.

He continued his activism, meeting with the Commissioner of Major League Baseball to argue that blacks should be allowed to play, and then with President Harry Truman to protest the wave of lynchings that followed the end of World War Two. Both meetings were failures (though MLB baseball was integrated a year later when Jackie Robinson joined the Brooklyn Dodgers). When Robeson told the President that if anti-lynching legislation was not enacted, "the negroes will defend themselves", Truman angrily terminated the meeting.

As America swung rapidly to the right in the late forties, Robeson was found increasingly in the crosshairs of The Man. A film he narrated, *Native Land,* was declared communist propaganda by the FBI. The organization he was closely affiliated with, the Civil Rights Congress, was placed on the Attorney General's *List of Subversive Organizations.* He was called before the United States Senate Committee on the Judiciary. When the committee demanded to know if he was connected with the Communist Party, he refused to answer, saying, "Some of the most brilliant and distinguished Americans are about to go to jail for failure to answer that question, and I am going to join them, if necessary."

He very well might have gone to jail, for refusing to answer that question both to the Judiciary Committee and later to the House Committee on Un-American Committee, and it took considerable bravery to stand his ground. Why did he do it? In his words, "Because by that time the Hollywood writers had gone to jail, and a great wave of anti-Communist hysteria had set in. To answer such questions would have meant that I was contributing to the hysteria. So as a matter of principle I felt I had to invoke my constitutional right to say that my political beliefs are nobody's business."

Just as Stalin was purging his political foes from history, so did America try to erase Robeson from sight. His recordings were withdrawn from record stores, and no companies would record him. Books about Robeson were removed from public libraries. Any journalist who did not condemn Robeson in harsh terms could count on losing their job. NBC-TV bluntly banned him from ever appearing in their studios. Rutgers University alumni tried to have Robeson's name pulled from the school's records, and the *American Sports Annual*, calling itself "the most complete record on college football" purged Robeson from ever having played on the Rutgers team.

Robeson's concerts were cancelled across America. The FBI openly followed him wherever he went and threatened the owners of concert halls who considered booking the singer. When Dodger Stadium booked a Robeson concert, the owner received death threats and the Los Angeles City Council passed a resolution banning the concert. As biographer Marie Seton wrote, "Robeson was a man to be marked down and hounded into submission by every means short of physical martyrdom, which appeared too dangerous since nobody could gauge what percentage of the sixteen million Negroes in America would rise in wrath if Robeson was arrested or mauled; but everything short of this was tried in the next few years."

The worst violence against Robeson and his fans took place in Peekskill, N.Y., a town on the Hudson River forty-one miles north of New York City. The events in Peekskill are described by Susan Robeson, the singer's granddaughter, as "one of the most frightening displays of racism and Nazi sentiment ever seen in America."

Robeson had been holding annual open-air summer concerts near Peekskill since 1946, but the times, they were a-changin'. When another was planned for August 26, 1949, the local press went nuts, egged on by all the national sentiment against the singer. The papers were filled with editorials and bold headlines reading "ROBESON AND

HIS FOLLOWERS ARE UNWELCOME" and "ROBESON CONCERT HERE AIDS SUBVERSIVE UNIT". The local Assistant District Attorney chaired a public meeting to devise a plan of action to stop the concert, and the Junior Chamber of Commerce attacked the concert as un-American and urged "group action to discourage it."

Local hoodlums, the Ku Klux Klan, and the American Legion took up the call, converging on Peekskill to create an "anti-Robeson" parade and demonstration outside the concert. Local police rounded up teenage boys, driving them to the river to collect buckets of stones and rocks to hurl at the concertgoers.

On the evening of the concert, 50 carloads of anti-Robeson demonstrators, plus hundreds more on foot, barricaded the concert grounds with a truck and wall of rocks. They began attacking those inside, with a barrage of rocks and bottles and screams of "No-one of you leaves here alive," "You come in, you don't get out!" and "We're going to get Robeson." Klan crosses burned on the perimeter of the grounds. People arriving for the concert were dragged from their cars and beaten, and then their cars overturned and smashed. A soldier had to drag a black man from a gang of white youths who were beating him and screaming, "Kill him! Let's finish him off!"

Robeson had not yet arrived for the concert, but hooligans were hunting the streets looking for him. The mob, now numbering about a thousand, charged into the concert area, forcing the concertgoers to retreat to the bandstand. Then, in a scene reminiscent of Nazi Germany, they made a giant bonfire of all the sheet music, books, pamphlets, and chairs. The state police finally arrived at ten PM and broke up the event. Not a single arrest was made.

Believing that the public's freedom and civil rights were at stake, organizers invited Robeson back for a second concert, on September 4th. This time, reports circulated that 50,000 would be protesting the concert. As September 4th arrived, 25,000 showed up to attend the concert, with another 2500 volunteering to form a human wall to protect them. Another "Chinese Wall", mostly of veterans, surrounded Robeson as he sang. There were confirmed reports that there were snipers with telescopic sights aimed at the singer in the surrounding hills.

As Robeson sang, Klan crosses began burning in northern Florida along with an effigy of him hanging in Valdosta, Florida. As the concert ended, the mob and the New York State Police became a single pack, lining the roads out of the grounds with stockpiles of rocks and bottles. A reporter from *The New York Age* described the scene:

"I still hear the frenzied roar of the crowds, the patter of stone against glass and flesh. I hear the wails of women, the impassioned screams of children, the jeers and taunts of wild-eyed youths. I still smell the sickening odour of blood flowing from freshly opened wounds, gasoline fumes from autos and buses valiantly trying to carry their human targets out of the range of bricks, bottles, bottles, and stones. I still feel the violence, the chaos which penetrated the air."

Eugene Bullard, the first black aviator of World War 1 and holder of the Croix de Guerre was photographed by the *New York Daily News* being attacked by two State Troopers, a local policeman and a deputy sheriff.

Tom Lloyd, one of the many union members who had attended the concert, remembers that "as I drove out on to the paved highway, a State Trooper slowed up the speed of our car by hand motions... Then a shower of rocks and pop-bottles hit our car and one broke the windshield, showering glass over the three of us in the front seat and inflicting cuts on the man sitting next to me...There were State Troopers and uniformed police in great numbers all along the road, but they did absolutely nothing to prevent the violence. In fact, I heard them laughing and jeering at us as we passed them with our battered cars."

Another man whose car had been hit said that he had asked a State Trooper to arrest the thrower. He said the policeman told him to "Go home, you dirty Jew kike, before you get your head split open."

Thomas Dewey, the Governor of New York and future Republican Presidential nominee ordered an investigation of the event, to be done by the same authorities who had supported and organized the anti-Robeson demonstrations. They completely exonerated the protestors and police of any wrongdoing. Instead they blamed the victims by saying that the concert was "initiated and sponsored for the purpose of deliberately inciting disorder and a breach of the peace, and...a part of the Communist strategy to foment racial and religious hatreds."

Nationally, the response against Robeson was even stronger. In 1950, the State Department revoked his passport, so that he could not spread his "seditious" songs and ideas outside the country. Robeson was now basically a prisoner in his own country. In 1952, when he was invited to sing at a meeting of the Mine, Mill and Smelter Workers union in Vancouver, he was told by President Truman that if he crossed into Canada he would be liable to five years imprisonment and a $10,000 fine.

Instead, Robeson had to come up with the idea of singing via telephone from the U.S. to a crowd of two thousand at an open meeting of the union held at Denman Auditorium. Even though he was only there by telephone line, his performance, ending with the fabled song, "I Dreamt I Saw Joe Hill", received a thunderous standing ovation.

Later that year the combined forces of the U.S. and Canadian governments again prevented him from performing in Canada. Instead, Robeson sang right at the edge of the border at the Peace Arch Park that straddles the two countries, playing across the 49th parallel to 30,000 on the Canadian side, 10,000 more in the U.S.

"It was the 'Woodstock' of the civil rights movement," says folk-music historian Gary Christall. "Think about it. It was 1952—at the height of McCarthyism, in the middle of the Korean War, and the Cold War was raging. Here was a guy with a strong antiwar stand who had been branded as one of the most dangerous men in the world singing about peace and they had more than 30,000 people there. That's a lot of folks. At the time, I don't think anybody could have outdrawn him. Maybe Sinatra. It was an enormous accomplishment for the labour movement, one of the big success stories—and a testament to Robeson's popularity."

Performances like the cross-border concert were highly charged with symbolic political meaning, but they didn't pay the bills. Robeson, once among the world's highest-paid performers, saw his income dwindle from over $100,000 in 1947 to about $6000 in 1952. Recording companies refused to record him or release his older records, and all American concert halls and theaters were closed to him. The jobs of people holding federal positions were threatened if they attended even his church basement concerts.

Robeson got little support from the public, but petitions from other artists like Harry Belafonte, Sydney Poitier, and the British musicians union did eventually begin to soften the US official stance. He was finally allowed to sing, he gave a powerful performance at Massey Hall in Toronto, one of the few concert halls that would have him. However, the reception to this was so intense that within a few weeks the ban on entering Canada was reinstated.

It was not until June 1958 that the United States Supreme Court ruled that the government could not arbitrarily withhold American citizens' passports and right to travel. Robeson returned to London, then set out on a world tour, where he took on new causes, most prominently, the plight of the Australian Aborigines, who at the time had no citizenship or other rights in their country.

In 1961 he was back in London, with plans to visit Russia, China and then Cuba before returning to the U.S. to join forces with Martin Luther King and Malcolm X in the newly created Civil Rights movement. This was highly worrisome to J. Edgar Hoover, who had a fear of what he called "Black Messiahs" springing up to fight for integration and freedom. At the same time, the CIA was concerned that Robeson would be in Cuba to witness their covert Bay of Pigs invasion, coincidently planned for exactly the date they learned he planned to be there—April 17. His son Paul Robeson Jr. believes there was considerable motive for silencing him and ending his proposed travel.

The singer flew to Moscow, had a series of concerts and meetings from March 23 to March 29 in which he seemed completely normal. Then, on the night of March 29, there was an uncharacteristically wild and suspicious party held in his hotel suite, at which Robeson began to act strangely before locking himself in his hotel bedroom. The next morning, he was found with slashed wrists.

His son, Paul Robson Jr., believes he was drugged with LSD at the party, a victim of the CIA's MKUltra mind-control/brainwashing program. When he began investigating what had happened at the event, which was mysteriously full of anti-Soviet dissidents, and mysteriously free of any KGB minders, he too was hit with what he believes was a huge dose of LSD. (Others believe it may have been BZ, a drug created in the late 50s and explored for its mind-control possibilities by the CIA).

After recovering from the overdose, the Soviets suggested that Paul Robeson return to the United States. They said that whatever happened to him he should not be given any heavy drugs or shock therapy. Instead, Robeson was forced to return to London, where he was placed under the care of Dr. William Sargant, a prominent but highly controversial and now discredited psychiatrist who was considered British Intelligence's expert on brainwashing. Sargant committed Robson to the Priory Psychiatric Hospital, where the singer was held for almost two years and given fifty-four electroconvulsive shock therapy treatments.

Robeson is not the only singer to have spent time inside Priory Hospital. Other celebrity patients there have included Eric Clapton, Susan Boyle, Sinéad O'Connor, Tom Chaplin, and Amy Winehouse.

During his stay at the British hospital, Robeson was under the surveillance of the CIA and Britain's MI5. His CIA file was under the personal control of Director of Covert Operations Richard Bissell Jr, who also masterminded the U-2 spyplane overflights, the Bay of Pigs invasion of Cuba, and the attempts to poison Fidel Castro and Congo Prime Minister Patrice Lumumba.

On the eve of a plan to give Robeson a series of even stronger shock treatments, his son, with the help of groups of supporters in the U.S. and Britain, got him out of the facility, and into the Buch Clinic in East Berlin. There, the doctors expressed "doubt and anger" about the high level of barbiturates and ECT that had been administered in London and stressed that "what little is left of Paul's health must be quietly conserved."

He returned to the U.S., but lived the rest of his life in seclusion due to his continued poor health and never performed again. On January 23, 1976, he died from complications from a stroke. He had spent thirty years in the wilderness, his singing career destroyed by political controversy. But dead singers are much safer than live ones, and so following his death he was honored with many awards—a star on the Hollywood Walk of Fame, a Lifetime Achievement Grammy Award, an award from the United Nations, a stamp in his honor by the U.S. Postal Service, a 40,000 ton tanker named for him, induction into the New Jersey Hall of Fame, an Academy Award for his filmed biography.

Nonetheless, he remains a controversial figure—a powerful leader and activist who more than any other singer or musician made an indelible impression on the politics of the twentieth century.

Leadbelly

For a hard-ass once described by *Time* magazine as a "murderous minstrel", who was born and spent most of his life in poverty, interrupted by some very long stretches behind bars and on prison chain gangs, Huddie Ledbetter gets mighty high praise these days from musicians like Bob Dylan, George Harrison and Van Morrison. Dylan, in his Nobel Prize acceptance speech, said of Ledbetter's song *Cotton Fields,* "that record changed my life…transported me into a world I'd never known. It was like an explosion went off. Like I'd been walking in darkness and all of a sudden the darkness was illuminated. It was like somebody laid hands on me. I must have played that record a hundred times." George Harrison once described the lineage as follows: "If there was no Leadbelly, there would have been no Lonnie Donegan; no Lonnie Donegan, no Beatles. Therefore, no Leadbelly, no Beatles." Van Morrison went further, calling Leadbelly a genius and saying he believed none of the British music scene of the 1960s would have happened without him.

Leadbelly's grandparents were slaves. His parents were sharecroppers, his father black, his mother a part-Cherokee Indian. They scratched out a living in Caddo Parish, Louisiana by working the land, fighting the boll weevils, and picking cotton. After eighth grade, Huddie left school, and joined them in the fields and the cotton gin. He was physically large and powerful, and so able to take on the back breaking work—able, according to his mother, to "do as much as two men." He also worked as a cowboy driving herds of cows for nearby Texan and Louisiana ranchers, a pistol strapped to his hip.

Like so many others in the rich musical stew of the Mississippi delta, he became what was then known as a "songster"—singing and accompanying himself on a variety of instruments— guitar, accordion, mandolin, reed organ and even jew's harp. He played mostly at what were known as *sukey jumps*. A "sukey" was a term dating from the 1820s meaning "slave" or "servant". A *Sukey jump*, then, was a rural black house-party involving food, moonshine liquor, dancing, and music. Neither jazz nor the blues had yet been created, so the songs were usually nineteenth century folk songs, some innocent, others less so. One, for instance, was titled *Take a Whiff On Me*. Although cocaine was still very legal at the time, the song warned against it, with lines like *Cocaine's for horses and not for men/ the doctor say it kill you, but he won't say when.*

It was still the Wild West in this remote corner of America in 1902, with disputes over women and bootleg liquor often ending in shootings and knife fights. At a sukie jump when he was sixteen, he got into a fight with another kid over a girl named Eula Lee. Huddie pulled out his gun and shot at his rival. Luckily, the gun misfired, or he might have had his first murder rap. Also, by luck his father was willing to get involved and persuaded the local sheriff to let the trigger-happy songster off with a $25 fine and a warning.

Leadbelly also twice managed to get his girlfriend pregnant. The first child died in infancy. Shortly after the second was born, the girl and her family moved away to Dallas, thereby relieving Ledbetter of the need to become a family man. However, he acquired a bad reputation because of the babies and the shooting, and so had to move away to the relatively big city of Shreveport. He took up residence in the whorehouses of the red-light district of the town known as St. Paul's Bottoms. For almost two years he scraped out a living playing what was then known as barrel-house music for the girls and their johns, singing slightly off-color songs like *Salty Dog* and *The Dirty Dozens*.

The carousing caught up with him, and he came down with what he called a "serious illness", presumably gonorrhea, that had him on death's door for six months. Conventional doctors couldn't seem to cure him so eventually he sought a remedy from an "old granny woman" who provided him with a cure for the STD called "Lafayette's Mixture", a potion that dated back the period of the American Revolution, named for the Marquis de Lafayette.

The close call with death got him thinking of salvation and so for a short while he "got religion and went to shouting." He was enlisted to lead songs in the small local church near his parents' home and got the spirit. "I was Jumpin' Judy—jumped all over the place, all around there. Everybody's trying to hold me, just jumping and shouting." The attraction of religion was very short-lived, though, and he soon went back to the devil's music.

He met and married a new woman who would become Lethe Ledbetter, and the pair moved to Dallas. He also picked up the instrument with which from then on he would be associated with—the twelve-string guitar—and began touring the saloons, dance halls and whorehouses of East Texas with another musical legend of the era, Blind Lemon Jefferson. In this early period, he also began singing his most successful song, *Goodnight, Irene*, and picked up the nickname "Leadbelly" that he carried for the rest of his life. There are various stories as to how he got it. Was it because he was tough and strong as hell? Because he could drink vast quantities of rot-gut moonshine and show no effects from it? Or because he once took a stomach full of shotgun birdshot at close quarters and lived to tell the tale? The truth is lost in the mists of time.

In 1915, he and his wife moved back to Harrison County, Louisiana, not far from the farm of his parents, who were by then in their sixties. Within a month Leadbelly was back in trouble. Big trouble. What exactly happened has again been lost due to destroyed court records and Leadbelly's very selective memory. One story has it that he attacked a woman after she rebuffed his advances. What is undisputed is that he ended up in jail for several weeks and his much-beleagured parents had to sign over their 68-acre farm to a law firm to try to get him out of the mess. The lawyers weren't able to prevent a conviction and he was sentenced to thirty days hard labor on a chain gang.

Leadbelly didn't like the idea of even thirty days without his freedom, so after only three he made a run for it, holding his leg-chains and awkwardly crab-walking as fast as possible away from the guards. Bullets flew past his head as he ran but he was finally able to dive into some woods and get away. He beseeched the first field hand he came upon to break his chains, but the frightened man told him to, "Pass by, nigger, pass by!" Eventually he was able to find some farmers who broke his leg chains, and then ran on, escaping the bloodhounds that were now on his trail by diving into a stream and wading away so the dogs could not follow his scent.

He went on the run, first to New Orleans, then, after changing his name to "Walter Boyd", hid out in the wild frontier of northeastern Texas. He laid low and steered clear of music for a few years, apparently listening to the advice of others that his "starvation box"—his guitar—would bring nothing but ruination, but eventually couldn't resist the call of the muse and returned to singing and playing in the local juke joints. In December of 1917 he was back in trouble. He was charged, under his adopted name of Walter Boyd, with the murder of an acquaintance, Will Stafford. While he was in jail awaiting trial, he overpowered the jailer, snagged his gun, and fled into the countryside. Three days later he was captured again. Within a month he was convicted and sentenced to twenty years in prison.

He was sent to the Shaw State Prison Farm in Bowie County, Texas where he attempted yet another escape. Again, he was re-captured, and nearly killed by the dogs and the white trackers. The violent incident was his last attempt to escape from prison. Instead, he tried a new tack, called by southern blacks, "yessing them to death." He became enough of a model prisoner that, for better or worse, he was transferred to the Sugarland Prison, a tough joint later immortalized in Steven Spielberg's first film, *Sugarland Express*.

Leadbelly spent seven years incarcerated inside Sugarland. While there he learnt or wrote many of the songs he later made famous. The most celebrated was *Midnight Special*, a song about the Southern Pacific train that passed by the prison every midnight—its lights flashing into the cells and its mournful whistle blowing. It is one of the most poignant of all songs about the law and incarceration, with lines like *You better not complain boy / You'll get in trouble with The Man*. The song has been covered by dozens of other artists, including Eric Clapton and Creedence Clearwater Revival, and a long-running TV music show was named for it.

In January 1924, Texas Governor Pat. M. Nuff, his wife and a group of women made a tour of Texan prisons. When they got to Sugarland, they found that the warden had organized a special concert for them, starring his best singer, Leadbelly. The "murderous minstrel" danced and sang many songs for the Guv'nor, including the favorites *Midnight Special* and *Ole Dan Tucker*, but he wasn't about to let the occasion go to waste, so he also sang a special song he had just written, imploring the state boss to give him a pardon so that he could go home to see his wife again. The Governor was most amused, but told him, "I'm going to turn you loose after a while, but I'm going to keep you here so you can pick and dance for me when I come down."

It took almost a year, but on January 16, 1925, in one of his last acts of office, Nuff signed a full pardon for Leadbelly. The singer had literally sung his way out of prison.

He moved to the biggest city in Texas, got a job and tried to abide by the commandment in his most famous song, *If you ever go to Houston/ Boy you better walk right/ You better not stagger, and you better not fight.* Eventually, though, he got back to playing in the frequently violent after-hours clubs. In one, he met a new woman named Era who would become his wife for the rest of his life. Things were not always peaceful with her either. "I'd be out playing for the niggers, drinking good whiskey, foolin' with the women, and having a good time," he recalled. "She got so mad with me one time that she broke my twelve-string box. I would have killed her then, but I know they'd put me in the pen."

On another occasion he and Era were attacked by two men at a house-party in Oil City. Even though Era fought "like a regular wild cat", Leadbelly got a vicious cut across his neck that left a giant scar he would wear for the rest of his life.

In 1930, he was involved in what became the most serious confrontation of his life. He was on the street, reportedly with a half bottle of rubbing alcohol in his pocket, when he came upon a Salvation Army band. He decided to start dancing to the music, which upset a group of white men, who, he said, "must have felt it was irreligious." Words were exchanged; knives were drawn. Soon Leadbelly had a gash across his head, and one of the whites, Dick Elliot, according to the story in the Shreveport *Journal,* was "in the Highland Sanitarium suffering from severe cuts inflicted by a drunk-crazed negro who attacked him late Wednesday afternoon."

Naturally, the white man went to the hospital and the black man went to jail. Once the newspaper report came out, a mob stormed the jail, and it was all the local police could do to prevent Leadbelly from being lynched. Within a month, he was found guilty, sentenced to six to ten years of hard labor, and sent to an institution that made Sugarland look like easy street. The notorious Angola Prison was described by Leadbelly biographers Charles Wolfe and Kip Lornell as, "probably as close to slavery as any person could come in 1930."

Twice, in November 1931 and June 1932, he was whipped—the first time for "laziness", the second time for "impudence."

In 1933, prominent musicologist, folklorist and self-styled "ballad-hunter" John Lomax went on a long expedition through the South on assignment for the Library of Congress to try and find and record the American folk music they felt was rapidly disappearing. He travelled with his son Alan, who would himself become a renowned collector of American folk music. "Alan and I," wrote Lomax Sr., "were looking particularly for the song of the Negro laborer, the words of which sometimes reflect the tragedies of imprisonment, cold, hunger, heat, and the injustice of the white man."

The Lomaxes had the good fortune to be able to get in to Angola Penitentiary, and the further good luck to be able to meet and record Leadbelly. With his booming baritone and equally powerful twelve string guitar, Leadbelly sang seven songs into their primitive portable disc recording equipment, including three that would become hits for others twenty years later—*Frankie and Johnnie* (for Elvis, Johnny Cash and many others), *Ella Speed* (for both Ian & Sylvia and Jim Kweskin's Jug Band) and *Goodnight Irene* (Number One song in the US in 1950, sung by The Weavers).

The Lomaxes were impressed with Leadbelly, and when they returned to Louisiana a year later, this time with improved recording gear, they decided to revisit Angola and record more songs with him. This time Leadbelly had a new plan. He had again written a song appealing for clemency, and he asked Lomax to record it and take it to Louisiana Governor O.K. Allen. Lomax agreed, and delivered the disc to the Governor's office. Within a month Allen had signed a commutation order, and Leadbelly was once again a free man. The legend of Leadbelly had been created—the singer who had sung his way out of prison—not once, but twice. There is now some revisionist thinking about how much the Lomax recording really contributed to the release, but the fact is that one month after the Governor received the disc, Leadbelly was free.

Leadbelly was extremely grateful to Lomax and offered his services to him as a driver and helper in the musicologist's quest to record more music through the roughest corners of the deep south. Lomax was intrigued but concerned about Leadbelly's fearsome reputation. He wanted to know if Leadbelly was carrying any weapons. The singer was no longer packing heat but he was carrying a long knife he showed to his new "Boss Man". Lomax nervously told him, "Whenever you decide that you are going to take my money and car, you won't have to use this knife on me. Just tell me what you want, and I'll give it to you without a struggle." Shocked that Lomax would talk to him this way, Leadbelly protested, "Boss, suh, don't talk that way…I'se yo man. You won't ever have to tie your shoes again if you don't want to. I'll slip in front of you if anybody tries to shoot you. I'm ready to die for you."

The pair travelled all through the South, with Leadbelly a great help getting old tunes out of other convicts, who were often suspicious about what the honky academic with his elaborate recording equipment was up to. After several months on the road together, they decided there might be commercial career possibilities for Leadbelly, and so they headed north to New York City. Lomax was more nervous about the operation than Leadbelly was. The black singer had to calm his white benefactor, telling him before a performance at the esteemed Bryn Mawr women's college that he shouldn't worry because, "maybe [the students] don't know it, but they is about to hear the famous-est nigger guitar player in the world." Leadbelly loved New York, especially after he was greeted with major newspaper stories like the one in the *Herald Tribune*, even if it was headed SWEET SINGER OF THE SWAMPLANDS HERE TO DO A FEW TUNES BETWEEN HOMICIDES. Lomax hated the sensationalism of the *Tribune* piece, and even more the *TIME* piece headed MURDEROUS MINSTREL, but he had to admit they helped with concert bookings for his protégé. "Leadbelly of this moment is the most famous [black man] in the world,' he wrote his wife, "and I the most notorious white man."

Of course, it was virtually impossible for Leadbelly to get hotel accommodation in New York. Eventually Lomax, Leadbelly, and the singer's wife, who they brought up from the South took up residence with two rich female patrons in Connecticut. Leadbelly and his wife were relegated to handyman and cook, but it became a base for Leadbelly's concerts, recordings, the filming of a *March of Time* newsreel about him, and a place where Lomax could write his new book, *Leadbelly and His Songs*. However, the professor proved to be a poor agent and somewhat of a rip-off artist. He negotiated a royalty of only two cents per record, and took two-thirds of Leadbelly's concert fees, leaving the artist with only a third of the take. After an eventful and sometimes acrimonious three months, the two parted ways and Leadbelly and his wife returned home to Shreveport and then moved on to Dallas. At one point the pair got in a wild domestic row and Leadbelly ended up in Parkland Hospital with a row of deep razor cuts around his midriff. Tough-as-nails, he serenaded the doctors and nurses as they stitched him up. "It was a most unusual Leadbelly concert," remembered his Texan friend Morris Fair.

A year later Leadbelly was back in New York, hoping for a comeback. The *Herald Tribune* writer who had written the piece the previous year now wrote a new one, headed LEADBELLY JINGLES INTO CITY, INHALES GIN, EXHALES RHYME. Leadbelly found a promoter who created a show for him that played first at the Lafayette Theater in Harlem, then at the famed Apollo in which Leadbelly, dressed in prison stripes, sang to an actor portraying the Governor who pardoned him. Unfortunately, the reviews were poor, the audiences stayed away in droves, and Leadbelly himself grew sick of having to always play up the pardoned con aspect of his life. He especially tired of it after the April 19, 1937 issue of *Life* magazine came out with an article titled BAD NIGGER MAKES GOOD MINSTREL, with a close-up picture of his weathered hands cradling his Stella twelve-string with the caption, "These hands once killed a man." Pete Seeger observed, "Every time a newspaper article was written about him, they said two-time murderer, spent twenty years in prison, and so on. Boy, did he never want to hear about that again."

Fortunately, he found a whole new set of friends in the rapidly growing left-wing political crowd based in Greenwich Village and Brooklyn that saw beyond the fearsome popular image. Celebrated black writer Richard Wright profiled him in the organ of the Communist Party, the *Daily Worker*, calling him a true "people's artist" and chronicled how he had been ripped off by John Lomax, in what he called "one of the most amazing cultural swindles in American history."

Leadbelly began to sing at events organized by the Worker's Alliance, the International Workers' Order, the Young Communist League, the Theater Arts Alliance and groups organizing for striking Kentucky miners and the Spanish Civil War. His new friends included activist singers like Burl Ives, Pete Seeger, Josh White and Woody Guthrie. Although Leadbelly himself never joined the Communist party, members of the party like Henrietta Yurchenko would later say, "We adored him, we loved him, we respected him." Leadbelly would joke about this. Hearing someone say to him, "You be careful now, or somebody will be calling you a communist," he laughingly replied, "Oh, all us niggers is communists, you know." The FBI weren't amused. They opened a file on Leadbelly in 1940.

He could not seem to escape violence. He was arrested for stabbing another black man with his knife. According to singer Brownie McGhee, Leadbelly had caught the man, an intruder, entering his apartment. However, sixteen stab wounds in the thief seemed excessive. A bondsman managed to get him out, and while out on bail Leadbelly stumbled into a store robbery, tackled the gunman and held him until police arrived. When it came time for his trial the judge took his brave actions at the robbery into account but seemed to ignore any evidence that Leadbelly had acted in self-defense in the stabbing incident. He sentenced the singer to a year (later reduced to eight months) in Rikers Island prison.

It was his last prison term. After getting out (without wild escapes or Governor's pardons), Leadbelly returned to live in a sixth-floor walk-up on the Lower East Side of Manhattan. He had considerable fame, but he seldom made more than $1100 a year from the five hundred songs in his repertoire. He did continue to record and perform. He registered for the draft for World War II but now over fifty, was never called up. Instead he moved to California to pursue some offers of movie work, but ultimately the film projects fell through. He had offers to make recordings in San Francisco, but the local of the Musician's Union there had a rule that forbade black musicians from playing with whites, so that too had to be aborted.

In 1949, he flew to Paris to do a series of concerts, and while there fell ill and was diagnosed with Lou Gehrig's disease. Six months later, he died in New York. Six months after that, The Weavers had their biggest hit with his song, *Goodnight Irene.* Even though they too were accused of being Communists and were at times the subject of blacklists, the song became the Number One single in the United States, playing, according to the *New York Times* "1400 times a minute" over "the 2583 radio stations, ninety-nine television stations and roughly 400,000 juke boxes in the United States." The royalties began pouring in, and even though Leadbelly shared the copyright to the song with John Lomax, had he lived another year he would have died a rich man. Instead, he was buried, shoeless, in Louisiana. There was no money for a marker.

Leadbelly's life was chronicled by celebrated black photographer, writer and film director Gordon Parks in a feature film, well reviewed but poorly released by Paramount Pictures in 1976. In 1988 he was posthumously inducted into the Rock and Roll Hall of Fame. The city of Shreveport renamed St. Paul's Bottoms, the funky red-light district where seventy-five years earlier Leadbelly had developed his musical chops. They now called it Ledbetter Heights in his honor, though apparently the renaming has not had the desired effect of improving the lot of the inhabitants of the area. In perhaps the most ironic tribute, the city also erected a life-sized statue of Leadbelly—right across the street from the city's courthouse.

Billie Holiday

Billie Holiday was the greatest female jazz singer from the 1930s to the 1950s. Perhaps, the greatest of all time.

"Lady Day is unquestionably the most important influence on American popular singing in the last twenty years," said Frank Sinatra. "It was Billie Holiday who was, and still remains, the greatest single musical influence on me. With few exceptions, every major pop singer in the US during her generation has been touched in some way by her genius."

She didn't just sing the blues—she lived them. Her life was tumultuous and unhappy—full of interactions with The Man from her birth to her death. Even her conception was illegal—she was born on April 7, 1915, to Sadie Fagan, when Sadie was thirteen years old. She would have been conceived sometime in July of 1914, when Sadie was twelve—much younger than the legal age of consent.

Her childhood makes Dickens' stories look tame. She was working as a cleaner in a whorehouse at age eight, first jailed (for being raped!) at ten, put into solitary confinement in a Girl's Reformatory at eleven, became a "five dollar call girl" at thirteen, and spent four months behind bars at Welfare Island Prison in her teens. Once she became a star concert singer and recording artist, she became the number one target of the corrupt Federal Bureau of Narcotics and was harassed, shot at, arrested and jailed many times. She died in a New York hospital room, handcuffed to the bed, illegally under arrest, and with two policemen guarding the door.

Billie Holiday was born Eleanora Fagan. She would later take her first name from the silent film star Billie Dove, and her last name from her father, Clarence Holiday. Her father abandoned the family to go on the road as a guitarist and banjo player. He eventually had some measure of success himself and performed for years with the Fletcher Henderson band. He died in 1937 of pneumonia. "But it wasn't the pneumonia that killed him," recalled Billie. "It was Dallas, Texas. That's where he was and where he walked around, going from hospital to hospital trying to get help. But none of them would even so much as take his temperature or take him in."

He was finally admitted to the Jim Crow ward of a veteran's hospital, but it was too late and he died there of a hemorrhage. Although his death was caused by racist intolerance and not by lynching, it was nonetheless the inspiration for some of the lines in his daughter's most famous song, *Strange Fruit*.

With an unwed, single teenage mother as her sole parent, she had a childhood that was rough-and-tumble in the extreme. She was certainly no shrinking violet herself. When her young cousin first tried to have childish sex with her, then tormented her by waving a giant squirming rat in her face, she clobbered him with a baseball bat, sending him to John Hopkins Hospital. She left school in Grade Five. From then on, her education, such as it was, came from the streets, or from her great-grandmother, who told her stories about her own youth on the plantations of Virginia. The old woman had been a slave—and a doxy—a forced mistress—to the plantation owner and had born sixteen children to him—themselves all slaves until emancipation.

Once out of school, Billie became a maid, first for Baltimore's rich white families, then for a whorehouse run by a madam named Alice Dean. It was there she first saw a Victrola and heard jazz—then often called "whorehouse music"—and became infatuated by the tunes of Louis Armstrong and Bessie Smith. She was not attracted to becoming a musician because of the glamour or excitement. As her obituary in *The New York Times* put it, "Miss Holiday became a singer more from desperation than desire."

When she was ten, she was accosted by a man remembered as "Mr. Dick" who tried to rape her. Dick was caught in the act and was taken to jail as was his bleeding victim. After spending a few nights in jail, both Dick and Billie were hauled into court. Dick got a five-year sentence. Billie was sent to a Catholic institution for "wayward" girls. The length of her sentence, according to the judge, was "until she was dead or twenty-one."

Her mother did what she could for her. On Easter, she brought her a basket of chicken, some hard-boiled eggs and other treats. However because of some infraction, the Mother Superior forced Billie to give it all away to the other girls, and stand watching as they ate it, then locked her overnight into the institution's morgue, alone with the body of a girl who had died in the home.

Eventually her mother sprung her from the dreadful place, and both mom and daughter, virtually penniless, moved north from Baltimore to New York City. Billie, fourteen, became a prostitute, but was only willing to hit the sack with white men, not black. She had already had too many bad experiences with men of her own race.

"With my regular white customers, it was a cinch," she remembers. "When they came to see me it was, wham, bang, they gave me the money and were gone. I made all the loot I needed. But Negroes would keep you up all the damn night, handing you that stuff about 'Is it good, baby?' and "Don't you want to be my old lady?'"

When she turned down a Harlem big shot named Big Blue Rainier, he set the cops on her. They charged into the whorehouse the next day and hauled her off to jail, as she says, "not for anything I did, but for something I wouldn't do."

She ended up in front of a female judge who sentenced her to a term in a Brooklyn city hospital, where, she remembers, a big dyke came after her. "They call them lesbians now, but we just called them dykes", she later wrote. "I took a poke at her and down the stairs she went."

She ended up back in front of the same judge, who called her "a girl of bad character", and this time sentenced her to four months at the Welfare Island prison on the East River.

At the time it was infested with the biggest rats in New York and even more belligerent dykes. A scuffle with one of them landed Billie in an unlit solitary cell for fifteen days on a bread, water and saltpeter diet.

Once out of the miserable place she hit the streets again, looking (unsuccessfully) for work as a dancer, and then (successfully) as a singer. She got her first singing gig at age fourteen, and for the next four years worked the many clubs on 132nd Street in Harlem. In 1932 she met the legendary producer John Hammond, who made two records with her singing with Benny Goodman's big band.

Billie Holiday and Benny Goodman were John Hammond's first big two finds but he went on to have an incredible career spanning four decades, in which he was instrumental in launching the careers of Count Basie, Bob Dylan, Bruce Springsteen, Pete Seeger, Aretha Franklin, George Benson, Leonard Cohen, Stevie Ray Vaughan, and countless others.

He also, like so many others in this book, incurred the interest of J. Edgar Hoover who had his G-Men investigate Hammond because of the producer's civil rights activism, and his ties to musicians, to the black community, and to members of the Communist Party.

Hammond signed Holiday to the Brunswick label and made many recordings with her through the late thirties. However, he didn't put much money in her pocket. She usually made $25 a recording, never more than $75, and no royalties. Consequently, as she was now supporting both herself and her mother, she had to go back to the streets to make a living. Pops Foster, who invited her to join his band, says when he first met her, she was "doing a little prostituting along 136th Street—that was kind of the main drag. She was a hustler, out of the clubs." Only when convinced she could make a living, however shaky, from singing, did she stop hustling.

Foster has lurid memories of the Harlem nightlife of the 1930s: "We had a place we all used to go to, and Billie went there too, what they called the Daisy Chain. It was a house of prostitution and drinks and everything. Billie used to frequent it just to see what was happening. And *everything* was happening. It was *faaaantastic!* Women going with women, men goin' with men. Nobody paid it any mind, everybody was gay and having a ball. Stayed open twenty-four hours a day. On 141st Street between Lenox and 7th they had a girl there called Sewing Machine Bertha and she'd go down on all the girls. The girl that owned that house—Hazel Valentine—very, very pretty girl—she was the landlady—an ex-chorus girl. Entertainers all went up there. Half colored, half white. Hell, yeah. Real integrated. All the lesbians went there. I couldn't quote names because some of them was real big-time stars, so it was husha-husha. The public didn't know anything about it. It was only show people."

It was also in this period that Billie began touring the mid-west and the south, and experiencing some of the raw racism of the country. If the experiences of classical pianist Don Shirley in the 1960s, as depicted in the film *The Green Book*, appear difficult, imagine what it was like for a young black woman, travelling with a white jazz band, in the 1930s.

The trouble began as soon as she began singing outside of Harlem, for in the 1930s New York City could at times exhibit racism just as strongly as could the Deep South. In October of 1938 she was the headliner for the Artie Shaw Band, appearing in the Blue Room of the Lincoln Hotel. The hotel's manager, Maria Kramer, asked Shaw to request Holiday to use the freight elevator so that hotel patrons would not assume that black people were staying in the hotel. Even the reactionary columnist Walter Winchell commented on the irony of this happening in a hotel named for the president who had freed the slaves, 65 years earlier.

Unlike the rather gentle Don Shirley, Holiday would give just as hard as she got. On one occasion at a New Year's Eve performance, a sailor saw her being served at the bar and yelled at the bartender, "When did you start serving nigger bitches?" Billie smashed her glass on the counter and reamed it into the guy's face creating what was described as a three-ring circus of cuts.

In another incident during the war when New York City was flooded with servicemen from all over the US, including the south, she experienced two sailors stubbing their cigarettes out on her mink coat. She asked them to join her outside the nightclub where she proceeded to deck both of them. When the NYPD arrived, they discovered, much to their amusement, two sailors lying in the gutter, and a sweetly feminine Holiday telling them they had attacked her.

The racism became more difficult for her to deal with once she was on the road. Touring with the Artie Shaw band, she could seldom find a restaurant that would serve her, a hotel that would give her a room, or even a washroom she was allowed to use. Indeed, the crackers that ran the clubs of the south and mid-west would not even let her stay on the bandstand after she had sung. Once finished, she had to go *back to where she belonged,* as they would put it.

The white band members would often, though not always, stick up for her. At one greasy roadside diner the manager and the waitresses refused to serve her. Trumpeter Chuck Peterson and sax player Tony Pastor told them "This is Lady Day. Now you feed her." Billie pleaded with them not to start anything saying she would eat in the bus, but they wouldn't listen, and instead began wrecking the joint. She remembers that as they ran out and their bus pulled out of the two-bit town, she could hear the sheriff's police siren coming after them.

In those days it was often just as bad in the North. In one incident, in Detroit, she was standing beside Peterson when a man approached them asking, "What the hell's going on? A man can't bring his wife in a bar without you tramp white men bringing a nigger woman in?" That insult quickly escalated into the racist beating and kicking Peterson in the mouth, while shouting at him that "I'll fix it so you don't play trumpet tonight."

The problems only stopped when they entered Canada. Mae Weiss, who travelled with the band as wife of bassist Sid Weiss, remembers the difference: "We played the Royal York in Toronto which would be comparable to the Waldorf in New York or the Plaza in Boston. It was wonderful to walk up to the front door and Billie walked in with us like anyone else and she got a room. No problem, no question. We all felt marvelous about it...She took it as she should have taken it, that was her right."

She did have allies on both coasts, if not in the so-called "fly-over states". In California, she was heckled by a patron calling her a "nigger" and cursing all "nigger singers." Bob Hope came to her rescue. Before the next set, Hope told her to get back out and sing." Let that sonofabitch say something and I'll take care of him."

"So I did, and he did," remembers Holiday. "It was a real mess. When that cracker boy started, I stopped singing and Bob took the floor. Hope traded insults with that cracker for five minutes before he had enough and left. After Hope finished with him, I went back singing."

While in California, she also became a good friend of Orson Welles, and claims to have watched nine previews of his classic but highly controversial "Citizen Kane" with him before its release in 1941. Welles may have had an affair with Holiday, as, almost certainly, Broadway actress Tallulah Bankhead did. Bankhead, who despite her outrageous and flamboyant behavior, had strong connections in Washington. She even called J. Edgar Hoover on her friend's behalf, asking him to help get the narcotics agents off Billie's tail. Hoover claimed he had no control over narcotics agents, to which Bankhead retorted, "Don't tell me that. You're the most powerful man in Washington. You know that every artist has to have a little something, sir, help her give the lift every once in a while."

Billie whispered anxiously to try to get her friend to stop, "Bankie, shut up. You're gonna get us all in jail".

While on the road the musicians were careful with the hotel rooms they stayed in—worried that narcs and local police would plant marijuana reefers in their rooms. Which brings us to the villain of our story, the man who is largely responsible for the downfall and the death of Billie Holiday, Harry Anslinger.

When Billie was put on trial in 1947, the case was titled, "The United States of America versus Billie Holiday", and, as she described it, "that's just the way it felt." The many battles between Music and The Man over the last hundred years have been a part of what has been called the culture war—the war between hip and straight, flamboyant and subdued, liberal and conservative, progressive and reactionary, often rural versus urban, often black versus white, often old versus young, usually the franchised versus the disenfranchised.

The authorities usually won these battles, but with the explosion of new technologies like phonograph records and movies, new ways of thinking and new kinds of music in the early years of the twentieth century, they began to think they needed new tools to fight this new Jazz Age. School principals might be able to bust students for how they dressed, how long they wore their hair, or the music they listened to, but it was not so easy for the police or the government to do that. They had to find a new tool for their arsenal, and they did—drugs.

When Billie Holiday was born in 1915, drugs were completely legal. Alcohol was widely available. Marijuana—both wild and cultivated was so common it was just referred to as a weed. Heroin and morphine were freely prescribed by doctors, and cocaine, first synthetically created in 1860 was so enthusiastically embraced that it was sold in soda fountain "elixirs"—the most famous of course being Coca-Cola. There were people addicted to the drugs in those days, but since they were legally available and inexpensive, addiction caused few societal problems.

North America changed radically with the prohibition of alcohol first in Canada from 1918 to 1920, and then in the US from 1920 to 1933. Prohibition had three completely unexpected effects. First, with the government out of being the largest beneficiary of liquor sales (through taxes), the void was filled by criminal organizations like the Mafia, who were soon making huge fortunes from bootleg booze. Second, with liquor suddenly harder to find, people turned to other stimulants, then still legal. Third, with alcohol now mostly available in illegal speakeasies, these new clandestine bars were an ideal place for the growth of clandestine music—no longer the square conservative music of the past, but now the raunchy outlaw wild sounds of blues and jazz.

A huge new policing infrastructure had to be set up to try to enforce Prohibition. Once set up, like all bureaucracies, it fought to perpetuate its existence. Harry Anslinger found himself a job with the US Department of Prohibition at the same time as Billie Holiday was finding her early work in the speakeasies and brothels of New York. Anslinger worked out of Nassau in the Bahamas, fighting the extensive smuggling of booze by schooners sailing from the islands to Florida and the Carolinas. After conveniently marrying a woman from the uber-wealthy Mellon family, a relative of the Treasury Secretary Andrew Mellon, Anslinger was promoted to a Washington desk job inside the Prohibition wing of the Treasury Department. He was appointed as the head of the new Federal Bureau of Narcotics. The United States' famous "War on Drugs" had just begun—and Billie Holiday would become one of its first casualties.

The Narcotics Department was originally a small and minor part of the Treasury Department. With the looming possibility that the 18th Amendment might be repealed, and Prohibition might end, Anslinger felt it possible he might be totally out of work. He could not countenance that. Not only did he, like everyone, need a job, but he was also on a mission. He was an out-and-out racist, and he saw it as his role in life to fight to preserve America as a bastion of white, conservative, Protestant values. Many Americans in the 1920's longed for the good old days, when whites ruled and blacks were slaves. Harry laid the groundwork for a return to slavery. By the twenty-first century, his war on drugs had almost done that. By 2005, more American black males were incarcerated in prisons, the majority on drug-related charges, than had been held in slavery until Emancipation.

Harry made no bones about his racial attitudes. He regularly called his few black agents and many black suspects by the N word. The senator from his home state of Pennsylvania demanded (unsuccessfully) his resignation, due to Anslinger's unbridled racism. He didn't stop with blacks, though. He also promoted the idea that West Indians, Central Americans, and Mexicans were full of what he called "loathsome and contagious diseases".

His problem, though, was that in those days, heroin, cocaine and morphine were only used by a small number of people—mostly rich people and mostly in the privacy of their own homes. Harry needed a more lurid story to excite the press, the public and his government bosses. He found it in marijuana. Unfortunately for Anslinger, it was still legal, so he began spreading nightmarish stories, both to the Hearst press and to the House Appropriations Committee about the insidious nature of the weed. One favorite was about black college students, hopped up on weed, "partying with female students (white) and getting their sympathy with stories of racial persecution. Result: pregnancy."

Another was a planted story in the July 6, 1927 edition of the *New York Times* reporting that a Mexican mother, unable to feed her children, had fed them the marijuana plants growing in her garden. Neighbors reported, "hearing outbursts of crazed laughter and rushed to the house to find the entire family insane." The woman, the paper assured its readers, would be insane "for the rest of her life."

Anecdotal evidence like this was one thing, but Harry wanted to go further with medical backup. He wrote to thirty scientific experts asking them their thoughts about marijuana. Twenty-nine responded saying it would be wrong to ban it and that they saw no harm in it, regardless of what was being reported in the press. Anslinger ignored them and instead quoted the one doctor out of thirty who believed it was a threat to society.

His department was involved in making the film *Reefer Madness* and his own writings about the drug are quite equal to the over-wrought narration in the cult classic. When you smoke grass, he wrote, you will fall into "a delirious rage", then be filled with "dreams…of an erotic character." Finally, it will turn you into "a mad beast". In fact, "if the hideous monster Frankenstein came face to face with the monster Marijuana, it would drop dead of fright". It is a lurid turn of phrase ridiculous on a number of counts, not least of which is that Frankenstein was not the name of the monster but rather of the doctor who created him—but it is a mistake that many people make.

Throughout the 1920s many states of the United States, Canada and England all added marijuana to the list of prohibited drugs, and by 1935 it was outlawed across the United States. It was very convenient timing for the gangsters who had lost their market in illegal alcohol with the end of Prohibition. They now had a much more lucrative product they could sell.

Anslinger went to work, creating the war on drugs by focusing on busting two groups of people—jazz musicians, and doctors. Jazz musicians, because they provided the potential for the kind of high-profile busts that The Man is always keen on, and, simply, because the uptight straight laced Anslinger simply hated jazz. "It sounds," his memos read, "like the jungles in the dead of night". The lives of the jazzmen "reek of filth" and their rhythms "resurrect the unbelievably ancient indecent rites of the East Indies." (The East Indies?? What—the Philippines? Indonesia?)

He went after doctors because thousands of them followed their Hippocratic Oath and ignored his new edicts. They continued to prescribe drugs for their sick and/or addicted patients. Over 20,000 doctors were charged with violating the Harrison Act, and even though many juries refused to convict them, seeing that they were only trying to treat the sick as well as they could, an astonishing 95 percent were convicted. Most received giant fines, others faced five-year sentences for each prescription filled.

One of the highest profile doctors Anslinger went after was Henry Smith Williams, a respected California expert on cancer, blood cells, and drugs. Williams fought back, penning a book (his 119th) titled *Drug Addicts are Human Beings* in which he posited that Anslinger had created the war on drugs because the Mafia had paid him to do so in order that they could corner the drug business for themselves. By making drugs illegal they drove the price up by over a thousand percent, thus turning addicts into thieves or whores to support their habit and creating a vast new income stream for the Mafia and other criminal syndicates. "The United States government, as represented by its (anti-drug) officers," wrote Williams, "has become the greatest and most potent maker of criminals in any recent century."

Williams' book, with uncanny accuracy, predicted that Anslinger's war would one day lead to the creation of a five billion dollar drug smuggling industry, but in the 1930's, it did little to slow down Anslinger, who merely shifted his focus away from doctors and back to musicians. "Not the good musicians," he reassured congressmen, "but the jazz type."

"Prepare all cases in your jurisdiction involving musicians in violation of the marijuana laws," he told his agents. "We will have a great national round-up arrest of all such persons on a single day. I will let you know what day," He also reminded them of his first rule when dealing with hopped up, reefer-toking jazz musicians: "Shoot first."

He made some busts. In November of 1930 Louis Armstrong was busted outside of Culver City's Cotton Club for smoking what he called by the slang name of "gage". Drummer Gene Krupa got a ninety-day prison term for possession of two joints. But Anslinger's bureau never had the success he expected in getting a mass incarceration of jazz musicians. He found that the community was too loyal. He could never get the snitches he needed to make the mass busts he wanted, so instead his bosses at the Treasury Department told him to focus on just one big one—the biggest female jazz singer in the world—Billie Holiday.

Anslinger undoubtedly went after Holiday largely because she was black. When it came to white addicts, it was a different story. Knowing that he could bust an even bigger star, Judy Garland, he had her come into his office, but then just had a friendly chat with her, recommended she take longer vacations between pictures, and then wrote her studio, assuring them she did not have a drug problem at all.

The new drug czar knew that if he was going to be able to infiltrate the Harlem world of Billie Holiday he would have to hire black agents, and so, although he was loath to have to do it, he hired an agent named Jimmy Fletcher to try to bust Holiday. His first attempt was memorable. Once inside her apartment, he tried to convince her to come clean, saying "If you've got anything, why don't you just turn it over to us? Then we won't be searching around, pulling out your clothes and everything." Pulling a good cop/bad cop routine, Fletcher's partner told her he would call headquarters to get a policewoman to join them to do a full body search of the singer.

"You don't have to do that. I'll strip," said Billie. "All I want to say is—will you search me and let me go? All that policewoman is going to do is look up my pussy."

She stood and stripped for them, then, to prove she had nothing secreted in her vagina, pissed in front of them—or so says a report by writer Johann Hari. It seems somewhat hard to believe, but then Billie did have a habit, if women's washrooms were overcrowded, of simply going into the men's, raising her dress and using a urinal. It was kind of the thing to do back then amongst a certain crowd, perhaps just to outrage the squares. This writer remembers seeing Holiday's friend Tallulah Bankhead at a boozy theater party in the early sixties hike her skirt up and use a bar sink for the same purpose.

The outlandish move worked and Holiday was not charged. Next time she was not so lucky. Holiday had a series of terrible pimps and managers throughout her life, and the worst and most brutal of them, Louis McKay, had decided she wasn't being obedient enough to him. "How come I got to take this from this bitch here? This low-class bitch," he asked. "I'm going to do her up so goddamn bad she going to remember as long as she lives." Knowing that Anslinger was aching to bust her, he went to Washington and made a deal with him.

In May 1947, after McKay had snitched on her, Anslinger sent a posse of Treasury agents to the Philadelphia hotel where Billie was staying for her gig with Louis Armstrong at the Earle Theater. As she was driven back to the hotel, she recognized that the car was being surrounded by Anslinger's agents, many of whom, by now, she knew by sight. She wanted to get away, and since her chauffeur seemed paralysed with fear, she pushed him out of the driver's seat, and then, although she had never driven a car before in her life, jumped in and roared away. One of the agents leaped in front of the car. She remembered it this way:

"He hollered "Halt!" and tried to stop the car by standing in the road. But I kept driving right on and he moved. I pulled away through a rain of bullets."

She somehow managed to drive the car back to New York, but soon after getting back was found and arrested at her quarters in the Hotel Grampion. Days later she was on trial, without a lawyer, charged with possession of drugs. She pleaded guilty, and further pleaded with the judge to convict her and send her to a hospital, where she could try to get off her heroin habit. Instead, he sentenced her to a year and a day and within hours she was on a train bound for the Federal Women's Reformatory in Alderston, West Virginia. She was put in the black section of the Jim Crow segregated prison, forced to go cold turkey, and given jobs in the prison's kitchen and pigsty.

She received thousands of letters of support from around the world but was not allowed to read any of them. The other women in the pen begged her to sing for them, but she turned them down. "I couldn't have sung if I'd wanted to", she later said. "If they'd understood my kind of singing, they'd have known I couldn't sing in a place like that. The whole basis of my singing is feeling. Unless I feel something, I can't sing. In the whole time I was there I didn't feel a thing."

Released in 1948, she and her promoters soon had her booked into Carnegie Hall for a comeback concert. Even though it was held on the Saturday night before Easter, traditionally thought to be the worst night of the year for show business, the show quickly sold out. An extra 200 seats were put up on the stage behind her (in contravention of the fire code) and 3,000 more turned away at the door.

However, she could no longer appear in New York's nightclubs. As a result of her conviction, she was stripped of her cabaret performer's license and so could barely make a living. She appealed the decision a year later but was turned down. Instead, the judge commended the police department for refusing to give her the card.

The cards were forever stacked against Billie Holiday. Anslinger, still anxious to get her, hired a new agent to go after her—a giant murderous tough guy named Colonel George White, who was famous for having killed an American citizen he referred to as a "Jap" during

World War II by strangling him with his bare hands. He told the authorities he had killed the man because he believed he was a spy, but he admitted later he had no idea who he was—he just liked the idea of killing him. When he had to undergo a personality test before joining Anslinger's Narcotics Bureau, it classified him as a sadist. Nonetheless, he was hired, and assigned the Billie Holiday file, which appealed to him. She looked to him to be "a very attractive customer", and he relished the idea that he might be the one "to kick her over."

Billie continued to tour and to record through the 1950s, as best she could. Critics sniped that she was past her prime, that the booze and drugs had ruined her voice. Don't believe it. Listen to her final albums, like *Lady in Satin* and *All or Nothing at All* and you'll hear the powerful, mature moving voice of one of the twentieth century's greatest song stylists.

In 1959, at age 44, she collapsed in her Manhattan apartment. She was rushed to the Knickerbocker Hospital, but they turned her away for being a drug addict. She ended up in the public ward of the city's Metropolitan Hospital. "You watch, baby," she told a friend. "They are going to arrest me in this damn bed."

Indeed, that's what happened, Narcotics agents, under Colonel White's direction, were sent to the hospital. They claimed to find an eighth of an ounce of heroin in a corner of the room. Connected to the bed with hospital tubes, she could not have hidden it there. The narcs took away her radio, record player, flowers, chocolates, and comic books (as well as heroin, she was also addicted to comic books), and handcuffed her to the bed. Her friend Maely Dufty screamed at them that it was against the law to arrest a person who was on the critical list. Laughing, they told her they had solved that problem: they had taken her off the list.

She was given methadone for a few days, but then the hospital took her off that, putting her into a panic. "They're going to kill me in here," she told Maely. "Don't let them."

On the streets in front of the hospital, protestors led by Harlem Reverend Eugene Callender holding signs reading "Let Lady Live" pleaded for her release, but to no avail. Harry and his men fingerprinted her in her hospital bed, took a mug shot of there and continued to grill her.

The singer had had enough. She smuggled a roll of cash she had hidden in her vagina out of the hospital with a friend to pay for her funeral. On July 17, 1959, she died.

Her funeral in Manhattan and burial in the Bronx were attended by hundreds, including swarms of police, concerned that their actions against her might cause a riot. The eulogy by Reverend Callender included the words, "we should not be here. This young lady was gifted by her creator with tremendous talent. She should have lived to be at least 80 years old."

In Washington, Harry Anslinger did not share the sentiment. Instead, he just grimly, sarcastically wrote that, "for her, there would be no more *Good Morning Heartache.*"

Chuck Berry

Chuck Berry holds a hallowed spot in the pantheon of rock and roll. John Lennon called him "one of the all-time great poets", and said, "If you had to give rock and roll another name it would have to be "Chuck Berry". Leonard Cohen claimed that "All of us are mere footnotes to the words of Chuck Berry." The plaque at the Rock and Roll Hall of Fame states that "While no one individual can be said to have invented rock and roll, Chuck Berry comes the closest of any single figure to being the one who put all the essential pieces together". Anthony Kiedis, singer for the Red Hot Chili Peppers, called him "a musical scientist who discovered a cure for the blues'. Stevie Wonder simply proclaimed, "There is only one King of Rock and Roll. His name is Chuck Berry."

He also, though, had more—and more serious—run-ins with The Man than almost any other musician. Those interactions with the law—almost all of them tinged with racism, injustice, and the authorities' hatred and fear of his music, made him a somewhat bitter, prickly and difficult personality. Dick Clark, with whom he had a long and complicated business relationship, said of him: "He's never gotten any easier to get along with; he's still an ornery son of a bitch, but I love him dearly". Keith Richards, another major fan and admirer of Berry, recalled this telling backstage incident: "In the dressing room I went up to say 'Hello' and he was just leaving with a bit of white tail. And I made the mistake of tapping him on the shoulder. I said, Hey Chuck, don't rush off without saying hello…' And he just turned around and just gave a hill shot right in the face. I was very proud of the fact that I didn't go down. He's the only guy that hit me that I never got back." A few years after that incident the pair ran into each other in Los Angeles Airport, and Berry promptly lit a match and threw it down Richards' shirt. "Every time him and me got in contact, whether its intentional or not, I end up getting wounded."

Many of his other musical colleagues reported his prickly nature. He was very bright, but also, it seemed, often very bitter. Following his lengthy trial and jail time from 1960 to 1963 for "transporting a woman across state lines with the intent of debauchery", other musicians noticed the changes in his demeanor. His longtime pianist Johnnie Johnson recalled, "I could see him, how he acted with other people, and I knew he had a chip on his shoulder. He was angry at how the law had treated him, and he thought that everyone wanted to cheat him. He was definitely a different person after he got out of prison." Fellow rocker Carl Perkins, who toured with Berry in the late 50's, also saw how he had gone downhill, when then toured Britain together in 1964. "I never saw a man so changed", said Perkins. "He had been an easygoing guy before, the kinda guy who would jam in dressing rooms, sit and swap licks and jokes. In England he was cold, real distant and bitter. It wasn't just jail, it was those years of one-nighters, grinding it out like that can kill a man, but I figured it was mostly jail."

Berry's first brush with the law was many years earlier—years before rock and roll. Born in 1926 in St. Louis to middle class parents (his father was a contractor and deacon of a Baptist church, his mother a high school principal), Berry began singing in 1941. In 1944 he skipped out of school and with two friends headed west on a road trip. Along with Lawrence "Skip" Hutchison and James Williams, he set out for California in a 1937 Oldsmobile, the trunk full of spare tires to ward against the flats they expected to (and did) have in those days of bad rubber and worse roads.

They were not far from St. Louis when they encountered the realities of Jim Crow segregation that was endemic in rural Missouri (and of course, all states further south) in the 1940's. The trio pulled into the "Southern Air" restaurant in Wentzville, where they were refused service and told they would have to go outside to the back where they were served food through a kitchen window designated for black service.

The trio of n'er-do-wells made it as far as Kansas City, where, having run out of money, they pulled off three armed robberies, with Berry using the barrel of a burnt-out revolver to relieve a barbershop, a bakery and a clothing store of about $150. In one of robberies the owner appeared to reach for a gun to protect his store, and only a shouted warning from Skip to Berry (known in those days as "Slick") prevented him, he would later say, from "pushing up daisies". (Yes, the nicknames and dialogue sound like they come from a Warner Brothers film of the era.)

The trio found their new lifestyle nerve-racking, and so decided to head back to St. Louis. En route, though, their car threw a rod, rattled to a stop and died. They tried to flag down passing motorists for help but received nothing but shouts of "Go home, niggers," until deep in the middle of the night when a man did stop to offer aid. Immediately Berry pulled the gun barrel on him, forced him out of the car, and began pushing the Oldsmobile down the road with the man's 1941 Chevy.

The victim, robbed of his car, naturally ran to a phone booth and called the police, and ten miles down the road the state troopers stopped the hapless trio, arrested them and put them in the Boone County jail. After five days Berry was finally allowed a phone call home, and his father put up $125 for a local lawyer to defend them. Twenty-two days later, they finally met with the lawyer, who told them they should plead guilty so that the judge would go easy on them (and no doubt so that the lawyer wouldn't have to do any work, and would stay in the good books of the local judge and police.) They did plead guilty, and then after a twenty-one minute trial, all three received the maximum sentence of ten years in prison.

They were sent to the Algoa Intermediate Reformatory in Jefferson City, Missouri. The incarceration began with a Lysol bath and mandatory venereal disease injections. Berry was given what was called "orientation", which was thirty days in solitary confinement. Once completed, he was put into the general population. The jail in those days was completely segregated, with the blacks having to bow and scrape to white guards who Berry recalls as being profoundly racist. It was a dangerous place. Lynchings were still happening in the 1940's and one of the most notorious was of a black oil worker dragged through the streets of a town close to the prison, then burned alive.

Berry soon learned to respectfully say "sir" to the guards, and also quickly learned the prison argot, some of which would serve him in his future songwriting. He and his two friends were "fall partners", having been convicted together, that had "copped a dime" (received ten years). "The Man" (the judge) had "thrown the book at them" and now, being newcomers who had no money, they were "short hairs and busted".

Berry learned to write in the prison—eventually writing for an illiterate preacher who attended to the cons. He also learned how to sing and created a gospel quartet that performed on Sunday services. Like so many other black performers, Berry got his start in gospel, then soon left it, morphing the group into what he called a "boogie" band—one that was accomplished enough that it was allowed out of the prison on occasion to perform dates in Jefferson City and even St. Louis.

Music would get him out of the prison, but it almost got him lynched within it. He became the object of infatuation of the wife of the Assistant Superintendent, and in one private concert for her and a nineteen-year-old female friend of hers (also white, of course), Berry ended up not just singing for the women but dancing with them. A mob of about 30 white prisoners managed to spy on the interracial trio, and a riot ensued, followed by several weeks of racial tension inside the prison.

It was only the first of what would be many problems with the law that were instigated by what would later be called "groupies" enthralled by Berry's music, or by the authorities unfairly targeting him because of their suspicion of such liaisons.

After three years inside the joint Barry was released and returned to St. Louis, where, true to form, he reports that he was "free, black, twenty-one, single and unbelievably horny" with nothing on his mind but finding "a mate to make love to."

Within a few months of his release Berry did find someone who became not just a one-night stand, but his future wife. Her name Themetta Suggs. After getting required approval from his parole officer, the pair were married on October 28, 1948. She began a long marriage and a life that she likely could never have imagined with this future wild man of rock and roll. She stuck with him through thick and thin.

The thin started soon. Within a year, Berry had met in the apartment building where he worked as a janitor a woman he remembers as a "single, unbiased Canadian woman". Although he had been warned by his father many many times of the potential dangers of a young black man even looking the wrong way at a white woman, he was nonetheless tempted by this one, especially when she, as he remembers, explained to him "the Canadian ideals of racial differences."

Though he was conflicted and resisted for some time, he eventually succumbed to her charms. Someone else, though, who had been unsuccessfully trying to date her, reported Berry's visits to the police, and the next day Berry was picked up by a patrolman and taken in to the station. There, the sergeant took up a position with a baseball bat aimed at his head, and Berry was told if he lied even once, the cop would "try for a home run".

Berry was then asked, by a hare-lipped cop, "Did you fugger?", and instantly replied "No sir. A white woman? No sir!"

He was eventually released, but because of the interaction with the police lost his janitorial job. He had to begin looking for other ways to earn money. By 1953 he had assembled a four-man combo, led by skilled piano player Johnnie Johnson, who would accompany him for most of his career. They mostly played across the Mississippi River in East St. Louis, which is in Illinois, a state at the time somewhat more tolerant than the still very racist Missouri. Though the clubs there were integrated, they were hardly mellow. Johnson recalls that one of the clubs "should have been named the 'Bucket of Blood'. There were fights on the floor every night. The owner, a policeman named Joe Lewis, would walk out in the middle of the crowd and fire his service revolver in the air to break up a fight." On another occasion Johnson was stabbed, and to the amazement of Berry and the other band-mates, kept playing the gig, wearing a makeshift bandage and covered in blood.

Within two years everything had changed, with Berry introduced to fabled studio owner Leonard Chess in Chicago, almost immediately recording his first huge hit, *Maybellene*, and soon playing gigs across the country. Just like Johnny B. Goode's mother would predict, "Maybe someday your name will be up in lights."

It was a tough racket. Studio boss Leonard Chess referred to the bar business as a "rough fuck". Berry had so many run-ins with bar owners who screwed the bands out of their fee that he soon became embittered and began to work only with very strict demands of what he expected from hiring venues. If they were not met, he had no compunction about refusing to perform. He also found that he was sharing writing credit—and thus splitting royalties—with managers and D.J's like Alan Freed, who had nothing to do with writing the songs, but were given credit in return for their promise to plug them on radio. No doubt, too, Berry had an ornery streak himself. In more than one incident, Berry tried to weasel his band mates out of their share of the proceeds, at least once coming to blows with his pianist over the matter.

There was lots to cause grief in those days—not least the fact that black performers like Berry could seldom find either hotels to stay in or restaurants to eat in the racist South of the 1950's. Frequently, even though he was headlining at a hotel or dinner club, Berry and his band were not allowed to enter the front door, or eat in the dining room. On at least one occasion, Berry was not even allowed to perform at shows he was booked for, with a local white band replacing him (and singing his hits) at the last moment when the promoter discovered he was black.

Nonetheless, both white and black teenagers began buying thousands of his records, and he became, arguably, the first rock and roll superstar. As he toured North America, he wrote his classic songs. The autobiographical *Johnny B. Goode*, the magnificent *Memphis, Tennessee*, with its great line "Cuz my uncle took the message and he wrote it on the wall" and its surprise twist that it is not a song about a lover, but rather a song about a six year old daughter of a broken marriage, and the anthem *Rock and Roll Music* were all written and recorded in this period.

He turned an observation of a young girl running around backstage hunting autographs at a concert he shared with a young Paul Anka in Anka's home town of Ottawa into *Sweet Little Sixteen*—the catchy melody a hit for Berry in 1958, and again five years later for The Beach Boys as *Surfing U.S.A.* (and yes, Berry successfully sued them for copyright infringement.)

Berry is one of the few songwriters to have used his interactions with The Man as the raw material for his songs. *Thirty Days* springs from his experiences as the Algoa juvenile detention center. *You Can't Catch Me* starts as a song about hot-rodding—a race on the New Jersey Turnpike between Berry in his *brand new airmobile* and a *souped up jitney* full of *flat-tops* (crew-cut teens). However, Berry then hears the *moaning siren of the state patrol*—but *Bye Bye New Jersey*—he becomes airborne and leaves the troopers, the flat tops and the state *just like a cool breeze*. Were that his own interactions with The Man were that simple. *Too Much Monkey Business* references the law, and *Brown Eyed Handsome Man* includes provocative lyrics about a judge's wife demanding that a District Attorney free a man who has been *arrested on charges of unemployment*. Finally, in *Reelin' and a Rockin'* , the kids at a teenage sock hop are *reelin' and rockin' till the break of dawn*—that is, until the police *come a knockin'* and close the party down.

In 1957 Berry met a woman named Francine Prager, hired her as manager, and the pair of them started a music company, Chuck Berry Music, a nightclub, Club Bandstand, and eventually an entertainment outdoor venue, Berry Park. Since Francine was white, she took lots of abuse from the St. Louis police for working for Berry—especially when the pair allowed integrated audiences into their nightclub.

However, as road manager she was able to shield Berry from the worst of southern racism. Other performers, in fact, had it worse than him. The leader of the racist White Citizen's Council of Birmingham, Alabama, Asa Carter, riled up the locals with a tract that read "We've set up a twenty-man committee to do away with this vulgar, animalistic Negro rock and roll bop. The obscenity and vulgarity of the rock and roll music is obviously a means by which the white man and his children can be driven down to the level of the nigger".

A few days later, on April 10, 1956, mellow crooner Nat King Cole performed in the Birmingham Civic Auditorium. A few minutes into the show, a group of members of the Citizen's Council stormed the stage, beating Cole in full view of the audience. The Alabama police, of course, did nothing to stop the beating.

Berry, too, had his share of violent encounters with angry mobs. Following a show in Little Rock, Arkansas, he was seen in an embrace with an admirer (a young, white, female one), and was chased out of the club by a white mob and as he tried to escape in his red Cadillac, was pelted with bottles and bricks, the mob trying to break the windows out.

Much, much worse was to come. The summer tours of 1958 and 1959 became more and more difficult, with scheduled shows of a variety of performers, with Chuck Berry and Jerry Lee Lewis as the headliners, frequently cancelled at the last moment by local authorities, fearful about what their kids were listening to. Boston's mayor John B. Hynes spoke for many of the uptight authorities across America when he was quoted by *Variety* saying "These so-called music programs are a disgrace. They must be stopped, and they will be stopped here—effective at once. As far as the City of Boston is concerned…if the kids are hungry for this kind of music they'll starve for it—until they learn to behave like citizens instead of hooligans. Boston will have no more rock and roll!"

The mayors and councilors provided the words – the police and local vigilante mobs supplied the action. On August 27, 1959 Berry was booked into Meridian, Mississippi (soon to become nationally notorious as the site of the "Freedom Summer" KKK and police-assisted murders of three civil rights workers). During the concert a girl threw herself at Berry, and after he "let her soul-searching kiss last a second too long", one of the frat boys began screaming that "this nigger asked my sister for a date". Berry escaped from the angry, beer-fueled crowd through a side door, and ended up in the local jail, where the local cops relieved him of the $700 they found in his pocket, and held him overnight, allegedly to protect him from the lynch mob assembled outside.

The problems of being on the road were often right on the road itself. Travelling home from a Kansas gig with teenage fan Joan Mathis, Berry's pink Cadillac got a flat tire (yes, there seem to have been a lot of flat tires in those days). While fumbling with the Continental spare, trying to fix it, Berry was spotted by police, who, as they later testified, were immediately suspicious. Black man, pink Cadillac, white girl, New York plates. It didn't help that they found a roll of $1900, an expired driver's license and a loaded revolver in the car. The St. Louis Globe-Democrat reported on the singer's automotive troubles with the headline ROCK 'N' ROLL STAR'S PINK CADDY REELS ON ROAD AND HE'S ROPED. Again, Berry was arrested and booked. At his arraignment, his lawyer was amazed to find "two hundred screaming girls around the building just fighting to touch him. One girl said "sign my sleeve!" and another who didn't have any paper said "Sign my hand!" and I heard her say, "I'm never going to wash this hand again". Whether the rabid fans affected the outcome of the trial is not recorded, but Silverstein managed to get him off the charges with nothing more than a stern warning from the judge.

He would not have as much luck with his next brush with the law. On December 1, 1959 a young Apache girl named Janice Escalante was released from the El Paso, Texas jail after a 25-day term for public drunkenness, vagrancy and prostitution, just as Berry and his band were rolling into town for an evening gig. They met her in a bar, Berry gave her a membership card in the Chuck Berry Fan Club, she confessed to being penniless, and to being a hooker, and before the afternoon was finished Berry had taken her under his wing, promising to save her from a life of sin and instead give her a job in his nightclub as a coat-checker.

Janice travelled with Berry for the rest of the tour, selling photographs of the singer before the show, and, as he freely admits, sharing his motel rooms and "parading around in the buff" while there.

Once they got back to St. Louis Berry did hire her to work the door at the Club Bandstand. However, within a week she proved herself to be a flakey, ineffectual worker, often missing her shifts entirely. Berry and his manager Francine fired her, and bought her a one-way ticket home to El Paso, but she refused to leave town.

Instead, she ended up telling her story to the St. Louis police, who, always keen to find a new reason to harass uppity Chuck Berry, charged him under the Mann Act with "white slavery", a crime that in his case could have led to twenty years in prison plus a $17,000 fine. Back in the 1910-1920 period the so-called "Progressive" Movement managed to pass a number of vice laws, including the banning of marijuana, the Mann Act and most famously, Prohibition. The Mann Act declared it illegal to transport a woman across state lines for the purpose of prostitution or debauchery, or, indeed, to engage "in any other immoral practice". It was created as a result of the hysteria whipped up by yellow journalists and by certain church and women's movements of the time over what many historians now believe to be a largely imaginary threat known as white slavery. By the 1920s, and certainly by the time of Berry's arrest in the late 1950s, the FBI and Federal prosecutors very seldom used the draconian act. However in Berry's case, given his race, his past criminal record, and his involvement in a revolutionary kind of music that the blue stockings of the day wanted to destroy, the old act was brought out, dusted off, and used to threaten him with very serious jail time.

Before the trial even began the city pulled out all the stops with its fire, liquor and zoning inspectors, and managed to close down Berry's nightclub. The state appointed Judge George H. Moore to adjudicate the trial—a man whom Berry's lawyer, Merle Silverstein, called, bluntly, "one of the greatest bigots of all time". Moore and the prosecutors used every opportunity to bring Berry's race into the case, even though it had nothing to do with the actual charges. Frequently Moore used the word "nigger" in the courtroom, and though Silverstein objected ("mildly objected", with a "weak voice", according to Berry), the lawyer knew there was little he could do without aggravating the judge and his handpicked, all-white jury.

Prosecutor Frederick Mayer, emboldened by the Judge, spared the jury no details of the sexual activity between Berry and Escalante, on their road trip through the American southwest. He also actively portrayed Berry's music as being jungle rhythms, and stoked the middle-aged, Middle American jury's fears that their teenage children would fall victim to the tantalizing, sinful appeal of rock and roll.

In the end, he succeeded. With a 15-minute rush to judgement that the local newspaper the *Argus* said stunned the courtroom, the jury brought in a guilty verdict. The judge lost no time in denouncing Berry, saying he would not be allowed any bail, because "I would not turn this man loose to go out and prey on a lot of ignorant Indian girls and colored girls and white girls...I have never sentenced a more vicious character than that kind [sic], I don't believe." He then gave Berry the maximum sentence—a five-year prison sentence and a $5,000 fine.

Immediately Silverstein appealed, and he and Berry were involved in a new round of trials throughout 1960. The continuing legal battles certainly hurt Berry's musical career, preventing him from touring and reducing his ability to record. He did release one new single in 1960—*Jaguar and Thunderbird*. It had some modest success, getting close to but not quite qualifying for the *Billboard Hot 100*. It chronicled a car race, between, obviously, a Jaguar and a Ford Thunderbird. Once again, Berry involved The Man in the story—a local sheriff who hoped to catch the speeding cars before they made the county line.

The appeal dragged on for some time in front of Missouri Judge Roy Harper—though perhaps not long enough, for within another year the FBI and the US Department of Justice handed down instructions to local prosecutors across the US, perhaps in some measure in reaction to the Chuck Berry case, that they were no longer to prosecute Mann Act violations unless it was for clear cases of "organized commercial" activity.

But in the fall of 1960 that wouldn't help Berry. Nor would Prosecutor Mayer's continual reminders to the jury of the business Berry was in. "Remember this is Charles Berry", he told them. "Chuck Berry, an entertainer. And his music and entertainment is directed to who? The teenagers of the country." Merle Silverstein immediately objected to the suggestion that rock and roll was on trial and his objection was sustained—but the damage had been done. The connection had been put in the jury's mind, and the appeal jury brought the same verdict as the first one—guilty.

Judge Moore pulled the defense and prosecution lawyers into his chambers and gave them a piece of homespun wisdom. "I learnt an old rule growing up down in southeast Missouri", he told them. "If you're going to fuck a whore, you've got to pay them." It was sage advice that Berry would have been wise to have followed back when he met Escalante in El Paso. Since he didn't, the judge then sentenced Berry—three years in prison, and a $10,000 fine.

Berry was again behind bars—first in the Leavenworth Federal Prison in Kansas, then back in Missouri at the Federal Medical Center. While there he took all the high school courses he needed to get the credits needed to pass Grade 12, focusing on the ones he felt he could use in running his music operation—business law, accounting and business management.

He also worked in the prison kitchen and the physical therapy wing of the prison—and more importantly, for our narrative, wrote several of his best songs there—*No Particular Place to Go, Nadine, Tulane, Promised Land* and *You Never Can Tell*. He not only met the famous Birdman of Alcatraz, who by then was also incarcerated there, but also Burt Lancaster, who was about to play the Birdman in the movie about the famous con.

Berry graduated with a high school diploma from the prison, and delivered the valedictory address. On his birthday, October 18,

1963, he was released, and returned to his home outside St. Louis at Berry Park.

Berry got back into his old routine running his various enterprises in and around St. Louis. He was recording, touring, fighting legal battles with various promoters and music publishers who throughout his long career continued to try to screw him out of returns and royalties. In 1968, he and his faithful business manager Francine Gillium opened a movie theater in the town of Wenztville, Missouri. However, he soon found that the farmers of the little backwater town could not handle the idea of a black man, partnered with a white woman, running an enterprise in their community. Someone threw a brick through the window of the theater office. Many bigoted comments were made on the streets. Many locals boycotted the theater and eventually they just closed it down.

He continued to run Berry Park, but on December 1, 1969, there was a major fire at the park. Berry says the "deliberately casual interest in fighting the fire was truly saddening." The fireman lazily fought the fire from behind the direction it was travelling, "allowing the salvageable portion of the structure to be consumed as they watered behind the blaze."

Berry re-built the amusement park but continued to be harassed by the local authorities. On August 24, 1974, following two years of observation and a two-week undercover operation, over 40 officers raided a Saturday night dance at the park. It was closed down for six months. Soon after it re-opened, Berry was hit with yet another lawsuit, this time by the parents of two girls who drowned in a swimming accident at the park.

Given the assorted bookkeepers and accountants who had run Berry's finances through the years, his various crooked music publishers, and his demands to be paid cash for his performances, it was no wonder Berry got in trouble with the tax authorities as well. Billy Peek, a guitarist who played with Berry and later with Rod Stewart, was approached by the IRS, attempting to entrap Barry.

"There was one guy – an IRS investigator", he recalls, "who was hot and heavy to get Chuck, saying, 'We're going to try and prosecute him here in Missouri. He can get eleven years for this."

In the end, he pled not guilty to charges of tax evasion, and was sentenced by Judge Harry Pragerson to three years suspended, 120 days in federal prison, four years of probation and 1,000 hours of community work. Ironically, only three days before the court hearing, Berry had been in Washington performing on the White House lawn for President Jimmy Carter and his wife and daughter.

Once again, Chuck Berry was back in prison—this time the Lompoc Federal Correctional Institute north of Los Angeles. As in his last stint, he used the time to do some writing—this time, the book he would title *The Autobiography.*

To promote the book, Berry appeared on *The Tonight Show* with Johnny Carson. Carson enjoyed talking to the singer so much that, in one of the rare times he ever did this, he turned over the entire show to Berry. During the long discussion Carson gingerly brought up the matter of Berry's various bouts with the law. Berry noted that his three major busts had each happened 17 years apart—in 1944, 1957 and 1974. He noted that the next 17 milestone was coming up that year.

Indeed, that is exactly what happened; within weeks of the Carson show, Berry was again arrested—this time in Manhattan on assault charges to a woman named Marilyn O'Brien Boteler. He managed to escape those charges with a minor fine, but within months was back in Missouri and in trouble again.

He opened a restaurant in Wentzville that he called the "Southern Air", named after the whites-only diner that led to his troubles back in 1944. However, in the process of trying to get the restaurant licensed, he somehow made an enemy out of a local private eye named Vincent Huck. Huck managed to get Berry embroiled in no end of legal difficulties through the 80's and 90's.

In March 1989 he was stopped at Lambert Field airport in Missouri by DEA agents hunting (unsuccessfully) for cocaine in his guitar case. Nine months later, in the most sordid accusation to date, Berry was charged with installing video cameras in the women's washrooms of his restaurant and collecting the tapes of his female clients using the premises. Eventually 200 women joined a class-action suit claiming they had been surreptitiously photographed.

Almost simultaneously, *High Society* magazine published a collection of private photos of Berry (naked) posing with a variety of women (white, also naked). Berry hired famed California attorney Melvin Belli to sue the magazine, naming Huck as the person who had stolen the photos and sold them to the magazine.

A few months later, Huck continued his battle against Berry. "He became obsessed with getting his hands on a big hunk of Berry's wealth and I think the racial issue bothered him a lot and really further clouded his judgement", said Missouri attorney Richard Schwartz. "He and a bunch of young lawyers and circuit judges up there in St. Charles County were going to have a nice big economic lynching, and I found it all very disturbing."

Huck convinced the DEA that Berry was trafficking in cocaine, and on June 23, 1990, they raided Berry Park, where they turned up guns, pornographic books and VHS tapes, marijuana and hash (but no cocaine). There were charges against Berry, civil rights violation charges against the prosecutor (who was facing re-election), dropped charges, and finally a plea deal, with Berry getting off with a $5,000 "contribution" to drug and alcohol programs, and two years of unsupervised probation.

That ended the criminal trials, but the civil trials continued through the courts for years afterward. Indeed, Berry's lawyer Richard Schwartz took it all the way to the United States Supreme Court. There, he argued again that Berry was the victim of a conspiracy—a witch-hunt. The times were certainly changing—but more rapidly in some places than others. At exactly the same time as Berry's civil rights to privacy and to possess nude photos and video pornography (under the First Amendment) were being challenged in the Supreme Court, Madonna was getting rich by getting naked in her lavish and expensive book, *Sex*. Today, of course, virtually everyone in the world has immediate access to material far more provocative than anything Berry had by simply typing "Pornhub" on their phone's web browser.

In 1993, though, things were different. Schwartz argued that "the singer was the victim of St. Charles County officials who were part of a racially motivated conspiracy to achieve financial destruction tantamount to an economic lynching of a uniquely American cultural icon." However, try as he might, the Supreme Court refused to take on the case. The details of it were all too sordid for the delicate sensibilities of the court, and they sent the singer, and his lawyers, packing.

In the end the civil class action suit was dealt with in a lower court. Again, Berry lost. The women were awarded $830,000, though most collected less than $5000 apiece. Most of the money was split between the instigator, Hoseanna Hucks, her brother, and their attorneys. The four-year long ordeal cost Berry $1,225,000, plus huge legal fees, so indeed it did turn into an "economic lynching" for him.

Fortunately, it was the last legal battle he would have to fight. He did continue to tour, but on a much-reduced basis—nothing like the three-hundred-gigs-a-year scale he had in the past. On March 18, 2017, Chuck Berry died, aged 90.

What an extraordinary, tumultuous, and creative life. His many, many incidents with The Man resist simple analysis. Certainly, many—most—were tinged with extreme racism, prejudice, and hatred by the authorities because of his success, his wealth, and his role in creating the revolutionary new music called rock and roll.

However, his cause was not helped by his own irresponsibility, orneriness, and astounding ability to get himself into trouble. It was a complex stew of conflicting elements that created the messy, dramatic life of Chuck Berry.

Nina Simone

Many of the singers and musicians in this book have battled with The Man on the streets, on arena stages, in the press or in the courts. None other than Nina Simone has fought The Man in her own bedroom. In 1961, she rather strangely married a New York City police detective, Andrew Stroud, and he became one of the largest, though by no means the only problem in her very troubled life. The battles between this police detective and widely acclaimed jazz singer were symptomatic of the larger issues in her career and life, and indeed of the problems America was experiencing at the time.

Nina Simone was born Eunice Waymon to a poor family in rural North Carolina. She began her musical career, like so many other black musicians, in church—but not, in her case, with gospel music, but rather as a young classical pianist. At her first concert, when she was only twelve, her parents were moved to the back of the hall to make way for white patrons. She refused to play until they were moved back to the front—her first political act of many to come.

Helped by a fund set up to support the precocious pianist, she was able to attend Julliard, but then not the Curtis Institute of

Music, which turned down her application, because, she believed, she was black. It may indeed have been the case, but that year of 72 applicants to the school, 68 others were also turned down. Nonetheless it meant she had to go out to work to support her parents and the family. She did this by first changing her name to Nina Simone to disguise herself, and then playing piano in a seedy Atlantic City joint called the Midtown Bar & Grill. There, she rapidly found she had to abandon Bach and Debussy and instead begin singing jazz and blues—the "Devil's Music" according to her straitlaced mother. It turned out she was very good at it.

Her big break was performing at the 1960 Newport Jazz Festival, and subsequently on Hugh Hefner's "Playboy's Penthouse" TV show, one of the first television shows in America to invite black performers. Shortly after, she met Andy Stroud, who soon convinced her to marry him. He promptly abandoned his career as a police sergeant to become her manager. Although she said he later "scared her to death", she fell for him because "he just took over." Her long-time musical director and guitarist Al Schackman remembers Stroud as being a "tough New York vice-squad cop who, when he stepped out of his car uptown, people ran. He had a way of just saying one word—'Eh!', and that could put a lot of fear in people."

At first he did well by her, making enough money from her touring and recording that they could live in a thirteen-room house in Mt. Vernon, NY, along with two cars ("one nigger, one classy—both paid for!", she wrote). Nine months later she gave birth to a daughter, Lisa, with whom she would have a stormy relationship throughout her life. By 1963 Stroud had her doing a solo concert in Carnegie Hall and performing across North America and Europe appearing alone or on double bills with stars like Miles Davis, Bill Cosby and Dick Gregory. She was not comfortable with the heavy work demands that Stroud put on her so that she could become what he called "a rich black bitch". She felt, to quote one of her signature songs, it was like *breaking up big rocks on the chain gang, breaking rocks and serving my time.*

The intense touring schedule soon soured her relationship with Stroud. She began reporting she had "no desire for sex...no desire to live...I had to take sleeping pills to sleep and yellow pills to go onstage." Schackman reports that "she came to resent Andy" because of the heavy touring, but "she was afraid of Andy."

"He wrapped himself around me like a snake," said Simone, "and I was scared of him. Andrew beat me up." One evening after a club date, "he started raining blows on me—bloody blows. He beat me all the way home-up the stairs, in the elevator, in my room, put a gun to my head, then he tied me up, and raped me." She escaped to her musical director's apartment, where she hid from her abusive husband for two weeks, her eyes black and her face covered with bruises.

"He was brutal, but I loved him," said Nina, and she returned to live with him. Her daughter Nina recalls her mother saying that Stroud was the best manager she ever had, "but on top of being charismatic, he could be a bully and be very mean, and she was on the receiving end of that more times than she should have been, which was never." Lisa says her mother told her that he rammed her head into a wall, and that he "punched her in the stomach when she was pregnant with me."

"He actually thinks I want to be hit. He told me so." wrote Simone. Stroud was not shy about remembering the beatings. On one occasion, while driving the family home, he reached around his daughter to give Nina a belt on the face. "Blood spurted," admits Stroud. "Over her eyebrow she had a one inch cut from my ring."

Nonetheless, she stayed with him. "I love physical violence," she once wrote. However, when the United States itself erupted in violence, she rapidly began to change. After the murder of Medger Evers on June 12, 1963, and the forty bombings of churches in September of that year including the Birmingham explosion that killed four young black girls, she began to explode with rage, writing and singing one of the angriest songs ever, *Mississippi Goddam*. The lyrics of the song were so incendiary, raw and real that southern radio stations would not only not play it but would smash the records and return the broken pieces to the distributors.

In 1965, Simone marched with Martin Luther King in the famous walk from Selma to Montgomery, Alabama, and performed *Mississippi Goddam* at an open-air concert surrounded by Federal Marshalls armed as snipers. She reported that she was so angry singing the song in Alabama that her voice broke and never again returned to its former octave. "But I think that mom's anger is what sustained her," says her daughter. "The energy and the creativity, and the passion of those days is really what kept her going."

However, her ex-cop manager/husband was unimpressed. "Andrew was noticeably cold," wrote Simone, "and very removed from the whole affair. None of it touched him at all."

Nina Simone is by no means the only black performer to be beaten by Amerika's white police. In the summer of 1959 Miles Davis was taking a smoke break between sets on the sidewalk outside Birdland, the famous New York jazz club where he was headlining. A cop came up to him and told him to move on. When Davis pointed to his name on the marquee, another cop charged in and smashed the jazzman in the face, knocking him to the sidewalk. Bloodied, Davis was taken to a Manhattan police station. When he was ultimately released, he returned to the club, his shirt and white suit covered in bloodstains. Thirty years later, little had changed. Tupac Shakur, walking on a street in Oakland, was stopped by police for jaywalking, thrown to the gutter and put in a chokehold. He was jailed for seven hours before being released.

All people who are treated like that get angry. Nina Simone got very angry and began to use her nightclub appearances as a forum for her increasingly radical politics. "I want to get rid of that din of those elegant people," she said, "with their old ideas, smugness, and just drive them insane." She abandoned King's non-violent ideals, siding instead with Malcolm X's ideas of violent armed revolution in order to create a separate black state. Her songs increasingly reflected Black Power and Black pride, and she became what black cultural critic Stanley Crouch calls her, not necessarily admiringly, the "patron saint of the rebellion."

"American society is nothing but a cancer," she said. "Are you ready to smash white things? To burn buildings? Are you ready to kill, if necessary?"

As her violent new songs became her focus, her commercial career shrank. She also began to tire of the road. She recognized that nineteen people (her band and management staff) were dependent on her performing, but "every night in these filthy rotten holes called dressing rooms is destroying me…I've wasted away to almost nothing. Inside I'm screaming 'Someone help me', but the sound isn't audible—like screaming without a voice."

All her relationships were disintegrating, especially the one with her manager/husband. She wrote in her diary, "I could kill them all", and on another occasion she wrote that "Andrew and I talked of my possible suicide. He let me know that he would not only not suffer, but he would be relieved. I hate him—I have every intention of leaving him, if I live. The beatings, Andy—those I can't take—they destroy everything within me."

According to Stroud her condition was a near-catatonic nervous breakdown mixed with a driving obsessive urge for sex. She described things differently. "I just wanted him to hold me sexually—he never was able to."

Immediately following the assassination of Dr. Martin Luther King on April 4, 1968, as America burst apart in riots and flames, she performed a powerful song memorializing him, then decided it was time to leave. "I knew I had to quit, and to leave the country, and to leave Andy", said Simone, "so I took my ring off and put it on the table, and I left the country."

At first, she headed for Barbados. When she briefly returned to America, many months later, she discovered a warrant had been issued for her arrest, for the taxes she had not paid as her protest against the Vietnam War. To avoid prosecution by the authorities, she escaped back to Barbados, and began a lengthy affair with the island nation's Prime Minister, Errol Barrow.

Persuaded by her friend Miriam Makeba that she should try living in Africa, Simone moved, with daughter Lisa, to Liberia, the West African nation created by ex-American slaves. While there she became estranged from her daughter. She beat her as she herself had been beaten by her ex-cop husband. Lisa herself considered suicide, but eventually left her mother and returned to America.

Simone eventually moved away from Liberia, not to the country she now called the "United Snakes of America", but to Switzerland, then to Holland, then France. She returned to touring and recording, but she still exhibited her ferocious temper. In 1985 she fired a gun at a record company executive, who she claimed had cheated her out of song royalties. She claimed she had "tried to kill him" but had missed. Ten years later she shot and wounded a neighbor's boy after claiming that his laughter disturbed her concentration.

Over the period of her troubled life she received fifteen Grammy Award nominations, a Grammy Hall of Fame Award, two honorary degrees in music and humanities, and was inducted into the Rock and Roll Hall of Fame. She sold over a million records. She was acclaimed by writer Maya Angelou, who wrote, "she is loved or feared, adored or disliked, but few who have met her music or glimpsed her soul react with moderation" Record producer Creed Taylor proclaimed that she possessed "a magnificent intensity" that "turns everything—even the most simple, mundane phrase or lyric—into a radiant, poetic message."

On April 19, 2003 she received an honorary degree from the Curtis Institute of Music, the Philadelphia music academy that had refused her admission at the beginning of her career. Two days later, she died in her home in southern France. She was seventy years old.

4. Music and Power

Music vs The Kremlin

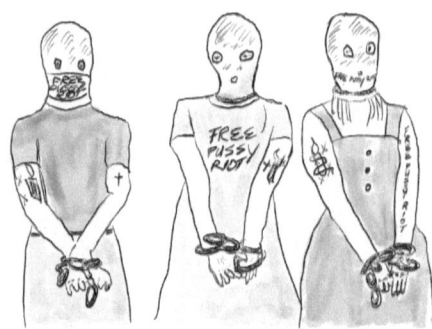

Throughout the twentieth century and right into the twenty-first, Russia has been led by a series of some of the worst tyrants the world has ever seen—first the Tsars; then the Soviets after the Russian Revolution of 1917; then the oligarchs and Vladimir Putin after the collapse of the Soviet Union in 1989.

Four seminal stories take shape in this chapter:

- The battles between Joseph Stalin and the leading Russian composers of the twentieth century, in particular Dmitri Shostakovich.

- The fight to ban jazz—even the word *dzhaz*—from the Soviet Union.

- The illicit fixation of Soviet youth with the Beatles and the profound effect it had on the fall of the U.S.S.R.

- The clashes between anarchic punk rockers Pussy Riot and Russian President Vladimir Putin.

Of all the gruesome tyrannical leaders Russia has seen through its long history, Joseph Stalin was almost certainly the most despicable. However, he was no fool. He was well read and passionately interested in all the arts—especially music. Following busy days of sending people to their death, he would frequently spend nights at the ballet, the opera, or at symphony concerts.

By 1936 he was well into his Great Purge, through which, in order to eradicate so-called "enemies of the working class", he and his secret police sent one million people to Siberian prisons and executed at least 700,000.

On January 26, 1936 Stalin went to the Bolshoi Theatre in Moscow for a performance of *Lady Macbeth of the Mtsensk District*—the latest work by the 29-year-old star Russian composer, Dmitri Shostakovich. Since the Russian leader was attending that night, the composer was also officially commanded to attend. He was seated directly across from Box A, where Stalin sat, hidden from most of the audience by a curtain hung as a security measure against possible assassination.

Although the audience embraced the new opera, Shostakovich watched in increasing horror as Stalin and his Politburo henchmen shuddered every time the brass and percussion played too loudly and laughed at the lovemaking scenes between the leads Sergei and Katerina. The composer was terrified to see Stalin and his gang walk out in the middle of the third act, and, according to eyewitnesses, was "white as a sheet" when he took his bow onstage at the end of the performance.

Two days later he learned how right he was to be worried. *Pravda*, the official organ of the party and the country, wrote an editorial with the headline "Muddle Instead of Music" in which the opera was condemned as an artistically obscure and morally obscene work. "From the first moment of the opera," the editorial read, "the listener is flabbergasted by the deliberately dissonant, muddled stream of sounds." Chillingly, the piece ended by stating that Shostakovich "was playing a game that may end very badly." The composer knew what that meant. Stalin, the Politburo and the NKVD secret police had executed or jailed thousands accused of being "enemies of the people." Would he be next?

Shostakovich was a complex individual, living in exceedingly dangerous times, but he was no political naïf. Early in his career he aligned himself with Mickhail Tukhachevsky, a Red Army hero notorious for having used poison gas against anti–Bolshevik peasants, and for commanding the 1920 Soviet invasion of Poland. However, by 1936 Shostakovich was no longer under the protection of the celebrated soldier. This was probably fortunate since Tukhachevsky had himself fallen out of favor with Stalin. He was tortured and then killed in the Great Purge, his wife and two brothers were shot, and his two sisters and young daughter all sent to the Gulag.

In 1936, Shostakovich came close to the same fate. He had already skirted prosecution by authorities twice before. In 1929 his avant-garde opera *The Nose* was accused of "formalism"—Soviet shorthand for anything that smacked of Western modernism or bourgeois culture by the government-sponsored Russian Association of Proletarian Musicians. In 1931 he bravely published a manifesto he called "Declarations of a Composer's Duties," which again riled up the more proletarian elements of the government.

Still, Shostakovich was no angry dissident bucking the Soviet system. His *Lady Macbeth* was an attempt to write music to defend and support Stalin's genocidal campaign to destroy the Kulaks—farmers who resisted the collectivization of Russian agriculture (or, in the words of Lenin, "bloodsuckers, vampires, plunderers of the people and profiteers who fatten on famine.") In one sense, then, his opera was written in the service of state-sponsored genocide. On the other hand, though, there were subtleties and complexities in it that led to its dismissal by Stalin and *Pravda.*

A day after the editorial, Stalin spoke directly about it, bemoaning Shostakovich's cacophonies and his "rebuses and riddles" (whatever that meant.) The composer was rebuked by Platon Kershentsev, the chairman of the Committee for Artistic Affairs, and told to wait by the phone for a call from Stalin himself. Shostakovich waited, but the call never came. Instead, his commissions, work and performances all slowly dried up. He watched as all around him his family and colleagues were systematically eliminated. His brother-in-law, mother-in-law, sister and uncle were imprisoned. Writers Maxim Gorky and Isaac Babel, who had defended him in print, were both killed by the state, as were composers Nikolai Zhilyayev and actor/director Vsevolod Meyerhold.

Shostakovich continued to compose, creating his grand 4th Symphony, scored for a massive orchestra of 130 players. It was unclear whether or not Shostakovich had repented and conformed to the Soviet dialectic. The Leningrad Philharmonic had begun rehearsals on the work when the government made a decision. Cultural government apparatchiks told the director of the orchestra that the composer had not responded properly to criticism of his previous opera and had now written a symphony of what they called "diabolical complexity," which was apparently a bad thing. The musicians were released. The performances were cancelled.

His symphony was dead but Shostakovich himself somehow survived the Great Terror and would also survive what the Russians call the Great Patriotic War. In June of 1941, shortly after the Nazi invasion of Russia began, he volunteered for duty. Rejected because of his poor eyesight, he instead joined the Leningrad Conservatory fire brigade and was tasked with the job of preserving the treasures of Soviet music. He also set to work on his 7th Symphony, written in Leningrad as German artillery shells were landing on the city during the 900-day siege.

The performance of the 7th Symphony may be the most dramatic story ever in the history of battles between Music and The Man. It was first performed in the city of Kuybyshev in March, 1942, and then the score was transferred to microfilm, put in a tin can, flown to Tehran, then driven to Cairo, flown to South America and finally flown to New York City. Italian conductor Arturo Toscanini, the

Musical Director of the NBC Symphony Orchestra, won the rights for the American premiere, which took place on July 18, 1942. *The New Yorker*'s "Talk of the Town" column detailed the long passage of the symphony around the world, and *TIME* Magazine put Shostakovich on the cover, in his firefighting regalia, with the caption "Amid bombs bursting in Leningrad he heard the chords of victory."

The score was also flown to Leningrad by military aircraft where a very depleted Leningrad Radio Orchestra began to learn it. After a gaggle of only fifteen musicians showed up for the first rehearsal, the commanding general ordered all competent musicians to report from the front lines. Following the rehearsals, the players would return to their military duties that included digging mass graves for victims of the siege. Three of them died of starvation before the premiere. When the German general learned of the date for the performance—August 9, 1942—he planned to disrupt it with artillery fire directed at the theater. But he was thwarted as the Red Army launched their own bombardment, which they called Operation Squall, to protect it. They also set up loudspeakers all along the No Man's Land separating the armies and broadcast the *Leningrad* symphony live to the troops on both sides. Imagine the morale boost it must have been to the Russians, and the downer to the soldiers from the land of Beethoven, Bach, and Brahms.

Was Shostakovich now back in the good books of the Politburo and Joseph Stalin? Not entirely. He kept trying to present himself in a manner that would keep him out of trouble. On New Year's Eve of 1943, he wrote, with overarching and probably duplicitous optimism, "A blizzard is raging outside the windows as 1944 approaches. It will be a year of happiness, of victory, a year that will bring us all much joy. The freedom-loving peoples will at last throw off the yoke of Hitlerism, peace will reign over the whole world, and we shall live once more in peace under the sun of Stalin's Constitution. Of this I am convinced, and I consequently experience feelings of unalloyed joy."

He was a year too early with his bright-eyed prediction, but finally in 1945 the Russians and their allies from around the world did of course defeat the Germans. Almost immediately, the Russians went back to their pre-war behavior of internecine backstabbing and betrayal in all fields, including music.

By 1948, at exactly the same time as the battles over Paul Robeson were starting to heat up in America, the Central Committee of the Kremlin held a conference about Russian music and then issued what became known as the "Historic Decree". It banned forty-two works by "formalists", including Shostakovich's 6th, 8th and 9th symphonies and Prokoviev's 6th and 8th sonatas.

Neither of the composers was sent to the Gulag, though in that period many artists were, including, on trumped up charges of spying against the state, Prokofiev's wife. She was jailed in Siberian hellholes for eight years. Shostakovich didn't want to follow her there, so he caved to the Committee with a mealy-mouthed speech of abject apology, clichés and jargon:

> *"The absence, in my works, of the interpretation of folk art, that great spirit by which our people lives, has been with utmost clarity and definiteness pointed out by the Central Committee of the All-Union Communist Party (Bolshevik), and in particular those that concern me personally, I accept as a stern but paternal solicitude for us, Soviet artists. Work— arduous, creative, joyous work on new compositions which will find their path to the heart of the Soviet people, which will be understandable to the people, loved by them, and which will be organically connected to the people's art, developed and enriched by the great traditions of Russian classicism— this will be a fitting response to the Resolution of the Central Committee of the All-Union Communist Party."*

On March 16, 1949 Shostakovich answered the phone and was told to hold for Stalin. The premier wanted to discuss a cultural and scientific mission to the United States in which Shostakovich had reluctantly agreed to participate. Bravely, he asked the dictator how he could represent Soviet culture abroad when so many of his compositions were forbidden in Russia. "How do you mean *forbidden*?" asked Stalin. "Forbidden by whom?" The Glavrepertkom, replied the composer, the Department of Repertoire. Stalin told him it must be a mistake and that he would take care of it. Later that day the Council of Ministers of the U.S.S.R. not only rescinded the ban on "formalist" music but reprimanded the Glavrepertkom for the mistake. Quite possibly someone from the agency was sent packing to Siberia to atone for it. Shostakovich wrote a letter of thanks to Stalin, telling the dictator that he had "supported me very much." He told one of his students that he could breathe again. The breathing would be short-lived, both for Shostakovich and the rest of the world. Five months later the Soviets exploded their first atomic bomb in the Kazakhstan desert.

As Stalin had requested, Shostakovich attended the Cultural and Scientific Conference for World Peace held at the Waldorf-Astoria Hotel in New York. It was a massive propaganda exercise and a clash of ideologies, attended by composers such as Aaron Copland and Nicholas Nabokov (Composer for the Ballet Russes and secret operative for the American military), writers like Arthur Miller and Lillian Hellman, scientists such as Albert Einstein, and a variety of spies, secret police, and government minders watching over them from both sides of the political fence. Protestors marched on Park Avenue outside the hotel with signs urging Shostakovich to defect and the rest of his party to "Go back to Russia." Shostakovich made a long, 5000-word speech denouncing both fellow Russian-born composer Igor Stravinsky (by now an American citizen) and the "new aspirants for world domination", which presumably referred to the cold warriors of the Truman administration.

Many of the participants in the conference had their reputations bruised. Shostakovich certainly suffered, and Aaron Copland, even more so. He was thought of as the "Dean of American Composers" for his powerful, populist compositions such as the *Grand Canyon Suite* and *Appalachian Spring*, but nonetheless the FBI opened a suspect file on him following his comments at the conference.

On January 20, 1953 Dwight Eisenhower was inaugurated as president of the United States. As part of the festivities, Copland's *Lincoln Portrait* was to be premiered, but Congressman Fred Busbey denounced the work as "Communist propaganda", citing Copland's involvement with organizations such as the National Council of American-Soviet Friendship and the National Committee for the Defense of Political Prisoners. Just as Shostakovich had to grovel in front of the Soviet Central Committee, Copland had to publicly announce, in the defensive jargon of the day: "I say unequivocally that I am not now and never have been a communist or member of the communist party or any organization that advocates or teaches in any way the overthrow of the United States Government."

His *mea culpa* was not good enough for the Inaugural Committee. He was uninvited; his music was not played for President-elect Eisenhower at Constitution Hall. For years later he had trouble travelling abroad. The State Department declined to renew his passport. He was repeatedly requested to demonstrate affiliations with anti-Communist organizations, and in 1953 several of his engagements were cancelled on political grounds.

Meanwhile, Shostakovich returned to the USSR, turned in his passport, as was required of all Soviet travelers, and (except for one brief trip to a music festival in England) lived in the country for the rest of his life. Stalin's death in 1953 was the beginning of his rehabilitation as an artist. He wrote three more symphonies in the 1950s. Listen to his powerful 10th, written only three months after Stalin's death, to get a sense of his skill and accomplishment. Musicologists posit that the violent Second Movement of the 10th was written to describe his true angry feelings about what Stalin had done to his life, and to the country.

In 1958, he succumbed to the scourge of the era, polio, which damaged the nerves in his right hand, forced him to give up the piano, and affected his ability to write music. In 1960, The Man again came calling. The new Premier, Nikita Khrushchev, asked him to lead the Composer's Union of the USSR, and then to become a candidate member of the Communist Party. Shostakovich had previously sworn to friends that he would never join an organization that used terror to carry out its aims, and now gave conflicting reports as to why he had agreed to become a delegate to the Supreme Soviet of the USSR. He told some people he was drunk when he agreed. He told his wife he had been blackmailed into the job. He claimed to his friend Isaak Glikman that "They've been pursuing me for years, hunting me down." The musicologist (and secret police agent) Lev Lebedinsky heard him say things like, "I am scared to death of them," "I'm a wretched alcoholic," and "I've been a whore, I am, and always will be a whore."

One of his last major works was the highly regarded score for the Russian film *Hamlet*. He also finally finished and presented the symphony he had been promising the Russian government authorities for years—an homage to Lenin he called *The Year 1917*. The founder of the Soviet Union would likely not have appreciated it. He once told Maxim Gorky "I can't listen to music too often. It affects your nerves, makes you want to say stupid nice things, and stroke the heads of people who could create such beauty while living in this vile hell."

In his later years Shostakovich was plagued not just with polio but also with Lou Gehrig's disease, two broken legs, two heart attacks and finally lung cancer. He died in August 1975. He received not just a civic funeral and many prizes from the Soviet Union, but also the honor of having a peninsula in Antarctica named after him.

* * * *

The struggles in the Soviet system over classical music and new Russian composers like Shostakovich were tame compared to the battles over Western pop music—first jazz, then rock and roll—specifically, as the Russians called them, "The Bitles".

The first 20 years of the twentieth century were one of the most revolutionary periods in history. Suffragettes marched, were imprisoned and died fighting for women's rights. The Industrial Workers of the World (the Wobblies) fought the police for workers' rights, emboldened by the songs of Joe Hill. There were general strikes, with pitched battles between the strikers and police in Winnipeg, Seattle, Spain and Australia. There were wild new movements in art and music—most especially, the creation of a new musical idiom—jazz. Most famously, of course, in 1917 there was the Russian Revolution.

Jazz presented a confusing challenge to the Russian revolutionaries. One might have thought they would have embraced this new, very revolutionary, unquestionably "proletarian" music, created by impoverished, disenfranchised, black musicians in New Orleans. American pop music was already popular in Russia by the eve of the revolution. Prince Felix Yusupov reported that as he poisoned Rasputin, "the gramophone was playing *Yankee Doodle Went to Town*."

However, the new hard-line Socialists demanded social engineering, wanted to control every aspect of life in the new workers' paradise, and rejected all influences from the West, certainly jazz, also pop music and European opera. The authority controlling what music Russia could listen to, the Proletkult, demanded only indigenous peasant folk music, with the lyrics reworked into ideologically correct propaganda and sung by factory workers collectives and military ensembles.

The Proletkult went so far as to not just ban jazz but also certain notes (that they referred to as "blue notes") and certain instruments. The saxophone was particularly singled out as being bourgeois, sexual, and evil, and for 60 years was neither manufactured in the U.S.S.R. nor allowed to be imported into the country.

However in the freakish hothouse of fledgling revolution and bureaucratic mania, there were aberrations in the official Soviet treatment of jazz. Russian émigré poet and essayist Valentin Parnakh sent missives back to Moscow from his outpost in Paris, extolling the films of Charlie Chaplin, the art of Pablo Picasso, and jazz, which he described as "a music of dissonances, syncopations, crashes, soaring brasses, howls and alarm sirens."

In 1922, he returned to Moscow with a collection of jazz instruments and a desire to turn Russia on to the wild new music. His timing proved to be perfect, for Lenin that year briefly opened the country up with his New Economic Plan and abandoned some of the collectivization and repression of the past.

On October 1, 1922, Parnakh's "First Eccentric Orchestra of the Russian State Federation and Socialist Republic" gave its first concert in Moscow. With a band made up of violins, a piano, a xylophone, a banjo, and drums, it is unlikely that its music would have been exactly considered "jazz" by the likes of Jelly Roll Morton or Louis Armstrong. However, the Eccentric Orchestra's music was popular with Russians, and was even accepted by the Commissar of Public Enlightenment, Anatoly Lunacharsky, who invited the band to play at a Congress on the Fifth Anniversary of the Bolshevik Revolution.

The Soviet press crowed that "for the first-time jazz music was performed at an official state function, something which has never happened in the West." Parnakh's jazz band flourished for the rest of the Twenties, supported by the state in a period when jazz was indeed being reviled and censored by the authorities in places like America and England.

The Eccentric Orchestra was followed by two authentically American brigades of the international jazz revolution—first a group of thirty-five black dancers and jazzmen called Sam Wooding and his Chocolate Kiddies, then Benny Peyton's Jazz Kings, with their star soloist Sidney Bechet, who electrified Soviet audiences with both his music and his wild, alcohol-fueled lifestyle. Bechet had spent eleven months in prison in Paris for shooting a woman in a duel over an insult about his musical abilities, precipitated by his claim that "Sidney Bechet never plays the wrong chord." Once Peyton and Bechet wore out their welcome in Russia, they were sent home and the Soviet Union would not welcome another band from the West for more than 30 years.

However, Commissar Lunacharsky did embark on an extraordinary initiative, dispatching Leningrad pianist Leopold Teplitsky to America to learn local jazz techniques, buy American instruments and arrangements, and return to Russia to introduce the masses to this new-fangled music. It all sounds a bit like the Billy Wilder/Greta Garbo screwball comedy *Ninotchka*, but it seems to have worked. By 1927 Teplitsky was touring Russia, playing an oddball mix of tunes like *Fascinating Rhythm* and *Yes Sir, That's My Baby* along with jazz versions of Liszt and Rimsky-Korsakov. The latter's son savaged the group, describing their efforts as "barbarous harmonies" and "a senseless parody of melody and chords", but the steelworkers and collective farmers of the Russian hinterlands responded warmly to these concerts of "the latest American music."

The brief period did not last long. By 1928 Lenin and Trotsky were dead, the New Economic Plan in retreat. Stalin was now firmly in power, his first Five Year Plan dedicated to rolling back recent liberations and instituting new campaigns that would devastate the lives of millions of Russians.

All foreign influences were to be exiled, smashed aside by the forced implementation of Russian peasant culture. Lunacharsky, who only two years earlier had dispatched his jazz ambassador to America, now savaged jazz as the "sonic idiocy of the bourgeois capitalist world." Russian writer Maxim Gorky wrote in *Pravda* an essay titled "On the Music of the Gross", describing jazz as being "the clamor of a metal pig; the amorous croaking of a monstrous frog."

Leopold Teplitsky was arrested and exiled. New laws decried that anyone caught importing or playing jazz records could be fined or imprisoned. Children were forced to confess to a love of jazz, and if they did, were expelled from school.

While it was now banned at home, the Soviets were not above using jazz to try to foment revolution abroad. The Sixth Congress of the Comintern—the Communist International—declared that the blacks of America's southern states were a separate nation, and instructed the American Communist Party to campaign for their independence. To help promote the idea, the Russian apparatchiks proposed that they would commission a film, to be titled *Red and Black*—the plot about a group of black steelworkers trying to organize a strike, the score black music—folk songs, spirituals, and jazz.

Twenty-two black Americans were assembled by the American Communist Party and sent to Russia to perform in the grand epic. Unfortunately, their Russian hosts were unimpressed. The group of mostly middle-class teachers, students, and aspiring actors from Greenwich Village and Brooklyn did not match their expectations to play tough proletarian steelworkers, nor, it turned out, could they either sing or dance. The project was abandoned and the wannabe Russian movie stars sent home.

Popular music in the Soviet Union from the 20s to the 80s was a bewildering confusion of advances and retreats, encouragement and repression. There was another thaw in the war against jazz in the mid 30s, but from 1936 on, Stalin's Great Terror consumed Russia, and the culture war was back on. Hundreds of musicians were rounded up and sent to labor camps in the Gulag. Valentin Parnakh, the leader of the pioneering Eccentric Jazz Orchestra, was exiled to Chistopol with the celebrated poet Marina Tsretaeva, a lover of his sister. With absolutely no means of support, and thousands of Russians literally dying of starvation, Parnakh applied for and got a job as a doorman. Tsretaeva applied to the same establishment as a dishwasher but was turned down. Within days, after pressure to become an informer by the NKVD (the precursor of the KGB), she committed suicide. Parnakh died in Moscow in 1951.

As thousands were being tortured and murdered in the Soviet prisons and gulags, a surreal debate emerged in Russia's two newspapers, *Pravda* and *Izvestia*, over music. The ferocious war of words, which raged over two months and 19 articles, debated the merits of jazz and classical music. *Pravda* supported jazz, and bizarrely accused *Izvestia* of "bourgeois fanaticism" for trumpeting the merits of symphonic music. The debate became savagely political, and in the end *Izvestia* lost. Its entire editorial board was purged, and many members were summarily executed.

It was a crazy era, with extreme experiments in social engineering. The Kremlin, as part of their effort to increase industrial productivity, re-wrote the calendar in 1929, outlawing the weekend by removing two days of the week. Saturday and Sunday were not restored until 1940.

The most lethal of Soviet experiments became a genocidal famine in the Ukraine, largely orchestrated by Stalin's fearsome Minister of Railways and Heavy Industry. Taking time out from starving millions of Ukranians to death, Lazar Kaganovich weighed in on the continuing debate about music. Arguing against the commissars who by the mid 30s tried to even ban the word *dzhaz* from the Russian language, Kaganovich wrote a "jazz guide leaflet" titled "How to Organize a Railway Ensemble of Song and Dance and Jazz Orchestras" in which he proposed that "there should be a '*dzhaz* band' at every Soviet station."

World War II, or "The Great Patriotic War", as the Russians call it, made new demands on the role of music in Soviet life. In 1944, *Pravda* editorialized that "popular music is called upon to fulfill serious social and political tasks." Now allied with America, the Soviets began importing wartime hits like *Honeysuckle Rose, Over There!* and *Chattanooga Choo Choo* and rewriting their lyrics to praise the heroism of the Red Army.

The war also saw the rise of the Soviet Union's most authentic and successful jazz musician. Eddie Rosner was a Polish Jew whose first success came in Germany, playing with the top jazz band in the country, Stefan Weintraub's Syncopators. Born Adolf Rosner, he sometimes regretted changing his name, saying, "It didn't help being a Jew playing Negro music, even if your name is Adolf." After being beaten up by Nazi storm troopers too many times, he escaped at the onslaught of the war to Russia, where he was welcomed and turned into the U.S.S.R.'s top jazzman.

A Communist Party boss, Comrade Panteleimon Ponomarenko offered him the job of heading the State Jazz Orchestra of the Byelorussian Republic. His first command performance was a bizarre event in 1941 in which he was summoned with his band to a theater in the Black Sea resort of Sochi, where he was expecting to play for Stalin. He found a totally empty auditorium, where he was ordered to play a two-hour concert, complete with comedy bits and interstitial patter. Not until the next morning was he told that Stalin had been listening, hidden behind a curtain, and had decided he approved of the trumpeter and his band.

With Stalin's endorsement, Rosner was booked across the Soviet Union throughout the next four years. However, the ending of the war in 1945 would bring much more troubled times for the musician, and, indeed, for Russia. By 1946 a new chill descended on the Soviet Union, and, as Winston Churchill described it, an "Iron Curtain" fell between east and west. All modern art, music and writing was declared "bourgeois decadence." Fanatical young vigilantes from the Komsomol patrolled bars, cafes and theaters, on the watch for the now forbidden jazz, "blue notes", vibratos, valved trumpets, and especially, saxophones.

Hundreds of musicians were rounded up and sent to the Gulag, including Rosner. Arrested with his wife, he was interrogated and tortured in Moscow's notorious Lubyanka prison, then shipped to Siberia. Luckily his musical skills meant he avoided hard labor building the "Road of Bones" to Magadan and instead was allowed to create an orchestra in the prison to tour the gulag to entertain the officials and guards.

Only after the death of Stalin in March of 1953 did the permafrost of Soviet life begin to thaw, and Rosner after eight years was released from prison. He then began applying to leave Russia, but it took almost twenty years before he was allowed to return to the West. He died in Berlin in 1976.

The death of Stalin led to the rise of a bohemian subculture known as the *Stilyagi* (loosely, the "Style-hunters"). This scandalous youth cult neither went to school nor worked in the smoking steel mills, instead hanging out in cafes and skating rinks, dressed in bright outfits decorated with images of monkeys, bathing beauties and palm trees. They gave themselves monikers like "Peter" and "Bob", and in imitation of Sinatra's Rat Pack, held "cocktail hours", where they created oddball dances called by names like "the Atomic", "the Canadian" and "the Triple Hamburg." The *Stiyagi* were the advance shock troops of an underground movement of young music lovers who would ultimately totally undermine the Soviet Union, not with guns or even protest signs, but with an illicit and passionate fascination and obsession with the music of the group they called "the Bitles".

The Beatles came of age at the height of the Cold War between the Soviet Union and the West. They were cutting their musical chops in Germany when the country was ground zero for intrigue between the two sides. They were playing the Cavern Club in Liverpool, sowing the seeds of Beatlemania, when the world came the closest it has ever come to nuclear Armageddon during the Cuban Missile Crisis. They released their major second album on November 22, 1963, the same day John F. Kennedy was assassinated. Very soon they became the biggest and best-selling musical artists of all time. They sold millions of records around the world, but not a single one behind the Iron Curtain, where they were banned. However the cult of the Beatles, and their profound effect on the country, was probably stronger in Russia than anywhere else on earth.

"Russia was held together by fear and belief," says Russian TV journalist Vladimir Pozner, "and the Beatles played a role in overcoming the fear and in showing that the belief was actually stupid."

Artemy Troitsky, the Russian rock historian, adds, "In the big bad west they had massive institutions that spent tens of millions of dollars to try to undermine the Soviet system, and I'm sure that the impact of all those dumb cold war institutions had a much smaller effect than the impact of the Beatles, who turned tens of millions of young people to another religion. And by the end of the 80s, the whole of Soviet ideology and Soviet power disappeared like fog in the morning."

The august Institute of Russian History confirms this by saying, "Beatlemania washed away the foundations of Soviet society. They helped a generation of free people to grow up in the Soviet Union."

The Soviet Union, determined to resist the Beatles, put up a mighty fight. President Nikita Krushchev declared the electric guitar "an enemy of the Soviet people." Shortwave radios that might pick up signals from the West were banned, and in case there were any illicit ones, stations playing rock music such as Radio Luxembourg were jammed. Border guards were equipped first with nails, later with more sophisticated scratchers, to destroy any Beatles records that might try to get into the country. The group was lampooned in sneering campaigns in the press as "the Bugs", with cartoons showing insect poison being shaken over the skittering Beatles.

Of course, the fact that their music was forbidden only made it more appealing to young Soviets. The music of the Beatles reverberated around the world through the 60's, exported on 45's and on 33 1/3 albums. It was very slow to come to Russia, though, since few Russians were allowed to travel abroad, and the few that did knew that it was forbidden to bring discs of the Beatles into the country. However, a few brave diplomats and officials would bring them in, as treasured gifts for their sons and daughters. Sailors too smuggled them in to the country, which is why Leningrad (now St. Petersburg) and in the east Vladivostok, both port cities, became hubs for the illicit Beatles records.

In 1960, Soviet-made reel-to-reel tape recorders—the Astra, the Chaika, the Nota and the Yauza 5 became available, and enterprising black marketers used them to tape Beatles music from the rare imported discs, and then make copies on what were known as either "flexis" or "music on bones". They discovered that X-Ray acetates, discarded from hospitals, could be used to burn new duplicates of *Revolver*, *Rubber Soul* or *Meet The Beatles*. Soon, thousands of these flexis were flooding the streets, with John, Paul, George and Ringo playing over the cloudy image of some old babushka's rib cage.

It was a dangerous business. Veteran Russian rock musician Vladimir Matietsky remembers that, "on the sidewalk, 'sharks' would sell you an X-Ray disc. You never knew what you might get, and it was risky with the vigilantes watching out. 'You want 'shakes?' they would ask. 'You want some rock 'n' roll flexis? Three rubles – good rock and roll.'" The flexis would be rolled up and slipped up a coat sleeve before the cultural vigilantes could spy the transaction, "but it was dangerous. Some guys who were mass-producing the flexis in Leningrad were sent to a gulag for seven years."

The state fought back by claiming that the flexi industry was fueling crime and even murder, and by flooding the street with fake flexis containing nothing but scratchy noise and then a message saying "You like rock 'n' roll? Fuck you, anti-Soviet slime." But the obsessed young Beatles addicts would not give up. Even as the authoritarian old grouch Leonid Brezhnev took over from Khrushchev in 1964, bringing in new repressions on Western music, young people began copying the style and later the music of the irreverent Liverpudlians. Collars were cut from coats to try to emulate the style of the Beatles' jackets, shoes were modified with "Cuban heels" to try to match the look of the British "winkle-picker" boots, and of course the few kids who had seen actual photos of the Beatles styled their hair to match that of the four Mop-Tops.

Since they could not listen to actual Beatles music, they tried to create their own. Kitchen tables were sawn up to create the bodies of electric guitars. Wires were pulled from model airplane kits, or pianos, to create strings. Teenagers discovered that the coils in telephone receivers could work as pickups, so scavenged them from pay telephones, or from the trucks of telephone repairmen. The loudspeakers hanging from every building to broadcast uplifting messages and propaganda were liberated to complete the makeshift, verboten rock set-ups.

It all sounds like grand teenage fun, but it was no joke. On the contrary, just jesting about the similarity between the names John Lennon and Vladimir Lenin was considered an offense that could get students expelled from school.

Yuri Pelyushonok was one of the thousands of Russian teens who was inspired by his love of The Beatles to create his own underground band. "The Beatles were a religion," he says, "Some bright light in a dreary life." Eventually he escaped, stowing away on a merchant ship and ending up in Canada, where he now lives, still writing and singing music. His song *The Yeah Yeah Virus* recalls the years when Beatlemania hit—and changed—Russia.

Pelyushonok was never able to turn his passion for music into a way of making a livelihood—but others did. Alexander Gradsky's uncle was a dancer with the Moiseyev Dance Troupe, one of the relatively few Russians able to travel to the West in the dark days of the 1960's. In 1963, his uncle brought his nephew a present—a copy of the LP *Meet The Beatles*. "I went into a state of shock," he remembers. "Everything except the Beatles became pointless." It made him, and thousands like him, question everything they were drilled into believing about Russia. "If such wonderful music is forbidden," he felt, "we knew there must be something wrong with our country."

Gradsky was a trained musician, a violinist and a singer with a range of three octaves, studying to sing Schubert. The Beatles changed his life. He gave up classical music and started his own

Beatle-emulating underground rock band, The Slavs, forming it with the grandson of Noble Prize-winning novelist Mikhail Sholokhov. The Slavs were only one of about 200 unauthorized bands playing in Moscow by the late 60's. "Hundreds of unofficial rock clubs sprung up," he recalls, "where young hustlers with a tape recorder and a sound system played rock music in borrowed rooms packed with sweating kids. They charged an entrance fee, which was risky, but the odd arrest didn't cure the rock epidemic. There were constant raids by the Komsomol vigilantes, and equipment was regularly confiscated. Organizers were imprisoned. But rock was resistant."

It took a very long time, but eventually Gradsky and his music became legitimized by the state. He began to tour the world, gave a concert at Carnegie Hall, recorded with Elton John and Liza Minnelli, and in 2000 was presented with a medal as a People's Artist of Russia by President Putin. But he has never forgotten where it all began. "The Beatles changed the Soviet Union", he insists, "The Kremlin lost the Beatles' generation, and then they lost the country."

The Beatles created a revolution in the West but unknown to them at the time, they created an even more potent revolution in the U.S.S.R. The irony, of course, is that Russia officially considered itself a "revolutionary" society. One might have expected that they would embrace the Beatles revolution, but instead they condemned, repressed and forbade it.

Sasha Lipnitsky, bass player with the Moscow band Zvuki Mu, remembers his exposure to the Beatles as providing him with "freedom—the wind of freedom. For many years we were told that the West was an enemy—nothing more. Not our neighbors on the planet, just "the enemy". The Beatles were the first to show us that there was something wrong with what we had always been taught by our Soviet rulers."

Though the repression was bad throughout the Cold War era, he remembers 1984 as being the worst. "That was when the KGB were hounding rock bands," he says. At one concert by his band, the KGB colonel shouted at him that the concert was "obviously a Western-inspired provocation," demanded to see official approval stamps on their lyrics and arrested him. "But we still wanted to have more concerts," he recalls. "For some reason I felt really brave."

George Harrison's comment that "we gave the people hope, we gave them freedom, we gave them the chance to forget boredom" applied nowhere as much as it did in the Soviet Union. Ultimately, the Beatles had a greater effect on the defeat of communism and the U.S.S.R. than all the militaristic posturing and anti-communist propaganda of the US and the West. One of the ironies of the story is that the Beatles themselves had no idea of the profound effect they were having behind the Iron Curtain. They did, of course write and record the song *Back in the U.S.S.R.* No-one really knew what to make of the message of the song (if there even was one) but it did inspire one of the many crazy Beatles myths and legends that swirled around Russia through the 60s and 70s. Fans there widely believed a story that en route to Japan, the Beatles' plane had to land at a remote Soviet military air base to re-fuel, and that the Fab Four emerged on to the wing of the plane to give an impromptu concert for the soldiers surrounding it while the fuel trucks filled it up.

Andrei Makarevich was another of the thousands of young Russians caught up in Beatlemania and starting a band to try to imitate his Liverpool heroes. His band, Time Machine, eventually became the biggest in the Soviet Union, but like all the others had many run-ins with The Man before becoming legit. One of the worst was a Moscow concert in November 1970 where the band was busted by the police. "We were stuck in prison for the night, and we were scared," remembers Makarevich. The cops peppered them with questions about their long hair, asked why they wanted to look like English or American youths, and told them they were now going to be under permanent surveillance.

The band continued to perform in secret gigs and continued to be arrested for performing their illicit music. The busts only added to the subversive underground allure—street cred that western stars like Neil Young, David Crosby and Rod Stewart could only dream of.

With the Moscow Olympics of 1980, the Soviet Union had to loosen up the rules a little, and in the brief thaw that followed, Time Machine flourished. They toured the country, their song *Povorot* stayed on top of the Russian hit parade for 18 months, and *Time* magazine reported that the excitement about them meant their concerts were "like a return to the early days of the Beatles."

However just as it had during the jazz era, official music policy lurched between glasnost and repression. By 1982, Yuri Andropov was in power, and Time Machine was again being denounced – now called "un-Russian" and "advocates of indifference." They were forced to wind up the band, and briefly did so, until Mikhail Gorbachev arrived in 1985 and monumentally changed the fate of the Soviet Union. "Every time I see Gorbachev," says Makarevich, "I say thank you for what you did."

As Gorbachev was born in 1931, he was in his early 30s when the Beatles appeared, so it is hard to know whether he was influenced by them. He was considered one of the more liberal apparatchiks during the Khrushchev thaw—one of the hosts of the 1961 World Youth Festival in Moscow, an event credited with introducing many young Russians to the bourgeois pleasures of jazz, blue jeans and rock and roll. Sasha Lipnitsky certainly thinks Gorbachev, along with thousands of other Russians, was influenced by the Beatles. "I reckon," he says, "Gorbachev is a result of The Beatles. Gorby's naïve and romantic attempts to change Russia are a result of that Beatles romance."

More than anyone else, Gorbachev was the architect of the end of the Soviet empire, and of communist oppression—although very quickly it was replaced by a new kind of repression under Putin and the oligarchs. His failed attempts to open up the authoritarian U.S.S.R. to the ideals of personal freedoms were once famously declared to be as impossible as "trying to fry snowballs", and ultimately his legacy is cloudy—but he did end the battles between Russian musicians and The Man, for a while.

In 2003, Paul McCartney, now Sir Paul finally played the Beatles' music in Russia, for a concert and television special titled *Paul McCartney in Red Square*. While there, he was summoned to a private audience with President Putin, who took him to his inner sanctum, dismissed his interpreter, and carried on a conversation with him in serviceable English. "He was fun," said McCartney. "He said, 'I really know your music.' He agreed the Beatles had been a force for freedom."

Forty years after the release of *Love Me Do*, Putin may have claimed enthusiasm for the Beatles. He was not as enthusiastic about a new musical phenomenon. On February 21, 2012, five members of the feminist punk rock group Pussy Riot, decked out in neon-colored balaclavas, staged an unauthorized performance at the alter of Moscow's Orthodox Cathedral of Christ the Savior. Shouting out that they were protesting the church's support of Vladimir Putin in the recent elections, they flailed at their electric guitars and tried to belt out their song *Putin Pissed Himself*.

Church security guards and parishioners quickly grabbed them and threw them out of the church. Two weeks later, three of the masked members of Pussy Riot—Nadezhda Tolokonnikova, Maria Alyokhina and Yekaterina Samutsevich were identified, arrested and charged with hooliganism for their illegal performance. They were all refused bail and spent the next 21 months in jail. It was not their first-time involvement with The Man. In 2008 Tolokonnikova had participated in an event in which she and a number of others stripped naked and had public sex in the Timiryazev State Biology Museum in Moscow, protesting President Dmitry Medvedev's call to increase the nation's birth rate. As Tolokonnikova was eight months pregnant at the time, she was singled out for censure for the provocative piece of performance art. Three years later, in 2011, she and Samutsevich participated in the Gay Pride rally in Moscow, which was broken up by the police. The same year, Pussy Riot performed an impromptu concert for the prisoners in the Moscow Detention Center No. 1 from the roof of a garage beside the prison, getting cheers from the incarcerated prisoners. A year later, they played at an anti-Putin rally, and were arrested and ultimately fined for setting off a smoke bomb during their act.

The three women now faced possible sentences of up to seven years in prison for their performance at the Moscow cathedral. Tolokonnikova and Alyokhina, both mothers, staged hunger strikes protesting being held in jail away from their young children. Paradoxically, though, they also managed to release a new song *Putin Lights Up the Fires* that included the lyric *Seven years* [imprisonment] *is not enough, give us eighteen* .

Putin said in a televised interview on the occasion of his 60th birthday that Pussy Riot had "undermined the moral foundations" of the country and "the girls got what they asked for," and thus himself was accused of muddying the judicial process. Patriarch Kirill, a leader of the Russian Orthodox church, condemned Pussy Riot's actions as blasphemous, saying that "the Devil has laughed at all of us," and said his heart "broke with bitterness" when he heard that some Orthodox Christians were asking for mercy and forgiveness for the band.

Meanwhile the Union of Solidarity With Political Prisoners declared the trio as political prisoners, and Amnesty International named them prisoners of conscience, due to "the severity of the response of the Russian authorities." As a 2800-page indictment against the band was being prepared, prominent Russians began protesting against what many saw as an excessive response by the state to the provocative performance. Opposition leader Sergei Udaltsov, protesting in support of the band, was detained by police. Former World Chess Champion Garry Kasparov was arrested and beaten for supporting the trio.

Over a year after their arrests, the trial began, with the three women held in a cage inside the courtroom, in a style reminiscent of Stalin's show trials of the 1930's. All three were found guilty and sentenced to two years in a penal colony. Their lawyer, Mark Feygin, announced he would appeal, but said that, "Under no circumstances will the girls ask for a pardon (from Putin). They will not beg and humiliate themselves before such a bastard."

The women were incarcerated in prison labor camps in Mordovia that were once part of the Dubravlag section of the Soviet gulag. Again, Tolokonnikova staged hunger strikes in protest against what she alleged were human rights abuses in the prison. The foreign ministries of the United States and the European Union countries called the sentences "disproportionate", with President Obama expressing disappointment and the White House saying it had "serious concerns about the way these young women have been treated by the Russian judicial system."

The trio appealed, with Samutsevich getting her sentence reduced to two years probation, but the others losing and returning to jail. The loss of the appeals sparked new protests around the world. Yoko Ono awarded the band the biennial Lennon-Ono Grant for Peace. Pussy Riot was announced as a finalist for the European Parliament's Sakharov Prize for Freedom of Thought, named for Soviet dissident Andrei Sakharov. One hundred and twenty members of the German parliament, the Bundestag sent a letter condemning the two-year jail sentences to the Russian ambassador to Germany. Hillary Clinton declared Pussy Riot a group of "strong and brave young women", who "refuse to let their voices be silenced."

Madonna stripped her blouse off at a Moscow concert, revealing the words "Pussy Riot" on her back, and invited the band, once released from prison, to perform with her. The women responded that "We're flattered, of course, that Madonna and Björk have offered to perform with us. But the only performances we'll participate in are illegal ones. We refuse to perform as part of the capitalist system, at concerts where they sell tickets."

There were large scale protests supporting the band in New York City, Edinburgh, Toronto, and Washington D.C. However, in their own country polls showed that the majority of Russians supported the draconian sentences received by the punk rockers. In Serbia, a first-person shooting video game was released with the balaclava-wearing band as targets.

Just before Christmas of 2013 President Putin, on the twentieth anniversary of Russia's post-Soviet constitution, declared a general amnesty for a number of high-profile prisoners, including the two Pussy Riot musicians and incarcerated members of Greenpeace. Tolokonnikova and Alyokhina were finally freed, three months ahead of their scheduled release date.

The pair participated in an Amnesty International concert in Brooklyn in 2014, invited onstage by Madonna. Two weeks later, they were at the Olympics in Sochi, Russia, attempting to film and perform a song titled *Putin Will Teach You to Love the Motherland*, when they were beaten by Cossacks working as security guards for the Olympics, and detained. A month later a group of unknown men wearing the controversial Ribbon of St. George doused the band with green dye, giving Alyokhina a concussion in the melee. In February, 2018, the band was again detained by Russian police, and a month later, arrested again and sentenced to fifteen days imprisonment for running on to the field during the FIFA World Cup final game, dressed as police, protesting the arrests of political prisoners.

Responding to the presidency of Donald Trump, Pussy Riot released the song and video *Make America Great Again*. The elaborate and skillfully made video displays a dystopian world in which Trump, played by one of the band members, enforces his values through beatings, shaming and branding of victims delivered by a Trump-led gang of storm troopers, over lyrics mocking and deriding Trump's ugly brand of politics.

Wagner, Strauss and Hitler

Richard Wagner is both one of the most revered and one of the most hated classical composers of all time. Adolf Hitler loved him. Today, his music is de facto banned in the state of Israel. While his music was acclaimed during his lifetime for its power, complexity and influence, his thinking was suspect, and his life a mess of poverty, political exile, turbulent love affairs, and repeated runs from his creditors.

He succeeded early as a choirmaster, conductor, and composer. He also became heavily involved in left-wing and anarchist politics, and was a supporter of the unsuccessful Dresden Uprising, part of the Revolutions of 1848/49 (which along with the upheavals in 1917/19 and 1968/70 was one of the most revolutionary periods in history). Warrants were issued against the revolutionaries and Wagner had to flee, first to Paris and then to Zurich, where he lived in exile and poverty for the next twelve years. While in Switzerland he continued to write music, including two of his most important works—*Tristan und Isolde* and *Der Ring des Nibelungen* (popularly called *"The Ring*

Cycle"). He also began muddying his reputation by writing political screeds such as the anti-Semitic essay *Judaism in Music.*

In 1859, Princess Pauline von Metternich and her husband, who was the Austrian ambassador to Paris, organized a staging of Wagner's opera *Tannhäuser* in Paris, but the presentation was hijacked by people wanting to use it as a protest against the pro-Austrian policies of Napoleon III, and had to be withdrawn after only three performances.

Three years later the political ban on Wagner was finally lifted and he returned to Germany. In 1864 Wagner's situation improved considerably when 18-year-old King Ludwig II succeeded to the throne of Bavaria. The very young king, who was homosexual, was a great admirer of Wagner, and expressed passionate adoration for the composer. To advance his musical career, Wagner was not shy about counterfeiting similar feelings for the king, who responded by settling the composer's many debts and organizing stagings of his masterpieces. It is odd that the king did not understand where Wagner's real romantic interests lay, since most of Germany knew the gossip that Wagner had a long string of very heterosexual dalliances, affairs and marriages that were worthy of a Mick Jagger.

Regardless, Wagner fell out of favor with the authorities. With the royal court deciding the composer had too much sway over the king, he was again banished to Switzerland. The king considered abdicating over the matter, and following his beloved composer into exile, but Wagner talked him out of it.

The king continued to support him, and in 1874 financed the construction of a new opera house for Wagner in Bayreuth, Germany. The construction of the building was difficult—Wagner said every stone in it was red with his blood—but the opening was attended by politicians and dignitaries from around the world, including Kaiser Wilhelm I and Emperor Pedro II of Brazil. The Bayreuth Festival has continued ever since. Today, it is one of the most important and popular festivals in Germany, with German authorities heavily involved in attempting to police the scalping and reselling of the coveted tickets.

However, the early years of the festival were financially ruinous for Wagner, and he returned to writing political articles, in part to attempt to stave off personal bankruptcy. Some of these articles returned to his old anti-Semitic themes. In others, just as Frank Sinatra would in his declining years, he repudiated his earlier liberal views and expressed reactionary viewpoints. In 1883 he died of a heart attack at his winter home in Venice.

Neither Wagner's music nor his wildly anti-Jewish writings were to disappear. As the new century dawned, many people began to recognize and lament the link between German music and reactionary political thought. Novelist Thomas Mann wrote in his essay *Reflections of a Nonpolitical Man* that art, especially German art "has a basically undependable, treacherous tendency, its joy in scandalous anti-reason, its tendency to beauty-creating 'barbarism' cannot be rooted out." French writer Romain Rolland accused the extravagant Teutonic symphonies and operas, especially those by Wagner, of promoting a cult of power—a "hypnotism of force." It can be no wonder, then, that they appealed immensely to Adolf Hitler.

Hitler first encountered Wagner's work in 1906, while he was living in bohemian poverty in Vienna, trying to make a living as an artist. On May 8 and 9 he attended the Court Opera to see Wagner's *Tristan und Isolde* and then *The Flying Dutchman*, both conducted by Gustav Mahler. Ignoring for the moment the fact that Mahler was Jewish, Hitler instead focused on what he saw as the dichotomy between the fantastic images and sounds coming from the stage, and the very Jewish city in which he was now living. "It's impossible to think of a more irreconcilable combination," he said. "This glorious mystery of the dying hero and this Jewish filth!"

Hitler not only adopted a lifelong passion for Wagner in Vienna but would imitate Mahler's flamboyant conducting style in the many speeches that would follow. The one hand, raised in a clenched, rotated fist, and the other, pulling back like the claw of a crab, were gestures he took directly from Mahler.

Although Hitler's early political success derived from his appeal to the roughnecks of Munich's beer halls, he rose to national attention through his carefully developed connections with Germany's musical and artistic elite. In the early 20s he began to get Wagner's heirs in his thrall. In 1923 Wagner's son Siegfried wrote a symphonic poem to celebrate Hitler's "Beer Hall Putsch". When the attempt to gain power failed, Wagner had to postpone the premiere, and instead spent the next few years keeping Hitler, who was now behind bars in Landsberg prison, well equipped with a gramophone, Wagner recordings, food, blankets and writing materials so that the future dictator could write his *Mein Kampf*.

Hitler responded with gratitude, telling the Wagner family that their Bayreuth Festival was "where the Master forged the spiritual sword we are wielding today," and was now "in the line of the march to Berlin." Once released from prison, Hitler would attend the Bayreuth Wagner Festival every summer from 1933 until 1940. Hitler was in many ways much more interested in art and culture than he was in military affairs or government. Just as he was himself an unsuccessful painter, his close sidekick Joseph Goebbels, who he appointed Minister of Propaganda, was an unsuccessful novelist. Hitler much preferred the company of artists to soldiers or bureaucrats—his closest associates were architect Albert Speer, filmmaker Leni Riefenstahl, various actresses and dancers, his photographer mistress Eva Braun, and the director of the Bayreuth Festival, Winnifred Wagner.

All culture fell under the command of Goebbels. Music came under the control of a division of the Reichskulturkammer called the Reich Music Chamber, whose first president was Richard Straus. Jewish musicians were deemed unfit, as were avant-garde, atonal, modern composers and musicians, all branded by the Nazis as being "degenerate". Many of the best known, such as Kurt Weill, Otto

Klemperer and Arnold Schoenberg defected in the early 30's. Those who stayed mostly died in the concentration camps. Entire schools of musical composition were wiped out by the Nazis.

Goebbels staged massive Nazi rallies that were choreographed to the approved German music of Beethoven, Bruckner and especially Wagner. Hitler, believing in a mantra of "music for all", commanded the building of large 3000 seat opera houses across the nation. However, Germans had developed a taste for American popular music and jazz during the 1920's, and had not much interest in the serious classical music Hitler tried to promote. The angry Fuhrer took to sending patrols out to the cafes and beer halls to round up both senior Nazi officials and SA Brownshirts to fill up the seats of the empty opera halls. During performances he was known to have to shake his minions awake whenever they dozed off.

No composer displayed the moral collapse of German music more than Richard Strauss, who served as president of the Reich Music Chamber from 1933 to 1935. "Thank God," he said after Hitler came to power, "finally a Reich Chancellor who is interested in art." He was so certain that Hitler would support artists by doing things like creating royalty schemes that would favor classical composers over popular ones, and extending composers' copyrights, that he largely ignored the violent excesses of the Nazis, even though his own family was partially Jewish. Finally, though, after his family was attacked, he began to fight back. In 1938 his two grandsons were stopped on the way to school and forced to spit on a group of Jews; then they too were spat upon. Strauss wrote about Nazi propagandists Goebbels and Julius Streicher, "I consider the Streicher-Goebbels Jew baiting as a disgrace to German honor, as evidence of incompetence, the basest weapon of untalented, lazy mediocrity against a higher intelligence and greater talent."

Those were dangerous words to be using in the violent atmosphere of late 30's Germany. In front of a large delegation of composers, Goebbels screamed at him "Stop once and for all your chatter about the significance of 'serious music'! You are not helping your case! The art of tomorrow is different from the art of yesterday! You, Herr Strauss, are yesterday!"

Somehow Strauss managed to survive the regime. Most others were not so lucky. His Jewish wife's grandmother Paula Neumann was deported to the Theresienstadt concentration camp. Strauss made several attempts to have her released, including a personal visit to the camp, where he announced himself to the guards by saying "I am the composer Richard Strauss". His demands fell on deaf ears, and his wife's grandmother eventually died in the camp.

Strauss continued to compose throughout the war, but most were not as lucky. Millions of individuals were killed in the camps, among them hundreds who had been prominent in the pre-war period, such as the Czech-Jewish composer Ervin Schulhoff, who died in the Wülzburg concentration camp in 1942. Many Czech-Jewish musicians and composers ended up in the Theresienstadt camp. When the Red Cross announced that it wanted to visit the camp, these musicians became pawns in an elaborate hoax, with a cast of children gamely singing a new opera by one of the incarcerated composers. Once a propaganda film had been made of the concert and the Red Cross had made their visit, the Nazis shipped off the children, the musicians and 18,000 other prisoners off to Auschwitz, where they were killed.

Even in Auschwitz there was music. An ambitious female SS guard organized a woman's orchestra from the inmates, led by Viennese conductor Alma Rosé, the niece of Gustav Mahler. She became obsessed and quite mad, once violently upbraiding a cello player for playing an F-natural instead of an F-sharp. Her musical perfectionism, though, was perhaps a tool she used to stave off insanity in the horrible conditions. In 1944 she fell ill to botulism. Dr. Josef Mengele tried to save her to preserve the sham orchestra, but she died, and by the end of the war, the rest of the musicians were all killed.

Meanwhile, as the war ground on, Hitler largely withdrew to his Berchtesgaden retreat, where he hosted musical soirees around his gramophone, and gave amateur music-appreciation lectures about the thousands of discs in his collection. By 1943 many of his associates thought he had gone crazy. He continued to obsess over music policy while the German Army began to retreat in tatters in North Africa, Russia and Italy. Following the Normandy invasion of 1944, Hitler was focused not on the campaign in France, but instead on how, or even if the Reich should honor Richard Strauss on his 80th birthday. Both he and Goebbels were inclined to ignore the event, as the composer had recently upset them by refusing to accept having wounded German soldiers billet in his villa. However, conductor Wilhelm Furtwängler absurdly advised them that international opinion would turn against the Nazis (as if it hadn't long ago) if Strauss' birthday were ignored. Hitler acquiesced. He had been considering sending him a new Mercedes and a ration card for 1000 litres of fuel. In the end he merely sent the composer a brief telegram.

On April 12, 1945 President Franklin Roosevelt died. The same day, Straus completed his latest symphony, *Metamorphosen*, and in the ruins of the German capital, the Berlin Philharmonic presented some of Hitler's favorite music—Beethoven's Violin Concerto, Bruckner's *Romantic* Symphony, and the immolation scene from *Gotterdämmerung*, the "Twilight of the Gods". Following the concert, the Hitler Youth, it is believed, passed out cyanide pills to the audience. On April 30, Hitler shot himself and his mistress (now wife), Eva Braun, took cyanide. The bodies were soaked in gasoline and burned. He had hoped that the violent music of Wagner would play as he died, but there is no evidence that anyone organized this for him.

It would take another 34 years before Wagner's music would be used to accompany the kind of hellish apocalypse that Hitler had in mind for his own death. In his 1979 film *Apocalypse Now* Francis Ford Coppola memorably used *The Ride of the Valkyries*, the opening of Act Three of the second of the four operas in Wagner's *Ring Cycle*. In the iconic scene, the music blasts from helicopter-mounted loudspeakers as the Air Cavalry squadron attacks and destroys a beachfront Vietnamese village, so that the squadron can surf on a particularly attractive point break in front of the settlement. It is one of the most distinctive uses of music in the highly acclaimed film— the other being the use of The Doors' song *The End* over a napalm bombing of the Vietnamese countryside.

Today, Wagner's music is still controversial. The Israel Philharmonic Orchestra refuses to play his music, and when Israel Public Radio has played it, it has later apologized to its listeners. Israeli authorities have not formally banned Wagner, but they do, in effect, support the ban. Along with Wagner, they have also effectively banned Pink Floyd's Roger Waters, because of what they consider his "odious" ideas about Israel, and his support of the BDS movement (Boycott, Divestment, Sanctions) and of Palestine.

Miriam Makeba

Many of the subjects of this book have spent time in jail, but none other than Miriam Makeba was already in jail at the age of 18 days. Born in 1932 in the black township of Prospect in Johannesburg, her father was a teacher, unable to find work. Her mother, the breadwinner of the family, was a domestic for white families, who also made and sold *Umqombothi* (homebrew African beer). At the time, one of the many draconian laws of South Africa made it illegal for blacks to drink beer, let alone make or sell it.

The police, always keen to find reasons to put blacks behind bars, raided their tiny home when Makeba was 18 days old, and sent her, and her mother, to jail—the future singer's home for the next six months. She would later report that while in prison she was described as a quiet and well-behaved infant: "the perfect baby, for a felon".

Released after six months, she and her mother returned to Prospect. Her childhood was a time of continual harassment by the police. Her home, and the homes of her extended family and neighbors, was frequently the target of midnight raids by the police, demanding to see the passes that all blacks had to carry, searching for illegal alcohol, or simply harassing them to keep them off-balance.

At the age of 16, in 1948, *apartheid* was enacted. Conditions for blacks in South Africa had been bad for many years, but they now became much, much worse. With the Boers focused on keeping blacks as uneducated as possible, most of their schools were closed, the teachers fired.

Makeba was forced to leave school and go to work as a domestic for white families. Twice, she was cheated out of her wages and fired by women who were jealous of the friendly attention the pretty teenager received from their husbands. She began singing, invited to join a local choir. Her first big gig was as a soloist with the choir, singing for England's King George VI and his daughter Princess Elizabeth on their royal visit. The song she had been chosen to sing, written by the choirmaster, would later be banned by the South African government, its lyrics thought to be subversive. But the king and princess never got to hear it. The heavens opened and it began to pour as the parade entourage got to the choir and so the limousines just roared past the bedraggled singers.

The king and princess ignored her, but others took note. She was invited to become the lead singer for a band called The Cuban Brothers. Although neither Cuban, nor brothers, nor, of course, even all male, nonetheless the quartet began to perform publicly. Soon Makeba got the attention of one of the biggest and most popular bands in South Africa – the Manhattans. She was invited to audition for them, got the job, and to her amazement became their lead singer.

The fame and success of the band did not mean the police hassles ended. Since they not only performed all over South Africa but also in neighboring countries Mozambique, Lesotho and Swaziland, they were frequently stopped by traffic police. One memorable night they were stopped three times, and on one of the stops forced to do a roadside performance for the cops. Makeba remembers ending up in jail a lot in those early years of *apartheid*. Worst would be the Friday night busts en route to weekend gigs, when, with the courts not open until Monday, the band would have to cancel their performances and spend the weekend in jail.

Makeba began to make 78 rpm recordings for Gallatone Records, both with the Manhattans, and as a solo artist. In 1955, she was returning from Durban to Jo-burg with a group of artists, when their car was involved in a major collision with another vehicle with three whites in it—all of whom were instantly killed. Makeba received a broken collarbone, and one of the other performers was much more seriously hurt. The police arrived, and pulled guns on the black musicians, threatening to kill them. An ambulance showed up, picked up the bodies of the three whites, but would not touch the injured black men. Makeba managed to get some Swiss tourists to drive her injured bandmates to a local hospital, but its emergency department refused to accept them. The group had to drive the injured man for hours to a black hospital in Jo-burg, but by the time they got there, he was dead.

Makeba's big break came when an American filmmaker, Lionel Rogosin, came to South Africa to surreptitiously make a film he titled *Come Back, Africa,* and discovered the young singer to star in it. Rogosin's film was accepted into the 1959 Venice Film Festival and he invited her to join him at the Italian festival. She managed to get a visa that allowed her to travel out of the country and took her first international airline flight. She was the only black face on the plane and was shunned by all the other passengers, no doubt shocked by her presence.

After Venice, where the film won the Critics Choice award, Makeba ended up in London, where she was startled on several occasions by the attitudes of the police. In one late night encounter, she assumed she would be arrested for being on the streets, but instead was given polite and friendly directions to her destination by a pair of London bobbies.

Rogosin organized a performance for her on the Steve Allen Show. Makeba had no idea who the celebrated TV host was, since television was banned in her homeland then, and until 1975. Rogosin also organized a gig for her at the Village Vanguard, a New York folk club. However, The Man was not impressed. Her travelling visa from South Africa was limited to Europe. Only after Steve Allen and Harry Belafonte interceded on her behalf was she able to able to travel to America.

Within days of her arrival in America Makeba was performing to an audience of 60 million on the Steve Allen show and to celebrities like Sidney Poitier, Duke Ellington, Nina Simone and Miles Davis at the Village Vanguard. "There are few cases in show business where a performer's life has changed more suddenly, more dramatically, and with so much promise," said the *New York Times*. *Newsweek* compared her to Ella Fitzgerald and Frank Sinatra, and Belafonte called her "easily the most revolutionary talent to appear in any medium in the last decade."

Her success was not the only revolutionary thing happening in 1960. Makeba began her involvement with the newly independent African nations of Ghana, Nigeria, Senegal, Ivory Coast and the Belgian Congo (re-named Zaire). In South Africa, things went from bad to worse, with the Sharpeville March, where the police shot sixty-nine people dead (including two of Makeba's uncles) and injured one hundred and eighty. Young lawyer and political activist Nelson Mandela was sent to prison for life. When Makeba's mother died, the singer went to the South African consulate in New York to get her visa renewed so she could travel home. Instead, the consulate stamped it "Invalid". She was exiled from her homeland.

Her inability to travel outside the US did not hinder her travels within it, and throughout 1961 and 1962 she toured with folk artists Odetta, Belafonte and the Chad Mitchell Trio all over the US and into Canada. She, like many black artists of the era, could not stay in the hotels she performed in (especially in the south), but she was increasingly involved with all levels of American society, even performing at the famous birthday party for President Kennedy at

Madison Square Gardens (as is also described in the chapter on Frank Sinatra). Her performance there is not quite as renowned as the notorious breathy lover's rendition of *Happy Birthday* by Marilyn Monroe, but the President was impressed enough to specially invite her back to the post-Gardens party at his New York hotel.

She was also asked to give a speech at the United Nations, in which she spoke about how South Africa's Verwoerd government had turned the country into a giant nightmarish prison for blacks. President Julius Nyerere of Tanzania learned of her exile from South Africa and her inability to travel and so offered her honorary citizenship and a Tanzanian passport. From then on, Makeba considered herself not just a native of South Africa, but of all Africa.

South Africa retaliated by banning her music. It was now illegal to play any of her records in the country. The same year they also banned the book *Black Beauty*, not realizing (or perhaps not caring) that it was a children's book about a horse.

Makeba continued with her activism. She went to Addis Ababa as the lead performer in the events surrounding the formation of the Organization of African States (and an informal delegate to the conference). She was also invited by President Kenyatta to attend Kenya's independence celebrations. While there, she met President Skou Touré of Guinea, a leader who would play a big part in the last half of her life.

Leader of one of the first African countries to gain independence, Touré, a big believer in supporting art and culture in his country, put artists and musicians on the public payroll, and held a major international music festival, with Makeba as the star performer. He toured the country with her and invited her to live in Guinea. While at the festival, Makeba met and began an affair with the fiery Trinidadian/American civil rights activist, Stokely Carmichael—leader of the Student Non-violent Coordinating Committee (SNCC), and later leader of the Black Panthers.

If Makeba's life was complicated and endangered by The Man before meeting Carmichael, it became doubly so after their marriage in 1968. Carmichael was deeply feared by the American establishment and was targeted by J. Edgar Hoover and the FBI's COINTELPRO (counter-intelligence program). He believed that he had been infected with cancer by the FBI—a claim that does not seem impossible, since it is well-documented that the FBI or CIA attempted to infect other leaders, such as Fidel Castro. Carmichael died of prostate cancer in 1998.

As a result of her association with Carmichael, Prime Minister Pindling kicked her out of the Bahamas, and then across America promoters began cancelling her tour dates. She still had supporters, though—some of them very well known. Marlon Brando intervened to insure that her California concerts went on as planned, and he introduced her at each of them.

However, her life became a nightmare. Both the FBI and the CIA began constant surveillance of her, in New York, and on the road. With her U.S. concert dates increasingly being cancelled, she traveled to Jamaica for a major concert. When she tried to fly back to America, she was refused entry, and the American Ambassador to Jamaica refused to give her a visa. Only through Carmichael, and his connections to the Congressional Black Caucus, did she get to return. Carmichael had his own travel problems too, for just as they did to Paul Robeson, the American government had revoked his passport.

Back in the USA, Makeba discovered that both her recording contract with Frank Sinatra's company Reprise Records and her performance contract with the William Morris Agency had been cancelled. She decided it was time to get out.

In 1970, Makeba and Carmichael left the US, and settled in Guinea, where she would live for the next 15 years. However, interactions with The Man did not end. When she arrived in France for a concert, she was taken off the plane by five machinegun-toting soldiers. In Senegal, Guinea's neighbor, she was targeted by government officials because of her close connection with Guinea's President Touré. The Senegal authorities cancelled her concerts and declared her *persona non grata* in the country.

Touré appointed her his country's Delegate to the United Nations and cultural emissary to the world. Touring in Latin America, she was about to perform at the Barradero Stadium when the police mysteriously shut down the concert. Nonetheless President Salvador Allende invited her to lunch the next day. Two weeks later, she learned that Allende had been assassinated, and that hundreds had been killed, including Chile's most popular singer, Victor Jara. The massacre (as is described in the chapter on the killing of Jara) took place at the same stadium where she had been scheduled to perform.

Although no longer performing in the US, she was still politically active there, working with the music community to try to enforce the boycott of *apartheid* South Africa. She personally appealed to Aretha Franklin not to play at Sun City, and successfully convinced the Queen of Soul never to go.

The 70's are of course a time of revolution—and counter-revolutions—around the world. Her adopted country of Guinea came under attack by mercenaries paid by what was then the fascist dictatorship of Portugal. All men and women of Guinea, including Makeba, joined a militia to defend the country. She was provided with an AK-47 machinegun and spent several weeks training on a firing range. Although she personally never had to fire the gun in anger, the militia did fight back, and ultimately the coup was defeated.

On a European tour, she was even arrested and jailed in Denmark, of all places. Touré heard of the crazy arrest and sent his European ambassador, Seydou Kerta, to extricate Makeba from the Danish prison. It was an odd life she led. She traveled with diplomatic passports given to her by eight countries—but none of them seemed to keep her out of hot water.

She received yet another passport, from Angola, when she visited to attend the southern African country's independence celebrations in 1975. Once again, there was trouble. A riot ensued at her concert, and thirty people were killed. Thirty! Four died at Altamont (as described in the chapter on the Rolling Stones). Eight times the number of deaths, and yet unlike the notorious California concert, I'll wager you've never before even heard of this one.

Although some of her tour dates dried up, new opportunities developed for her. She began playing at big European rock festivals with headliners such as The Who. The rock crowds were at first mystified by Makeba's music, but eventually warmed to it and to her fierce political stance. She continued to speak out against the Pretoria regime of South Africa. She was sometimes, she says, scared of the things she said on stage, "but the next time comes and I don't care. If I die on stage I guess I'll be the happiest person because I'll be dying like a soldier on the battlefield."

In 1984, Guinea President Sekou Touré died. He had been virtual dictator of the country since 1958, had imprisoned or exiled all possible opponents, and according to some had killed over 50,000 people during his reign. Still, he had tremendous support from the people of Guinea, and from Miriam Makeba. She, along with her friend Nina Simone, and dignitaries from around the world, attended his funeral. Three days later, there was a coup d'état. Again, police and soldiers were breaking down the door of her house, taking away her passport and telling her she was under house arrest.

For the third time, she was forced to leave her country. This time, she went into exile in Belgium. Within two years she joined Paul Simon's famous *Graceland* tour. Again, there was more hot water with a huge controversy about Simon performing and recording in South Africa. Even though he was playing with South African artists such as Makeba, her ex-lover Hugh Masekela, and Ladysmith Black Mambazo, anti-apartheid activists felt that he was breaking the boycott and that Makeba and Masekela were sell-outs.

On February 11, 1990 Nelson Mandela was released from prison, and South African President FW de Klerk announced the unbanning of all political associations, including the ANC, and the potential for the return of exiles. Makela at the time was on another European tour but organized to meet Mandela on his first trip out of the country, in Stockholm, where he was addressing the Swedish parliament. Mandala encouraged her to return home.

It was not easy. Even though she had honorary citizenships from many countries, the South African authorities still stalled her on her request for a visa. Finally, they allowed her to return—for only six days!—with a visa attached to her French passport. Her arrival back in South Africa, after over thirty years of exile, was a powerful, wrenching moment both for her and for the South African people. And though she could only stay for six days, she returned the next year to perform two sold-out concerts at Johannesburg's huge Standard Bank Arena.

Two years later, at age sixty-two, she got to vote for the first time in her life in the election that brought Nelson Mandela to power as the new President. In the late 90s and early 2000s she began living in South Africa again. She recorded new albums there (one with Dizzy Gillespie and Nina Simone), starred in the feature film *Sarafina* about the Soweto student revolts that ultimately brought down the old *apartheid* regime, and was appointed as South Africa's Goodwill Ambassador to Africa.

She also received numerous awards including the Polar Music Prize (previous recipients—Bob Dylan, Paul McCartney, Elton John), the highest honor of Tunisia, presented to her by President Zine Ben Ali, and the Legion d'Honneur, presented to her by French President Jacques Chirac. As she remembers it, "There are only three South Africans who have been awarded the Légion of Honour—President Nelson Mandela, Archbishop Desmond Tutu, and little me."

On November 7, 2008 she was performing in Caserta, Italy—a benefit for the Italian writer Roberto Saviano in his stand against the Camorra, a criminal organization like the Mafia. After singing her hit *Pata Pata* she suffered a heart attack and died soon after.

Her extraordinary career ended as it had begun—singing for a cause she believed in. No cause, of course, was more important to her than bringing the plight of South Africans to the attention of the world, and helping to end *apartheid*, and in that she was unquestionably successful. Her story is one of the victories for music in the battle against oppression and for freedom.

Singing for a Cause

If The Man got exercised about instrumental musical genres like classical and jazz, and largely non-political ones like pop and rock, you can bet that the overtly left-wing political genre of folk and protest music caught the attention of the authorities. The genre peaked in popularity in the early 60s, and it is only because the era was somewhat more liberal than those that proceeded or followed it that folksingers did not get more harassment than they did from the establishment.

Folk songs were an important tool in the most important battle of the era—the fight in America for Civil Rights and against segregation. The two most important battlesongs of the era, sung in marches, sit-ins and in jail cells thoughout the segregated south, were *This Land is Your Land* and *We Shall Overcome*. *This Land is Your Land* was written as a rejoinder to Irving Berlin's *God Bless America,* which itself has frequently been considered an alternative to the American national anthem, Francis Scott Keys' *The Star Spangled Banner.*

The Star Spangled Banner is not, musically speaking, one of the world's great national anthems. It is not really even about America, but rather about a fairly obscure minor battle in one of America's least significant wars.

America The Beautiful, written by Katherine Lee Bates, is much prefered by many people, and has been proposed as an alternate anthem, as has *God Bless America*, written by Irving Berlin and made wildly popular by singer Kate Smith in the 1930s and the early years of the Second World War. However Berlin's song was not without controversy. The Ku Klux Klan and other right-wing groups condemned it for having been written by a Russian-Jewish immigrant. Leftwing groups thought it sappy and jingoistic. Itinerant songsmith Woody Guthrie was certainly in the latter camp. Guthrie did not believe that an America that he saw as being controlled by rapacious capitalists and bankers, in which kids were going to bed hungry and cops were beating up workers and strikers was a nation that was "blessed" by God. On February 23, 1940, the wildly prolific Guthrie banged out another song—a rebuttal to Berlin's *God Bless America* that he called *God Blessed America*. Little did he realize he had written a classic. Once it morphed into *This Land is Your Land* it would become a staple of the 1960s battle for civil rights, and would itself be proposed as a new anthem for the United States.

Guthrie was rough-around-the-edges, very much a man of the people. He was arrested a few times for vagrancy and similar charges. Frankly, in the lean years of the Depression, the only thing that saved him from more police harassment was his white skin. A black man acting in the uppity way Guthrie did would have ended up with long stretches in one of the nation's many prisons. Instead, Guthrie was mostly able to hitch around the United States, playing his topical songs at union meetings, labor camps and small theaters. He often performed with Appalachian singers like Aunt Molly Johnson, who had been forced to run from her Kentucky home after receiving death threats from mining officials who thought her songs dangerous and subversive. They likely thought the same of *God Blessed America / This Land is Your Land*, with lyrics like *Was a big high wall there* that tried to stop me/ A sign was painted said Private Property / But on the back side, it didn't say nothing—God blessed America for me.

Guthrie was accused of being a communist. While he never for a minute denied his sympathy for the working class, he denied affiliation with the Party. "They called me a communist and a wild man and everything you can think of," he said, "but I don't care what they call me. I ain't a member of any earthly organization." He did, though, become a close friend of fellow singer Pete Seeger, and the pair started an unabashedly leftwing group called the Almanac Singers that moved rapidly from singing at "hootenannies" in Greenwich Village lofts to giant union rallies surveilled by the FBI at Madison Square Gardens. Woody enscribed his guitar with the words, *This Machine Kills Fascists* and Seeger encircled his banjo with *This Machine Surrounds Hate and Forces it to Surrender*. Guthrie wrote dozens of songs about a wide variety of social issues. He even wrote one condemning Fred Trump, father of the 45th President, for his discriminatory rental policies in his Coney Island apartment blocks.

Following the war, in the wildly idealistic late 1940s, Pete Seeger transformed what was left of the Almanac Singers into a more radical group called People's Songs. Following the socialist principles of collective musical action, the group enthusiastically supported the Progressive Party candidate in the 1948 presidential election, Henry Wallace. Wallace was trounced by Harry Truman, and America began rapidly sliding to the right. People's Songs was disbanded. Seeger was a witness to the attacks on Paul Robeson at the Peekskill Riots of 1949. Woody Guthrie began to physically deteriorate as he began to succumb to Huntington's Disease.

Seeger helped start a new folk group called The Weavers, which had several huge hits including a cover of Leadbelly's *Goodnight Irene*. They sang a gentler brand of folk music, but they still had many enemies. Duncan Emrich, a Columbia professor and head of the Library of Congress' Archive of American Folk Song wrote a memo to the FBI telling them he was concerned about "the efforts of Communists and Communist sympathizers to infiltrate and gain control of folksinging." In February of 1952 Harvey Matusow, a friend of the Weavers and a volunteer member of People's Songs, testified to the House Un-American Activites Committee that Seeger and his group were Communists. Matusow told Senator McCarthy and his cronies at HUAC that the Weavers were using "their appeal to the young people as a means of getting the young people down to the meetings of the Communist fronts and indoctrinating them with the party line and later recruiting them." It was a complete lie, but it worked. Their label Decca dropped them. All their performances were cancelled.

Three years after his accusations, Matusow admitted to having been a paid informant who, at the behest of Roy Cohn, lied in order to incriminate musicians, artists and writers, including the Weavers. As a result Matusow was convicted of perjury and spent nearly three years in prison. (Shark-like Roy Cohn moved on from being counsel for Joe McCarthy's committee to becoming the lawyer, mentor and role model for both Donald Trump and Roger Stone, until he was disbarred for ethical violations just before his death from AIDS in 1986.)

Pete Seeger was called before HUAC and grilled by counsel Frank Tavenner, who used an old concert listing in the *Daily Worker* to try to get Seeger to admit that he was a Communist. Seeger responded: "Sir, I refuse to answer that question, whether it was a quote from *The New York Times* or the *Vegetarian Journal*. I am not going to answer any questions as to my association, my philosophical or my religious beliefs, or my political beliefs, or how I voted in any election, or any of these private affairs. I think these are very improper questions for any American to be asked, especially under such compulsion as this."

The questioning continued for a long time, but eventually Seeger wore them down and he was released from the hearings. He had been one of the bravest of the people hauled before HUAC. He did not admit to anything, he did not name names, and he did not hide behind the shield of the Fifth Amendment. He simply, politely refused to follow the committee's dark line of questioning. The *New York Post* sarcastically reported HUAC's harassment of Pete Seeger under the headline DANGEROUS MINSTREL NABBED HERE. "Amid our larger tribulations," read the *Post* editorial, "the Justice Department has moved fearlessly and decisively against ballad singer Pete Seeger. . .That the combined powers of the House Committee and the Justice Department should be rallied to imprison him is a bitter burlesque. Some jail will be a more joyous place if he lands there, and things will be bleaker on the outside."

Seeger did not go to jail, but he was blacklisted. No longer able to record or publically perform, he instead developed a new audience for his music, one that as it grew up would become a major force in the "New Left" of the 1960s. He began singing and playing his banjo for kids in schoolrooms and summer camps across the American Northeast. He taught the kids the songs, and they sang them together, as singalongs. The favourites were the social justice anthems, *If I Had a Hammer* and *This Land is Your Land*. Eight years later, the kids that learned the songs in summer camp would be singing them at sit-ins, protest marches and in jail cells in Arkansas and Mississippi.

Other young people learned Guthrie's songs from old records from the late 40s. One of them, then known as Bob Zimmerman, recalled the moment he first discovered Woody Guthrie. "I put one on the turntable and when the needle dropped, I was stunned—didn't know if I was stoned or straight. . .All these songs, one after another made my head spin. It was like the land parted." Zimmerman became so obsessed with Guthrie that he left Minnesota to head for New York with the twin goals of meeting Woody Guthrie and becoming a folksinger himself. After changing his name to Bob Dylan, he succeeded at both. He genuflected before his idol at the New Jersey sanatorium where Guthrie was living out his last days. Only months after arriving in New York he was performing and then recording songs, including his skillful tribute to his dying mentor, *Song to Woody*.

Within the next two years Dylan had created a catalogue of masterful topical and protest songs that became immediate classics: *Blowin' In The Wind, A Hard Rain's A-Gonna Fall, Chimes of Freedom, Masters of War, The Times They Are A-Changin'* and others. He was adopted as the voice of the generation that wanted to see major change in an era of nuclear brinkmanship, racial injustice, Barry Goldwater, Bull Conner, John Wayne and the John Birch Society.

Meanwhile in California a teenaged girl with an incredible soprano voice named Joan Baez had attended a Pete Seeger concert in Palo Alto and then immediately bought herself a guitar and begun to teach herself the Seeger/Guthrie repertoire. Within a few years she and Dylan would be considered the queen and king of folk music. They played together, most famously at the Newport Folk Festival. Together, with her beautiful voice and his horrible one, they sang his songs—the best protest songs that have ever been written. But, says Baez, "I think his active commitment to social change was limited to songwriting. To my knowledge he never went on a march. He certainly never did any civil disobedience, at least that I knew about. I've always felt he just didn't want the responsibility."

Joan, on the other hand, became likely the most politically and socially active singer in history. The story of the many causes she has marched for, sung for, been arrested for could fill the rest of this book. Let's look just at one two-week period at the end of 1972. In early December, Baez was invited to participate in a tour of North Vietnam, to see what American bombing was doing to the country, and what treatment the Vietnamese were giving to captured American pilots. It was thought to be a relatively safe time to visit. American bombing of the North had slowed, and there was a total lull expected for the Christmas period, but politically it was a very dangerous thing to do. Baez hated long night flights, unfamiliar foreign food, visiting war memorials and traveling with strangers.

However, it was an opportunity to see the "enemy" up close in the most important war of her lifetime. She agreed to go, travelling with a conservative lawyer, an Episcopalian minister, and an angry, Maoist Vietnam Veteran Against the War. The four of them crossed the Pacific and travelled through Bangkok and Laos into Hanoi. What they did not know was that Richard Nixon had just made what he would claim was "the most difficult decision he ever made," authorizing over the Christmas period the heaviest bombing in the history of the world.

For a few days the situation was relatively quiet, with Baez and the others being shown the bombed-out city, war memorials, and movies showing the effects of American napalm on the children and countryside of Vietnam. Then, however, the bombing started, with waves of B-52s conducting night raids, raining down thousands of bombs on the city. Baez would be sometimes woken eight times a night by her minders and hustled down into underground bomb shelters. The concussion blasts were so intense that she had to sit down, for fear of being knocked to the ground. Eventually she began taking her guitar down to the shelter to help calm the nerves of the others trapped underground with her.

She and the visiting group were also taken to meet American POWs, most of them pilots whose planes had been downed by Russian missiles. She offered to sing for them too, and reports that the unanimous request was for Robbie Robertson's *The Night They Drove Old Dixie Down*. Why Joan Baez ever chose to record this dirge-like paean to the sick cause of the slaveholding Confederacy, or why a group of American military would want to hear a song glorifying traitors to their country is a mystery, but there it is.

The bombing continued night after night, with noon bombings sometimes mixed in to keep the Vietnamese on their toes. There are a variety of violent and difficult interactions described in this book, but none other are as dangerous or as metaphorical as a musician being a potential target of a massive carpet bombing operation by airplanes from her own country. Of course, Nixon knew she was there. She was almost certainly on his "enemies list"; the FBI was almost certainly tracking her whereabouts.

Bob Dylan certainly did *not* travel to North Vietnam at the height of the war. Unlike Baez, he hated the mantle of being a spokesman for his generation. He is a poet. He has certainly not abandoned his muse, his art, or his audience, but he did largely abandon politics a long time ago. He has had a life largely free of any unwanted involvement with The Man, but he did have at least two interactions which could easily have ended his career. In the summer of 1964, Dylan made a tour of the South and West of America. In those simple days the singer toured in a station wagon with his pal Victor Maymudes driving and managing the tour, and a couple of other guys along for the ride. After playing at Emory University in Atlanta, at an event organized by Martin Luther King's Southern Christian Leadership Conference (SCLC), Dylan's gang drove south toward New Orleans, shocked by the backward, poverty-wracked states of Mississippi and Louisiana, with Dylan writing *Chimes of Freedom* in the back seat. Wanting to experience the music of New Orleans, they tried to get into bars, but were refused entrance. In that unenlightened era, blacks were not allowed into white establishments, and whites were often not allowed into black ones.

After another concert, at Tougaloo College, a black teacher's college, the marijuana-fueled odyssey continued north to Denver, for another concert, then through the mountains heading for a concert in Reno and then a rendezvous with Baez in California. At one point, they became stuck in a long lineup of slow-moving traffic. Maymudes, nervous that they were going to be late for the concert, executed a ridiculous manoever of clambering over the seat back and trading positions with the driver, while the wagon was winding through the mountain passes, then passing cars on blind corners to get ahead. Eventually they discovered the cause of the hold-up—a funeral for a local mayor. Again he tried to pass the procession. A highway patrol officer spotted them and took chase. Rather than pull over, Maymudes sped up, giving the others in the car an opportunity to hide their illicit drugs. If the crazy driving didn't kill Dylan, the potential of a bust could have killed his musical career. In the end Maymudes did pull over and though he was berated by the cop, he was not charged, and Dylan made his Reno gig on time.

On the next tour—across Europe, a overly enthusiastic roadie attracted police attention to the revolutionary folk singer. Local police awoke tour manager Maymudes at five AM wanting him to direct them to the hotel room of the star. Maymudes did, but shrewdly managed to warn Dylan, who managed to hide the grass he had in his room in his hat just before the police stormed in. Again, it was a very close call that could have ended Dylan's singing career. But didn't.

What of the Beatles? Where were they during the massive civil rights and other battles of the early 1960s? Largely, like most people, MIA. In recent years Paul McCartney has been putting out a claim that the Beatles cared passionately about the Civil Rights Movement. If they did, they certainly did not use the massive megaphone they had in the 60s to respond to the crisis. He claims to have been present when a black woman was being handcuffed and beaten for the crime of sitting in a section reserved for whites, and being shocked by television images of white racists screaming that 15-year-old black girl Elizabeth Eckford should be lynched for attempting to enter Little Rock Central High School. No doubt he was shocked by both incidents, but this shock did not translate into commenting on either in any of the dozens of Beatles' press conferences, or using them as material for a song. He now claims that *Blackbird*, recorded in 1968 for *The White Album*, was all about racial inequality, that by using the term "black bird" he was referring to a black woman. It all seems revisionist and faintly absurd. No-one listening to the song, either in 1968 or today could have any idea from the lyrics that it had anything whatsoever to do with civil rights or racial inequality. Indeed back in the day he originally said he got the idea for the song while listening to a blackbird (a real avian, not a woman) in Rishikesh,

India. The British slang expression "bird" was thrown around in lines like, "Oie, Ringo! Check out the dolly bird in the mini-dress! She's a bit of all right, in't she?" It was never used to describe a black woman (actually, a "negro woman" would have been the expression used in those days) being beaten up by southern cops. Even if one wants to stretch credulity and accept that *Blackbird* was in some way a protest against racial intolerance, it was written and released five years too late to make any difference.

So the singing of protest songs about the horrible conditions in the south was largely left to southern women themselves. One of the most powerful was Bernice Johnson Reagon, who early in the struggle in November 1961 was arrested and jailed for her participation in a civil rights protest in Albany, Georgia against the segregation on interstate buses. Singing in the jail cell was a new tool for the non-violent protest movement, and it changed her. After jail, she says, her voice was bigger than she had ever heard it before. "It had this ringing in it. It filled all the space of the church. I thought that was because I had been to jail. It was because I had stepped out of the safety zone. I tell people, if you don't sometimes walk through trouble, you'll never get to meet the rest of yourself...And maybe if I'd never gone to jail, I would not have ever gotten to know that part of my singing. It was a blessing."

She did not think it a blessing at the time, though, since she was immediately expelled from Albany State College for her involvement in the protest. She instead became a fulltime activist in the Civil Rights Movement and a founding member of the Freedom Singers, an a cappella quartet that performed at rallies, sit-ins and in prisons. Pete Seeger encouraged the group to link forces with SNCC, the Student Nonviolent Coordinating Committee.

Reagon and her Freedom Singers were in the thick of the ugly battles against racist white mobs, the Klan, and the police in the long hot summers of the 1960s. She and her group used their "freedom songs" to help pull their community together and inspire confidence when it would be natural to lose it. They mostly sang spirituals like *Ain't Gonna Let Nobody Turn Me Around* with modified lyrics like, *Ain't gonna let segregation, Lordy, turn me round, turn me round. Ain't gonna let segregation, Lordy, turn me around. I keep on a-walkin', keep on-talkin', marching up to Freedom Land.*

Others sung by the movement included *Hold On, Eyes on the Prize, We Shall Not Be Moved,* and of course, *We Shall Overcome*, which became, along with Guthrie's *This Land is Your Land*, the number one anthem. It was originally a gospel hymn, written in 1900 by Charles Albert Tindley and re-discovered by Pete Seeger's Peoples Songs in 1947. It has probably been sung in southern prison cells more than any other song.

Another favourite of Raygon's was *This May Be the Last Time*, which she called "a powerful mood-setter. You can't really sing the song without thinking about the statement you're making. It says *this may be the last time, this could be the last time – I don't know.* Maybe the last time we all sing together, maybe the last time we all pray together. Many times, that song would be done just before a march, and it would make you know something of the potential cost that you were going into in taking the stand you were taking." The song was sung by the Staple Singers, then covered by the Rolling Stones, produced by Phil Spector, and became the third Number One hit for the Stones. Their version, performed on *The Ed Sullivan Show* on an absurd set made up of ridiculous chandeliers hanging over their heads, unfortunately expunges any and all hints of its provenance as a song of defiant protest.

By the end of the decade the genre of protest music seemed to have hit its Best Before date, eclipsed by the more violent and provocative actions of the Black Panthers and the Nation of Islam. Reagon eventually disbanded her Freedom Singers, but in 1973 she joined forces with Carol Maillard to create a new group called Sweet Honey in the Rock that performed for over thirty years, received several Grammy nominations, and sang original songs addressing issues such as police shootings, domestic violence, and the environment. Reagon moved on to become a noted academic—Director of the Smithsonian's Program in Black American Culture, curator of National Museum of American History and the 1989 winner of the $275,000 MacArthur Genius Grant.

The success of the protest song in the Black Civil Rights Movement inspired people from other communities. Buffy Sainte-Marie was born on the Piapot First Nation in the Qu'Appelle Valley of Saskatchewan. The date of her birth and the names of her parents were unrecorded, and like many native children of the period, she was whisked away from the reserve by the authorities, not, in her case to a Residential School, but rather to adoptive parents living across the continent in New England. She was almost the only non-white living in what she now calls, "Javex, USA" and was ostracized both for her status as an adopted child and a Native. Her brother "let me know in no uncertain terms that my mom was not my mom and that I didn't belong in that family." The boy moved on from psychological bullying to physical and sexual abuse, and then for many years Buffy was also sexually abused by another older family member.

In 1961, the same year Bernice Johnson Reagon began protesting and singing in Georgia, Buffy Sainte-Marie visited Washington and met members of the newly formed National Indian Youth Council. The 50s and 60s were just as bad for Natives as they were for Blacks. Arguably worse, with the Indian Relocation Act of 1956 displacing natives off their land, and 109 Indigenous tribes and bands terminated by the US government. She travelled with the group to Oklahoma, where she and the others witnessed signs in store windows reading, "Help Wanted. Indians Need Not Apply" and on houses for sale or rent reading, "No Indians." At 23 she returned to Saskatchewan and was adopted (in Cree Nation context) back into the Piapot nation.

She transformed these experiences into two powerful songs about the native experience—*Now That the Buffalo's Gone* and *My Country 'Tis of Thy People You're Dying*. She was subsequently named

Billboard Magazine's Best New Artist. Like so many other committed artists of the era, she linked up with Pete Seeger, appearing with him on his TV show *Rainbow Quest*. Travelling through San Francisco Airport, she witnessed the return of dead American soldiers in body bags. She was inspired by the macabre sight to write one of her biggest and most important songs, *Universal Soldier*. It is a powerful indictment of war, blaming not just the the politicians and arms-makers but the soldiers themselves for continuing the never-ending business of warfare.

Sainte-Marie got the attention of the folk music crowds in New York's Greenwich Village and Toronto's Yorkville Village. She became good friends with Dylan, Joni Mitchell, Neil Young and Leonard Cohen. Her songs were very successfully covered by Donovan and Glen Campbell. Forced into an unecessary addiction to codeine by a corrupt Florida doctor, she turned that experience into another hit, *Cod'ine*. Meanwhile, her powerful protest songs and her activism were getting the attention of The Man. The FBI opened a file on her in the mid 1960s.

Her career was also stymied by the sexism of the 60s. She was conned into selling the publishing rights to *Universal Soldier* for one dollar. Many people attributed the writing of *Universal Soldier* and *Cod'ine* to Donovan. Paul Simon, years before he became a major name, toured as an opening act with her, but soon demanded top billing. When Elvis Presley recorded her song *Until It's Time for You to Go*, his people demanded that she split the publishing rights with him, even though he had nothing at all to do with the writing of the song, and it had already been recorded by Sainte-Marie and covered by Barbra Streisand and Neil Diamond.

By 1970, when the American Indian Movement (AIM) was actively resisting racist US government policies, protesting broken treaties, and fighting the strip mining and industrial pollution of native lands, Buffy Sainte-Marie became involved in the fight, especially in the actions at Wounded Knee, South Dakota and Gresham,

Wisconsin. In Wisconsin, she and other activists were ducking bullets fired by local vigilantes. "The National Guard saved our butts," she remembers, "and helped us to not get killed when those vigilantes began attacking Indian people."

Although the National Guard perhaps saved her life, she was nonetheless lumped in with other activists and singers by the government, and was put on a virtual blacklist by both the Johnson and Nixon administrations. She didn't learn the truth until years later when she was shown a letter addressed to a government agent commending him for suppressing her music "which deserved to be suppressed." Her music was not played on the radio, and shipments of her records would simply vanish—and the FBI and CIA continued to monitor her movements.

She again got involved with a violent, manipulating man, record producer and composer Jack Nitzsche. The pair wrote *Up Where We Belong*, the theme song for the film *An Officer and a Gentleman*, for which they won an Academy Award for Best Song. They also wrote the music for *Performance,* the brilliant film about Music and The Man that starred Mick Jagger, Anita Pallenberg and James Fox. However Nitzsche was a horrible, violent person very much in the mold of his mentor Phil Spector. "I think I probably slept with one eye open all the time I was married to Jack," she says. "One time, when I was asleep, he did assault me but not by hitting me: he shot me up. He skin-popped me with heroin while I was asleep."

It wasn't his first assault. Nitzsche had been charged with raping his previous girlfriend, the actress Carrie Snodgrass, with the barrel of a gun. The sordid heroin incident was the last straw for Sainte-Marie. A few weeks later she grabbed their young son in the middle of the night and escaped from Nitzsche, returning to her home in Hawaii.

Her recording and performing dried up for some years, but she continued to write. It took fourteen years to get her song *Bury My Heart at Wounded Knee* to where she wanted it to be. In the meantime she became an expert and original visual artist. She was one of the earliest and most skilled users of the Apple computer, using it to create art, record albums, and communicate. She was using the internet as early as 1990, years before most people had even heard of it. Her album *Coincidence and Likely Stories*, made with an audio linkup she created between her farm in Hawaii and a studio in London is considered the first record ever made over the Internet.

Buffy Sainte-Marie continues to record and perform today. Over the years, she has supported causes of civil rights, peace, the environment, and native land claims with her songs. Her work is often done in more subtle ways than placard-waving marches. For years, she used the musical platform of *Sesame Street* to inform children about indigenous lives. In 1996 she launched a digital and musical teaching project called *Cradleboard* to teach North American kids about native culture. Her goal was to change the attitudes of children so that as they grew into adults they would shift away from the systemic racism against native North Americans. This policy, she says, began with the 1493 Papal Bull from Pope Alexander VI that commanded Europeans to overthrow and destroy the "barbarous nations" of the New World, and continues to this day. She and her music have definitely had the effect of upsetting the establishment's applecart.

"I wasn't trying to disrupt the power agenda," she says, "but I'm awfully glad I did."

Narcocorridos: Mexico's Deadly Music Business

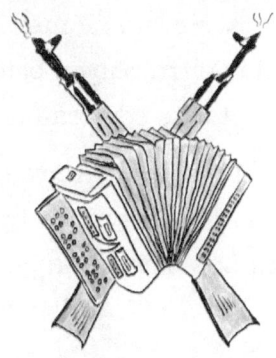

Being a musician in Mexico can be very dangerous. Consider the appalling death toll over the course of just one year. On November 25, 2006, singer Valentín Elizalde was ambushed and shot to death along with his driver and assistant after leaving a concert in Reynosa, a border city in the state of Tamaulipas. It is believed he was killed by members of the Los Zetas drug cartel for singing the *narcocorrido To All My Enemies,* a song that drug kingpin Osiel Cardenas found offensive.

Less than two weeks later, Javier Morales Sergio Gómez, leader of the popular band Los Implacables del Norte, was gunned down in Michoacan only three days after 6000 soldiers and police had been sent to the state to try to keep the peace. Gómez' *narcocorridos* included songs such as *Death Contract* and *Drug Tragedy.*

About the same time, singer Lupillo Rivera's SUV was hit by seven bullets in Guadalajara. He survived. But then four members of Banda Fugaz were shot dead barely two months later after a concert in the town of Puruaran.

In late November, in a motel room in Matamoros, across the border from Brownsville, Texas, Zayda Peña, the 28-year-old singer of Zayda y Los Culpables was shot in the neck. She was rushed to hospital but a gunman came into her room the very next day and blasted her with a bullet to the heart instantly killing her. The date was December 1.

On December 2, ten hours away in the city of Morelia, one of the biggest Mexican stars, Sergio Gómez, lead performer for the top-selling group K-Paz de la Sierra played before 20,000 people. After the show he was kidnapped, tortured, beaten and strangled to death.

The violence was still not over. A few days later, the police in the southern state of Oaxaca discovered the body of José Luis Aquino, a trumpeter with the band Los Conde—a group made up mostly of brothers and cousins. His feet and hands were bound and his head was encased in a plastic bag.

Much of the death and violence stems from the close intertwined relationship between Mexican musicians and the Mexican drug cartels. Mexican singers and bands sing songs—*narcocorridos*— about the drug barons. The *corridistas* are frequently bankrolled by the drug cartels to launder their drug profits. The gangsters often taunt The Man by jamming police radio frequencies with *narcocorridos*. Sometimes the songs entertain the top drug dealers, and sometimes they upset them, usually with tragic results.

The tradition of songs about outlaws in Mexico goes back to the late nineteenth and early twentieth century ballads that commemorated revolutionaries such as Emiliano Zapata and Pancho Villa. The first *narcocorrido*, titled *El Contrabandista* was recorded in 1934. It was written by Juan Gaytan and sung by the duo Gaytan y Cantú. It tells the sad tale of a smuggler's journey from liquor to drugs, following the end of Prohibition.

Comencí a vender champán, tequila y vino habanero.

Pero este yo no sabía lo que sufre un prisionero

Muy pronto compré automóvil, propedad con residencia,
Sin saber que en poco tiempo iba a ir la penitencia.
Por vender la cocaine, la morfina y mariguana
Me llevaron prisionero a las dos de la mañana.

I began selling champagne, tequila and Havana wine,
But I did not know what a prisoner suffers.
Soon I bought an automobile, property with a house,
Without knowing that in a short time I would be going to jail
For selling cocaine, morphine and marijuana,
They took me prisoner at two in the morning.

The genre began to explode in the late 1960's with the success of the group that is to this day the most famous and successful of *narcocorrido* bands—Los Tigres del Norte. They have sold well over 30 million records, won seven Grammy Awards, and have a star on the Hollywood Walk of Fame. They began composing songs about the usual themes of love and betrayal but by the 1980s were writing and singing songs about the narcotics trade and immigration to *el otro lado*—the other side (the United States). In 1988, for their hit album *Corridos Prohibitos* (Forbidden Songs), they shed their usual fancy cowboy duds and appeared on the cover as a bunch of street toughs in a police lineup. In the 1990s they began recording political *corridos* attacking corruption in the Mexican government. Their album *Jefe de Jefes* (Boss of Bosses) is a portrait of contemporary Mexicans from peasant farmers to immigrants, drug smugglers to greedy politicians. It was ambitious, but Mexican intellectuals still dismissed them as making *música naca*—music for hicks. Nonetheless they developed a faithful audience of millions, in Mexico, Latin America, and in the giant Latino Diaspora in the USA.

The huge success of Los Tigres del Norte and the many other bands and singers who have followed in their wake is particularly remarkable considering the fact that they sing in Spanish, and that their traditional, old-fashioned melodies are led by the unsexiest instrument ever invented—the accordion. These constraints have prevented their music from migrating through to the larger, mainstream audience outside of Mexico. And while they believe that their songs provide a "voice for the voiceless", they also write many commissioned songs for brutally violent gangsters, who buy *corridos* as status symbols alongside pricey cars, fancy haciendas and hot women. As a result, their music is often in trouble with The Man. Most *narcocorridos* are banned by radio and TV stations in Mexico and the United States and so are instead primarily sold as CDs in giant *tienguis*—the outdoor flea markets that are ubiquitous across Mexico, California and Arizona.

Giving credit where it is due, the creation of Mexico's most violent and reviled musical genre really comes not from Los Tigres del Norte but from Angel Gonzalez, the nearly-forgotten composer who wrote many tunes for them and for other *narcocorrido* bands. Gonzalez, from his hometown village of Basuchil, began his long songwriting career with a shocking and ground-breaking *corrido* called *Contrabando y Traición* (Smuggling and Betrayal).

> *Salieron de San Ysidro, procedentes de Tijuana,*
> *Traian las llantas del carro repletas de hierba mala*
> *Eran Emilio Varela y Camelia la tejana*

> They left San Ysidro, coming from Tijuana,
> They had their tires filled with bad grass,
> They were Emilio Verela and Camelia the Texan.

The song seemed revolutionary not just because it glorified drug smugglers, but because it glorified Camelia, a female drug smuggler and murderer. In the ballad, when Camelia discovers her partner/lover has betrayed her, she shoots him dead. The song became a huge hit. It was adapted into a movie. Camelia became a legend. Soon there were spin-offs and dozens of other songwriters trying to replicate the formula and write *corridos* each more violent and lurid than the last. Angel Gonzalez was not just a popular songwriter but the father of a new genre, and Camelia was leading lady in many more songs, shooting out rival gangs, getting betrayed by narcs, ending up in Texan prisons, and dying—always bravely—in hails of bullets.

Camelia, and all the characters in Gonzalez' songs, are fictional. Paulino Vargas, who has superseded Gonzalez so that to the Mexican songwriting community he is now considered the grandmaster of the *narco* genre, has taken *narco* songwriting to a more interesting and much more dangerous level. Vargas' songs are not about fictional characters, but real ones. Some recently deceased. Others still very much alive. Vargas researches his stories like a reporter.

"When I have to make a *corrido* about someone, I go where the incident happened," says Vargas. "I see something on television, the radio, in the newspaper, and if the character interests me I make a trip and see how it was, what happened, to have some idea of what I'm going to say. I investigate the story. If there are relatives, I ask their permission, and if not I just shoot it out there without permission. But I have to be sure it is factual. I don't like to invent things. It has to be true. You know, the public knows the difference. They can tell what isn't real and what is. The public is a monster that you can't fool. For me, what works best is what's closest to the truth—though of course you have to add a bit of a *morbo*." (a morbid twist.)

Vargas has written over a thousand songs—an impressive number. Not even Bob Dylan, considered one of the most prolific songwriters ever, has written quite that many (though most would agree his are, shall we say, of considerably higher quality.) Most of

Vargas' are specifically about the melodramatic exploits of particular drug smugglers, and of the DEA agents or rival dealers who brought them down. Sometimes, though, he writes of the broader themes of the drug trade, such as his hit song, *Les Super Capos*, that explores the George Bush/CIA/Contras/cocaine affair.

Rosalino "Chalino" Sánchez, another, perhaps even bigger star of the illicit Mexican music scene, stayed closer to the traditions of the *narcocorrido*. At fifteen Chalino shot another kid who he believed had raped his sister, and went on the run to Los Angeles. In 1984 he began a career as a low-level smuggler of drugs and people across the border. After being caught and jailed, he discovered a new avocation—writing songs about the other crooks who were behind bars with him. On his release he discovered a way to record the songs and find an audience for them. Mexican and American street toughs responded enthusiastically to him, and many of these *valientes* (brave men, or knaves, depending on your point of view) commissioned him to write songs about their exploits. He was the real thing. He once bluntly described his musical style saying, "I don't sing, I bark." He was not a pop dude wearing fancy white leather cowboy togs singing about Camelia, but rather a raw voice that listeners felt was authentic and true.

Chalino developed a new twist to the *narcocorrido*. Prior to him, most of the songs were murder ballads—songs about the recently deceased. Indeed, it was claimed that young *valientes* would get into fights with the crazy goal of getting shot and becoming *corrido* heroes. Realizing that there was probably more business to be had celebrating live gangsters than commemorating dead ones, Chalino began writing songs, usually under commission, praising the bravery of various gangland characters. He found many customers, their jeans filled with rolls of Benjamins, who were pleased to pay him for his work.

The Man, of course, was not impressed with his music, and though Chalino tried to get airplay many times, neither U.S. nor Mexican radio stations would carry his songs. It didn't slow his career down, though, as his records and fame spread across Mexico and California, especially after a wild incident on January 20, 1992. Chalino was singing in a club in Coachella, California (long before the town's now-famous music festival) when a man approached the stage, pulled out a gun and shot him in the side. True to badass form, Chalino pulled out his own gun and shot back. By the time the incident was over, the would-be assassin had been shot in the mouth with his own gun, a member of Chalino's band and five audience members were wounded, and one killed. Back in Sinaloa it was said the toll was really much higher, except that many of the injured were "illegals" who ran from the club and hightailed it for the border before the police showed up.

The deadly incident was widely reported both in Mexico and the US—even making ABC's *World News Tonight*. Chalino's record sales skyrocketed and his concerts sold out. Drug lords were offering him $20,000 or $30,000 to write a song about them. Four months after the Coachella shooting, he performed at the Salon Bugambilias in Culiacán. Chalino left the concert with his brother, a cousin, and several young women. Before the entourage got far they were pulled over by a group of armed men flashing police badges. Chalino was taken away at gunpoint. The next morning, May 16, 1992, his body was found in an irrigation canal, blindfolded with two bullets in the back of his head.

Were they really police? *¿Quien sabe?* Some say they were. Others claim the killers were thugs with fake police ID's hired by a big-time narco to rub out the bard. Still others claim they <u>were</u> police, but working off-hours as security for a drug cartel—a not-uncommon occurrence in northwestern Mexico in the 1990s.

Chalino's death did nothing to slow down his popularity. Not only did his own cassettes and CD's continue to sell, but Mexican *corridistas* rushed out dozens of verses in honor of the martyred singer. His widow claims she knows of over 150 songs dedicated to her dead husband. There were also hundreds of imitators—*Chalinitos*, as they were called, trying to sing, dress, and live like their idol. At least one of them, Saúl Viera, *El Gavilancillo* (the Little Hawk), died as Chalino did—assassinated in 1997. Most of these aspirants to narco-musical glory were male, but at least one, Lolita Capilla, *La Brona de Sonora* was a very young girl. Her cassette covers depict her in a frilly white confirmation dress with an assault rifle in her slim arms.

The Man was not impressed. In 1987 the Governor of Sinaloa made a formal call to "suppress the exaltation of violence" in radio programming, and there were similar efforts made by the authorities in Sonora, Chihuahua, and Baja California. *Narcocorridos* cannot be heard on Mexican radio, but the ban has actually increased the sales of the illicit tunes. Since the music cannot be heard on the radio, and since people often think that if something is prohibited it must be good, the records sell like hot *tamales* in stores and flea markets across the country.

Writing and singing *narcocorridos* is a dangerous business, both for the musicians and for the gangsters they write about, though many of the drug barons have a very cavalier attitude towards it. El Al de la Sierra, now considered the most popular of the Sinaloan *chalinitos,* describes his work this way:

"This singing thing is a job, like being a journalist, you might say. Someone pays me to make a *corrido* and I do it. Why not? To me, it's no crime, because it's my job. So if a drug trafficker comes to me, wants me to compose a *corrido* for him, I do it with pleasure. Sure, I try to protect him, I say to him, 'Give me a nickname to use' but a lot of them don't want that:

"I want my own name!"

"Okay, fine, it's your problem. I'll do it with your name,"

The lust for infamy gets absurd. The *narcocorrido* songwriters even report completely straight businessmen, innocent of any crime, who commission songs written about themselves, using their real names, glorifying their fictitious gun battles. Songwriter and studio owner Antonio Uriarte recalls being kidnapped by some *narcos* and locked in a room until he had composed a song of their misdeeds. Others are a little less forceful with their demands. "They give me a list, telling me the name of their *rancho*, what they do for a living—if they want me to mention what they do for a living—just stuff like that. They say 'Put it in there that I like women a lot,' that he's had three, four women, and that kind of thing. So I take down the most important information and then, based on the list, I go and write the verses and it's done. Some want their name to be used, some not—they give me some code, because if a *corrido* comes out saying that somebody has two, three women, and he has a wife at home, when he gets back she'll be after him with a broomstick."

Angry wives with broomsticks seem like only a fairly minor consideration. The Man can buy cheap discs and listen to *narcocorridos* as well. While police do not divulge their investigation techniques, it surely seems likely that they would be interested in hearing recorded songs extolling illegal activities by named conspirators. It might not stand up as evidence in court, but it would certainly be a good start for some scrutiny of malfeasance.

Acapulco-based singer Gabriel Villanueva Noyola confirms this with a story about a *corrido* he was asked to write by a young thug who told him he killed another guy with a machete. Noyola told the man he would write it for him but warned him that "the day that record comes out they'll take you prisoner." The notoriety-hungry hoodlum insisted, and so "I wrote the *corrido*, and about two months later the *judiciales* grabbed him. All because of the *corrido*. Because if something is under cover and you shake the hive, the bees get stirred up, no? This kid didn't want to believe me, but the family of the fellow who was killed heard the record or the cassette, they listened, and two months later the police grabbed him, and it seems he had to pay about fifteen thousand bills before they let him go."

As for the singers and songwriters themselves, the dangers can come both from the police and from their gangster patrons. Monterey-based star singer-songwriter Julián Garza tells a gruesome story of one of the many parties he has been hired to play at that make him question his choice of profession.

"There were a lot of people, and the man who had hired me was some kind of policeman, because they had improvised a police force there, armed with 30-30's. I've always been scared of those kind of people, I'm scared of them because there are some *cabrónes* who don't reason—fucking savages. As on this occasion. So we began to sing, and I see these policemen who were going around plastered, sticking their rifles in people's faces, clearing their way through the crowd, holding them by the barrel, all fucked up. They got shit-faced on mescal or who the hell knows what. And suddenly a *cabrón* comes up and pulls out a goddamn pistol and says 'Sing me *Las Tres Tumbas, cabrón*! Three times, or else you die!'"

Garza complied, but as soon as he finished, another drunken lout demanded that the band play *his* favorite tune, *El Bayo de Cara Blanca*, again three times. They wearily complied, and the repeated renditions of the song wound up the huge crowd so much that in the middle of the third repeat, two of the hooligans (or cops, or whatever the hell they were) pulled out guns and began shooting at each other. None of the bullets hit their intended mark, and instead a young kid, standing by the bandstand fell to the floor, struck in the chest.

Garza stopped playing and went down to the floor to tend to the wounded boy, but then, he says, "up comes the *cabrón* who hired us, completely shit-faced already, and says to me, 'Listen, why aren't you playing?'

"'There's a kid hurt here. How am I going to play?'

"'No, leave the kid there. You have a contract with me.'

"*Hijo de su pinche madre!*"

The band left the body on the floor and returned to the stage but wrapped things up as soon as they could and got out vowing never to play again for the unruly cops and their rowdy friends. To

Garza's chagrin, a few months later, he was expected to do a return engagement. He reports his response as follows:

"No, you know what? Go off and fuck your mother, go tame that bunch of goddamn savages of yours. Your place there, I don't want to even go over it in an airplane, *cabrón*."

Perhaps by now the reader is feeling the same way about this moronically violent musical sub-culture. *Adelanté!* Let's move on. *Si vamanos.*

Music vs Donald Trump

The battle between Music and The Man can take many forms. Sometimes it is about The Man harassing musicians; other times it is about The Man wanting to use musicians, and their music—and the musicians resisting.

Donald Trump was impressed for many years with the Rolling Stones. It was probably not their music that attracted him, but their reputation. They've been known for years as "The World's Greatest Rock and Roll Band", and Trump loves anything that is called "the greatest", "the biggest" or "the best." So when he began to campaign for the American Presidency in 2016, he consistently used the songs of the Stones—in particular, *Start Me Up* and *You Can't Always Get What You Want* as fanfares for his grand entrances and exits to-and-from his high-octane campaign rallies.

He didn't ask the Stones for permission, and they didn't give it. The band's lawyers fired off cease-and-desist orders, and their publicist, Fran Curtis, announced, "The Rolling Stones have never given permission to the Trump campaign to use their songs and have requested that they cease all use immediately." Trump in standard fashion just deflected questions about the dispute, saying "I have no problem with that. I like Mick Jagger," and continued using the music though out the campaign and subsequently during his Presidential rallies.

It wasn't the first time he had locked horns with the band. In 1989, he came up with the idea that he wanted to impress his friends by hiring the Stones to play at his Trump Plaza Casino in Atlantic City, New Jersey. According to John R. O'Donnell, an executive at the casino, Trump forced O'Donnell to negotiate a bad deal—$4.2 million for three shows—that made it impossible to make a profit. Trump was convinced he could sell tickets for $250 - $1000 apiece, and even though O'Donnell warned him he was going to lose money, Trump insisted, "I want the fucking Rolling Stones. I told everybody the Rolling Stones are going to be playing at Trump Plaza. I'm coming down to watch them. My friends are coming down. Don't lose this deal, Jack."

The concerts were indeed a disaster—the casino lost $800,000, and the Stones refused to have their picture taken with Trump's arms draped around them, which he desperately wanted them to do. O'Donnell had been promised a bonus for organizing the concerts, but Trump stiffed him out of it. He complained to Trump, saying, "You wanted to do this deal. We told you not to do it. You did it anyway. But who's going to get beat up now? Me! Because it's my bottom line."

O'Donnell reports that Trump was silent for a minute, then exclaimed, "Well, sue the bastards."

"Sue who? The Rolling Stones?"

"Yeah."

"What?"

"Fucking sue them, Jack. I want to sue them. It's their fault we took the loss."

O'Donnell went to the trouble of discussing the matter with Trump's general counsel, who advised that there were no grounds for a lawsuit. Trump continued to press for one, but eventually forgot about it, and the idea was dropped. The incident was revisited four years later in an episode of *The Simpsons* titled *Rosebud* in which Trump surrogate Montgomery Burns hires The Ramones to play at his birthday party, then, when displeased with the band's performance of *Happy Birthday*, tells his factotum Smithers to "Have the Rolling Stones killed."

"But sir, they're not The R-"

"Do as I say!"

The Stones were not the only musicians who locked horns with Trump during his years as a casino-owner. Trump booked Frank Sinatra and Sammy Davis Jr. for a twelve-night run to open his new Atlantic City casino in 1990. When Trump learned that Davis had become diagnosed with cancer, he cancelled the song-and-dance man's booking and tried to beat down Sinatra's fee. Sinatra sent his manager Eliot Weisman with a message to give to the casino owner. The exact message, Weisman recalls, was, "Sinatra says to go fuck yourself."

Trump's battles with the Rolling Stones (and, as we will see, with many other musicians) during the 2016 election campaign was not the first time that a right-wing Republican presidential candidate had crossed swords with a musician. In 1984, handlers for Ronald Reagan wanted to use Bruce Springsteen's anthem, *Born in the USA* for the President's re-election campaign, apparently not concerned the song's lyrics protest the same conservative policies that Reagan was himself enacting. Springsteen did not give permission, so instead Reagan just invoked Springsteen's name in a speech in the blue-collar town of Hammonton, New Jersey, saying, "America's future rests in a thousand dreams inside your hearts; it rests in the message of hope in songs so many young Americans admire: New Jersey's own Bruce Springsteen. And helping you make those dreams come true is what this job of mine is all about."

Springsteen was furious at being co-opted by the President, and responded at a concert in Pittsburgh, saying, "There's really something dangerous happening to us out there. We're slowly getting split up into two different Americas. Things are getting taken away from people that need them and given to people that don't need them, and there's a promise getting broken. In the beginning the idea was that we all live here a little bit like a family, where the strong can help the weak ones, and the rich can help the poor ones. I don't think the American dream was that everybody was going to make it or that everybody was going to make a billion dollars, but it was that everybody was going to have an opportunity and the chance to live a life with some decency and some dignity and a chance for some self-respect."

If that wasn't clear enough, Springsteen continued, in an interview with *Rolling Stone*, "You see the Reagan reelection ads on TV—you know, 'It's morning in America.' And you say, well, it's not morning in Pittsburgh. It's not morning above 125th Street in New York. It's midnight, and, like, there's a bad moon risin'. And that's why when Reagan mentioned my name in New Jersey, I felt it was another manipulation, and I had to disassociate myself from the President's kind words."

Reagan was not the first Republican presidential candidate to co-opt music for his own use. Abraham Lincoln had the lyrics of the old folk song *Rosin The Bow* turned into campaign theme song *Lincoln and Liberty*.

More recently, the battles continued during the Bush-Cheney campaigns in 2000 and 2004, the McCain-Palin campaign in 2008, the Obama-Romney battle in 2012, and others. Both Sting and Tom Petty had to force George W. Bush from using their songs. John Mellencamp, who describes himself as being "as left-wing as you can get," has repeatedly had to stop the use of his songs by Ronald Reagan and George W. Bush.

One way to make sure your songs won't be co-opted by politicians you don't like is to publicly announce what you think of them. During the sabre-rattling run-up to the very controversial Gulf War,

Natalie Maines, lead singer of the Dixie Chicks, told her audience in the Shepherds Bush Empire theatre in London, "Just so you know, we're on the good side with y'all. We do not want this war, this violence, and we're ashamed that the President of the United States is from Texas."

The comment set off a firestorm of response back in the USA. There were the predictable yowls of reaction from Rush Limbaugh and other conservative commentators. Radio stations sponsored bulldozer crushes of Dixie Chicks CD's. The group's latest records sank in the ratings. Disc Jockeys who played their songs were fired. Tour sponsors Lipton and Pepsi were threatened with boycotts.

Maines was forced to make an apology, saying, "As a concerned American citizen I apologize to President Bush because my remark was disrespectful. I feel that whoever holds that office should be treated with the utmost respect. We are currently in Europe and witnessing a huge anti-American sentiment as a result of the perceived rush to war. While war may remain a viable option, as a mother, I just want to see every possible alternative exhausted before children and American lives are lost. I love my country. I am a proud American."

Three years later, the controversy had still not gone away and neither had President Bush, Vice-President Dick Cheney or the war in Iraq. Haines recanted her previous apology, saying, "I apologized for disrespecting the office of the President, but I don't feel that way anymore. I don't feel he is owed any respect whatsoever."

Bush never used Dixie Chicks tunes as backdrop scores for his rallies, but the next Republican nominee for President was very keen on having musical accompaniment. Abba had to demand that John McCain's campaign stop using their song *Take a Chance on Me*, and John Bon Jovi, who had thrown $30,000 fundraising dinners for Barack Obama at his home, had to fight to stop McCain from using his *Who Says You Can't Go Home* at campaign rallies. Jackson Browne successfully sued John McCain for what Browne's lawyer described as an "utterly reprehensible misappropriation of Jackson Browne's endorsement."

Dave Grohl of the Foo-Fighters had to fight the McCain campaign's use of their *My Hero*. McCain was definitely not their hero. Van Halen told the McCain campaign that "permission was not sought or granted nor would it have been given," for the use at rallies of their *Right Now*. Sarah Wilson of Heart said she felt "completely fucked over by Sarah Palin's use of her song *Barracuda*." Palin may have been attracted to the song because her high school nickname, which she apparently wore proudly, was "Sarah Barracuda." Wilson, in her cease-and-desist letter, said that Palin had "views and values that in no way represent us as American women."

The most interesting skirmish of Music vs The Man—actually Music vs The Woman—was when Sarah Palin used country singer Gretchen Peters' CMA song-of-the-year *Independence Day* without permission. Peters lashed out, saying that the song, which described the plight of an abused woman, was being totally co-opted, and that it was "beyond irony" that it would be used by Palin, who "would ban abortion even in cases of rape and incest," and would "set women's rights back decades." However instead of suing the campaign to make them stop playing the song, Peters donated all her election season royalties from the song to Planned Parenthood, and encouraged others to make similar donations, under the name "Sarah Palin", thus helping to raise one million dollars for the organization, to the chagrin of the Vice-Presidential candidate.

The battle continued. Tea Party favorite Newt Gingrich was smacked with cease-and-desist orders from Survivor (for using *Eye of the Tiger* without authorization) and The Heavy, for *How Do You Like Me Now?* (Answer: not much). Cyndi Lauper rejected the use of her classic *True Colors* in an attack-ad by the DNC on Mitt Romney, saying, "Mitt Romney can discredit himself without the use of my work."

Romney's campaign was threatened with lawsuits from both Al Green and Somali-Canadian singer K'Naan, whose hit song *Waving Flag* had been properly licensed by Coca-Cola for use as the anthem of the FIFA World Cup in South Africa, but then used without authorization by Mitt Romney's campaign. K'Naan stated that, "I'm for immigrants. I'm for poor people, and that doesn't seem to be what he's endorsing." To add insult to injury, he offered the Obama campaign use of the song, if they wanted it, for free.

Don Henley successfully sued California Republican senatorial candidate Chuck Devore for using a re-written version of The Eagles' *The Boys of Summer* in an attack ad on Obama and liberalism. Devore's team argued it was a "parody", but the judge ruled it was not, and so the Senate aspirant had to settle financially with The Eagles and apologize for the unauthorized use.

The battle went international with the unapproved use of MBMT's song *Kids* by French Presidential candidate Nicholas Sarkozy. The President's party, the UMP (Union Movement Populaire) offered a token one euro in compensation. Ultimately the American psychedelic band received 29,000 Euros, which they donated to an artists' rights organization.

In 2012, Twisted Sister's tattooed frontman Dee Snider stated, "I emphatically denounce Paul Ryan's use of the song *We're Not Gonna Take It* as recorded by my band. There is almost nothing I agree with Paul Ryan, except perhaps the use of the P90X," which is a home fitness workout system.

The libertarian Senator Rand Paul apparently loves Rush, calling the prog-rock band his favorite group and used their lyrics in his speeches. The group, which seems to have libertarian tendencies themselves, and once quoted Ayn Rand in their liner notes, nonetheless hit Paul with a cease-and-desist letter over the unapproved use in a campaign video of one of their songs. The band stated that as Canadians they did not want to get into American politics. Then drummer/lyricist Neil Peart went further, saying he would never vote for Rand Paul and that, "it is very obvious the politician hates women and brown people."

Once Donald Trump descended on his gold-plated escalator to begin his 2016 Presidential campaign, the battle got even uglier. Trump used Rolling Stones songs without concern for repeated cease-and-desist letters, and also stole a wide variety of other songs from other artists for his rallies. The campaign employed REM's *It's the End of the World as we Know It*. Singer and lyricist Michael Stipe responded by saying, "Go fuck yourselves, the lot of you—you sad, attention-grabbing, power-hungry little men. Do not use our music or my voice for your moronic charade of a campaign."

Barbra Streisand's music was used to pump up Trump rallies to the MAGA crowds, apparently unaware that she has strong liberal sentiments stretching back to the 1960s. She hated it. "I'm just so saddened by this thing happening to our country. It's making me fat. I hear what he said, and I have to go eat pancakes now, and pancakes are very fattening."

Adele objected to Trump playing her songs *Skyfall* and *Rolling in the Deep*. Steven Tyler of Aerosmith asked him to stop using his *Dream On* at rallies. Trump played the song anyway, then haughtily tweeted that he had "a better one to take its place." The "better one" was Neil Young's *Rockin' in the Free World*. Young's management company responded with a release stating, "Donald Trump was not authorized to use *Rockin' in the Free World*. Neil Young, a Canadian citizen, is a supporter of Bernie Sanders for President of the United States of America."

Trump then moved on to use the Queen anthem *We are the Champions,* a song so bombastic that the band's guitarist Brian May resisted recording it back in 1977. He resisted even more the use of it by the Trump campaign, which he described as "unsavory," posting to his website that "I can confirm that permission to use the track was neither sought nor given."

Pharrell was even less happy about the use of his song *Happy*, especially just hours after a mass shooting at a Pittsburgh synagogue. "On the day of a mass murder of 11 human beings at the hands of a deranged 'nationalist'," his cease-and-desist letter told Trump, "you played the song *Happy* to a crowd at a political event in Indiana. There was nothing "happy" about the tragedy inflicted upon the country on Saturday and no permission was granted for the use of this song for this purpose."

None of these musical controversies slowed Trump down, of course. In January 2017 he became President. Unlike previous inaugurations, almost no singers or other show business personalities attended. After his election he took to slamming various singers including Bette Midler, Beyonce, Jay Z, and Bruce Springsteen in rally speeches. The only well-known singer who aligned himself with Trump, other than rock dinosaur Ted Nugent, is rapper Kanye West, who was invited to the White House and arrived with a red MAGA hat on, crowing, "Trump is on his hero's journey right now. He might not have thought he'd have a crazy motherfucker like me."

Trump has a strange and rich connection with rap. His name has been referenced, not by any means always positively, though neither always negatively, in over 300 rap songs over the past 30 years. Obviously his much larger-than-life personality is part of the reason. Perhaps it is simply because there are lots of words that rhyme with his name. Try finding a good rhyme for Clinton, Gingrich, Merkel, Sarkozy or Trudeau.

In the summer of 2019 Trump got involved with another of the many bizarre events that have peppered his Presidency. Trump learned, from fellow ex-reality-TV star Kim Kardashian, that American rapper A$AP Rocky had been arrested in Sweden and was in jail on charges stemming from a street brawl in Stockholm. Why Trump chose to get involved in the matter is unknown, but perhaps it was a combination of being able to use the arrest to try to get some street cred with black voters in the 2020 election, and also the opportunity to get in some digs at Sweden for their Social Democratic government and especially their liberal immigration policies.

"Give A$AP Rocky his FREEDOM," Trump tweeted. "We do so much for Sweden but it doesn't seem to work the other way around. Sweden should focus on its real crime problem." Of course, Sweden's "real crime problem" was caused, in his mind, by recent immigrants to the country from Africa and Eastern Europe.

Trump sent his top hostage negotiator and national security advisor Robert O'Brien to Sweden to work on the case, then personally called Swedish Prime Minister Stefan Löfven asking him to drop the charges, and telling him he would personally pay for A$AP's bail. Chuck Berry and Jerry Lee Lewis would have been so lucky to have President Dwight Eisenhower intercede in the same way during their legal battles in the 1950s. Löfven told Trump that in Sweden, politicians had no control over legal cases, and also that the country did not use a bail system.

Trump's subsequent attempts to interfere in the case were only revealed publicly during the Congressional hearings in December that led to his impeachment. U.S. diplomat David Holmes testified that he was present when US Ambassador to the European Union (and Trump donor) Gordon Sondland called President Trump from a Kiev restaurant to discuss two matters—the upcoming A$AP trial, and Trump's attempts to persuade Ukraine President Volodymyr Zelensky to try to find dirt on Joe Biden and his son, Hunter Biden. Sondland advised Trump to stay out of the Swedish matter, and "let A$AP get sentenced, play the racism card, give him a ticker tape when he comes home." He added that Sweden should have released the rapper on Trump's word, but that the President could at least tell the Kardashians that he tried.

The trial began in Stockholm on July 30. Trump's hostage guy O'Brien demanded that A$AP be given a hotel room by the Swedish court and threatened "negative consequences" if the case was not resolved quickly. It was. On August 14, A$AP flew out of the country on his private jet. Trump, according to a White House official familiar with the episode, fumed that he did not get enough credit from the public for the rapper's quick release.

Much of President Trump's fourth year in office was spent dealing, in his idiosyncratic way, with the Covid-19 pandemic. At the height of the first wave of the crisis in March and April of 2020, Trump stayed inside the White House, not venturing out, except for a brief visit to see the departure of the hospital ship USNS Comfort from Norfolk, Virginia. On May 5, 2020 he flew to Arizona to visit the Honeywell factory that was by then making masks for the deadly health crisis. In a totally surreal moment, television cameras photographed Trump, himself maskless and not observing the mandated six feet of social distance, inspecting the manufacturing process while Guns and Roses' version of the song *Live and Let Die* played over background speakers. Once this way-too-appropriate song ended, Trump made a rally-style speech, then faux-dramatically left the facility to the beat of his fave campaign song, the Stones' *You Can't Always Get What You Want*. When the band's lawyers sent yet another cease-and-desist letter, Trump complained that the British band's resistance to his using their music meant that he felt they were "un-American". Meanwhile his lawyers got to work responding to a new lawsuit, this one from Neil Young over the use of his music in the 2020 Trump Presidential campaign.

5. Only in America

Frank Sinatra

Frank Sinatra hated the police. Through his entire life, he referred to all of them—from the New Jersey beat police of his youth, to the FBI agents who trailed him through most of the 50's and 60's, to J. Edgar Hoover, to Attorney General Robert Kennedy—as "fuckin' cops". The phrase he usually used was "fuckin' cops and reporters." In a fine turn of irony, though, he actually got named "Frank" because of a policeman.

His mother, Dolly, was the terror of Hoboken. She was an incredibly foul-mouthed and colorful character. Frank's lifelong valet, George Jacobs, said that he'd never heard a woman curse like Dolly. "Fuck you, you fucking son of a bitch fucking bastard motherfucker" was apparently a typical Dolly sentence. It probably came in handy when she needed to muscle up votes or favors. She muscled up a lot of votes in the dock-towns of New Jersey. Her specialty was her own people—the Italian immigrants who had arrived in large numbers (frequently entered "Without Papers"—hence the derogatory nickname "WOP") in the first twenty years of the twentieth century.

However she had much bigger political goals, most of which involved the Irish who ran the tough towns in those days. Instead of picking an Italian godfather for her newborn son, she picked an Irish one—a local journalist with close ties to a Hoboken police captain. The most famous entertainer in the world was supposed to be named Martin, after his own father, but a befuddled priest at his christening instead named him Francis Albert Sinatra, after his Irish godfather.

Sinatra would have many other godfathers in his life—the rest of them Italian, most of them leading hoodlums in the Mafia. Indeed, the famous scene in the book and film *The Godfather* involving the decapitated head of a racehorse and the classic line about "making him an offer he can't refuse" are popularly thought to be based on gangster Johnny "Don Giovanni" Roselli's real-life efforts (denied by both Sinatra and Roselli) to influence Columbia boss Harry Cohn to give Sinatra the role of Angelo Maggio in *From Here to Eternity*.

The pampered only child of Dolly and Marty Sinatra was brought up in the snazziest home in one of the roughest neighborhoods of Hoboken. He got to meet The Man early in life. His mother was an abortionist who frequently found herself in courthouses charged with what was then of course an illegal, but for many young women, a life-saving, operation. His father had worked as a driver for the Mob, and had been arrested for receiving stolen goods. His uncle Dominick, a boxer (under the name Champ Sieger), was charged with malicious mischief. Another uncle, Gus was arrested several times for running numbers. A third, Babe was convicted of murder and sent to the slammer for fifteen years.

Frank's own first serious run-in with the law came in 1938, when as a young singer of 23, he was charged first with "seduction" and then a few weeks later with adultery. Sinatra was one of the most infamous stickmen of show business, bedding hundreds of women over the eighty-three years of his life. He got in trouble with lots of them, but only Antoinette Della Penta Francke pressed a charge of "seduction" against him.

The charges were eventually dropped, but to the chagrin of the "Chairman of the Board", the famous mugshot taken of him has lived on. It now hangs in bars around the world, a tribute of sorts to this notorious "Bad Boy" of music. But the saga of "Sinatra vs The Man" is quite unlike that of any of the other stories chronicled in these pages. You think rock stars invented the hedonistic lifestyle? Hardly. Sinatra out-drank, out-spent, out-lived all of them—and not just for a few wild years, but for five decades! Think the young generation that arrived in the 60s invented the idea of flaunting authority and living outside the law? Frank had been doing that since the 1940s. Think stars like John Lennon had big FBI files? Sinatra's was 2400 pages long!

Here's how Bono paid tribute as he presented Sinatra with the Grammy Legend Award in 1994, "Rock 'n Roll people love Frank Sinatra because Frank Sinatra has got what we want—swagger and attitude. Rock 'n Roll plays at being tough, but this guy, well, he's the boss. The boss of bosses. The Man. The big bang of pop. I'm not going to mess with him—are you?"

Sinatra, though, didn't just waste his confidence and swagger on Vegas audiences, Hollywood starlets, Mafia crime bosses or fawning entertainment columnists. And certainly not on low-level cops or politicians. He was up there—working with the real Man. He was on close terms with every American President from Franklin Roosevelt to Ronald Reagan, as well as a couple of Vice-Presidents—Hubert Humphrey and Spiro Agnew. He didn't just sing for them or organize their inauguration events—he played a major role in getting two of them, John F. Kennedy and Ronald Reagan, elected, and, it will be argued shortly, played a major role in a scenario that possibly led to JFK being killed.

"Look, make no mistake about it. Sinatra's a thug," said President Kennedy to his political advisors. "Let's face it. Let's be aware of it and let's try to use it to our advantage."

The Chairman of the Board, the biggest entertainer of his time, played on the very biggest stages of the twentieth century —in music, in movies and in politics. Moreover, said bandleader Tommy

Dorsey, "He's the most fascinating man in the world—just don't put your hand in the cage."

It was no cakewalk for Sinatra advancing from being a singing waiter in the mob-controlled roadhouses of New Jersey to being the biggest singer in the world. He began with a group called the Hoboken Four, then got an offer to join Harry James' big band. James thought the name "Sinatra" sounded too Italian, so offered him the gig if he would change his name to "Frankie Satin". The future Frankie Satin asked his mother Dolly, his de facto manager, for advice.

"I'll give him 'Frankie Satin' with a shot to knock him cold," she offered. "Your name is Sinatra, and it's going to stay Sinatra. So tell him to fuck off with this 'Frankie Satin' crap."

Sinatra passed this on, probably not in quite those words, to the bandleader, who acquiesced, and Sinatra began touring and headlining with him. As always, his eyes were on the brass ring. Sinatra left Harry James after a few years to join the Tommy Dorsey Band—one of the biggest in America. With the Dorsey band, he became a huge star. By 1942 he decided it was time to go solo. Dorsey, a powerful and testy personality himself, refused to let Sinatra out of his contract, until, it is believed, the singer's godfather, Mafia don Willie Moretti persuaded the bandleader, with several thousand dollars and, more to the point, a gun held to his head, to let Frank go.

The move worked. Within a year Sinatra was playing at the Paramount Theater in Manhattan to sold-out concerts thousands of screaming, swooning teenagers—so-called "bobbysoxers". His sidekick Nick Sevano described it as "absolute pandemonium—the girls throwing their panties and brassieres at him and going nuts, absolutely nuts."

The Man took note—and was not impressed. "The hysteria which accompanies his presence in public is in no way part of an artistic manifestation", said the New York *Herald-Tribune*. Doctors called the swooning "a nervous disease and a harmful thing", "mass frustrated love without direction" and "mammary hyperesthesia" (a previously undiagnosed ailment that presumably translates as overly sensitive breasts).

The head of the New York Police Department's missing persons bureau blamed the singer for the problem of runaway girls and recommended he be exiled to New Guinea. One Member of Congress called him the "main instigator of juvenile delinquency in America", and the Education Commissioner of New York City threatened to press charges against him for encouraging truancy, because thousands of girls were skipping school to attend his concerts. "We can't tolerate young people making a public display of losing control of their emotions," he whined.

Even worse was the resentment of servicemen during the war years. One soldier famously yelled at him in a nightclub, "Hey wop! Why aren't you in uniform?" Writer William Manchester claimed that Sinatra was "the most hated man of World War II, much more than Hitler," because all the sex-starved soldiers on the frontlines of the battles in the Pacific and Europe resented the many newspaper pictures of Sinatra, surrounded by enthusiastic girls. Sinatra publicly claimed he would love to join the Marines, but privately was relieved when he was rejected for service with a 4-F classification because of the perforated eardrum that had been damaged in childbirth.

Popular syndicated columnist Walter Winchell received an anonymous letter which he printed in his column alleging that Sinatra had paid $40,000 to bribe doctors to get him the 4-F classification. Even though the FBI investigated and cleared him of the claim, the damage was done. Frank's gilded reputation was beginning to be tarnished.

During the war years Sinatra began his 50-year-long association with politicians. Singing at a rally for the Democratic candidate for Governor of New Jersey, he also spoke on behalf of the wildly corrupt Mayor of Jersey City, Frank Hague. Fifty thousand people showed up to hear him. The pandemonium at the Paramount also continued. At a return date at the Manhattan theater, his performance required two hundred detectives, seventy patrolmen, fifty traffic cops, four hundred police reserves, twelve mounted police, twenty radio cars, two emergency trucks, and twenty policewomen to subdue the rioting music-loving teens. It is a reminder that the relationship is not always "Music *vs* The Man." Sometimes The Man is out in force, protecting music, and musicians—and not even charging for it.

Sinatra's fame now eclipsed that of the president. So the president, Franklin Roosevelt, invited him to the White House. The pair got along famously. "I told the President how well he looked," said Frank. "He kidded me about making girls faint and asked me how I do it. I said I wished to hell I knew."

The meeting outraged columnists in the right-wing Hearst newspapers, which only stiffened Frank's resolve. He donated $5,000 to the Roosevelt re-election campaign, made radio recordings and spoke at Carnegie Hall on behalf of the Democratic Party and the President.

In 1945 he truly established his liberal bona fides by starring in a short film called *The House I Live In*. The film, which would win Frank his first Academy Award, was made by RKO Pictures, directed by Mervyn Leroy and written by Albert Maltz. Maltz, whose unabashed leftwing loyalties would get him blacklisted from Hollywood by the House Un-American Activities Committee, will return in 1962 to our chronicle of Frank's battles with authority. In 1945, he had Sinatra talking tough to a gang of antisocial street-kids on a set portraying what looked like the mean streets of Hoboken:

"Look, fellas, religion makes no difference except maybe to a Nazi or somebody stupid. Why, people all over the world worship God in many different ways. God created everybody. He didn't create one people better than another…This wonderful country is made up of a hundred different kinds of people and a hundred different ways of talking and a hundred different ways of going to church. But they're all American ways."

Frank then burst into song, announcing that "the house he lived in" included all—black, white, Italian, Irish, Protestant, Catholic. The liberal sentiments of the short film were well received by some elements of post-war America. *Time* Magazine called it a "well-meaning project, part of a larger Sinatra crusade, whose message should be clear enough to anyone." *Cue* described the "microphone-hugging crooner" as now being "one of filmdom's leading and most vocal battlers for a democratic way of life." But not everyone agreed.

The success of the film led to Sinatra being invited to Gary, Indiana to try to settle a strike by the white students of a high school against the "pro-Negro" policies of their new principal, who had allowed the school's black students to share classrooms with whites, join the school orchestra, and swim in the school pool one day a week. Frank was greeted by five thousand angry, catcalling, whistling, foot-stomping white students and their blue-collar parents. He folded his arms and stared down at them for a full two minutes until they finally fell silent.

"I can lick any son of a bitch in this joint" were his first words to the racially charged crowd. That got their attention, and he followed it by imploring them to end their strike. "We've all done it," he told them. "We've all used the words *nigger* or *kike* or *mick* or *polack* or *dago*. Cut it out, kids. Go back to school."

Sharing the stage with Sinatra were the mayor of Gary, an influential local priest, and a group of politicians who supported the strike and opposed the integrationist policies of the new principal. Frank called one of them out, labeling the leader of the segregationists a "cheap meddler" and a "two-bit politician". "Surely you're not going to let a man like this influence you," he told the students. "You ought to run this bum out of town."

The priest stalked off the stage, and the mayor, red-faced with anger, told Sinatra, "Your remarks were most unfortunate. You were ill-advised in your statements, and what you said was a disservice to the cause and to the community."

Others disagreed. Sinatra received numerous awards for his work in Gary. The right-wing, though, also began to notice him. Gerald L.K. Smith, leader of the conservative America First party, testified before HUAC that Sinatra "acts as a front for Communist organizations". California senator Jack B. Tenney produced a list of Hollywood celebrities who he claimed had Communist leanings— Katherine Hepburn, Gregory Peck, Danny Kaye, John Garfield, and Frank Sinatra. Another right-winger, Gerval Murphy, director of the supreme council of the Knights of Columbus, also accused the singer of being aligned with Communists.

Sinatra did not back down for a minute. "The minute anyone tries to help the little guy, he's called a Communist. I'm getting so I expect crackpots to say things like that. The guy's a jerk."

Even more damaging to Frank's reputation than his passion for helping the little guy was his passion for power, specifically the dangerous, illicit power of the Mob. Once Frank had moved to Los Angeles in the 40s, he became entranced by Bugsy Siegel, the West Coast chief for Murder, Inc. Siegel was himself originally from New York, where he had been associated with gangsters Meyer Lansky, Frank Costello and Lucky Luciano. He was indicted for murder in 1940, but managed to beat the rap and hang out with the cream of Beverly Hills society.

Jo-Carroll Silvers, wife of comedian Phil Silvers, remembered how Sinatra and Silvers reacted to Siegel: "They were like two children seeing Santa Claus, or two little altar boys standing to pay homage to the Pope. They were wide-eyed and so very impressed by this man, who was then the chairman of the Mafia board. Bugsy was handsome, charming and very pleasant, but he also had an aura of danger about him that Frank would later cultivate. Phil and Frank were enthralled by him. They would brag about Bugsy and what he'd done and how many people he had killed. Sometimes they'd argue about whether Bugsy preferred to shoot his victims or simply chop them up with axes, and although I forget which was his preference, I will always remember the awe Frank had in his voice when he talked about him. He wanted to emulate Bugsy."

Both men had similar, grandiose ambitions. Bugsy want to build a city in the Nevada desert full of mob-controlled casinos. Sinatra wanted to be the king of that city. Both their dreams would come to pass.

In 1947, Joe Fischetti, the Chicago mob boss who had started as a foot-soldier in the Al Capone gang, invited Frank to sing at what was to be the first major gathering of the Mafia since 1932. Held in Havana, the get-together included Frank Costello, Albert "The Executioner" Anastasia, Meyer Lansky, Vito Genovese, Joe "The Fat Man" Magliocco, Mike Miranda, and Lucky Luciano. The point of the meeting was to declare Luciano the head of the crime syndicate—the *capo di tutti capo*. Along for the merry holiday in the sunny Cuban capital were a number of FBI agents, surreptitiously keeping a watch on the hoodlums—and on their favorite singer.

The story came out that Frank arrived in Havana carrying a suitcase containing two million dollars—supposedly as a tribute that was to be paid to Luciano. Whether or not this was true, or where, if it was, the money came from, are both unknown. Walter Winchell wrote that Sinatra's earnings in 1944 were "more than any other individual in the world," but it seems unlikely that he would personally have seen fit to hand over two million dollars of his cash to Lucky Luciano. Presumably it was Mob money, more easily able to cross into Cuba in the famous singer's hands than in the luggage of any of the gangsters.

After the sojourn in Havana, the FBI file on Sinatra continued to grow. Unfortunately, his career did not. From 1946 to 1953 his reputation, both as a singer and a movie actor, tanked. Widely thought to be washed up, he was reduced to singing dreadful novelty songs for middle-of-the-road Columbia Records producer Mitch Miller and performing in lowbrow comedies and risible musicals like *The Kissing Bandit* ("Uninspired and very dull," said *Picturegoer* Magazine). His torrid extramarital romance with Ava Gardner did not help his image with Middle America. Nor did his tangles with the press that would continue throughout his lifetime.

Frank hated newspaper reporters nearly as much as he hated cops. One who particularly stuck in his craw was Lee Mortimer, the entertainment editor of the New York *Daily Mirror*, who had derided the film *The House We Live In* as "foreign *isms* posing as entertainment," and called Sinatra's fans "morons" for idolizing a man who socialized with gangsters.

In April of 1947 Frank and his usual entourage encountered Mortimer in Ciro's, a Hollywood nightclub. Sinatra lunged at the diminutive, 120 pound Mortimer, called him a "fucking homosexual" and a "degenerate." While Sinatra's buddies held Mortimer on the ground, Sinatra repeatedly slugged him, screaming at him, "I'll kill you the next time I see you. I'll kill you."

Mortimer ended up in hospital, but somehow Frank's lawyers and PR agents kept the police out of it. However the cops did get involved in Frank's next idiotic escapade. Following a very late-night party in Indio, California, a drunken Sinatra and his paramour Ava Gardner decided to take his .38 revolver and shoot out all the streetlights in the town. They managed to not only hit the lights (and some shop windows), but also a passer-by who was grazed in the stomach by one of Frank's bullets. They were both arrested, and Sinatra phoned his press agent, who quickly flew in from Burbank with $30,000 that he used to pay off the cops, shopkeepers and injured man to hush the matter up.

His various absurd shenanigans with Ava Gardner, which included a faked suicide attempt that the New York police spent days investigating, were matched by his boorish behavior on his CBS TV series *The Frank Sinatra Show*. He couldn't even get a gig entertaining the troops in Korea, since the Army denied him security clearance, citing his "Communist affiliations." Even a simple application for a passport prompted a full-scale FBI investigation. The insanity with both Gardner and the press continued, with the pair involved in an incident in which a screaming Sinatra almost killed a Mexican photographer by running him over. Gardner cranked up the worst in Sinatra with her own abrasive personality—so aggressive and combative that Frank's longtime pal Jimmy Van Heusen took to calling her "The Man."

The "Dark Ages" (as Frank called them) of 1946-1953 ended, and one of the great comebacks in show business history began when he landed the role of Angelo Maggio in *From Here to Eternity*. The possible involvement of the Mob in helping to convince Columbia to cast Frank in the part inspired the horse-head scene in *The Godfather*. The film made Sinatra a star all over again—and won him an Academy Award.

It was the beginning of an incredible twelve-year run as an entertainer, only slowed (but certainly not stopped) by the arrival of the Beatles in the mid-60s. Even the Beatles, wildly successful though they were, cannot really compare with Sinatra's remarkable career. The Beatles made thirteen studio albums. Frank made fifty-nine. The Beatles made two movies (three, if you count the animated *Yellow Submarine*). Sinatra made forty-five, all of which he starred in, and a couple of which he also produced and directed.

He loved to perform, and generally, if he wasn't fighting with his record company, loved to record. He did not love making movies, mainly because he didn't have the patience for it, and didn't respect most of the studio bosses, producers or directors he worked for, or the actors he worked with. One big exception was Humphrey Bogart, who he admired, and even, to hear some tell it, venerated. Bogart in turn was amused by the brash kid from Hoboken. "He's kind of a Don Quixote, tilting at windmills, fighting people who don't want to fight," he was quoted. "He's a cop-hater. If he doesn't know who you are and you ask him a question, he thinks you're a cop. Sinatra is terribly funny. He's just amusing because he's a skinny little bastard and his bones rattle together."

Bogie, his wife Lauren Bacall, and Sinatra began a group they called the "Rat Pack", dedicated to drinking, laughing at each other's jokes, staying up late and not caring about what anyone else thought of them. They were also linked in their liberal politics and support of Democrats such as Adlai Stevenson. When Bogie died in 1956, Frank took over as leader, with Dean Martin, Sammy Davis, Peter Lawford, Joey Bishop and Shirley MacLaine as his main sidekicks, with the main goals being boozing, cavorting with party girls, random acts of violence and delinquency, and putting on the squares. Sinatra ran the Rat Pack much the same way Sonny Barger ran the Hell's Angels—except that the Rat Pack dressed in snappy suits instead of leathers and travelled by private jet instead of on Harley-Davidsons.

Sinatra's numerous brushes with the law are almost too many to recount. In 1954 he and baseball star Joe DiMaggio were arrested after a nutty incident in which the two celebrities broke down the door of a Los Angeles apartment, searching for DiMaggio's wife Marilyn Monroe, who was supposedly inside, either in the arms of actress Sheila Stewart, or of jazz pianist Hal Schaefer (depending on who is reporting the story). Sinatra threatened to sue the chief of police of Los Angeles over the incident.

At the 1956 Democratic convention, he was (in his mind) mauled by House Speaker Sam Rayburn, who wanted him to sing *The Yellow Rose of Texas* to the big crowd. "Get your hands off the suit, creep," replied Frank—an insult that would reverberate in the 1960 convention, when Rayburn's Texas friend Lyndon Johnson wanted the job that Sinatra's friend, John F. Kennedy ultimately got.

In the late 50s Sinatra became not only a minority owner (and number one headliner) of the Mafia-run Sands Casino in Las Vegas, but also the front-man for another mob-owned resort further north in Nevada, the Cal-Neva Lodge. Through the Cal-Neva he became good friends with two men who would have a profound effect not just on Sinatra's future, but on the future of the world. One of them was Chicago mafia boss Sam Giancana, the successor to Al Capone, top member of the national crime syndicate *La Cosa Nostra* and a man who police believed had the blood of over two hundred men on his hands. The other was Joe Kennedy—one of the richest men in America, subject of numerous scandals, United States Ambassador to Great Britain, and father of the future U.S. president.

It was an unholy trinity, with each of the men on a very particular mission. Frank's goal was to get closer to Jack Kennedy, a man he admired and worshipped, and thus gain power by getting close to the most powerful office in the world—the U.S. Presidency. Giancana's goal was to use Frank to try to get the Kennedy brothers off his back with their attempts—Jack's as a powerful member of Senate Rackets Committee, Robert's as Attorney-General—to break the Mafia. Joe's goal was to use the illicit power that Giancana wielded, especially in Illinois and West Virginia, to help him buy the votes to get his son elected as President. Jack once publicly joked that his father had told him to not break the bank—"I just need to buy you a victory, I don't need to buy you a landslide."

The fly in the ointment for all of them was a good-looking woman named Judith Campbell Exner. While everyone agrees she was gorgeous—"in the Elizabeth Taylor category," according to AP Hollywood reporter James Bacon—not everyone could exactly define her work status. To some, including both George Jacobs and Kennedy's brother-in-law and Sinatra pal Peter Lawford, she was a working girl—a prostitute. Lawford said in those heady days leading up to the swinging sixties, he pimped for Frank, and Frank pimped for Kennedy. He told his agent Milt Ebbins, "She was a hooker. Frank gave her $200 to go to bed with Jack." Others disagreed, describing her as simply a woman who liked to party—"and sleep around a lot."

She certainly slept with all the players in this yarn. She started with Sinatra, though he tired of her after she refused to participate in a threesome with Frank and a black girl he brought to their bed. "You're so square," he told her. "Get with it. Swing a little."

Since she wouldn't, Frank introduced her first to Kennedy Sr., who apparently patronized her, without payment, on several occasions in Palm Springs. Then, more importantly, Frank introduced her to both his friends Jack Kennedy and Sam Giancana, both of whom fell for her in a big way. Of course Giancana had a well-known romantic streak. He was rumored to be the driver and a gunman in the 1929 St. Valentine's Day Massacre.

Kennedy, for a candidate in a Presidential election, was playing with fire. It almost cost him the nomination. It may have cost him his life.

J. Edgar Hoover had no love for any of the Kennedys. Nor did Lyndon Baines Johnson, who was involved in a bitter battle for the nomination in the summer of 1960. When he lost the nomination for President, he began a campaign to get on the ticket as Vice-President (even though he referred to the job, quoting former VP John Nance Garner, as "not worth a bucket of warm piss."). Through Hoover, and his G-Men's surveillance of Sinatra, he learned all about Kennedy's torrid affair with Exner, and thus his inadvertently close ties to The Mob. He then proceeded to blackmail Kennedy to add him to the ticket as the Vice-President. He wasn't interested in the job, but he saw it as a steppingstone to the job he had craved since childhood—the Presidency. And, if the arguments of researchers like Phillip Nelson are to be believed, in his *LBJ - The Mastermind of the JFK Assassination*, it was Johnson who ordered the assassination of Kennedy three years later, using the skills of Sam Giancana to organize it, French paid assassins to execute it, Lee Harvey Oswald to be the fall guy for it, and Mobster Jack Ruby, the CIA and Hoover's FBI to kill the patsy, hide or destroy the evidence, and cover it up.

That was in 1963. Back in 1959, it was all still fun and games, with Sinatra partying with the future President, energetically fund-raising for him, and campaigning with him, singing a re-written version of one of his big hits, *High Hopes*, at all the big rallies.

Life, though, was never simple for Sinatra. As he was partying and working with Jack, he was also turning out some of his most spectacular albums with his musical partner and arranger Nelson Riddle and continuing to make movies. He decided he wanted to produce, direct and star in an adaptation of a book about the only American soldier executed for desertion in World War II—*The Execution of Private Slovak*. The story was a total downer, but as Frank said, "You don't win Oscars for comedies", and he wanted another Oscar.

Frank had the perfect writer in mind for the screenplay—Albert Maltz, who had written the paean to brotherhood, *The House I Live In* back in the 1940s that had won him his first Oscar. The only trouble was, Maltz had never repented from his membership in the American Communist Party, had refused to "name names" to HUAC, and so was one of the Hollywood Ten writers and directors blacklisted by the film industry. He was now living in Mexico. However, the blacklist now was beginning to crumble. Blacklisted writers had been hired to write the films *Spartacus, Exodus,* and *Inherit the Wind.* Sinatra wanted Maltz to write *Private Slovak* and offered him $75,000 to do it.

The conservative press, led by William Randolph Hearst and columnist Hedda Hopper, went crazy with a campaign against Sinatra. He could care less—he was on top of the world. He had just made $400,000 for 19 packed nights performing at the Mob-owned Fountainbleu Hotel in Miami. But much more important than what newspapers thought was what the Kennedys did, and both the senior strategists of Kennedy's campaign—father Joe and brother Bob thought it very dangerous that Jack should be so closely tied with a man who was not just tied to the somewhat seedy world of show business, not just tied to numerous mobsters, but now also tied to a known Communist.

When Roman Catholic Cardinals Spellman and Cushing, and right-wing actor John Wayne all railed against him for wanting to hire Maltz, Sinatra took out ads in *Variety* and the *Hollywood Reporter* reading "This type of partisan politics is hitting below the belt. I make movies. I do not ask the advice of Senator Kennedy whom I should hire. Senator Kennedy does not ask me how he should vote in the Senate. . .Under our Bill of Rights I was taught that no one may prescribe what shall be orthodox in politics, religion or other matters of opinion."

Old Joe disagreed. He called Frank and said, "It's either Maltz or us. Make up your mind." Sinatra, furious, but recognizing that Kennedy as President meant more to him than Maltz as screenwriter, caved. He dumped Maltz that day, paid him the full $75,000 he had promised, and abandoned his plans to direct and produce the film. Then, remembers George Jacobs, "he went on a three-day Jack Daniel's binge and totally destroyed his office at the Bowmont house. 'Who gives a shit? I'm outta this fucking business!' he screamed, ripping up books and scripts, hurling over bookcases. This time I felt his rage and frustration were understandable."

Kennedy narrowly won the election against Nixon and became the 35th President, albeit with considerable help from his father's money that Sam Giancana and his mob cronies were able to use to buy votes in Chicago and West Virginia. Who would be invited to produce and star in the big inaugural gala? Who else—Mr. Frank Sinatra. Never has there ever been a closer alignment between Music and The Man. "This is the most exciting assignment of my life," said Frank. "It will be the biggest one-night gross in the history of show-business." He managed to close down two major Broadway shows so that Ethel Merman, Sir Lawrence Olivier and Anthony Quinn could participate. He worked the phones for weeks, roping in Ella Fitzgerald, Mahalia Jackson, Tony Curtis, and many others. He persuaded Leonard Bernstein to write a special composition and Nelson Riddle to bring a full orchestra.

Still, there were major hiccups. Frank's pal Sammy Davis Jr. was supposed to sing, but the new president put the kibosh on that, citing concerns about backlash over Davis' recent interracial marriage to Swedish actress May Britt. And even though Kennedy announced to all that "we are all indebted to a great friend, Frank Sinatra," the next day, at the inauguration itself, Frank found himself uninvited (possibly by Jackie, who hated him.) He showed up, in a specially constructed Inverness cape and top hat, with matching silver cane, and announced to a resistant security guy controlling the stands that he was Frank Sinatra. "We don't care if you're the Pope," he was told. "You're not on the list."

The early years of the Camelot Presidency were incredibly complicated, with the aborted Bay of Pigs invasion of Cuba, the Cuban missile crisis, and the early buildup to the war in Vietnam. Sam Giancana and his mafia henchmen felt their deal with Sinatra and the Kennedys, which was supposed to have created big results, had totally soured. Fidel Castro had kicked the mobsters out of Cuba and closed their casinos, smashing the slot machines and symbolically, and literally, turning Meyer Lansky's *Riviera* into a pigsty. Giancana felt betrayed that Kennedy hadn't got Cuba back for him, betrayed that the Kennedys—particularly Robert Kennedy, were investigating the Mafia more actively than ever, and betrayed by Frank Sinatra.

Giancana was so disgusted by what he characterized as Sinatra's failure to help get the Justice Department off his back, that he considered having the singer killed. He always backed away from the idea, he told his cronies, because he couldn't bear the thought of destroying that incredible voice. He just liked hearing Sinatra sing too much to kill him.

The Kennedys continued to live dangerously, with both JFK and Bobby becoming involved with Marilyn Monroe—after she was introduced to them by Frank. He and Monroe had themselves enjoyed a brief but torrid romance, but like so many of his women, he inelegantly ditched her. Both John and Robert Kennedy are reported to have had brief flings with her, the future president's in Sinatra's Palm Springs "compound". Famously, in one of the most celebrated mashups of Music and The Man in history, she seductively sang "Happy

Birthday, Mr. President" to Kennedy at Madison Square Gardens, sewn into one of the sexiest, sheer dresses of all time.

On August 5, 1962, Marilyn was found dead in her Los Angeles home—an apparent suicide. Did she kill herself, or was someone else to blame for her death? Her estranged husband, Joe Dimaggio, certainly knew whom to blame. A friend of his remembers Dimaggio cursing Hollywood, on the day of her death, for chewing Marilyn up and spitting her out, at "the fucking Kennedys", as he called them, in particular Bobby Kennedy, "and Sinatra—Joe cursed Sinatra." The Kennedys certainly had a motive to silence Monroe, so there have forever been rumors—but never proof—that they were somehow involved in her death.

Another theory has it that Giancana had her killed, after she confessed to him that she was going to go public about her affairs with the Kennedys. He saw it, the theory goes, as a way to destroy Robert Kennedy (who was actively investigating him) by implicating him in her death, and at the same time increasing his sway over both Sinatra and the President.

It is remarkable how close Kennedy and his crooner pal were in the early years of the new Presidency. For instance, Sinatra wanted to star in and co-produce a film of Richard Condon's novel *The Manchurian Candidate.* However the president of United Artists, Arthur Krim, hated the book, fearing that its volatile mix of political skullduggery, brainwashing, and assassinations was far too close to the actual American reality. The studio boss' reticence to finance the property didn't slow down Sinatra. He simply went to Kennedy, who loved the book, and asked him to phone Krim and tell him so. Kennedy did, Krim agreed, and Sinatra, with John Frankenheimer directing and Angela Lansbury co-starring, created a classic. It proved to be an amazingly prescient film, foreshadowing the waves of killings that would cloud the next twenty years, both Kennedy brothers, Martin Luther King, Malcolm X, and singers such John Lennon, Sam Cooke, and Victor Jara.

By 1962, major cracks were developing in the Sinatra-Kennedy relationship. Sinatra, who had nicknames for everyone, openly referred to JFK as "Prez", which others felt was disrespectful and far too familiar. Jackie absolutely hated Sinatra, and Bobby felt that Sinatra's close ties to the Mob were wildly dangerous to the President. Both the President of the USA and the Chairman of the Board continued to ignore the signs. When the President planned to visit California, Sinatra got it into his head that he could turn his Palm Springs "compound" into the western White House—Jack Kennedy's home away from home. As Jackie would be away in India for the period of the upcoming visit, a jolly time was planned, probably with Judith Exner and other fun-loving girls in attendance.

Sinatra went into overdrive, having a helipad built, a children's bungalow transformed into housing for the Secret Service, a giant flagpole raised, presidential plaques attached, parties planned, and itineraries set. Then, to Sinatra's utter shock, Kennedy's people cancelled the visit. It was felt that it was just way too dangerous for the President to be seen hanging out with the singing hooligan. Not only did Kennedy cancel, but, Sinatra learned, to his shock, that he would be instead staying at the home of his main rival—Bing Crosby. Crosby, of all people—a Nixon-supporting Republican!

Sinatra, in his usual style, went into a towering rage—destroying his collection of JFK photographs, kicking in the door of the presidential guest room, trying to rip the gold plaque off the door, and according to some reports, taking a sledgehammer to the new helipad. The incident only confirmed to Frank what he always suspected—that despite his vast wealth and his many artistic accomplishments, his Italian origins would make him persona non grata to the American establishment.

Frank had bigger problems in Nevada, where his mob ties meant that the gaming commission took away the license for his lodge's gambling license (aka its license to print money). Further, his drift away from the Kennedys, and Robert Kennedy's increasingly active efforts to shut down the Syndicate, meant that he was not holding up his end of his deal with Giancana and his mobster associates.

"Lying (expletive)!" he described Sinatra, in a phone call recorded and selectively transcribed by the FBI. "I figured with that guy, maybe we'll be all right. I might have known that guy would (expletive) me."

At that point his underling Johnny Formosa suggested a solution. "Let's show 'em. Let's show these asshole Hollywood fruitcakes that they can't get away with it as if nothing's happened. Let's hit Sinatra. Or I could whack out a couple of those other guys. Lawford and that Martin, and I could take the nigger and put his other eye out."

At which point, Giancana replied, ominously, "No. I've got other plans for them."

Sinatra blithely acted like no one could lay hands on him. When the Chairman of the Nevada Gaming Control Board, Edward Olsen, began investigating Sinatra, this is how the singer talked to him:

"You just try to find me, and if you do you can look for a big, fat surprise—a big fat fucking surprise. You remember that. Now listen to me, Ed...don't fuck with me. Don't fuck with me. Just don't fuck with me. And you can tell that to your fucking board and that fucking commission, too."

When Olsen did not back down from Sinatra's threats, but instead took away his gaming license, it affected not just the singer but other partners in his gambling lodge, including the always intimidating Sam Giancana. Kennedy tried to help his pal, asking the Governor of Nevada, Grant Sawyer, whether his people "were being a little hard on Frank out here?" He asked whether there was "anything you can do for Frank." The Governor simply told the president, "No."

Giancana, too, responded to Sinatra's petulant tirade against the gaming commissioner that had cost the gangster some $465,000.

Singer Phyllis McGuire, of the McGuire Sisters, with whom Giancana was having yet another affair, remembers the gangster saying, "If he'd only shut his damned mouth."

"Sam could never figure out why Frank would deliberately pick fights...he would always say to him, *Piano, piano*—'take it easy, take it easy'. He could never get over the hot-headed way Frank acted."

It is obviously quite remarkable and ironic that a murderous gangster like Giancana would have to try to tell a supposedly mellow lounge singer like Sinatra to try to curb his out-of-control temper.

The worst was still to come.

In 1963 Frank became involved with a married cocktail waitress at his Cal-Neva Lodge. When her husband, local sheriff Richard Anderson came around the lodge, a scuffle ensued in which Sinatra ended up getting punched hard enough that he was not able to perform for two days. Frank retaliated—getting the sheriff thrown off the police force. Two weeks later, Anderson and his wife were driving to dinner when a car driving at high speed in the wrong lane forced them off the road, and they were both killed. The car never stopped; no charges were ever laid.

Incidents like this continued to dog Sinatra for the rest of his life. Famously, his son Frankie Jr. was kidnapped in a bizarre scenario that rattled Sinatra and fascinated the world. Dozens of FBI agents and police were put on the case, trying to find Junior. Frank Sr., in classic form screamed his instructions to them: "Call Bobby Kennedy! Call Hoover! Jesus Christ, call the president, I don't care! Wake up the fucking president. Somebody *do* something!"

To quote film director Billy Wilder, "Wherever Frank is, there is a certain electricity permeating the air. It's like Mack the Knife is in town, and the action is starting."

On June 8, 1966, Frank took nine people to dinner at the Polo Lounge of the Beverly Hills Hotel to celebrate Dean Martin's forty-ninth birthday. Dining beside their noisy table were Frederick

Weisman, the president of Hunt's Foods, and Boston businessman Frederick Fox. Weissman asked the Sinatra party to keep it down, and suggested their language was offensive to women in the dining room. One thing led quickly to another, and soon, Weissman was lying unconscious on the floor in a pool of blood—according to some, decked with one of the Polo Lounge's famous table phones by Mr. Frank Sinatra.

Weissman was rushed to intensive care at Mt. Sinai Hospital, where he was in critical condition for 48 hours, and not expected to live. The police investigated the brawl but could not locate any of the Sinatra group. "Sinatra has been in hiding," said Police Chief Clinton Anderson, "but we'll get him. We want to find out the cause of the fight."

Sinatra flew to Palm Springs with his wife Mia Farrow and with casino manager Jack Entratter and his wife Corinne. "Now I've gone and done it," moaned Sinatra. "I've really fucked up. If this guy croaks, I'm fucking finished." Corinne Entratter reported, "It was the only time I think I've seen that man scared."

The police continued to try to investigate, but got nowhere. Martin, following the Italian code of *Omerta*, told the police he saw nothing. A year later he admitted to journalist Oriana Fallaci, "The cops came. We said we didn't know who did it and walked out. But we did, yeah."

In the end Weissman recovered, and as he convalesced his family received anonymous, threatening phone calls advising him not to press charges. They duly complied, and the police abandoned the investigation.

The cops were called in on many other occasions, some of them over Frank's actions against other entertainers. Jackie Mason was a former rabbi, turned lacerating, take-no-prisoners standup comic. He mined rich material from Sinatra's life, particularly the thirty-year age difference between Sinatra and his wife Mia Farrow. "Frank soaks his dentures and Mia brushes her braces," Mason joked. "Then she takes off her roller skates and puts them next to his cane. . .and he peels of his toupee and she unbraids her hair."

Sinatra was not amused. Next thing Mason knew, three shots were fired through the patio door at his suite in Las Vegas' Aladdin Hotel. The Clark County Sheriff investigated, but couldn't make any provable connections to Sinatra. Mason, certain there were some, excised all Mia jokes from his act but then, one night, couldn't stop himself, telling the audience that "I have no idea who it was who tried to shoot me. . .after the shots were fired all I heard was someone singing: 'Doobie, doobie, doo.'" Only a few days later he was sitting in a car with a lady friend when someone pulled the door open and smashed him in the face "with some kind of a ring on that's supposed to cut your face open." As his friend fled, she heard the assailant telling Mason, "This is not the worst that can happen if you don't keep your mouth shut about Frank Sinatra." The comic ended up in hospital with many face lacerations and a broken nose. Again, the police investigation into the possible involvement of the biggest star on the Las Vegas Strip went nowhere.

Sinatra continued to have strange altercations with people in very high places. Many of the singers and musicians in this book have gone up against The Man—but none others have gone *mano a mano* with the most powerful person in the world, certainly none while that man was standing, only in his pajama bottoms, at close to midnight, in his White House bedroom, contemptuously dismissing him. In the spring of 1968, Sinatra, newspaper columnist Drew Pearson, and soon-to-be presidential candidate Hubert Humphrey ended up in Lyndon Johnson's suite, with both Lyndon and wife Lady Bird getting ready for bed.

Knowing of the 5'7" singer's affection for both John Kennedy and for Humphrey, the 6'4" President towered over Sinatra, offering him a souvenir booklet about the White House. "I don't suppose you read," he told Frank, "but this has lots of pictures." He then also handed him a souvenir tube of lipstick with the White House seal on it. "It's a conversation piece," he told him. "It'll make a big man of you with your women." Sinatra did not smash the president with the hotline telephone, but he did angrily storm out of the room.

Humphrey would be the last Democrat that Sinatra would campaign for—which he did less out of love for the Minnesota senator than for his deep hatred of Richard Nixon. With Nixon's victory, Sinatra began to slide shockingly to the right.

Shirley MacLaine reported that Sinatra hated Nixon "with deep vitriol." Songwriter Jimmy Van Heusen claimed Sinatra hated Ronald Reagan even more. "We'd be at some party, and if the Reagans arrived, Frank would snap his fingers and say 'C'mon, Chester. We're leaving. I can't stand that fucking Ronnie. He's such a bore. Every time you get near the bastard, he makes a speech and he never knows what he's talking about. The trouble with Reagan is no-one would give him a job.' This happened time and time again because Frank could not abide being in the same room with the Reagans. Every time they'd walk in, we'd have to walk out, and each time we'd have to listen to Frank's diatribe against Reagan all over again."

"It's true that Sinatra despised Ronnie almost as much as Richard Nixon", said Peter Lawford. "He said he thought he was a real right-wing John Birch Society nut—'dumb and dangerous,' he'd say, and so simple-minded. He swore he'd move out of California if Reagan ever got elected to public office. 'I couldn't stand listening to his gee whiz, golly shucks crap,' he said. Frank couldn't stand Nancy Reagan either; he said she was a dope with fat ankles who could never make it as an actress."

But as the sixties morphed into the seventies, Sinatra was hanging out with Nixon's deplorable Vice-President Spiro Agnew, and organizing inauguration events for Ronald Reagan. In some measure this was because Sinatra felt betrayed by the Kennedys, and thought the Republicans might possibly be more helpful to him in getting the gaming license back for his Nevada casino.

In 1972, he even threw his official support behind the re-election campaign of Richard Nixon, to the consternation of many, including his daughter Tina. "My hair was on fire," she later wrote. " 'Damn it, Dad,' I told him. 'I've been killing myself for McGovern, and now you come out for *Nixon?*'"

"That's the way it goes, kid—it's a free country", said her father.

In the end, she wrote, "I decided to forgive him his appalling lapse of judgement, and we agreed to disagree."

One can only imagine what his daughter thought of Sinatra's courting of Nixon's disgustingly corrupt and ultimately disgraced Vice-President, Spiro Agnew. Sinatra applauded Agnew's "politics of polarization" and extreme right-wing opinions, so much so that Agnew made eighteen trips to Sinatra's Palm Springs compound in the eighteen months after he was elected (and before he was forced to resign). Sinatra treated him like royalty, re-naming the guesthouse he had built for Kennedy as "Agnew House" and filling it with monogrammed stationary and trinkets.

In 1973, the Nixon team asked Sinatra to come out of his supposed "retirement" to emcee and sing at the second inauguration concert. However security clearance issues and a drunken tirade from Frank at a pre-concert party ended that plan. A well-lubricated Frank spotted *Washington Post* gossip columnist Maxine Cheshire at the party.

"You're nothing but a two-dollar broad," he told the woman. "You're a cunt. That's spelled C-U-N-T!" He then took two dollars from his pocket and stuffed them in her drink glass. "Here's two dollars, baby," he said. "That's what you're used to."

His outlandish comments spelled the end of Frank's involvement in that event, but not even H. R. Haldeman could convince Nixon to cancel Frank's private concert at a later dinner for the President and the Italian Prime Minister Giulio Andreotti. It was that evening, the story goes, that Nixon himself finally convinced

Sinatra that he should come out of retirement (though perhaps the singer's extravagant lifestyle and $10,000 a day expenses also had something to do with it).

Some of Sinatra's expenses were donations to his new political friends. He gave the Nixon campaign a $50,000 contribution and followed that with an "unrecorded" (and illegal) further contribution of $100,000. In return, according to some FBI reports, he was able to persuade the President to commute the twelve-year sentence of a distant relative, and underboss of the New York Mafia, Angelo "Gyp" DeCarlo.

After Agnew was forced to resign in 1973, Sinatra gave the disgraced VP $30,000 to pay his tax evasion fine, and lent him $200,000 to pay all the back taxes, interest and penalties Agnew had avoided. Music vs The Man? Not this time. This time it was Music Bankrolling The Man.

Ten years later, he was supporting the even more reactionary politics of Ronald Reagan. Once again, there was a *quid pro quo*. Sinatra supported Reagan; Reagan maneuvered to get the singer back the gaming license he coveted for his Mob-connected Cal-Neva Lodge.

Frank's politics had shifted dramatically. He began as a staunch defender of "the little guy", so solidly and defiantly to the left that he was accused of being a communist, and an enthusiastic supporter of liberal leaders like Roosevelt, Stevenson and the Kennedys. By the end of his life he had moved totally to the right, supporting Nixon, Spiro Agnew and Reagan. If that surprised or shocked anyone, he couldn't have cared less. As Humphrey Bogart said, he hated cops and authority, railed against them his whole life, and accepted no-one's rules but his own. In his many dealings with The Man, from the 1930s to the 1980s, there can be no doubt—just as his signature song said, he did it His Way.

Rock and Roll

There has never been a period when music created so much strife between the generations as the early years of rock and roll between 1954 and 1959. Two men were at the center of the storm—the disc jockey who gave rock and roll its name and then became its first victim, Alan Freed, and the wild boogie-woogie pianist and singer, Jerry Lee Lewis.

It is impossible to give rock and roll an exact definition, or an exact birthdate, but it is plain where it came from, and what it evolved from. It was born in the American south, primarily in the Mississippi Delta, and it grew out of an unholy combination of gospel music, "the devil's music", the wild tunes *Variety* and *Billboard* once defined as "Race Music", and Rhythm and Blues. The expression is heard as early as 1910, in a recording of an up-tempo spiritual called *The Camp Meeting Jubilee*. It is referenced again, this time with a nautical meaning, in Buddy Jones 1939 tune *Rockin' Rollin' Mama*.

By the 1940s, the expression was understood to mean, at least by the hep cats of the south, sex. That certainly is what Sister Rosetta Tharpe's *Rock Me* (1941), Roy Brown's 1947 release *Good Rocking Tonight*, and Wynonie Harris' *All She Wants to do is Rock* (1949) are all about.

From its beginnings, it was outlaw music. When did it actually become Rock and Roll? Maybe when Alan Freed gave it a name, which was as early as 1951, when he used to howl along to the "race" records he played on his WJW radio show in Cleveland, drinking beer, banging the beat on a phone book and shouting "Rock and Roll!" into his microphone. Perhaps, though, singer Ruth Brown was on point when she said the defining moment of when rhyhm and blues morphed into rock and roll was "once the white kids started dancing to it."

There were a number of factors that allowed that to happen—some cultural, some legal, some technological. First, the technological ones. In 1931, Adolph Rickenbacher invented the electric guitar. In 1933, Laurens Hammond invented the Hammond organ. In 1946, jukeboxes began to be mass produced. On March 31, 1949, RCA released the first 45 rpm record, and although the very first records by Elvis and others were released on the archaic 78 rpm format, 45 singles rapidly became the favored format of rock and roll. In 1950, Leo Fender created the solid body Fender Telecaster guitar, followed by the Stratocaster model in 1954. With the explosion of wealth in the 1950s, lucky teenagers began to own their own cars—always with radios in them, tuned to Top 40 rock and roll stations. Just as importantly, battery powered transistor radios were introduced by Texas Intruments in 1954 and popularized by Sony in 1955. Suddenly, teenagers had three new ways of listening to *their* music, outside of parental supervision—jukeboxes, cars and transistor radios.

Meanwhile, The Man got involved, first with legislation about what people could and could not listen to on radio, and second with the much more explosive and important issue of race. When radio began broadcasting in the US in the 1920s, the Federal Radio Commission was instituted to control it. As unbelievable as it would seem 40 years later (let alone today), virtually all music on radio was then performed live, with the FRC "attempting everything this side of public hangings" to curb the practice of playing records on the radio. Indeed they called it, "in effect a fraud upon the listening public," and demanded that recorded music always be identified as such, with an audio version of a scarlet letter. The Man kept radio on a very tight leash, and in fact, in the US, even banned the recording of music from 1942 to 1946.

In the late 40s a brash irreverant radio man named Arthur Godfrey arrived on the scene, replacing the staid, stentorian style of radio with a new free spirit and earthy disposition. He wasn't Wolfman Jack or Cousin Brucie, but he did start to loosen things up. He exuberently smashed records he didn't like on the microphone and poked fun at his own commercials. The Man responded to these winds of change by ending some of their regulations on music and commercial radio. In Great Britain and Canada, the government-controlled BBC and CBC were even more straightlaced than in America, but that too began to change. Radio Luxembourg began aiming a much freer style of radio into England and Ireland. With the loosening of radio regulations in Washington, Canadians at least in border cities were now able to receive signals—and rock and roll—from big 50,000 watt clear channel AM stations like WKBW Buffalo and WWVA Wheeling, West Virginia.

Even more important was the profoundly important *Brown vs Department of Education of Topeka* which fundamentally began to change the relationship between blacks and whites in America. While focused on the issue of segregated schools, it began to integrate all aspects of America, including music. Before *Brown* only the bravest of boys, like Elvis Presley and Jerry Lee Lewis, would have the nerve to secretly visit the black juke joints of the American South, but now the ears of many white teenagers were starting to open to black music.

What was the very first rock and roll song? Some argument can be made for Sister Rosetta Tharpe's 1945 hit, *Strange Things Happening Every Day*. Tharpe is certainly one of the world's first rock and roll electric guitar players, and well deserves her long-overdue 2017 induction as an "Early Influencer" into the Rock and Roll Hall of Fame. Ike Turner's *Rocket 88* (1951) also gets some votes as the first rock and roll song. Most famously, Elvis' *That's Alright, Mama*, released on July 5, 1954 is considered by many to be the first. For my money, its provenance disqualifies it, as some of its verses are cribbed from an old song (from 1926!) by Blind Lemon Jefferson. For the first genuine rock and roll song, I believe we have to wait for *Whole Lotta Shakin' Goin' On*, recorded by Big Maybelle (and produced by Quincy Jones) in 1955, then turned into a megahit in 1957 by Jerry Lee Lewis.

Lewis is the quintessential rock and roll speed demon—a product of the Deep, Deep South, old time religion, hellfire, brimstone, liquor, fast cars, broken marriages and battles with The Man. He was born in Ferriday, Louisiana, as were his two cousins, Mickey Gilley and Jimmy Lee Swaggart. Mickey Gilley would grow up to become a singer as well, and proprietor of "the world's biggest honky tonk", a massive rock and roll and country music complex in Dallas. Jimmy Lee Swaggart was tempted by the riches his cousin was making in the 1950s, but eventually resisted the call of Mammon and became a televangelist preacher for the Assembly of God. Nonethless he was unable to resist the pleasures of the flesh, and was brought down and ultimately defrocked because of several scandals involving prostitutes and police. Even without his lost affiliation with the church, he has managed to suck ten million dollars from his followers, only marginally less than his cousin has made out of sixty years of rock and roll.

All three cousins grew up attending the services of the Assemblies of God, a severe Pentacostal sect that believed in the sinfulness not just of liquor, tobacco, movies, and dancing but also of swimming, medicine and life insurance. The most extreme members also handled poisonous snakes and sipped "salvation cocktails" made of strychnine and water as part of their worship of Jesus. Members of the little Ferriday church, including Jerry Lee's mother, frequently found themselves "overcome by the Holy Ghost" and with eyes rolling to the back of their head began shrieking in unknown tongues. Is it any wonder Southern rockers like Jerry Lee Lewis and Little Richard grew up to belt out lyrics like *Awopbopalooobop Alopbamboom*?

Jerry Lee's father was a moonshiner, busted twice and given long prison terms for making whiskey. He may not have been missed by his son, since when he was around he frequently beat the boy, usually for his son's terrible school attendance and all-F's report cards. He only stopped when his wife Mamie screamed at him, "Elmo, stop, you're killing that child." Elmo did recognize Jerry Lee's extraordinary musical talent, and eventually bought him a cheap piano. He even served as his prodigal son's first roadie, driving Jerry Lee and the piano around to early gigs at car dealerships and store openings in rural Louisiana.

Jerry Lee and Jimmy Lee would sneak out together at night to explore the other side of the tracks—especially a forbidden black juke joint called Haney's Big House. "I sure heard a lot of good piano playin' down there," reported Lewis. "Man, these old black cats come through in them old buses, feet stickin' out the windows, eatin' sardines. But I tell you, they could really play some music—that's a guaranteed fact."

The pair would also go out to rob stores. After robbing them they would boldly drop by the police station to ask Police Chief Harrison if there was any news about the thieves. "Well, boys," he would reply, "we ain't got 'em yet, but we're on their trail." The pair would then ask how many men he figured were involved. "It's a gang of 'em," he would tell them.

Lewis, without a lick of formal training, became such a fearsome piano player that he discovered he could make more money by playing music than he could from stealing. Still, there were suspicions. After bringing home $200 in tips from a weekend playing at a joint called the Domino Lounge, his mother freaked out.

"My God, Elmo!" she cried. "He broke into a store!"

He became a regular customer—and in-house pianist, at Nellie Jackson's, an establishment in Natchez that he would extol throughout his life as, "the greatest whorehouse in the south." Meanwhile, he began composing sermons, and preaching them on Sundays in the tiny Church of God in Ferriday. At fifteen, he began studying for the ministry at the Southwestern Bible College in Texas, but within months was expelled for carousing and pounding out hymns with a boogie-woogie beat in the chapel. By 1953 he had two wives—a bigamist, at seventeen! He had also acquired the nickname, *Killer,* that he would be saddled with forever.

"I hated that damn name ever since I was a kid, but I've been stuck with it," he would later say. "I don't think they meant it *killer* like, like I *kill* people. I think they meant it music'ly speakin'. But I am one mean sonofabitch."

He was also a convicted felon. In 1953 he was sentenced to two years in jail for stealing a .45 handgun, but his lawyer managed to get him off on a suspended sentence, "because of his tenduh age."

Soon after, he met a disc jockey and bandleader named Johnny Littlejohn, who was from the home of the soon-to-be King, Tupelo, Mississippi. The pair began playing dates in dives from Shreveport to Nashville, but Littlejohn never knew what he'd get from his temperamental pianist.

"He was tortured," said Littlejohn. "He was torn between music and that Assembly of God. He'd get into that thing about God and Mammon, get on that preacher kick. I'd drive over to Ferriday to get him and he'd tell me he was going to become a preacher. 'I ain't gonna play in no more clubs. I'm gonna live for the Lord,' he'd say. I'd beg him to come. Sometimes he would, sometimes he wouldn't. Once he stayed away for two full weeks, then he called me and said, 'Well, John, y'know, things are getting bad and I need the bread.'"

In the summer of 1954, the greatest revolution in the history of the music business since the invention of sound recording by Thomas Edison was underway. It is hard to know if Jerry Lee Lewis, or anyone else really sensed it at the time, but Lewis knew something was going on, and eventually decided it was time to act. The place to be was Memphis. The exact place to be was Sam Phillips' Sun Records Recording Studio.

It was Sam Phillips who had discovered and first recorded Elvis. Or. . .was it? Phillips' secretary, Marion Kreisker claims it was not in fact Phillips but she who first recorded Elvis' first record. According to her (and it seems somewhat unlikely she would make it up, though Phillips disputes it), it was she who first got Elvis into the studio, after asking him, "What do you sing?"

"I sing all kinds," replied Elvis.

"Well, who do you sound like?"

"I don't sound like nobody."

At that, Kreisker got him into the booth and made that first, virginal recording of his incredible voice.

We saw in the opening chapter the influence of women on outlaw music. It is certainly true of Elvis and all early rock and roll. Macho though they were, it is plain that both Presley and Lewis were strongly influenced by proto-rockers like Sister Roseta Tharp and Big Mama Thornton. Also, of course, neither Elvis nor Lewis would have become the phenomena they did without women. Just as with Sinatra before him and the Beatles after, the first response to them was from females—teenage girls.

The world went wild for Elvis, but as far as Lewis was concerned, "The Pelvis" was just another southern cracker like he was from across the river in Mississippi. If Elvis could make a million, so could he. And so he loaded up his piano on his daddy's pickup, and headed north to Memphis.

Meanwhile, the other major figure in our story of early rock and roll was well on his way to musical fame and fortune.

Alan Freed began as a jazz musician in Ohio until an ear infection ended his career. In 1945 he began working as a disc jockey at

WAKR in Akron, then moved north up the roads beside the winding Cuyahoga River to Cleveland in 1948, where he joined WXEL-TV, spinning platters in the afternoons and evenings. Freed was a big drinker, and in 1950 he met a man named Leo Mintz, owner of a Cleveland music store called Record Rendezvous, in a Cleveland bar. Mintz told Freed about this interesting new phenomenon. Rhythm and Blues records, or "race records" as they were then called, once a tiny part of his business, were now selling in huge numbers—and not just to black teenagers, but to white as well.

After witnessing first hand the excited buyers at Mintz' store, Freed was intrigued. Seeing the opportunity, he managed to convince the very skeptical station management at WXEL that there was a market for this black music. Freed is famous for naming it "rock and roll", but his main contribution to American musical history is that he popularized and championed black music to white audiences, thus in a certain sense not just naming, but *creating* rock and roll. It wasn't always easy. One of the first tunes he helped move from the black charts to the white-dominated national pop charts was *Sixty-Minute Man* by the Dominoes, which featured lyrics promoting the sexual prowess of the singer, of being able to satisfy his "girls" with fifteen minutes each of *kissin'*, *teasin'*, and *squeezin'*, before his climatic fifteen minutes of *blowin' his top.*

Calling himself "The King of the Moondoggers," Freed adopted a persona as wild as any of the artists whose records he played. In 1952, he had the first of what would be many run-ins with the authorities over rock and roll. Freed booked the Cleveland Arena for an event he called "The Moondog Coronation Ball." No one in 1952 recognized the extraordinary popularity of this new music and a combination of that and a printing snafu meant that twice as many tickets were sold as the venue could handle.

It was a raucous, high-energy night, with a crowd that was about 80 percent black who were very surprised to see that the man who they'd been listening to on the radio was white. They were a little shocked, but not upset. Times were changing, and when he walked out on stage, "he generated the same kind of electricity as Mickey Mantle or Judy Garland." The crowd around the stage went nuts, and so did the huge throng of ticket holders locked outside, unable to get into the packed arena. Door windows got broken, and the scene turned wild, with the authorities turning fire hoses on the crowd, and shutting down the show. It was Freed's first "rock and roll riot", but not his last.

The new music was dismissed as "garbage trash, a shocking display of gutbucket blues and lowdown rhythms" and the fans called "trained squeals" by the newspapers, but any publicity is good publicity, and the uproar over the Coronation Ball gave more notoriety to both rock and roll and to Alan Freed. In 1954 he landed a job at WINS in the Big Apple. New Yorkers went just as crazy for Freed and his noisy radio shows as his listeners had back in Cleveland.

"He jumped into radio like a stripper into Swan Lake," wrote Clark Whelton in the *New York Times*. "Freed knocked down the buildings you hated and turned the rest into dance floors—the musical equivalent of a front-row seat for the San Francisco earthquake."

He almost singlehandedly gave major careers to acts like The Drifters, Clyde McPhatter, Fats Domino, Joe Turner, Frankie Lymon and the Teenagers, and Little Anthony and the Imperials. Instead of eking out a living on the old chitlin circuit, they were now selling huge numbers of records to white buyers as well as black.

Neither the authorities, nor even fellow radiomen were much impressed with Freed's choice of music or his crazy jive talk. Paul Sherman, a staff announcer at WINS, described Freed's show as "crap...loud, phony, unpleasant and artificial." Frank Sinatra, asked about the new music, said it "smells phony and false. It is sung, played and written for the most part by cretinous goons, and by means of its almost imbecilic reiteration and sly, lewd, in plain fact dirty lyrics it manages to be the rancid aphrodisiac and martial music of every side-burned delinquent on the face of the earth."

Freed just ignored the old farts. At 100 mph, he perorated to his teen listeners: "Now we're gonna send El and Jimmy, Peggy and Reno, Judy and Rick, Joyce and Teddy, Marlene and Don, Yvonne and Buddy, Elaine and Vinny and Bootsie, and Carol and Johnny Accosella; Mary and Jerry and little Junior Lucadamo, Antoinette and Dominic, Carmine Mangarelli and Ralph Reya, and especially to Charlie Accosella, who's been going steady for fifteen months with Lucy who says, 'I know I getcha mad honey, but I don't mean to. It's just love, that's all!'

"And good luck to the Phi Zeta Sorority on your dance, from Lucy Mangarelli of Mount Vernon, New York, Kenneth Cook of St. Albans, from Joan Harding, who still loves him, and Frankie Johnson of Flushing, from Olga in Springfield Gardens, Long Island." And now, Freed would ring his cowbell, hit the turbocharger, turn the volume to 11 and the speed to 120. "All the kids of Andrew Jackson High—Gail, Jackie, Helena, Dorie, Kenneth, Jerry, Billy, Shadow, Baby, Joan, Olga, Clifford, Connie, Jose, Slim, Mousie, and Tommy—here's Varetta Dillard, Savoy Records' *Mercy, Mr. Percy*!!"

The magic of radio went pumping out into the night. Some radio frequencies are better than others, and WINS lucked into a good one. Freed's crazy jive talk was heard not just in New York City, but up and down the Eastern Seaboard from Canada to the Carolinas, turning on all manner of future revolutionaries and regular folk to rock and roll. Late 60s Yippie activist Abbie Hoffman remembered how as a kid living near Boston he "had to rig up a roof antenna to hear ol' Alan Freed bang a telephone book on the table while he spun the Sound."

The squares and over-20s were distinctly unimpressed. Paul Sherman's fellow WINS announcer Lew Fisher listened to Freed's verbal diarrhea and grimaced at his pal, "Oh my God, I give him three months."

"You're crazy" replied Sherman. "I give him one week."

Neither were right. Freed lasted until 1958, when he was finally fired from the station after being charged by the police with inciting to riot and anarchy.

Freed wanted to continue using the "Moondog" moniker he'd used in Cleveland for his TV show and live concerts, but the name was taken by an eccentric New York street musician, who successfully sued Freed to retain it. The jock decided he would instead call his show the "Rock and Roll Party", even though his right-hand man Jack Hooke warned him that the phrase "rock and roll" was widely considered a euphemism used by blacks for sexual intercourse. "I don't give a shit," exclaimed Freed. "That's what I'm going to call it!"

On April 12, 1955, the marquee of the giant Brooklyn Paramount Theater read, "Alan Freed Presents the Rock 'n' Roll Easter Jubilee". It was a smash hit, drawing ninety seven thousand people and producing a box-office gross of $107,000 that shattered the theater's all time record. However a group of teenagers leaving the concert created a disturbance on a subway car, and the widely publicized ruckus was blamed on Alan Freed and rock and roll. Nonetheless, Freed continued to organize big live shows for every Easter, Labor Day and Christmas from 1955 to 1958. Increasingly, there was consternation from the press and from The Man.

Some of it was based on the old issue of race. No one before Freed had created big public events that drew large numbers of both blacks and whites to hear performers of both races, and even in New York, many people found it shocking. Freed's personal propensity for close physical contact with his performers was also a point of contention. He would frequently kiss black female singers or embrace black males following their performances. He was also photographed sharing cigarettes or drinking from the same glass as the black musicians. Freed's go-fer Ray Reneri said that when Freed, "this so-called 'madman' walked on the stage with 99 percent of his show black... a lot of people hated him."

The other issue about rock and roll was that it was digging deep into the revenue earned by America's traditional music makers on Tin Pan Alley. Until the 50s, the members of ASCAP—the American Society of Composers, Artists and Publishers—held a virtual monopoly on the writing and publishing of America's music. The cream of American pop composers—the Gershwins, Kerns, Porters and Berlins—were represented by ASCAP, and the organization wanted to keep it that way. They perceived that "good music" was created in New York City and Los Angeles, and had little interest in music from anywhere else, certainly not music that originated from do-wop street singers from Philadelphia or kids with guitars in gunny sacks playing beside the railroad tracks. The organization also had longstanding issues with the use of their licensed music on radio. In 1941, radio broadcasters, fed up with ASCAP, had decided to start their own alternative licensing society, which they called BMI – Broadcast Music International. By the 1950s, with the explosive growth of rhythm and blues, rock and roll, and country music, ASCAP members were shocked and panic-stricken to learn that BMI-licensed songs comprised over 80% of the music heard on the radio.

ASCAP went on the warpath, with a campaign in newspapers and to politicians slagging BMI-licensed music. Lyricist and ASCAP-board member Billy Rose (writer of *Me and My Shadow* and *It's Only a Paper Moon*) called BMI songs, "obscene...junk...on a level with dirty comic magazines." Jimmy Kennedy, in *Variety* wrote, "The most astonishing thing about the current craze for rhythm and blues records and their accompanying *leer-ics* is that they were ever permitted to happen."

ASCAP's favorite target was Alan Freed, and they would spearhead the political effort to shut down his live rock and roll shows, get him off the airways, and eventually get him criminally charged during the Payola hearings.

Freed's notoriety grew with his appearance in the 1956 film, *Rock Around the Clock*. The film achieved infamy after a large group of teens snake-danced out of a screening in Minneapolis, smashing windows and causing the theater to cancel future showings. Riots were reported from as far away as Dublin, Ireland. West German theaters attempted to get anti-riot insurance before showing the film. In Egypt, authorities claimed the film was an "Eisenhower-led plot" to encourage Middle-Eastern turmoil by undermining the nation's morale. In Iran the Shah banned it, claiming that it was a threat to Iranian civilization.

City fathers across America began pulling up the drawbridges against the onslaught of Alan Freed and his raucous new music. In his old town of Cleveland, politicians dug up an ordinance barring anyone under eighteen from dancing in a public place. In Cambridge, Massachusetts, the city council approved a bylaw barring disc jockeys from appearing at record hops. In Hartford, Connecticut the police tried to have the Hartford State Theater's license revoked when it booked a Freed concert, claiming that "public safety was endangered." In Washington, D.C. the police chief urged a ban on rock and roll shows at the National Guard Armory. The press inflamed the issue. *Billboard* (a pro-ASCAP trade paper) described the block-long lineup of teenagers waiting to get into a Freed concert as restless "natives." *Look* magazine said attending a rock and roll show was like "attending the rites of some obscure tribe whose means of communication are incomprehensible" and could be frightening for an adult.

To paraphrase singer Al Jolson, "America, watch out. You ain't seen nuttin' yet!" The wild man of rock and roll was still to come. In late March 1957, Jerry Lee Lewis signed with Sam Phillips and recorded *Whole Lotta Shakin' Goin' On* at Sun Records in Memphis. Phillips released the record on April 15, and on April 21 sent Lewis out on the road to promote it. Along with Johnny Cash, Carl Perkins, and the Queen of Rockabilly, Wanda Jackson, Jerry Lee set out on a tour of western Canada. They began in Sault Sainte Marie, Ontario, and headed west at a blistering pace, through Manitoba, Saskatchewan, Alberta and British Columbia, then circled back to some towns and cities they had missed, travelling up to five hundred miles a day with Cash teaching Lewis how popping amphetamines could ease the ordeals of touring. When Lewis finally got back to Memphis, he reported the financial rewards of the long spring tour. "I left home with fifty dollars in my pocket, an' when I came back I had about twenty-five. Don't know how it happened, but it did."

That would soon change. By the end of July, his soon-to-be signature rock anthem had sold 100,000 copies. Preachers began railing against Lewis and his sinful song, and radio stations began to ban it. But Sam Phillips' brother, Judd, took Jerry to New York and got him an interview with the hippest TV host on television, Steve Allen, then placed a giant order of the records and sent them to record stores across the country. Allen liked Lewis, and booked him. Lewis *howled,* jumped off his piano stool towards the end of the song and kicked it towards the TV host. Ed Sullivan would have had a conniption, but Allen just laughed, threw the stool back at him, then threw more furniture at the piano. Jerry played some high notes with the heel of his shoe. The audience went crazy, giving the loudest applause either Allen or Lewis had ever heard.

Only a few days later, Lewis was invited to perform on Alan Freed's ABC-TV show, *The Big Beat.* The song, with its down and dirty lyrics intact, exploded. By the end of August it held the number one position on all three charts, Pop, R&B, and Country, and had sold well over a million copies—one of them to this writer—the first record he ever purchased.

Lewis didn't just have a hit, but he established a new sub-genre of rock and roll, proving that the piano could anchor the new music just as hardily as the electric guitar. He (and Little Richard) were the first of a great string of rock and roll pianists—Leon Russell, Billy Preston, Burton Cummings, Billy Joel, and of course Elton John.

In mid August Lewis recorded his second great profane hit, *Great Balls of Fire.* It was one of the craziest recording sessions ever, with a long inebriated liturgical argument preceding it that was fortunately recorded by engineer Jack Clement.

"H-E-L-L!" spelled out Lewis

"I don't believe this," muttered the boss, Sam Phillips.

"Great Godamighty, great balls of fire!" shouted James Van Eaton from behind his drums.

"That's right!" confirmed guitarist Billy Lee Riley.

"I don't believe this," moaned Sam.

"It says make merry with the joy of God *only*," yelled Jerry. "But when it comes to *worldly* music, rock 'n' roll –"

"Pluck it out!" shouted Billy Lee Riley.

"You have done brought yourself into the world, and you're in the world, and you're still a sinner," exhorted The Killer. "You're a sinner, and unless you be saved and borned again and made as a little chile and walk before God and be holy—and brother, I mean you got to be *so* pure. No sin shall enter there—*no sin!* For it says *no sin*. It don't say just a little bit; it says *no sin shall enter there.* Brother, not one little bit. You got to *walk* and *talk* with God to go to heaven. You got to be *so* good."

Jerry carried on, praising the Lord and damning rock and roll—the devil's music. His bible-thumping mother Mamie and TV preachin' cousin Jimmy Lee Swaggart would both have been proud of him. *Finally*, late in the night, Sam Phillips got the recording session back on track, and Jerry laid down one of the wildest pieces of rock and roll ever.

For the next eight months Lewis' two rock masterpieces dominated the airwaves. They even penetrated a Louisiana hospital where Jimmy Lee Swaggart lay, recuperating from a bout of pneumonia acquired at an outdoor revival meeting. "The airwaves were filled with the heavy rock 'n' roll beat of Jerry Lee's music," he remembered. "Dark, gloomy thoughts roamed through my mind. It seemed as if every demon in hell had crawled out to do battle with me. 'Look at Jerry Lee,' the voices said. 'He used to be a preacher but he got smart.' I cried out for God's help. Finally I reached over and picked up my Bible. It fell open to Joshua 1:9, 'Have not I commanded thee? Be strong and of good courage; be not afraid, neither be thou dismayed, for the LORD thy God is with thee whithersoever thou goest.' God's healing power surged through my body. It was like fire in my veins. 'Jerry Lee can have *Great Balls of Fire*,' I declared, but I'll take the fire of the Holy Ghost! Hallelujah!"

Well, that was all very well, but meanwhile his cousin was laughing all the way to the bank. The new song was the biggest selling record in the history of Sun—bigger than any of Elvis' many hits. Jerry Lee told his daddy that there were almost as many zeros on his checks as there had been F's on his third-grade report card.

On March 28, 1958, Lewis flew to New York to join Alan Freed's rock and tour titled The Big Beat. With Lewis, Chuck Berry, Buddy Holly, Frankie Lymon and the Chantels as the headliners, the tour kicked off in Freed's favorite venue, the Brooklyn Paramount. However, there was a problem. For over a year Lewis had been adamant that he close every show. For even longer, Berry had demanded the same. With them playing together for the first time, they fought about who was to go on before whom. The impresario finally laid down the law, and made a decision. Freed decreed that since Chuck Berry had musical seniority over Lewis, he would close the show.

Lewis did as he was told, performing before Berry, and had the crowd screaming to his music. But he had a trick up his sleeve. At the climax of his show, he kicked the stool away and broke into *Great Balls of Fire*. As he continued to bang out the song with his left hand, he pulled a can of lighter fluid out with his right and sprayed it over the piano, then tossed a match on it. The piano burst into flames, and like a madman, he kept pounding the blazing keys. The audience went berserk. Reeking of sweat, burnt lacquer and lighter fluid, he finished the song and left the stage. As he passed Chuck

Berry in the wings, he turned to him and calmly told him, "Follow that, nigger."

"Burned that damned piano to the ground," he later recalled. "They forced me to do it, tellin' me I had to go on before Chuck."

Berry and Lewis made peace with each other and became friends. Together, they worked a grueling grind—forty-six cities in forty-four days.

The tour ran into trouble when the bands and singers arrived in Boston to play a big gig at the Boston Arena. The city, of course, was notorious for its authoritarian censorship. The phrase "Banned in Boston" had entered the public lexicon back in the nineteenth century. Over the years many musical acts, plays and books had been banned by city's prudish censors. Boston even once declared exchanging gifts at Christmas forbidden, and tried to ban the American $5 bill, after a new version in 1896 included images of partially nude allegorical figures.

According Ray Reneri, Freed "hated Boston." After his first concert there in 1955, he was hauled into Police headquarters. He was so fearful that he was going to get beaten up by the Boston police that he would only go with his assistant Renari. "If they're going to hit me, I want a witness," Freed told him. After being released unharmed, he told a crowd of reporters gathered in front of the station house that he thought the Boston police were "a bunch of red-necked old men."

Now, three years later, Freed was back in Boston, having to deal with his old nemesis, the city's police force. This time, he had two much wilder performers as his headliners—Jerry Lee Lewis and Chuck Berry. There were police all over the stage and standing beside it in the wings. Once the lineup came to its penultimate performer, Jerry Lee Lewis, wanting as usual to upstage his rival Chuck Berry, the Killer went into a wild medley of his two biggest songs. He didn't light the piano on fire this time, but instead climbed on top of it, hitting the keys with the toe of his shoe while belting the lyrics into his mike. The kids went crazy, leaving their arena seats, dancing in the aisles and rushing the stage. The panicked police told another of Freed's assistants, Jack Hooke, that if Freed didn't get the kids back in their seats, he would. By force. Hooke ran to Freed and shouted to him, "Alan, you better get 'em back in the seats or we're going to have trouble. You know how they [the police] are in this town!"

Freed reluctantly stopped Lewis in mid-performance and addressed the audience, "Alright, listen, hold it! I have to stop the show for a minute, kids. You have to sit down. I want everybody back in their seats. The show won't go on unless you all get back in your seats!"

The audience, also reluctantly, complied. Even though there was now *not* a whole lot of shaking going on, Lewis returned to his song claiming there was. He was then followed by Chuck Berry, who launched into *Sweet Little Sixteen*. The kids again leapt up and began dancing. Once again, the police sergeant freaked out, and snapped his fingers ordering the building staff to turn on the house lights. As the lights came on, Freed screamed at the cop, "Hold it!"

The policeman screamed back, "This show is not going on until everybody's in their seats!"

Berry, his band and the audience fell eerily silent, cowed by this loud verbal stand off between the impresario and the police.

"Alright, kids," begged Freed. "I told you before, this is the way it has to be. You have to go back to your seats for the show to go on. Please go back." As they returned again to their seats, Freed gave the signal for Berry to continue and the houselights to be turned out.

"I'm not putting the houselights out!" snapped the policeman. Freed went ballistic. "You can't do that! These kids paid $3 a ticket and they didn't come to see a show with bright lights on!" The cop would not back down, and his partner told Freed why in no uncertain terms. "We don't like your kind of music here," he hissed at him.

Freed, boiling mad, grabbed his mike and addressed the crowd with a statement that would be the beginning of his downfall:

"Kids, the police in Boston won't put out the lights. I guess the police in Boston don't want you to have a good time." Freed later denied using exactly those words, but whatever was said, it did get "the kids" going. Loose chairs and other debris began raining down on the stage. Chuck Berry abandoned his mike stand, ran to the back and took refuge behind his drummer. The concert ended in chaos, with Freed exiting out a fire door, his assistants running for safety, and the crowd surging for the exits.

Fighting broke out in the streets. A sailor was stabbed and fifteen other people, according to questionable press reports, were beaten, robbed or raped in front of the Boston Arena. Two teenaged girls attacked a woman in the subway, carving swearwords in her arms with switchblades. Freed and the musicians jumped on a plane for Canada to perform a concert the next night at the Montreal Forum. As they returned the following day they discovered they were big news in the American press, now full of exaggerated stories about the aftermath of the Boston concert. Teenaged gangs "raced through the streets, knifing, beating and robbing." The *New York Times* story was headlined, ROCK AND ROLL STABBING. The *New York Herald Tribune* ran an editorial titled ROCK 'N' RIOT saying that Freed had lured in "20,000 shrieking juveniles" and had "touched off a riot." The paper continued, "There was a time when cities boarded their gates against the plague," and while that action might no longer be necessary, "most communities still try to keep known thugs at bay." With the exception of the Pied Piper of Hamelin, the newspaper continued, "musicians are not generally thought to be dangerous... Now another pied piper seems to have turned up."

The nation's city fathers seemed to be newspaper readers. Freed's cavalcade received cancellation notices from the cities of Troy, New York and Providence, Rhode Island. New Haven Mayor Richard C. Lee announced, "Not only will this show not be permitted, but while I am Mayor there will be no further rock and roll melees in this city." The chief of the Newark National Guard, Major General

James Cantwell cancelled, out of concern for "the public's safety" the Freed Cavalcade show booked for the Newark National Armory. Massachusetts Senator William D. Fleming introduced a bill to ban rock and roll from all state-owned buildings.

On May 8, a grand jury handed down an indictment against Freed, charging him with "inciting the unlawful destruction of property during a riot touched off at a performance at his rock and roll show." Six days later, they added new charges: "unlawfully, wickedly, and maliciously inciting to riot during a rock and roll show," and "incitement of anarchism." Freed's attorney, Warren Troob, announced that he was "enraged" over the charges, which he charged was "the work of the [Catholic] church" and its anti-rock and roll crusade. He was concerned. The charges were serious. Freed faced a possible twenty years in jail.

J. Edgar Hoover, Director of the FBI, made a public statement denouncing the Boston concert and warning the nation about rock and roll's "corrupting influence on America's youth." The FBI began to compile a file marked with the name of the main scapegoat on it—"Alan Freed".

Freed's son Lance Freed is convinced that his father was "set up" in Boston because "he was seen by many at ASCAP as the leader of the movement that made BMI a viable organization." He claims to have seen documents that suggest there was communication between the Boston Archdiocese and the FBI concerning his dad and how they could "get him there" in Boston.

J. Elroy McCaw, the owner of WINS, wasted no time waiting for a trial to determine Freed's guilt or innocence. The same day the Boston grand jury handed down the indictment, McCaw fired their star D.J. To add insult to injury, he replaced him with Freed's old nemesis at the station, Paul Sherman—the announcer who had predicted Freed would only last a week.

Jerry Lee Lewis, on the other hand, was still on top of the world, though his fall from grace would come shortly, and it would be even more terrible than Freed's. For now he was still loved by his fans, his bosses, and the press. *Billboard* reporter Ren Grevatt wrote:

"*Really breaking it up for the Paramount audiences is Sun Records' phenomenal Jerry Lee Lewis. The Ferriday, La. rockabilly is one of the most dynamic chanters on the current scene, and according to Sam Phillips, chief of Sun: 'He's the most sensational performer I've ever watched, bar none.' This comes from the man who also developed Elvis Presley and Carl Perkins.*"

Another piece of very good news for Lewis, if not for music fans, was that his rival Elvis had been drafted into the army. Was the induction another deliberate attack on rock and roll? His fans certainly thought so. Thousands wrote letters to the Army begging them to give the King a deferment. The draft board would hear nothing of it. One member of the Memphis draft panel exulted in putting the greasy singer in his place. "After all," he growled, "when you take him out of the entertainment business, what have you got left? A truck driver."

The establishment had much motivation to try to end Presley's career by sending him off to Germany. They knew the revolutionary effect he had on teenagers. "Hearing him for the first time," said Bob Dylan, "was like busting out of jail." One report in the thick FBI file on Presley described a Presley concert in La Crosse, Wisconsin as "the filthiest and most harmful production that ever came to La Crosse for exhibition to teenagers. . .nothing less than sexual gratification on stage. . .a strip-tease with clothes on."

So The Man was happy to see The King get his sideburns shaved off and demoted to a lowly private in the US Army and, for other reasons, so was Jerry Lee Lewis. He celebrated—returning to Ferriday to receive the key to the city from the mayor, and then, to top things off, by secretly marrying his thirteen year old cousin, Myra Gale Brown. She entered into the spirit of things by dropping out of grade eight.

On May 21 the bride and groom flew to New York, en route to England, where the William Morris Agency had organized a thirty-seven day, thirty-show tour for Jerry Lee. Before he left, Judd Phillips wanted to consult with the singer to try to keep him out of hot water in what he perceived to be the much more conservative, potentially hostile climate of England. How, he asked, did Jerry Lee propose that he was going to introduce his wife to the British press?

"She's my wife," said Lewis. "There ain't nothing wrong about that."

"Right an' wrong don't have anything to do with it," replied Phillips. "Those people ain't gonna like it."

"Look," said Jerry Lee, "People want me, and they're gonna take me, no matter what."

"You're not gonna do like Sam and me think you should, then, huh?"

"Hell, no. Gotta do what's right."

Sure enough, as soon as Jerry Lee and Myra stepped off the plane at Heathrow, they were surrounded by a sea of reporters and photographers from every London paper except the *Times*. They immediately asked who the little girl beside the rocker was. Lewis as promised boldly told them she was his new wife, and when asked how old she was, told them she was fifteen. They asked if she was his first wife; Jerry told them no, he'd been married twice before. One of them then asked Myra if she didn't think that fifteen was too young an age to be married.

"Oh, no. Not at all," she sweetly replied. "Age doesn't matter back home. You can marry at ten if you can find a husband."

The next day, the story in the London *Daily Herald* was headed

'ROCK' STAR'S WIFE IS 15

And It's His Third Marriage!

Further digging by a reporter at the Memphis *Press-Scimitar* revealed to the British press that Myra was born on July 11, 1944. She wasn't fifteen, she was thirteen—and further, she and Jerry had been married five months before Lewis divorced his previous wife. For the second time in his life, he was a bigamist.

Lewis began his tour at the Regal Cinema in Edmonton. A panning review in the *Daily Sketch* claimed that Jerry Lee "throws together everything that is bad in rock and roll. Drooling at the piano, Lewis moans, grunts, wails and sneezes so close to the microphone that he might be eating it." In *The People*, the front-page editorial called for all teenage subjects of the crown to boycott Lewis' concerts in order to "show that even rock and roll hasn't robbed them of their sanity." It went on to urge the Home Secretary to have Jerry Lee immediately deported from the United Kingdom.

The London *Evening Star* was even more explicit. "Lewis should not be allowed to parade his charms before British teenagers," read their editorial. "He should be deported at once. He is an undesirable alien." The next day, the British agent who had organized the tour, Leslie Grade, met with the president of the Rank Organization, owner of the theaters Lewis was booked to play in. Within an hour an announcement was made. The tour was cancelled. That afternoon, Lewis and his entourage left their hotel, headed to the airport and got on a plane to fly back to America. At both Heathrow and Idlewilde they were besieged by reporters. The London *Daily Herald* gloated BABY-SNATCHER QUITS.

In New York, one of the reporters asked Myra Gale what she thought of it all. "I think what Jerry thinks about it," she replied. A reporter from the *Daily News* asked Jerry if it wasn't a bit odd to marry a thirteen-year-old girl.

"You can put this down," he replied, starting to lose his patience with the press. "She's a woman."

The press continued to snipe at him. In the *New York Herald Tribune*, columnist Hy Gardner jibed that, "The Jerry Lee Lewises are going to have an addition to the family. He bought her a new doll." He then got serious, adding his opinion that Jerry Lee's music possessed "the contagious, almost frightening beat of a tribal drummer." As always in the bad reviews, the underlying, unspoken message was that rock and roll was black, was African, was evil.

Elvis stuck by his fellow Sun recording artist. Asked by a reporter about Lewis' travails, he replied, "He's a great artist. I'd rather not talk about his marriage, except that if he really loves her I guess it's all right." Presley learned a lesson from the Jerry Lee debacle. In Germany, he met a fourteen-year-old girl named Priscilla Beaulieu, but instead of marrying her, he secretly took her home to Graceland, waiting until 1967 to marry her without risking tarnish. Years later, when asked his thoughts about marriage, Elvis famously replied, "Why buy a cow when you can get milk through the fence?"

The worst news for the new music was yet to come. Because Alan Freed's concert tours of big Eastern venues had been shut down, rock and rollers took to touring much smaller Midwestern halls though the winter of 1958-59. One of these tours, the Winter Dance party, featured Buddy Holly, Waylon Jennings, J.P. Richardson (The Big Bopper) and Ritchie Valens. The organizers failed to take the winter weather into account, the lack of heating on the tour buses, or the long distances between the venues. Holly's drummer Carl Bunch ended up hospitalized with frostbite, so Holly decided to look for alternative transportation. On February 27, 1959, Holly, Ritchie Valens and the Big Bopper took off from Mason City, Iowa in a small charter plane heading for the next gig in Moorhead, Minnesota. Within minutes of takeoff the plane was caught in a snowstorm and crashed, killing all three of them, plus the pilot. It was, as denoted in Don McLain's *American Pie*, "the day the music died."

A week later the Boston Attorney General's office announced they were dropping the "anarchism" charge against Freed, but the other charges stood, with no trial date yet set. In Washington, The

Man had come up with a new and potentially much more serious way of taking down Alan Freed and rock and roll.

The House Subcommittee on Legislative Oversight decided in the 1950s that one of its jobs was to probe the morals of radio and television. In today's climate it may seem hard to believe that the US Congress saw fit to spend its time investigating whether answers were slipped to contestants on TV shows, or whether DJ's took $100 gifts to play rock and roll tunes, but that's the way things were in the 1950s. The culture wars were so intense at the time that Washington saw itself as a bastion of morality in a sea of declining values. Washington had just successfully taken on the film industry with the anti-Red witchhunt of the House on Un-American Activities Committee, and now the politicians decided to take on other media, starting with television.

The focus of both commercial radio and television was originally drama, but drama is expensive to make. Once TV was introduced in the late 40s, it rapidly took drama, sports and big live event presentations away from radio, leaving it with headline news and recorded music shows hosted by jocks like Freed. By the mid-50s, the "Golden Age" of TV drama was mostly already over, replaced by quiz shows, that proved to be both cheaper to produce and wildly popular.

The first blockbuster quiz show was *The $64,000 Question* on CBS, but the most successful one was NBC's *Twenty-One*. In November of 1956 a New Yorker named Herb Stempel began a long successful run on the game show, ultimately broken by a charming egghead professor and poet named Charles Van Doren. Months after losing, Stempel made accusations that the show had been rigged, that he had received the correct answers to the difficult questions by the producers, and then in the end told he would have to "take a dive" to Van Doren.

The allegations made their way to a grand jury investigation in lower Manhattan, but it too appeared to be tainted. It is estimated that of the one hundred and fifty contestants who testified before it, over one hundred were lying, and when the judge in a highly unusual and still not understood move sealed the testimony from the public, the House Subcommittee took over with its own investigation.

The press and public took a great interest in the hearings, and President Eisenhower weighed in, calling the quiz show hoax a "terrible thing" to do to the American public. The star witness at the hearings was Charles Van Doren, who confessed to the committee that he had been specifically cast by producers Jack Berry and Dan Enright as a foil to the rough-around-the-edges Stampel, had been given the answers to the questions and had knowingly participated in the fraud of battling Stempel and ultimately beating him.

The revelations were damning. Van Doren was fired from his jobs at NBC and Columbia University, the lead sponsor (Revlon) of *Twenty-One* dropped its sponsorship of the show, and within a week all of producers Barry & Enright's shows were pulled from the air.

ASCAP and other anti-rock and roll forces were buoyed by the television hearings, especially when they learned that Barry and Enright also owned Top Forty AM radio stations. Thinking that the House committee might bring down BMI and rock and roll for them the same way it had demolished the quiz shows, they searched for a way to convince the Congressmen to put radio in their sights the same way they had TV. They had a perfect scapegoat in mind—Alan Freed.

There was nothing new about Payola. The business of paying to get songs heard can be traced back to the middle of the nineteenth century. The famed British songwriting team of Gilbert and Sullivan paid substantial sums to persuade performers to sing their compositions. The widespread practice was known as song plugging. By 1905, Tin Pan Alley was paying out half a million dollars a year to convince singers to sing certain songs.

By the time of the rock and roll era, the only way to sell a record was to get it first played on the radio, and with the dozens of new recordings released every week, the only way to do that, especially for unknown groups on tiny indy labels, was to pay disc jockeys to listen to them, and hopefully play them. It was disparaged as "Payola", but it was not illegal, and it is hard to see why it was even unethical. Why was it considered fine for an oil company to give a politician tens of thousands of dollars for a political campaign, or a big record company to pay thousands to advertise on big billboards or ads in *Variety*, but pernicious for a promoter for the Penguins to offer a DJ $200 to play their latest effort, *Earth Angel?*

Whether or not the foes of rock and roll really thought Payola was evil, they saw it as a way of taking down the new music. They managed to convince the Washington legislators to hold hearings on the earth-shattering issue that they hoped might be the demise of rock and roll, and the demise of BMI. As a political issue, it had little downside for the politicians. Rock and Roll radio was a much easier target than taking on corruption, waste or ineptitude in the Army, the CIA or the Administration. The only people who were in favor of rock and roll were teenagers, and they couldn't vote anyway (the voting age didn't drop from twenty-one to eighteen until 1971.)

The newspapers, openly antagonistic to radio and television in the 1950s, jumped on the anti-radio bandwagon with glee. When Freed was called to testify, the *New York Daily News* proclaimed FREED FACES PAYOLA PROBE with a front-page headline. After his unrestrained testimony, the *New York Post* hit the stands with a full-page headline reading ALAN FREED TELLING ALL TO PAYOLA PROBERS in type that record executive Morris Levy called, "the same size (as) when World War II ended."

Freed was bold in defense of the practice. Some people might call it bribery, but he said "he would look like an idiot" for rejecting a gift of something like a fur stole for his wife after having done somebody "a hell of a turn, inadvertently helping a company by playing a record for it." He called the taking of cash gifts, "the backbone of American business." Asked, "If somebody sent you a Cadillac, would you send it back?" he brazenly replied, "It would depend on the color."

As a result of the scandal, Freed was fired from his "Big Beat" dance show on WNEW-TV. Many of his teenage fans wept openly on his final show, as Freed tried to console them, saying, "Now, don't cry." One girl claimed that the station was, "trying to get rid of rock and roll," and another told reporters the show gave teens something to do after school and "kept them off the streets." "What," she asked, "are we going to do with ourselves now?"

By now sobbing himself, Freed told his studio audience he felt he had done no wrong and urged them to stay calm and shed no more tears. "We know we are more adult than adults," he said. "By no means is this goodbye. I'm not going anywhere. I'll be back on the air soon. Payola may stink, but it's here and I didn't start it. I know a lot of ASCAP publishers who will be glad I'm off the air."

Freed put a brave face on things, but others were concerned. His long-time loyal assistant Ray Reneri told him, "You have to get out of New York. Don't you understand? They're going to get you. They're not going to be satisfied until you're out!"

Indeed, on February 25, 1960, New York District Attorney Frank Hogan received Criminal Court Judge Gerald Gulkin's order to file an information from the grand jury charging Freed with "requesting and accepting" $10,000 from Roulette Records in February, 1958. The next day, Freed was charged with a count of commercial bribery.

Despite his glib and confident public façade, the pressure on Freed began to take its toll. He was now under the scrutiny of the FBI, the New York State Attorney General, the House Committee on Legislative Oversight, and the Internal Revenue Service, and his enormous legal bills were growing every day. His ex-wife Betty Lou Greene described him as being so strung out that "he couldn't sit down." His daughter Alana said that, "for the first time in his life he felt total panic. He didn't know what he was going to do. He didn't know which way to turn."

Freed got almost no support from anyone other than his teen fans, which is not surprising since there was an almost visceral hatred of rock and roll by almost all of the adult world. Journalist Jeff Greenfield says adults in the 50s considered rock and roll, "like masturbation: exciting, but shameful," Elton John remembers, "it was incredible how much [older] people fucking *hated* rock and roll." Even the hipper and more progressive elements of 1950s society jumped on the bandwagon of belittling the music and the disc jockeys who played it. The *New York Herald Tribune* editorialized that the payola scandal proved that, "the music played by disc jockeys was so bad that's it's almost a relief to learn that they had to be paid to play it." The influential *Music Journal*, playing the race card again, pontificated that teenagers, "were definitely influenced in their lawlessness by this throwback to jungle rhythms. Either it actually stirs them to orgies of sex and violence (as it did for the savages themselves), or they use it as an excuse for the removal of all inhibitions and complete disregard of the conventions of decency."

Neither the press nor the authorities were able to end rock and roll. Nor did the hearings make a dent on BMI, or on the record companies who offered cash inducements to persuade DJs to play their songs. Even though ASCAP's goal was to try to break rock and roll by breaking BMI and the radio stations that owned it, the publishing rights organization came out unscathed. It was the disc jockeys who took one hundred per cent of the fall in the payola hearings—especially Alan Freed.

Freed was in debt, and in need of a job. Any job. He was offered one, by KDAY Los Angeles. It was a small station, begun by the "singing cowboy", Gene Autry. Freed took the job, but his New York style did not seem to work in California, and heavy drinking, exacerbated by his legal problems, noticeably affected his on-air manner. Within a few months, he was fired.

In September, 1962 he managed to get another gig, this time at WQAM Miami, but drinking, his oversized ego, and his moonlighting as a promoter of live rock and roll events upset the station's management, and he was gone by November. In December, weary of the long, drawn out legal battle with the government, he entered into a plea bargain, pleading guilty to taking a $700 "gift" from a record company called Superior Record Sales. He was given a fine of $500 that his lawyer managed to persuade the judge to reduce to $300, due to what he described as Freed's "lack of funds." In March of 1963, now awash in a sea of alcohol, facing both gigantic legal fees and the potential of tax-evasion charges, Freed paid the $300 fine, and headed back to Palm Springs, California. According to his daughter, he basically gave up. Despondent over his inability to hold a job or hang on to his old audience, he resorted to alcohol. He "would fix himself a drink when he got up in the morning, he would drink all day, and he would go to bed with one."

He died on January 20, 1965. New York jock Paul Sherman believed Freed deliberately drank himself to death in a long-term suicide. Buffalo D.J. George "Hound Dog" Lorenz attributed Freed's death to a broken heart, "which of course no hospital could mend."

Freed is one of the most high-profile fatalities in the war between Music and The Man. Certainly, his own failings contributed to his death, but so did the intense hounding of him by the government agencies, the police, and the mayors and city councils, and the corporate elements of the music industry such as ASCAP and the traditional record companies who wanted desperately to shut down Alan Freed and the music he stood for.

His star Jerry Lee Lewis was one of the many shocked and saddened to hear of Freed's death. Lewis was having hard times of his own. In 1962 his three-year-old son had fallen into a swimming pool and drowned. He hadn't had a hit record in the new decade. He kept working—he even returned to England to make a film and do a tour, which proved more successful than the disastrous first one—but he was certainly no longer a contender for the title of the King of Rock and Roll. The music had changed. Lewis' fellow rocker Chuck Berry was in jail. Elvis was out of the army, singing soft ballads and mostly focused on making movies—twenty-seven of them in the 60s, all dismissed by critic Andrew Caine as a "pantheon of bad taste," but all money-makers. Radio playlist decision-making had been taken from the D.J's and given to the suits in management. Rock and roll had been taken over by the likes of Connie Francis, Neil Sedaka and what Lewis dismissively referred to as "all the Bobbies—Bobbie Vee, Bobby Vinton, and Bobby Rydell."

Jerry Lee's life spiraled into a hot mess. In 1965, following a show in Grand Prairie, Texas, police surrounded his Cadillac as it pulled into their motel, and after searching the car found 200 pills. Although it was Jerry's car and mostly Jerry's drugs, his young band members took the fall for it. His drummer, Robert "Tarp" Tarrant ended up in the Memphis penitentiary, where he recalled life in the Jerry Lee Lewis band:

"With Jerry Lee it got to the point where he didn't try to hide it anymore, and he didn't try to do it in proportion. Never enough of nothin', that's the way it was. It got worse and worse, and he started havin' a lot of goons around. They were buyin' him dope, and of course, they were totin' dope too. They were totin' a lot of money for him, 'cause everything was always cash with Jerry. Guns. Hell, man, we had guns galore."

Lewis never for a minute denied his wild antics. He once shouted at a reporter, "Hell, I smoke pot. Pills, dope, needle, Ex-Lax. I drink whiskey, Scotch, gin, vodka, piss, vinegar—whadaya think of that? Snuff queens? Hell, where they at? I'd like t'meet 'em. They done all faded out." In 1968, he got involved in one of the most unlikely events in the history of rock and roll—playing the part of Iago in a Los Angeles musical version of Shakespeare's *Othello*. He was impressed both by the amount of verbiage in the play, saying, "I never thought there was so many words," and by the playwright, saying, "This Shakespeare was really somethin'. I wonder what he woulda thought of my records."

The cast and director were impressed with him. He was the only actor who had all his lines memorized at the first rehearsal.

The play, titled *Catch My Soul,* was not well received, but Jerry Lee got great notices." The *Toronto Star* wrote "Jerry Lee Lewis is genuinely diabolical as Iago. It is astonishing what new implications of evil he can find in words as simple as 'Go to, very well, go to.'" The *Christian Science Monitor* called him a "Louisiana-born genius" and "a unique Iago."

By 1969, his long fallow period was over. In September, along with fellow rock pioneers Chuck Berry, Little Richard and Bo Diddley played at a major rock and roll revival event captured as a concert film by D.A. Pennebaker called *Sweet Toronto.* The concert and film not only revived their careers but created a new giant interest in 1950s rock. Two months later, astronaut Charles Conrad on Apollo 12 carried a ninety-minute cassette of Lewis' music to the moon.

Suddenly, Lewis was hot again. He had seventeen Top 10 hit singles in the 70s, and along with them a string of divorces, lawsuits and arrests. In 1970 he bought a Convair turbojet airplane, hired a full time pilot, and began flying to his gigs, charging $10,000 a night for them. By 1974, the Cappaert Investment Corporation was suing him for $100,838 for payments he had not made on the plane. His bass player Hawk Hawkins and his steel guitarist Charlie Owens both quit his band and filed suit against him for $8000 in back salaries. On top of that his ex-wife Myra Gale was suing him for $19,700 in unpaid back alimony. Lewis, instead of showing up to the court hearing, flew to perform at Wembley Stadium, leaving his lawyer to explain that the check was in the mail.

"Mr. Lewis has the keys to the jail in his back pocket," warned Judge J. Brugge. "I don't want him back here troubling the court again." Fat chance. In February 1975, returning from a concert in Vancouver, Lewis' plane was surrounded on the tarmac in Denver, and he and twelve others on the plane were charged with international drug smuggling.

He continued to give mesmerizing performances around the world. He is one of the most entertaining and talented pianists the world has ever seen, performing with shockingly arrogant and appealing cocky self-confidence.

His cousin Jimmy Lee Swaggart was also a major celebrity by the 70s. He was defrocked by his church for his dalliances with prostitutes, but he still had a huge flock of TV worshippers. In one of his big Sunday morning televised sermons, he made a plea for the salvation of his cousin's soul. Once Lewis was drinking, he would respond to his cousin's sermons by carrying on to people around him about how he had wasted his life singing the devil's music. Or else he would start playing with his guns. One drunken night he accidently shot two holes in the chest of his bass player, Norman "Butch" Owens. Lewis' fourth wife, Jaren Pate screamed at Owens for dripping blood on her new white carpet. Lewis was charged with shooting a firearm inside the city limits, a misdemeanor.

Two weeks later, he was charged with disorderly conduct for shouting obscenities at his wife's neighbors.

A month after that, he totaled his $46,000 Rolls-Royce and again ended up in police custody. Ten hours after being released, he drove his Lincoln Continental, late at night, up the driveway of Elvis' Graceland, crashing into the gate and bellowing at the security guard, "I want to see Elvis. You just tell him the Killer's here."

The security guard, Robert Lloyd, recognized Lewis and told him Elvis did not want to be disturbed. Lewis pulled out a .38 derringer and shouted back, "Git on that damn house phone and call him! Who the hell does that sonofabitch think he is? Doesn't wanna be disturbed! He ain't no damn better 'n anybody else."

The guard phoned into the mansion, but was told by someone from the King's entourage, "Elvis says to call the cops."

Within a minute a patrol car arrived. Officer B.J. Kirkpatrick pulled Lewis' door open, disarmed him of the derringer, and ordered him out of the car. "I'll have your fuckin' job, boy," hissed the Killer.

There was another drunk driving charge for the Graceland incident, but it was small potatoes in comparison with Lewis' issues with the IRS. The tax liens that the IRS had been filing since 1958 against Jerry Lee Lewis had grown by 1979 to a whopping $274,000. On February 27 IRS agents showed up at his ranch with a fleet of eight tow trucks, and hauled away five motorcycles, two Lincoln Continentals, a Corvette Stingray, a 1954 black and gold Cadillac, a jeep and a tractor. They also wanted his new $68,000 Rolls-Royce, but it turned out the Memphis Rolls dealer already had a lien on it, for non-payment.

Five months later he was suing his wife for "habitual, cruel and inhuman treatment," and she was countersuing him for "cruel and inhuman treatment, adultery, habitual drunkenness, and habitual use of drugs."

In September, a court ordered him to pay $125,000 in damages to Butch Owens over the shooting incident three years earlier. Seven days later IRS agents returned to his ranch to claim more of his possessions. While there they discovered controlled substances, and so Lewis was arrested once again.

Two months later, on November 24, Lewis locked himself in his dressing room at the Orpheum Theater in Memphis, where he was booked to perform at 8 PM. Outside the door, US Marshalls, armed with a writ of attachment, ordered him to unbolt the lock. They had been instructed to seize all monies held by him, along with any jewelry or musical equipment in his possession, in order to satisfy the $125,000 court judgement regarding the Owens case. Meanwhile, the audience waited restlessly for the stand-off to end.

At 10:20, the Marshalls finally gave up and left, and Jerry Lee Lewis emerged and strode to the stage. With his band laying down the backbeat, he was introduced:

"Ladies and gentlemen, the man the FBI wants, the IRS wants, the US Marshalls want—but you've got him! The Killer!"

Louie Louie and the FBI

Conventional musical history has it that rock and roll died in 1959. Elvis was in the Army. Chuck Berry was in jail. Jerry Lee Lewis was in disgrace over his bigamy and marriage to his thirteen-year-old cousin. Buddy Holly along with The Big Bopper and Ritchie Valens was killed in the plane crash, and Alan Freed's career destroyed by the Payola hearings. That conventional and oft-told story—even as reported in the previous chapter—has it that The Man had won and that rock and roll was moribund until revived by the Beatles and the "British Invasion" of 1964.

Don't believe it. There was lots of great rock and roll in the first four years of the sixties. Just for instance: *Heat Wave* by Martha and the Vandellas, *Only the Lonely* by Roy Orbison, *Stagger Lee* by Lloyd Price, *What'd I Say* by Ray Charles, *Do You Love Me?* By The Contours, *Be My Baby* by The Ronettes, *Wipe Out* by The Safaris, *Duke of Earl* by Gene Chandler, *He's So Fine* by The Chiffons, *Da Doo Ron Ron* by The Crystals, *Quarter to Three* by Gary U.S. Bonds, and the Number One hit *The Loco-Motion*, written by Carole King and Gerry Goffin and sung by their teenage babysitter Little Eva.

Great though all those tunes were, none compares with the greatest song of all time, *Louie Louie*. No, wait a minute. *Louie Louie* is *not* the greatest song of all time. It is the *worst* song of all time—an egregiously horrible, dumb piece of pop drek, most probably obscene, a definite sign that Western Civilization is sinking into the abyss. *Louie Louie was* certainly worthy of a two-year FBI investigation. Certainly deserving of being banned by the Governor of Indiana. But... *Louie Louie* is definitely fun to dance to.

Let's start at the beginning of the tale and investigate the absurd and nonsensical notion that this simple-minded, romantic sea shanty is really a revolutionary, pornographic call to arms. Pound out the primitive beat as you read along—you remember, it's just 1,2,3/1,2, 1,2,3/1,2. Only three chords—the three basics taught on first day of guitar school—A, D, E-minor. If E-minor is too tricky for you, just play E—likely no one will notice.

The song was born as *El Loco Cha Cha*, written by Cuban composer and songwriter René Touzet. It makes sense that he was Cuban, because notwithstanding the buckets of ink that have been wasted on coming up with other meanings for the song, it is simply a song about a sailor, a single-handed sailor, presumably Cuban, who sails the Caribbean, all alone, while thinking of his girl. He wishes he was seeing his girl, but instead he only sees the coast of Jamaica. He confirms this several times with choruses of *yeah, yeah, yeah, yeah, yeah, yeah*. It is unclear whether his name is "Louie" or hers (seems odd) is, but the name is repeated numerous times throughout the song.

Touzet provided the basic structure, but the song went through several more incarnations before it was injected, like Clorox-bleach-into-lungs, in the popular culture of the 1960s. First, and perhaps most importantly, a young black singer and songwriter named Richard Berry took Touzet's cha-cha beat and wrote new English lyrics (on a few sheets of toilet paper, as the story goes), and thus turned *El Loco Cha Cha* into *Louie Louie*. Although the song has been recorded over two thousand times, Berry never made much money from it. His original recording did not click and he sold the copyright to it for $750 to pay for his wedding. The tune did not make a dent in Berry's hometown of Los Angeles, but it did meander up the coast to the Pacific Northwest where it was covered by Little Bill and the Bluenotes, and then by Rockin' Robin Roberts and the Wailers, both of Tacoma, Washington. The kids of Washington and northern Oregon loved the song, and it was repeatedly played at sock hops and "Battle of the Bands" events, where it was heard by two slightly younger bands, the Kingsmen, and Paul Revere and the Raiders. Both bands recorded the song in the spring of 1963.

With their superior musicianship, bigger name, distinctive if faintly absurd stage act decked out in tricorn hats and Revolutionary War outfits, and especially with their connection to powerful Columbia A&R man Terry Melcher (who you'll meet in an upcoming chapter through his unfortunate connection with wannabe rocker Charlie Manson), everyone expected that Paul Revere and the Raiders would be the group to make a hit out of *Louie Louie.* However, it was not to be. It was the Kingsmen who turned the song into gold, even though their version, hastily recorded in Portland, Oregon in a single take with poorly placed microphones, is often maligned as the worst recording of all time. Seattle rock historian Peter Bletcha describes it as "the Kingsmen's chaotic version—with its clubfooted drum beat, insane cymbal crashes, ultra-cheezy keyboard figures, lead guitar spazzout/solo, and that famous fluffed third verse, as well as Ely's generally slurred and unintelligible vocals. . ."

It didn't matter. It was, as we say, close enough for rock and roll, and it had fantastic youthful energy, with singer Jack Ely peppering the song with hoarse demented asides of *Let's give it to 'em, right now!* and *Let's go!.* The song was released by indie label Wand Records, and soon caught fire, getting radio play and sales across North America. By the end of 1963, it was the Number One song on the *Cash Box* chart in the US, and Number One on the CHUM Chart in Canada. By February of the new year, though, there was trouble brewing. INDIANA GOV. PUTS DOWN 'PORNOGRAPHIC' WAND TUNE blared the headline in *Billboard* Magazine. The sub-head read SAY KIDS BLEW THE WHISTLE. The story revealed that after hearing the Kingsmen's recording of *Louie,* Governor Matthew Welsh's "ears tingled," and he immediately fired off a letter to Reid Chapman, president of the Indiana Broadcasters Association, requesting that the song be banned from all radio stations in the state. Thirty years later, he would sheepishly claim that, "at no time did I ever pressure anybody to take the song off the air. I [just] suggested to him [Chapman] that it might be better all round if it wasn't played." Whatever he exactly said, Chapman did enact the edict, and the record was banned from Indiana airplay.

The Marion County, Indiana prosecutor's chief trial deputy, Leroy K. New got into the act with his own critique of the song, saying "The record is an abomination of out-of-tune guitars, an overbearing jungle rhythm and clanging cymbals." The term "jungle rhythm" is of course a dog-whistle codeword for "black". Wand received a threatening letter from the National Association of Broadcasters (NAB) stating that it had "received a number of inquiries and complaints from member stations on the recording *Louie Louie* being circulated on the Wand label." Soon the Federal Communications Commission (FCC), the US Post Office and the US Justice Department were investigating the song. Why, one might ask. The lyrics are a bit slurred, the audio a bit muddy, but listen to it and it seems to contain the rather tame lyrics about the lovesick sailor that Touzet and Berry originally composed. The guy gripping the tiller may have ants in his pants, but it is hardly *Tropic of Cancer.*

It appears Governor Walsh, Trial Deputy New and untold numbers of FBI G-men were the victims of a teenage prank. Richard Berry described it to the Indianapolis News as follows: "What happened is that a bunch of college kids back in Indiana got hold of a printing press and started printing up and distributing their own ideas of what they thought they heard." Someone knew how easy it to put a burr under the saddle of The Man regarding the subject of rock and roll, and they did it masterfully. Copies of these new, quite obscene lyrics began circulating in school buses and school yards and school rooms, and some little snitchs passed them on to their teachers or their vice-principal or their parents, and the hook was set. Soon they were in the hands of the FBI.

Here, for the record, are the completely inaccurate lyrics to *Louie Louie*, as created by the dirty minds of some Indiana frat house:

> *There is a fine little girl waiting for me*
> *She is just a girl across the way*
> *When I take her all alone*
> *She's never the girl I lay at home*
>
> *Tonight at ten I'll lay her again*
> *We'll fuck your girl and by the way*
> *And...on that chair, I'll lay her there*
> *I felt a boner in her hair*
>
> *She had a rag on, I moved above*
> *It won't be long she'll slip it off.*
> *I held her in my arms and then*
> *I told her I'd rather lay her again.*

Not Shakespeare, but much more exciting than listening to Mr. Greene drone on about *Twelfth Night* in Grade Nine English class.

A March 27, 1964 memo from the Indianapolis office of the FBI reports that a local woman (name blacked out) reported to the

FBI that "about November, 1963, purchased a record under Wand label at Blanchard's, a record store in Crown Point, Indiana...Record was publicly displayed, was routinely priced, and was not suspected of being obscene when purchased.

"Sometime after buying the record [blacked out] heard from various acquaintances the record had obscene lyrics if the "Louie Louie" side were played at a speed of 33 1/3 instead of the normal 45 rpm. About 1/29/64, a co-worker gave [blacked out] a typed sheet of lyrics, which were allegedly transcribed from the record when played in this manner, and which appear obscene.

"She said that the record was widely played in the area and was once ranked first on the WLS Radio (Chicago) record survey." The memo also noted that on March 25, Assistant US Attorney (AUSA) Lester R. Irvin of Hammond, Indiana, asked the FBI to see if the record violated US Code Section 1465, Title 18 ITOM [the Federal law against Interstate Transportation of Obscene Material]. Irvin noted if the FBI found that it did, he would arrest the perpetrators.

Another letter, sent to Attorney General Robert Kennedy, read: "Dear Mr. Kennedy...My daughter brought home a record of LOUIE LOUIE and I...proceeded to try and decipher the jumble of words. The lyrics are so filthy that I can-not [sic] enclose them in this letter. ..We all know there is obscene materials [sic] available for those who seem it, but when they start sneaking in this material in the guise of the latest teen age rock & roll hit record these morons have gone too far...This land of ours is headed for an extreme state of moral degradation...How can we stamp out this menace????"

In the light of these complaints, the FBI charged off like Don Quixote on a mad quest, keen to prosecute the song. The Indianapolis investigation ultimately grew to become a two-and-a-half-year-long case, involving FBI gumshoes from six major field offices, and the Washington headquarters itself. For fear that the agents would be themselves be contaminated by the suspected obscene record, the FBI destroyed the first *Louie* specimens it considered, but then acquired more, which it laboriously played at 33 1/3, 45 and any number of speeds in-between. They didn't interview either the singer of the Paul Revere and the Raiders version of the song, or Jack Ely, singer of the Kingsmen's. In fairness, it probably wouldn't have helped anyway. Ely later admitted to a reporter that he had slurred the words because he had learned the song from a jukebox in a noisy dance hall, and couldn't understand all the lyrics.

The G-Men did visit Richard Berry, and told the shocked songwriter that he could go to jail for the song, since the lyrics had crossed state lines and thus he could face federal obscenity charges. The agents were not yet certain if the song was obscene, so they shipped off more copies of the record, and the typewritten lyrics concocted in the Indiana frat house in a specially-marked "Obscene" cover envelope normally used to ship copies of books like D. H. Lawrence's *Lady Chatterley's Lover*, to the agency's Washington laboratory.

Even though the FBI's main focus in the early 60s was on hunting down criminals and communists and trying to sully the reputation of civil rights leaders like Martin Luther King, they still found time to continue to spend tax dollars on the quest to attack rock and roll. Agents from the New York office were sent to visit Marv Schlachter, President of Wand Records. Schlachter took the visit, and the threat to *Louie Louie* in stride. In fact, he welcomed the news that The Man was still sniffing around the tune. "There were a number of times when, in effect, the record was banned," he later said. "Every time that happened, we would re-release the record and sell another million copies."

More than a year after it had begun, the earth-shattering case of *Louie Louie vs Federal Bureau of Investigation* moved up to the very highest level of the agency. In June 1965, Director J. Edgar Hoover received a personal letter from a "concerned citizen" in Flint, Michigan. The letter described in detail the concerned citizen's concern about the million-dollar, possibly pornographic platter, and asked what the FBI was doing to fight it. "We have also been in contact with Mr. Lawrence Gubow, US Attorney in Detroit, and he informed us that your bureau was investigating the record in question," wrote "Concerned Citizen". "He wasn't too explicit, however. *Can you tell us what is being done? What can we do to help?* Mr. Hoover, do you think more of these type records are inevitable? Is there perhaps a subliminal type of perversion involved?"

Hoover replied promptly. "I strongly believe that the easy accessibility of such material cannot help but divert the minds of young people into unhealthy channels and negate the wholesome training they have already been afforded by their parents," pontificated the man who was thought by many to be in a homosexual relationship involving cross-dressing with his lifelong housemate and assistant, Clyde Tolson. "With reference to the record you described," he told "Concerned Citizen", "I am unable to make any comment concerning current investigations being conducted by the FBI. You may be assured, however, that this Bureau is continuing to make every effort to discharge its responsibilities with the highest degree of thoroughness and dispatch."

He also attached for his correspondent copies of the Bureau's pamphlets *Poison for Our Youth* and *Combating Merchants of Filth: The Role of the FBI*.

The new involvement of the boss got the attention of all the field agents across the land of the free and home of the brave, and they continued to see what they could do about shutting down the filthy song, until finally, two years and multitudinous tax dollars after it had begun, it was left to Detroit's Assistant US Attorney Robert J. Grace to make a decision. Grace, likely getting sick of the whole matter, "advised that in his opinion the investigation of instant matter disclosed no evidence of a ITOM [remember, that's FBI-speak for Interstate Transport of Obscene Materials] violation and that he was, therefore, recommending that no further investigation be conducted."

So that was the final end of the FBI's involvement, but by no means the end of the story. Partially as a result of Jack Ely and the

Kingsmen's overwrought and maniacally joyful rendition of Berry's tune, and partially as a result of the FBI's frenzied interest, the song soon became the ultimate frat house garage band anthem. Not only did it become a staple of every pickup dance band everywhere, with *Mustang Sally* as the only possible contender for climatic final song of the evening, but it also was recorded by literally hundreds of other singers and bands. The Beach Boys did it. So did the Angels, the Bobby Fuller Four, the Ventures, Frank Zappa, Jan & Dean, and Otis Redding.

The best version, IMHO, is by Tina Turner. Not only does the song make a lot more sense being sung by a woman, but Tina's version gets rid of the archaic nineteenth century sea shanty elements, and makes it very specifically about a contemporary cat with a sailboat (named Louis), sailing the Caribbean, searching for gold with a very enthusiastic Tina Turner by his side. What more perfect image of paradise is there than that? The YouTube version comes with the sexiest pic ever of Tina and the Ikettes dancing up a storm as she belts it out.

The song cemented its apparent immortality by being featured in dozens of movies, including, but certainly not limited to *American Graffiti, Animal House, Quadrophenia, The Naked Gun, Coupe de Ville, Wayne's World 2,* and *Mr. Holland's Opus.*

In the summer of 1981 a disc jockey at KFJC in Los Altos Hills, California named Jeff Riedle (known as "Stretch", due to his six-foot-five-inch frame) came up with the idea of programming a marathon of different versions of the song. In its first incarnation, Stretch's playlist consisted of thirty-three renditions. It was a modest beginning, but the stunt was such a hit with listeners that he repeated it six months later with fifty. By the summer of 1982 he had stretched the torrent of *Louie Louie*'s to eighty-eight, and the following December the station broadcast a wicked "Lou-a-thon" that ran for twelve hours and featured two hundred versions of the song.

They didn't stop there. On Friday, August 1983 they began broadcasting what they called *Maximum Louie Louie,* an exhausting transmission of *eight hundred* versions of the song that lasted all weekend—well-known, obscure, professional, amateur, Chinese, Italian, French, Spanish, reggae and even classical versions of the noxious, notorious tune.

Two years later, the city of Philadelphia, not wanting to be out-Louied by California, had its first official *Louie Louie* parade, with four hundred participants and five thousand spectators. As with everything *Louie*-related, the event grew like Topsy. A year later, they had one thousand marchers, sixty thousand spectators. In 1987, twelve hundred marchers, ninety-five thousand spectators. That one, *People* Magazine called "The *Louie* heard around the world. Or at least in Scranton." By 1987 the parades were being franchised, sponsored by Taco Bell, and raised $120,000 for the American Leukemia Society.

Meanwhile, in Washington, the ultimate gentrification of the song was underway. Richard Berry's birthday, April 12, was officially declared *Louie Louie* Day at the State capitol in Olympia. In March of 1985 a resolution was introduced in the Washington state Senate to make *Louie Louie* the official state song. Senator Al Williams introduced the motion grandly, pronouncing, "Whereas 'Rock and Roll' musicians have provided some of our citizens the ability to express their pride, energy and creativity through the art of dance," and "Whereas Rockin' Robin Roberts, singer for the 'Wailers', a Washington musical group, was the original vocalist for the song *Louie Louie"* [plainly not true, but hardly the first time René Touzet and Richard Berry's seminal role in the song's history had been ignored]. Finally, "Whereas some of our legislators, citizens, and even the governor are not familiar with the song *Louie Louie*. . ." This third clause was mighty rich. Had there ever been a time before when a career politician had been rebuked for not being an enthusiast of something that only a few years previous the FBI had treated as a moral threat to America?

It would be *Louie Louie's* greatest opportunity to stick it to The Man. The song that had once been banned by a state would now be the sanctioned official song of a state. However, it was not to be. For whatever reasons, Governor Booth Gardner and Washington House did not pass the bill. Richard Berry, who after years in the wilderness had finally got the copyright back to his song, and so now had taken to wearing a peaked sailor's cap and calling himself "Captain Louie," did not complain about the song's non-official status. He said he was "really flattered" by the effort to make *Louie Louie* official, "but can you imagine someone going to meet a dignitary at an airport and playing *duh duh duh, duh duh?*"

For a final ironic beat in the story of Richard Berry, his daughter Christy became so intrigued by the legal history of her father's song that she went into training herself to become. . .an FBI agent. Berry died in 1997, knowing he had written the greatest song of all time. Or maybe the worst.

Van Halen

The story of Van Halen is a classic tale from the most decadently successful period in music—the mid-70s to the late 80s, when teenage kids could determine to become rich rock stars, create groups that succeeded beyond their wildest dreams, then ultimately come crashing down in a sea of alcohol, cocaine and acrimony.

Edward and Alex Van Halen were two brothers living in Pasadena, California. They were not rich, like their collaborator, David Lee Roth, whose father was a very wealthy doctor, but they and their Dutch immigrant parents lived in a decent house in a nice part of town. Nor did they want for parental support. Their parents bought them Edward's first guitar—a Gibson Goldtop, and Alex's first good quality drum set. Nonetheless they were first busted by The Man before their first public performance. While practicing at the house of a young friend named Brian Box, the police showed up three times in an hour to tell them that the neighbors were complaining about the noise. On the third visit the exasperated cop told them, "If I hear one more note, somebody's going to jail." Alex took that as his cue to hit the snare drum, so the cop slapped handcuffs on Box and shut down the rehearsal.

Undaunted, the two brothers rehearsed incessantly and formed a group that became known as not just one of the loudest but also one of the best amateur bands in Pasadena. By the age of seventeen

Edward was already recognized as an amazing guitar virtuoso. Today, he is considered one of the best rock guitarists of all time. The band, though, had a reputation for causing trouble. A 1971 concert in the basement of a Jewish temple in Whittier ended with the Whittier cops charging in after a report of a fight. Their friend Brian Box was again there, and remembers, "I was sitting down, watching the band. Then the next thing I knew all these cops came walking in and all these kids pointed right at me. These cops grabbed me by the back of the hair and were dragging me out of the place." Box's friends leapt to his defense. The police responded by pulling out their batons and cans of Mace. The band stopped playing, and joined in the melee. Soon dozens of the kids were getting arrested and thrown in the back of squad cars. "Those cops were really out of line. That really pissed me off," recalls Box. Alex and Edward had to call home, and their father, Jan Van Halen had to go down to the police station to bail them out.

The Van Halen's band, first named the Trojan Rubber Company, then Genesis, then Mammoth got a reputation. "Schools wouldn't hire us, [and] nobody wanted anything to do with us," remembered Edward. But while school administrators hated their loud abrasive heavy metal sound, teenagers loved it. They were also amazed by the musicianship of the two teenaged brothers. Guitarist Eric Hensel says, "Ed was better than anyone I had ever seen in town by about a mile." However, he emphasizes, "I don't want to discount [Alex's] contribution, because when you saw them it was the combination of the two. It was a two-man show. They had a synergy between them that was just unbelievable. It was like they could read each other's minds."

They had musical skills, but they weren't accomplished singers, and had little rock and roll razzmatazz. Meanwhile, across town, a kid named David Lee Roth was preening himself in front of any mirror he passed, convinced he would become a rock star, but without a band to accompany him. He did already have charm, popularity, and a bevy of female admirers, many of them young pretty black girls.

Friends thought he felt he was a cool black dude trapped in a white body. His high school pal Vincent Carberry recalls, "he certainly had star quality and showmanship and God knows the gift of gab and self-confidence."

Roth's cocky self-confidence meant he had no trouble walking over to the house of the Van Halen's and telling them he wanted to be the singer for their fledgling band. The brothers agreed he could audition for them. He failed the first one, but they allowed he could return for a second, but he failed that too. "It was terrible," remembers Edward. "He couldn't sing. I was completely and thoroughly appalled."

Roth decided if the Van Halen bros wouldn't let him into their band, he would start his own. If he couldn't beat the Van Halens with musicianship, he would beat them with flash. He created a band he called "Red Ball Jet" and proceeded to careen around the stages of the schools and churches they played in, dressed in tight pants and midriff-baring sequined shirts. Red Ball was constantly in trouble with The Man—or sometimes, The Woman. At a concert at St. Francis High School, a stern nun told him she forbade his skimpy stage outfit, and had to change into something more suitable for the audience of Catholic schoolgirls. There was a tense exchange of words between the nun and the budding rock star, and then, remembers guitarist Dan Hernandez, "He wouldn't change, so we didn't play."

In another gig in a church basement, the band learned that they had only been hired to serve as an example of the evils of the "Devil's work." The band decided if that was why they were there, then they would live up to their billing. They stripped off their shirts and Roth pulled his pants as low as they would go without falling down. They caused such pandemonium they had to escape by exiting through the window of their dressing room.

They would often play in the Mexican barrio of Pasadena, attracting the attention of the police, who were suspicious about why this all-white teenage band was playing parties in the Mexican side of town. The reason seems to have been simple—David Lee Roth, with his good looks, leather pants and long hair. "The girls, man they would line up," remembers George Perez, who first met the singer in grade seven, "They'd wet their panties going to look at this guy."

Roth, with his rich father helping, tried hard to make his band a success. They played gigs at a downtown Los Angeles police station, a USO concert and a girls' prison. They played backyard pool parties, one of which was illuminated by a police helicopter hovering above with Roth dancing around the giant spotlight until the cops angrily shut the party down. The chopper gave the band an idea—they'd rent one of their own to land at their next gig at Eliot Junior High School, as the Stones did at Altamont. Roth papered San Gabriel Valley with 3000 posters advertising the gig showing a photo of the band stark naked, with only guitars covering their dangly bits. When the city administrator heard the news about helicopters and naked teenage rock musicians, he hit the roof. The concert at least made the local newspaper. The Pasadena *Star-News* ran an article under the headline ALTADENA ROCK FEST CANCELLED.

The city official wasn't the only one who had problems with the flamboyant Roth. "Ed and I couldn't stand the motherfucker," said his future band-mate Alex Van Halen. "We couldn't stand the band. We couldn't stand the music. " His brother concurred, claiming that Red Ball Jet was "totally into showmanship, except that they… couldn't play a note." Nor did Roth get a much better reaction when he auditioned his band at the big clubs on Sunset Strip. By 1973, Red Ball Jet had given up and broken up. Roth was left with nothing other than a high quality PA system. However, his fancy gear proved to be his entrée into the orbit of the Van Halens, who had plenty of backyard gigs to play, but no PA system. They began renting Roth's gear, but eventually, recalls Edward, "we were renting his PA every weekend for thirty-five dollars and getting fifty dollars for the gigs. So it was cheaper to get him into the band." Roth was insistent, telling the Van Halens that they could no longer use his gear unless they let him sing.

The band, with their new singer, soon became the hottest act in Pasadena, though most of their outdoor backyard gigs didn't last long. Rudy Leiren, who became Edward's guitar tech once the band hit the big time, remembers that once the very loud band began playing, "the cops were going to be there in ten minutes and bust the party. I think it was very rare that a party went to ten o'clock, let alone past ten."

Even in their abbreviated form, the dozens of backyard gigs helped the band hone their tight, distinctive style. They did though need a new name, for just as they had with Genesis, the band received a cease and desist order from another band named Mammoth. The politically astute Roth suggested the name "Van Halen", which the brothers at first resisted, "because we didn't want to appear conceited" but eventually agreed to. No one could take that name away from them.

The band had big plans to perform on the club circuit, but within the first few months of Roth joining the two brothers, they were turned down by *nineteen* venues. Instead, they carved out a new path for themselves, becoming Pasadena's biggest outdoor party band. It was not terribly lucrative, but it was a chance to continue to hone their musical chops, it was fun, and gave them notoriety, not just with young audiences, but with the police and authorities of the San Gabriel Valley.

The first ended with a giant knife and gunfight, with a teen named Charles Levor getting what was described as "fifty buckshot wounds on his backside." The next was a big outdoor event on the steps of Pasadena's city hall supporting the centennial of the city. Two thousand rowdy patrons showed up and celebrated the civic anniversary by drinking, and fighting. Local police and organizers tried to rope Roth into cooling things down, but when that didn't work, the cops waded into the crowd, confiscating the crowd's alcohol, pouring out, according to the Pasadena *Star-News,* "enough booze to fill a liquor store."

A month later the band had another gig. It was a perfect venue—a giant mansion with a two and a half acre backyard with tennis courts and a pool, with a keen wannabe host, teen Jack Van Furche. Most importantly, his parents were away for the weekend. Jack ordered some kegs of beer, papered the local high schools with hand-drawn notices, rented a little stage and some lights, and hired Van Halen.

By 9:30, remembers the Van Furche's girlfriend, Debbie Hannaford Lorenz, the party was raging. "It's packed like sardines in this whole backyard. It was solid people—there were thousands of people there." At that point a police helicopter appeared overhead, and hovered above the noisy party, shining its three and a half million candlepower spotlight down on the stage and yard. It was exactly the sort of spotlight David Van Roth had always wanted. He began leaping around more intently, singing more loudly, shouting at the young crowd to get crazy. The pilot began ordering the teens to disperse over the chopper's loudspeaker.

Meanwhile, dozens of San Marino squad cars began arriving, and the police officers began fighting their way into the tony yard. The kids began pouring out of the yard to the front, where they began rocking the cop cars back and forth to flip them over. Alex remembers that "four cop cars got turned over," and Edward recalls that nineteen of the partygoers were arrested and that, "I'll never forget a group of guys took one cop and they took his handcuffs and they handcuffed him around a tree with his own handcuffs!"

It was only the beginning. That month the band rounded out their ensemble with a bass player and back-up singer named Michael Anthony, and continued to play backyard parties in Pasadena, all of which turned into bacchanalian battles with the authorities. The wildest of them became known as "The Battle of Pasadena."

Don Imler had recently retired from his position as deputy inspector from the L.A. County Sherriff's Department. Now that he was retired, he, his wife and sometimes their friends would head south to spend months at their retirement home on Rosarito Beach in Mexico, leaving their twenty-two year son Denis and teenage daughters Debbie and Karen in command of their Pasadena ranch home. The three kids liked to party, and in November 1974 they determined to organize the best backyard party in Pasadena history. They figured twenty kegs of beer, some serious stage lights, and Van Halen would get the party started.

They even provided the band with a rehearsal space for the week before the party—their father's den, incongruously full of Sheriff's Department plaques and memorabilia. The band enjoyed practicing and playing at the Imler's house, since the parents were gone and instead it was full of pretty girls who would teasingly answer the phone, "Mustang Ranch," referencing the infamous Nevada whorehouse.

For the night of the big party, Roth got things underway by firing off pyrotechnic flash pots while the Van Halen brothers managed to increase the volume of the band to an absurd new level. "I have that memory of walking down the street with all the cars and the music just echoing everywhere, and you know it's a Van Halen party," remembers Debbie Lorenz. "It was just such an exciting, electrical feeling. You were excited to get to go. I loved it. I loved that sensation that you'd get through your whole body."

The neighbors were less enthusiastic about the sensation they were getting through their whole bodies, and were soon on the phone to the police. Karen Imler admits, "It was crazy. Huntington Drive turned into and sounded like a drag strip." By eight the backyard was packed with kids, drinking, laughing and dancing to the music of Van Halen. Partygoer Jeff Touchie recalls, "People were throwing each other in the pool. Girls were running around half naked and drunk and jumping in." Another guest, Dana Anderson remembers, "I dropped PCP that night, so I was bouncing off the walls." He managed to walk right through a sliding glass door behind the band, shattering it into hundreds of pieces. Others through the giant house and yard were stoned on quaaludes, mescaline, cocaine, mushrooms and peyote.

Police began to appear, and told Denis he'd have to get the band to turn the volume down, but it was almost impossible for him to make his way though the densely-packed crowd, let alone persuade Roth to tone down his act. The cops called for re-enforcements, and soon a helicopter was overhead and dozens of squad cars and a paddy wagon were on their way. With the helicopter overhead, Roth fired his remaining smoke pots. The deafening noise, smoke, sparks and whirring helicopter blades created a scene that was like something out of the Vietnam war. Musician Eric Hensel describes what he saw as he exited the party—"Fifty or sixty cop cars and four guys in each one with full riot gear. . .it was an amazing thing to watch. I'd never seen anything like it in Pasadena."

One kid, trying to get away by hopping the fence, managed to break the water supply line to the pool. Water sprayed all over, threatening the band's electrically charged equipment. The band grabbed brooms to push the water away, with Edward later confessing he was "very afraid he was going to get electrocuted." Edward's friend Peter Burke recalls, "The sheriff's department showed up and started shoving people around really brutally. I mean girls. It was pretty hairy." Another friend, Art Agajanian recalls, "The Temple City Sheriff's Department was very hard on kids. They used Mace and tear gas. They billy-clubbed kids."

It was a baptism of fire for the band's new bass player, Michael Anthony, who remembers, "The cops said they were going to arrest us. I thought we were going to jail. That really scared us. Yeah, those backyard parties were something incredible. There were like two thousand people in this backyard."

None of the band members were arrested, but twenty-one partygoers were hauled away in the paddy wagons, with charges from narcotics possession to "suspicion of failure to disperse."

The irrepressible David Lee Roth, knowing he was the main cause of all the mayhem, took it in stride. "Cop cars showed up parked in a line, all with the flashing lights and lots of flares. It was all very exciting and kind of scary, and you might go to jail, and your parents might have to come get you out, and maybe even pay for a friend or two. It was great."

Eventually the band moved on from playing to stoned teens and phalanxes of Pasadena riot police. They weren't able to crack Hollywood yet, which still dismissed them as merely a cover band, so instead criss-crossed the vast sprawling smog-choked suburbs of Southern California, from Pomona to Palmdale, La Cañada to Redondo Beach. The band could not seem to shake the attention of The Man. In Mitty's, one of the notorious biker bars they performed in, their music was frequently the soundtrack for violent fights. "One time late in the evening," remembers Edward, "we just saw a guy's intestines hanging out of his gut." At other events, less violent but still considered illegal, they provided the musical groove for wet tee-shirt contests that would frequently be attended by undercover cops who would alert their uniformed brethren to swarm into the clubs to arrest the organizers and bare-breasted participants.

Finally, in 1976, the band cracked the resistance from the music industry and made it on to the clubs of Sunset Strip and Hollywood Boulevard. Even though the prevailing wisdom was that the kind of heavy rock Van Halen played was outdated, and that the public wanted the softer "L.A. Sound" of performers like Jackson Browne, Fleetwood Mac, CSNY and The Eagles, nonetheless Warner Brothers finally signed them to make a record. It was one of the most successful debut albums of all time, making diamond status, eventually selling over ten million units. Further, in an era of wretched recording excess, it was recorded in only three weeks for a total cost of $54,000. By comparison, Fleetwood Mac's *Rumours*, recorded in the same period, went *over budget* by $400,000.

Warner Brothers also managed to secure some major venues for the band, including the Los Angeles Civic Auditorium. Again, though, the band would attract the wrath of the authorities. Promoter Steve Tortomasi remembers, "There was an angry, drunken asshole named Jack, who was a Civic stage manager. He hated rock music. He told me before this show, 'If they use fireworks, I'm calling the fire department and shutting your show down.'" Tortomasi passed this on to the band, but they ignored his advice. They restrained themselves until their last number, then exploded twenty-five smoke pots at once, smoking out the windowless 4500 seat auditorium. Within minutes the sound of Van Halen rock was conjoined with the wail of sirens. "Then," laughed Roth, "it was like right out of the movies. All the doorways flew open at once, and all you can see [were] those rolling red lights on top of the fire trucks and all of these guys with gas masks and hoses and full-blast fire boots and gear. . .bursting through the door to throw 4500 of our closest friends out of the building."

The band rapidly exploded into an international touring act. At first they were sent out as an opening band for acts like Journey, Black Sabbath and Ted Nugent, but they very rapidly began to outshine the headliners. Initially nervous about playing in the big leagues, the fantastic response they got from audiences and critics gave the band new confidence. Roth told a reporter that Van Halen and its crew were comparable to the hordes of Attila the Hun, because both were "a group of barbarians who are sweeping around the world non-stop and have a few basic goals in mind and when it's done have a good old barbarian party—after each city is conquered." Even the critics who were cool to their music admitted their success and popularity with audiences. The reporter for the *San Francisco Chronicle* predicted, "Van Halen purveys rock at its lowest common denominator—and will be very big before long."

Discombobulated Black Sabbath frontman Ozzy Osbourne admitted that Van Halen "are so good they ought to be headlining the tour." Ted Nugent, seeing that his star had been eclipsed by the newcomers, announced, "I don't ever want Van Halen on the same bill as me!"

The young band celebrated their success by beginning a pattern of ridiculous misbehavior. In Aberdeen, Scotland, they learned that their first album had gone gold, so they found some gold paint and began redecorating the hallways of their hotel. Roth admitted in his memoir that the Scottish police "escorted" them out of the country, telling them, "Don't ever come back."

In order to attempt some measure of control over them, their label assigned a tough young streetwise New Yorker, Noel Monk as their road manager. Within a year he graduated to becoming their manager, taking an equal share in the band's fortunes in return for running the complex operation. In Madison, Wisconsin, Monk came upon the four musketeers in a hotel room smeared with ketchup with most of the furniture broken or thrown out the window. With the musicians were two naked groupies, having ketchup squeezed into what Monk describes as "every available orifice (and some that, frankly, were not available)."

"It was the kind of scene that would have made Caligula proud," says Monk. He left the boys and girls to their fun. His only interest, he says, was to avoid any sort of police involvement. The next morning, he simply brought the hotel manager up to view the damage, and wrote a check to cover it. The lads were pleased to hear that Warner Brothers paid for their destructive shenanigans. It took them several years to understand how the music business works. These expenses, and all others, would ultimately be deducted from their earnings. Who cared? The money was pouring in, so the high jinks continued. At the Tangerine Bowl in Orlando, the band opened for the Rolling Stones. They needed to cross the Bowl in order to get to their dressing room, so were given a high-end limousine to make the short trip. By the end of it, the young rock gods had destroyed it, ripping out seat rests, bending the doors off their hinges and pummeling the hood and roof. Again, Monk had to make a large payment of tens of thousands of dollars to cover the damage and keep the idiotic incident out of the courts.

Like many pampered rock stars of the era, the band resented having to do promotional appearances at radio stations and record stores. Monk attempted to jazz up their interest by having them make grand entrances. On one occasion they appeared on the back of four Harley-Davidsons. They topped that by showing up once in an armoured Brink's truck, having several uniformed gun-toting "security guards" (actually roadies) jump out, then the four band members made their appearance, waving to their adoring fans.

Their grandest entrance, and perhaps the grandest entrance ever made in show biz history, was at Anaheim Stadium. This time, it was a quadruple bill. Keen to outshine the three other bands they were performing with, they concocted an outlandish scheme. While the other groups were partying away the afternoon before the show began, the four members of Van Halen slipped away and hung out in a trailer behind the arena. When it came time for their appearance, fans noticed a plane appear above the arena, and four skydivers leap from it and begin drifting down towards the arena. As the crowd began to focus on the action above them, the announcer blared over the PA system, "From out of the sky, Van Halen is coming into the stadium." Tracy "G" Grijalra, a guitarist attending the concert, remembers it vividly: "As they got closer, you can see they've got the big VH on their fucking parachutes. They got closer and closer and the whole fucking place was roaring. I'm like, 'There's no fucking way.' Talk about getting the crowd before they even walk on! Now I don't think it was them, but it didn't fucking matter, because everybody thought it was. They land in the backstage area, and then they come running out in parachute outfits. I'm like *Fuck me!* They rip off the jumpsuits and they've got their fucking rock star clothes on. They throw Eddie his guitar and that's it. I'm like *Fuck it*; they had everything, and they thought of everything!"

It was of course not real, but it was a spectacular piece of showmanship. Once the skydivers landed behind the arena they ran in to the trailer, and the four band members came running out, wearing identical jumpsuits. It certainly became part of the lore of the band. Another even better known story, always told to prove that by the end of the 70s musicians had become utterly coddled and pampered, was the one about how the rider of demands for every show was that the band's dressing room had to be provided with a long list of drinks, food and candy, including a bowl of M&M's *with all the brown ones removed*. The demand seems so ludicrously over the top that it could not be real, but it was, and, according to Monk, here's why:

"It acted as a sort of insurance clause that proved that the things that really did matter in our contract (safety matters and the like) had been given proper weight and consideration. We figured that if a promoter took the time to remove all the brown M&M's from the bowl before putting them in our dressing room, it was far less likely he'd screwed up any of the other, really important stuff. It gave the promoters a headache and made us look like a bunch of dickheads, sure, but it saved me time, and it prevented something going wrong for the band."

The band didn't need the brown M&M's clause to make them look like dickheads, since as they grew in stature, they often managed to do it on their own. The two Van Halen brothers began to have an increasingly acrimonious relationship with their front man David Lee Roth, and eventually fired him from the band. They also began to fight with each other. On one occasion Monk discovered the pair of them battling in a hotel room. "They began screaming at each other in what I later learned was Dutch—the tongue of their motherland. It was one of the strangest things I had ever seen—these two ordinarily placid Southern California rockers, who usually spoke in a sort of pothead surf patois, suddenly nose to nose, spitting and snarling, and growling at each other in a foreign language, as if they had become possessed. I started to leave the room as their voices got louder—it was all just too crazy and pathetic, even for rock and roll. But before I could exit, they were on each other, slamming their fists in each other's face grabbing great fistfuls of hair, and rolling around on the floor like drunken idiots. As we separated them, all I could think was, 'Holy shit...I've got a couple of madmen on my hands.'"

The violence spilled out into the streets as the band attempted to protect the vast secondary income it was making from merchandizing tee shirts, hats, vests, and all manner of other clothing and chachkas bearing the name, imagery or logo of the band. Monk, with a family background in New York's schmata business, convinced the band they should control merchandizing themselves, rather than license it to others, as most bands do. "I considered it an untapped vein of gold," he said.

The easy part proved to be convincing the teen fans to buy the stuff. Heavy metal rock fans are even more loonily willing to part with their money than sports fans in order to dress up to prove their allegiance to the cause. By the end of 1982, Van Halen was making a quarter of a million dollars a night in sales of merchandise—as much as they were making by playing music. Further, in those days it was all cash, so by the end of a weekend their manager might be carrying three quarters of a million dollars on him. To protect himself, and the band, he assembled a staff of ten very intimidating guys. "Trust me when I say this: you did not want to fuck with these guys. Hell, I didn't want to fuck with them, and I was their boss (they called me L'il Caesar, the nickname Edward had come up with a couple years earlier.)"

Local entrepreneurs felt that if the band could make money selling Van Halen tee shirts, they could too. The band strenuously disagreed. "The Bootleg Wars, as I like to refer to this period in Van Halen history, was a vicious but essential stage of the band's development, at least from a business perspective," says their manager. "Van Halen might have been a party band that espoused mainly the time-honored teenage pursuits of inebriation and sex, but behind the scenes, they were an entity seriously devoted to protecting and furthering their own brand. Merchandizing was central to this pursuit, and we crushed anyone who attempted to illegally infringe on our business."

In order to do this, Monk interacted with US Marshalls and local police in a manner quite unlike the other bands and musicians chronicled in this book. "It was important to us to maintain at least a cordial relationship with police departments across the country. After all, we needed cops to get our job done. Every concert involved heavy interaction with the local police force, as they were responsible for traffic management, crowd control, security, and a dozen other issues. At every show, the cops could make your job harder or easier, so it only made sense to develop an atmosphere of mutual trust and respect. I like cops and appreciated the fact that they had a difficult and dangerous mission. I understood that if they wanted to make our lives miserable—ours, after all, was a business in which illicit activity of one type or another was an everyday occurrence—they could easily do that."

Convincing the band of that was not always an easy matter. *Wait a minute. . .Noel likes cops? What's that about? We fucking hate cops.*

Returning backstage at the end of a set, the band would often be shocked to find uniformed cops, guests of their manager, chowing down on pastries and bowls of brown-free M&M's from their craft service table. Recognizing the intense cultural divide, the manager would usually hustle the cops out, but often thanking them for coming with $50 bills.

Greasing the cops usually kept them on the side of the band, but not always. Monk and his group of security goons would often take it upon themselves to violently confront the parking lot clothing bootleggers, and sometimes the locals would complain to the police about their heavy-handed tactics. At a show in Fort Wayne, Indiana, the cops got sick of a screaming match between the band management and the bootleggers, so arrested the lot of them, and they all spent the night in the city's drunk tank.

A similar fracas developed over the band's attempts to control photography at a big arena concert in San Diego. It may be hard to fathom for those who have grown up in an era where everyone over the age of five carries a high quality camera in their pocket, and uses it all the time, but before the era of the IPhone it was completely forbidden to take cameras into musical events. Van Halen and their security heavies protected the band's photographic rights just as voraciously as they did their merchandizing. If security found photographers, as they did in San Diego, they would grab their cameras from them, open them up, pull the film out of them and hand them back empty, usually with a warning peppered with four letter words not to do it again.

In San Diego, one of these confrontations escalated into an angry argument. With the band belting out their music in the background, the local police decided that manager Noel Monk was getting out of line. Again, he was hauled to the police station and spent the night in a holding cell.

Once he got out he discovered that the band was highly amused by what had happened. "Here I was," he confesses, "the guy who supposedly knew how to keep the cops off their backs in every city in the country, and I was the one who ended up getting arrested."

"You don't mess with the cops in San Diego," a laughing Roth told him. "Everybody knows that. These guys are real pricks down here."

Michael Jackson

In January of 1993, when Michael Jackson was invited to perform at the inauguration of President Bill Clinton, he was on top of the world. The *Guinness Book of Records* of that year described him as follows: "Most successful entertainer of all time; highest grossing live performer in history; best-selling album of all time; youngest vocalist to top the U.S. singles chart at number one; longest number of weeks at the top of U.S. album charts; most successful music video; and highest paid entertainer of all time."

On top of that, he was renowned for his philanthropic efforts. He donated all the profits of his recent "Dangerous" World Tour to the Heal the World Foundation to fight illness, hunger, homelessness and abuse of the world's children. He invited hundreds of low income, hospitalized and minority children to play at his vast Neverland Ranch in Santa Ynez, California. No one was surprised that he dedicated a song at the inauguration to "all the children of the world".

A few months later, his world came crashing down amid vile accusations that would haunt him for the rest of his life. Even though he was twice found not guilty of all charges, the accusations would in fact continue until his 2009 death and would be resurrected a decade later with new accusers leveling new charges at him.

It is true that many of Jackson's problems with The Man were self-created. Much of his strange personality quirks and his naïve, childlike behavior seems to have stemmed from his obsession with his virtually non-existent childhood. From the age of six he was constantly performing and recording with his family. The Jackson Five was managed by their father Joe Jackson, who regularly held his belt in his hand, ready to whip any of his sons, but particularly Michael, the youngest, if they made any mistakes during rehearsals.

In adulthood, Michael Jackson saw himself as Peter Pan, the leader of the Lost Boys, who lived in the perpetual childhood fantasy world of Neverland. It was more than just an interest in the story that was originally written in 1902 by Scottish novelist J.M.Barrie and later turned into numerous films, plays and TV series. "Peter represents something that's very special in my heart," he told journalist Martin Bashir a hundred years after the book's original publication.

"You know, he represents youth, childhood, never growing up, magic, flying, everything I think that children and wonderment and magic, what it's all about. And to me, I have just never, ever grown out of loving that or thinking that it's very special."

Bashir: "You identify with him?"

Jackson: "Totally."

Bashir: "You don't want to grow up?"

Jackson: "No, I am Peter Pan."

Bashir: "No you're not, you're Michael Jackson."

Jackson: "I'm Peter Pan in my heart."

As he told Oprah Winfrey in a 1993 interview, "People wonder why I always have children around. It's because I find the thing I never had with them, you know. When I was little it was always work, work, work, from one concert to the next. If it wasn't a concert, it was the recording studio. If it wasn't that, it was TV shows or picture sessions."

Jackson told a group of kids visiting Neverland that "I'm only happy when I'm with children," and he began hanging out with young kids in the early 80s. His first and most famous "special friends" were *Webster* star Emmanuel Lewis and *Home Alone* star Macauley Culkin. Both have adamantly denied that there was anything untoward about their relationship with the famous singer. "Nothing the least unusual ever happened," says Culkin. "It was just clean fun. I know it sounds weird to somebody who doesn't know that scene. Looking back, I guess it was a bit weird. But at the time, it just seemed so harmless, so normal. Michael is just Michael and if you really knew him, you would know how stupid the accusations are."

The accusations, though, were flying like Tinkerbell, and with them the harassment by The Man that would last for the rest of his life. Many, in fact, have characterized the authorities—especially the Santa Barbara Attorney's General office, of having a vendetta against Jackson. The reasons why Michael Jackson was the target of The Man, and the target of so many lawsuits are many—he was a musician, he was young, he was black, he was incredibly famous, incredibly rich, he seemed childlike, innocent, possibly weak, he appeared to be homosexual, or at least bisexual, he was eccentric, and he lead a lifestyle that at very least left him open to suspicion of misbehavior.

He did not hide his wildly unorthodox activities. He toured Japan with his pet chimpanzee Bubbles. He collaborated with Freddie Mercury on an album, although Mercury and the producers had to abandon the project after Jackson repeatedly insisted on bringing a llama into the studio. He attempted to purchase—for one million dollars—the skeleton of the nineteenth century British carnival freak Joseph Merrick—the "Elephant Man". His skin color and appearance seemed to radically change through the 80s and 90s. And he hung around with young boys.

In August 1993 Jackson was accused of child sexual abuse by a thirteen-year-old, Jordan Chandler, and his father, Evan Chandler. Even though from the outset there was considerable question about the veracity of the accusations (the boy's mother, for instance, told the police she did not believe them, and thought the boy had been coerced into making them) the police were sufficiently convinced, and raided Jackson's Neverland Ranch, where they seized fifty boxes of books, videos, clothing and other paraphernalia. They also forced Jackson to strip off his clothing in order to examine his penis.

The press, led by the tabloid trash TV show *Hard Copy* and the supermarket weekly *National Enquirer*, had a field day. The police, though, began to be suspicious of the motivations of Evan Chandler, who seemed more interested in money than justice. He was quoted saying, "If I go through with this I win big time. . .I will get everything I want. . .they will be destroyed forever. I will take anybody down that harms a child. This man is going to be humiliated beyond belief. He will not believe what is going to happen to him. Beyond his worst nightmares. He will not sell one more record." He hired the meanest lawyer he could find, who he claimed would "destroy everybody in sight in any devious, nasty, cruel way he can do it."

Chandler, a dentist and a screenwriter, with a writing credit on the Mel Brooks film *Robin Hood: Men in Tights*, proposed, through his lawyer, that he would drop his lawsuit against Jackson if the singer would purchase four screenplays from him for $5 million each. That deal fell apart with the dentist/screenwriter being accused of extortion. Meanwhile a reporter from Los Angeles TV station KCBS uncovered information that Jordan Chandler had told his father about the alleged molestation while in his dad's dentist chair under the influence of sodium amytal, a drug rarely used in dentistry but instead one that has become associated in recent years with False Memory Syndrome.

Santa Barbara District Attorney Tom Snedden continued on what some called his crusade to crucify Michael Jackson, but the investigation was proving to be unsuccessful. The police department's humiliating strip search ended with an admission by the police that "photos of Michael Jackson's genitalia do not match descriptions given by the boy who accused the singer of sexual misconduct." By December 1993, as many as twelve investigators from Santa Barbara and Los Angeles were working full time on the case, the team had spent over $2 million on it, had interviewed more than two hundred witnesses, sent cops off as far away as Manila on wild goose chases, all without finding a single piece of credible evidence against the singer. Although Snedden, obsessed with the case, refused to give up, he and his team were beginning to despair. While they could find numerous kids who had been invited by organizations like the Make a Wish Foundation to visit and play at Neverland, they could not find a single one who would state that anything improper had happened there.

In January of 1994, Sneddon and a four man team flew off to Melbourne, Australia to interview another boy, Brett Barnes, who they thought might testify against Michael Jackson. Again, they came back empty handed. Barnes and his family were outraged at the suggestion, and Brett completely denied that Jackson had tried to molest him.

Meanwhile, Jackson's insurance company decided to settle the civil lawsuit from the Chandlers. Over the protests of Jackson and his advisors, the insurance company paid Jordie Chandler $15,331,250, each of his parents $1.5 million, and their lawyers millions more. There were hundreds of media accounts claiming that the payment implied an admission of Jackson's guilt, and that it somehow prevented a criminal prosecution. In fact, neither are true. Insurance lawyer Lewis Kaplan explains, "Insurance companies almost always settle. That's what they do. It's not an admission of guilt. It's an attempt to avoid a long, costly legal process and one where there's always a risk. You never know what a jury might do. In this case, with the defendant worth hundreds of millions of dollars, settling is a no-brainer. Of course they would settle."

Meanwhile two District Attorneys, Tom Snedden of Santa Barbara and Gil Garcetti of Los Angeles opened Grand Jury hearings on the case. However after another eight months and millions of dollars spent on trying to make the case against Michael Jackson, the pair gave up. They held a joint press conference on September 21, 1994 and announced they had dropped all criminal charges.

Also that year, Michael Jackson needed the services of another representative of The Man. Dominican Republic Judge Hugo Alvarez Perez formally asked the Prince of Pop whether he would take the hand of the daughter of the King of Rock and Roll, Lisa Marie Presley, to be his wife.

"Why not?" replied Jackson.

The rock and royal wedding shocked the world, and surprised even the judge, who agreed with the throng of reporters outside the courthouse that, "It was all very strange, but it is not my job to ask why people are getting married." Judge Perez later said that the marriage lasted longer than he thought it would. "I gave them a year. They lasted a year and a half." In December 1995, the pair separated.

The following year, Jackson married Debbie Rowe, a 37-year old nurse working in his dermatologist's office. She offered to be artificially inseminated, for a fee of six million dollars. With an eight-year old boy serving as the best man, the Jackson-Rowe wedding held to the singer's usual high standards of bizzaro. Rowe gave birth to two children, named Prince Michael I and Paris-Michael. Immediately after birth the children were whisked away from Rowe and raised at Neverland by a team of six nurses and six nannies and their doting father.

Famously, Jackson was photographed and seen by hundreds of screaming fans dangling Prince off the balcony of his Berlin hotel suite. The Man pontificated, many child protection experts responded and even Donald Trump got involved contributing the comment "I couldn't believe what I saw. Obviously Michael is somehow out of control." In the end, though, the Berlin police did not press charges.

Jackson would probably have been wise to leave his troubled dealings with The Man alone, but instead, he released a new album, HIStory, with a song about his main tormentor, D.A. Tom Snedden (who he disguises as "Dom Sheldon" in the lyric sheet, though not in the actual song). He calls Dom Sheldon a "cold man", who wants to "get my ass dead or alive" and asks whether he is "a brother to the K.K.K." Also on the album is the song *Tabloid Junkie* that attacks the media for its continuing persecution.

Through the late 90s and early 2000s Jackson continued with his increasingly extreme lifestyle. Although at one point Elizabeth Taylor got him into extensive rehabilitation in a Swiss clinic for his overuse of morphine, demerol and various anti-anxiety drugs. He was constantly getting cosmetic surgery operations (twenty to thirty in his life, it is believed) and using skin-lightening creams to counter the effects of the skin disorder vitiligo, which causes white patches to appear on the skin. He got into a bitter battle with his record label, Sony, calling its president, Tommy Mottola, "mean, racist and very, very devilish," and accusing Sony of stealing and cheating from musicians, especially black musicians, in its stable.

For all its particular complexity, much of Jackson's personality, like that of many black artists, was formed by his memories of childhood racism. He never forgot going door-to-door with his siblings, selling the magazine of the Jehovah's Witnesses, *The Watchtower*, and being greeted with the words, "Get lost, nigger." He had to take it as a boy, but now he was in a position to tell his perceived enemies to beat it.

Feeling that he was being pilloried by The Man, slandered by the press, screwed by his record company, and abandoned by some of his friends and family, Jackson decided that he had to fight back in order to try to restore his reputation and career. His friend

Lady Diana, the Princess of Wales, in a similar position after the hot mess of her breakup with Prince Charles, had done this by working with a British journalist named Martin Bashir to create a televised interview/documentary shown worldwide that had done wonders for her reputation. The technique worked for Lady Di. It imploded for Michael Jackson.

After guiding the viewers through the maze of Jackson's life, career success, and various eccentricities, Bashir skillfully asked him about the stories of the many young boys and girls who had shared the singer's bed at Neverland. Jackson freely agreed that he had slept with many children, arguing that it was "a beautiful thing," and nothing to be ashamed of.

"When you say 'bed' you're thinking sexual," he responded. "It's not sexual. We're going to sleep. I tuck them in. I put little, like, music on. Story time. I read a book. Very sweet, put the fireplace on. Give them hot milk. You know, we have little cookies. It's very charming, very sweet."

Neither Bashir, the public, the tabloid press nor The Man agreed with Jackson's televised assessment of his sleepovers, even though Bashir's editing and approach on the doc would later be seriously challenged. D.A. Tom Sneddon, though he continued to deny it, was still on a vendetta against Jackson—one that has been compared to Inspector Javert's crusade to track down Jean Valjean in *Les Miserables*. In November 2003, a few months after the Bashir documentary aired in the U.S., more than sixty police officers and investigators from Sneddon's office raided Neverland. The police team was twice the size of those usually used to raid the premises of most wanted serial killers. Armed with a search warrant, the giant team removed material from the fantasy ranch, and this time also chopped pieces out of every mattress on the property, looking for DNA evidence. On December 18, 2003, the Santa Barbara D.A.'s office charged Jackson with seven counts of child molestation and two of intoxicating a minor with alcohol.

The Prince of Pop, now facing the possibility of forty-five years in prison, responded in his usual showbiz manner—by going on television. On Christmas Day 2003, he sat for an interview with *Sixty Minutes'* Ed Bradley. Again he did not deny but rather defended his actions, responding to Bradley's questions about whether he still considered it appropriate to share his bed with underage kids. "Of course. Of course. Why not?" he said. "If you going to be a pedophile, if you're gonna be Jack the Ripper, if you're gonna be a murderer, it's not a good idea. That I'm not. That's not how we were raised. And I met. . .I didn't sleep in the bed with the child. Even if I did, it's okay. I slept on the floor. I give the bed to the child."

Jackson also told Bradley he had been roughed up by police during his arrest, saying "They manhandled me very roughly. My shoulder is dislocated, literally. It's hurting me very badly. I'm in pain all the time. This is, see this arm? This is as far as I can reach it. Same with the other side." The cops responded to this by releasing a video showing Jackson waving to his fans after leaving their custody, thus, they said, proving he was lying.

The media circus, with its two headliners Michael Jackson and Tom Snedden was back in town. The new charges brought out all manner of con artists, extortionists and fame-seekers, eager to get in on the action. One of the many examples of this was a fifteen-year-old Toronto boy claiming to have been molested by Jackson after meeting him in a Canadian video arcade. The tabloid TV show *Hard Copy* got very excited about the story and sent Diane Dimond, their number one attack dog reporter on the Wacko Jacko beat to Toronto to interview the kid. Dimond eventually took the teen to Toronto police headquarters where he was questioned for six straight hours. Although Detective Darryl Campbell at first reported they found his story to be "fairly believable," they began cross-referencing it with that of Rodney Allen from the neighboring city of Mississauga—a man they had been following, and discovered the entire tale was a scam. The police charged both the boy and Allen with public mischief for fabricating the story about Jackson. Diane Dimond returned to Los Angeles empty-handed.

Four years later, Allen was arrested again, this time for himself molesting a number of boys. He was found guilty and sentenced to life in Warkworth Penal Institution in Campbellford, Ontario.

A large number of experts were enlisted to give their thoughts on both Jackson and his accusers. Santa Barbara Sherriff's Department Detective Paul Zelis asked Los Angeles psychologist Stanley Katz for his assessment of Jackson, and got this as a response. "Jackson," he said, "is a guy that's like a ten year old child. And, you know, he's doing what a ten year old would do with his little buddies. You know, they're going to jack off, watch movies, drink wine, you know. And, you know, he doesn't even really qualify as a pedophile. He's really just this regressed ten year old." Detective Zelis concurred, saying, "Yeah, yeah, I agree."

On February 28, 2005, the case of *The People of the State of California vs Michael Joseph Jackson* went to trial in a Santa Barbara courtroom. Snedden began by carefully weeding out anyone from the jury pool who might be sympathetic to the singer, above all Michael Jackson fans and black people, and so, over Jackson's attorney Tom Mesereau's objections, the judge approved an all-white jury to decide the singer's fate.

It was, naturally, a sensationalistic trial, even though the prosecution's main witnesses, the Arviso family, proved highly unreliable, and much of Snedden's expected physical evidence proved to be nonexistent. But of course the defendant, always the drama queen, kept the proceedings interesting. At one point, hospitalized because of a minor accident, he was forced to attend by the judge and so finally appeared at the courtroom wearing pajamas, with an aide, as always, shading him with an umbrella against the bright California sun.

Several other celebrities appeared on Jackson's behalf. Comedian Jay Leno testified that the same boy who now claimed

Jackson had molested him had once, earlier, attempted to extort money from the *Tonight Show* host. CNN talk show host Larry King reported to the court information very damaging to the credibility to the family of the lead prosecution witness, but the court ruled it inadmissible, so the jury never heard it. Indeed, after the trial, the boy's mother was charged with perjury and welfare fraud.

To the dismay of prosecutor Tom Snedden, defense attorney Tom Mesereau eviscerated the credibility of the Arviso family, successfully portraying them as con artists trying to profit from Michael Jackson. In a last-ditch attempt to throw the book at Jackson, Snedden's team fiercely cross-examined Macauley Culkin, and two former "special friends", Brett Barnes and fellow-Australian Wade Robson. (Robson has a featured role in the next phase of the Jackson saga.) All three of the young men stuck by their stories, defended the singer, and vehemently denied that anything inappropriate had happened between them and Jackson.

After ten days of deliberations, the jury returned their verdict—Michael Jackson was declared not guilty of every charge.

He had won in the courtroom, but his life was in shambles. The legal fees for the 2005 trial were over $30 million. His career, he felt, had been largely destroyed. Believing that Neverland had been "defiled" by the police raid, he vowed never to return, and instead began looking at properties in Montreal, Berlin, and Bahrain. His health was also a mess and he had to spend much time with medical specialists in Los Angeles. He did receive some performance offers—$3 million for a private concert for a Russian oligarch, $100 million to play Las Vegas for six months, but his singing voice was now so bad he felt he could do neither.

By 2009 Jackson had fallen under the thrall of the Nation of Islam, and while there is no evidence he had become a Muslim, this shadowy group had become his de facto security force and managers, now controlling his life and career. Believed to be $400 million in debt, Michael and his new handlers agreed to a plan that he would play a series of fifty concerts at London's O2 Arena.

Wildly underweight and popping proscription drugs including a new favorite, Oxycontin, neither he nor many of his huge entourage felt he would able to survive the grueling performance schedule, but he and his dancers began to shakily rehearse the elaborate show. It was, said Jackson, "an act of futility."

On June 25, 2009, less than three weeks before the first show in London, with all the concerts sold out, Jackson died of cardiac arrest, his bloodstream flowing with propofol, lorazepam, and midazolam. His death was huge news around the world, causing servers to slow and crash, and radio and TV outlets to move to non-stop Jackson coverage. More than a million and a half fans attempted to attend his memorial service, and nearly three billion streamed the event. It was likely the most watched funeral in history.

The Man was not through with his investigations of Michael Jackson. In August, his death was declared a homicide and six months later his personal physician, Dr. Conrad Murray, was charged with involuntary manslaughter. He was found guilty and received a sentence of four years in prison. He was released after two years, due to California prison overcrowding, and good behavior. So ironically, while Michael Jackson never went to jail, his doctor, and at least two of his accusers did.

Jackson's death ended neither his phenomenal success nor the extreme slagging of his reputation. In the year after his death, he sold thirty-five million albums worldwide. Sony Music renewed his contract, signing with his estate for $250 million. The *Cirque du Soleil* mounted a lavish $57 million tribute to Jackson, opening it in their home city of Montreal and then moving it to Las Vegas. While the show was in early pre-production, Wade Robson, one of Jackson's "special friends", and a staunch defender of him in the 2005 court hearings, applied for the position of choreographer for the show. He was considered, but eventually did not get the gig.

Devastated, and with his career as a dancer and choreographer in tatters, Robson began to revise his story about Michael Jackson. As a young teen, Robson had developed a crush on Jackson's niece, Brandi Jackson, and asked the singer's help in getting him together with her. Jackson's matchmaking worked, and Brandi and Robson had a seven-year teen romance, ending only when Brandi learned that he was having affairs with other girls, including Britney Spears, who he thought could do more to advance his budding career.

With his love-life now turning sour and work drying up, he decided, according to his deposition, that "it was time for me to get mine," from the connection to the Jackson. After he was turned down for the job of choreographer for the Michael Jackson Cirque de Soleil show, Robson made the decision to go after belated benefits from his connections with the late singer in whatever way he could. In 2012, he began trying to hustle a book about his alleged abuse by Jackson, but no publisher picked it up. In May 2013, he filed a civil lawsuit against the Jackson estate, but it was twice thrown out of court. He then began to shop around the idea of a tell-all interview about his days at Neverland.

In 2017, the editors at Britain's Channel 4 decided to re-open the case against Michael Jackson, and so commissioned filmmaker Dan Reed to make a four hour film telling the stories of Wade Robson and James Safechuck.

Robson had testified in the defense of Jackson both in 1993 and again in 2005. In fact, in the 2005 trial, according to Private Investigator Scott Ross, who worked on the Jackson defense team, he was considered their "most credible, strongest witness, which was why he was put on as the lead witness for the defense in the Michael Jackson trial. The three tough prosecuting attorneys went very hard in their cross examination of Robson, much harder than they did on Macaulay Culkin and a lot harder than they did on Brett Barnes, and the reason he didn't change his story is that he was telling the truth—there's nothing to change."

However, change it he did. In the Dan Reed film, he describes, in detail, a very different story of his relationship with Michael Jackson, and the time he spent at Neverland. Either he is guilty of perjury in his depositions in the 2005 trial, or his statements in the film are incorrect. His new allegations were backed up by those of fellow "special friend" James Safechuck. Safechuck's statements are new, as the judge in 2005 ruled him to be an unreliable witness, so he was not allowed to testify.

Reed's film premiered at the 2019 Sundance Film Festival, and then played on HBO in North America and Channel 4 in Great Britain, both to huge ratings. The reaction was swift—a backlash against Jackson, a surge in sales of his music, and a new ban on it by radio stations in Canada, the Netherlands and New Zealand, and the withdrawal from circulation of the *Simpsons* episode that Jackson had starred in. The Children's Museum of Indianapolis closed their Jackson exhibit and Louis Vuitton cancelled plans for Jackson-inspired products.

Nonetheless, many fought back against the new charges. Two documentaries were created, refuting many of the claims made in *Leaving Neverland*, and a video of Wade Robson's 2016 deposition was leaked, in which he completely contradicted the allegations he and his mother Joy make in the HBO/Channel 4 documentary.

The Man was hauled back into the fight, when the Jackson estate filed a $100 million lawsuit against HBO, claiming the network had violated a 1992 agreement never to disparage Jackson's public image. In return, HBO filed an anti-SLAPP motion against the estate. Judge George Wu is ruling on the decision.

For millions of people, the legacy of Michael Jackson is now destroyed. Even though he was never found guilty, the man once considered, in Berry Gordy's words, "the greatest entertainer who ever lived" is now mainly remembered as a pedophile. Before leaving the sad story, let's examine it one last time. The main charge, that Michael Jackson showed boys how to masturbate, is absolutely not recommended behavior, not for anyone, certainly not for a world-famous pop star. But *if* that is all there was to it, it is insignificant compared to the vast amount of documented pedophillia by people in authority that has been revealed over the last fifty years.

Let us leave the last word to the dean of rock critics, Robert Christgau, who in his obituary of Jackson wrote that "his troubling life began to shape an arc not merely of promise fulfilled and outlived, but of something approaching tragedy: a phenomenally ebullient child star tops himself like none before, only to transmute audibly into a lost weirdo. . .so that the fact that he's a great musician is now often forgotten."

6. But Wait! There's More!

Sir Paul McCartney

During the crazed years of Beatlemania, Paul McCartney was known as just being the cute one. John Lennon was considered the wild one, the artistic one, and the revolutionary and creative Beatle. The truth is Lennon's partner was certainly as creative, certainly as musically and artistically talented, and arguably just as rebellious and rambunctious as his bud. He had more interaction with The Man, and definitely spent more time behind bars.

Born in Liverpool during the Second World War, the future knight spent his childhood playing in what he and his Scouser pals called "bombies" (shattered bomb sites.) His first interaction with The Man was when he found a one-pound note in one of them, and his father insisted he hand it in to the local police station. Over the years, McCartney has spent considerable time in British courtrooms litigating the break up of the Beatles, and of his unsuccessful second marriage. His first time was as a seven-year-old, testifying in a Liverpool courtroom against two bullies who had robbed him of a wristwatch in a back alley.

His mother died of breast cancer when he was fourteen. While his relationship with his father was nowhere as acrimonious as others we have chronicled in this book, it did have its ups and downs, and usually involved the familiar issues of school, hair, clothes, and music. Elvis was a seismic influence, as he was on so many other teens of the era, and Paul's attempts to emulate him by getting local tailors to turn his baggy school uniform pants into an approximation of Presley's tight "drain pipe" jeans caused issues with both his dad and with the notoriously tough headmaster of his school, J.R. Edwards, who was known by the boys as "the Baz"—short for "the bastard". Even more contentious was when Paul went to a barber (a man commemorated twelve years later in *Penny Lane*) to get an Elvis-inspired haircut called a "DA", vernacular for 'Duck's Arse'. It featured a big pomaded quiff on top with two side wings interwoven at the back giving it the slang moniker.

McCartney was not much of a student—"sagging off" from classes with his friend George Harrison, passing only one subject at his first attempt of the onerous "O-Level" tests that graded sixteen year olds in England, and again failing history, geography, religious knowledge and German on his second. His passion was not school, but playing guitar in the group founded by Lennon, the Quarrymen. To add to the discord on the home front, he also managed to get his girlfriend Dot Rhone pregnant when he was seventeen and she sixteen. The decision made by the pair's families was that they would have to marry. To support wife and kid Paul would have to leave school, give up music, and get a real job. Unfortunately for the unborn baby, but very fortunately for the rest of us, Dot had a miscarriage. Paul's musical future was back on track. "Where are we going, Johnny?" he would hurl at Lennon. "Macca, we going to the toppermost of the poppermost!" Lennon would shout back.

The band played at illegal strip clubs and at dances in unprepossessing village halls around northern England—mostly to tough "Teds" who, amped up by the band's versions of hard driving 50s rock and roll tunes like *Hully Gully* and *Be Bop a Lula*, would turn the events into rancorous rumbles. Those venues were upscale compared to the band's next gig—a succession of seedy clubs on the notorious St. Pauli red-light district of Hamburg known as the Reeperbahn.

Fueled by Preludin, 'Purple Hearts', trays of beers and schnapps sent on stage at the Kaiserkeller nightclub by their noisy German customers, the band, by now named the Silver Beetles, played five hours a night, seven days a week. While Lennon clowned around, goose-stepping across the stage, wearing a comb to turn his upper lip into a Hitler-style moustache and drunkenly accusing the customers of being "Fuckin' Nazis", McCartney pressed on, doggedly making his way though languid Elvis hits like *It's Now or Never* even as the dance floor erupted into fist- or knife-fights.

The fun wouldn't last forever. In November of 1960, the St. Pauli police discovered that George Harrison was under eighteen, thus working illegally, and booted him out of the country. Within a month, McCartney and the band's drummer Pete Best got into an argument with the owner of the Kaiserkeller, Bruno Koschmider, that ended their gig with the club. As they were leaving, they made a stupid and halfhearted attempt to light the joint on fire. Koschminder called the cops and soon McCartney and Best were charged with arson and found themselves behind bars in the main Reeperbahn police station. It was McCartney's first, though as we'll see not his last visit to jail. This one was short. After a night, the police hustled them onto a plane, and deported the pair back to Britain.

The future of what would become the world's most successful musical group looked bleak. Their only hope was with one of their patrons, promoter Allan Williams, who offered them the job of house band at a new spot he opened in Liverpool modeled on the Hamburg clubs. Unfortunately, the similarity went a bit too far. Within six days of opening the club burnt down—torched, police suspected, by a rival club-owner. The Beatles (the 'Silver' part of the name had now been dropped and the second "e" changed to an "a") were again unemployed. Offered a possible return gig to Germany, McCartney was assigned the task of writing a groveling letter to the Hamburg authorities:

> *We both swear that we had no intention of burning the cinema or maliciously damaging the property. The whole incident had no motive to prompt it, in fact there was no reason at all behind the burning. It was just a stupid trick which we feel we ought to have been punished for in a less drastic manner.*

The letter appeased the German cops and in 1961 the group, still with Stu Sutcliff on bass and Pete Best on drums returned to Hamburg. McCartney was aggravated by his perception that Sutcliff was an inferior bass player who refused to rehearse or try to improve. There are several stories of physical altercations involving Sutcliff—one with McCartney, the other, more serious, either with Lennon or with some local hooligans, depending on who is telling the story. Sutcliff, never terribly serious about music, and much more interested in visual art, quit the band in a huff. A year later, he died in Hamburg of a brain aneurysm, possibly caused by the fighting a year earlier.

With Sutcliff gone, McCartney was obliged to take over the role of bass player. "There's a theory that I ruthlessly worked Stu out of the group in order to get the prize chair of bass," he says. "Forget it. . .nobody wants to play bass, or nobody did in those days. Bass was the thing that fat boys were asked to stand at the back and play. So I didn't want to do it, but Stuart left and I got lumbered with it."

It is odd that McCartney continued to play bass, arguably the least important and certainly least sexy instrument of rock and roll when he was very skilled at both piano and drums. He composes on the piano, but he let Billy Preston play keyboards when the Beatles required them, and to the scorn of fans taught his wife Linda Eastman to play them for his band Wings. He is also a very good drummer, thus prompting the (malicious, and probably inaccurate) response to the question, "Is Ringo Starr the best drummer in the world?" "No, Ringo Starr isn't even the best drummer in The Beatles."

McCartney's bass playing was also hampered by the fact that he is left-handed. Fortunately, he was able to purchase a very rare left-handed German-made Hofner "violin" bass in Hamburg, and he has played it ever since. It was one of the many fortuitously cool things about the group—the fact that McCartney's bass and Lennon's rhythm guitar bookended the visual image of the band—Paul's pointing left, John's pointing right. McCartney's original bass was stolen, but Hofner specially made him—by then their most celebrated customer—a replica of the discontinued model. Today the replica, now insured for two million US dollars, is still being played by Sir Paul, while the original, according to one of his biographers, Philip Norman, has somehow mysteriously absconded to Ottawa, the capital of Canada, not generally thought of as a home for hot instruments.

After their apprenticeship in Germany, the lads returned to Liverpool and from their base at the Cavern Club over the next two years moved on to conquer first Britain and then Europe, North America, and the world. Paul was the favorite of the millions of girls who swooned over the band in waves of crazed adulation. Amazingly, by today's standards, the Beatles travelled in those heady days with only one manager, one roadie and no security. It was left up to the police to form phalanxes to protect them from the screaming hysterical teens. Generally the cops looked out for the golden boys of music but as the craze continued, cracks began to develop between the Beatles and The Man.

In 1963, McCartney was pulled over (the third time that year) for speeding. There was little Beatlemania in the courtroom where instead the presiding Judge W.O. Halstead told him "It's time you were taught a lesson," banned him from driving for twelve months and fined him twenty-five pounds. No matter, he could well afford a driver, though no red-blooded 24-year-old wanted one in the car-crazed 60s. The band's security staff, though, was still very lightweight, a point driven home on their 1966 tour of North America and the Far East. In Tokyo, the band received death threats from Japanese nationalists who objected to the martial-arts-sanctified Budokan Hall being used for their concert. It was little wonder that thugs and crazed evangelicals got violent as right-wing commentators in America and Japan began writing hysterical diatribes condemning the band. Archconservative columnist William F. Buckley wrote that the Beatles were "not merely awful, but so unbelievably horrible, so appallingly unmusical. . .that they qualify as the crowned heads of anti-music." Dog whistle lines like that were mere lisping words to the effetely erudite Buckley, but red meat for the Blue Meanies out in Pepperland.

In the Philippines, they set off a firestorm by turning down an invitation to breakfast by Imelda Marcos, the shoe-crazed wife of corrupt dictator Ferdinand Marcos. With officials wildly screaming they had insulted the First Lady, they were surrounded by gun-toting cops, roughed up at their concert, maligned by the official newspapers, lost all hotel privileges and told they could not leave the country until paying a massive government tax bill that should have been covered by the local promoter. They were assaulted and spat on by Filipino demonstrators and police as they tried to get to the airport and barely got out of the country alive. "Beatles, *alis diyan*! Beatles, go home," shouted the Marcos-organized Beatle-haters. Ringo had to duck to miss getting punched in the face, and the two Beatles road managers were both kicked and bloodied by the airport police.

"If we ever go back," said the band, "It will be with an H-bomb. We wouldn't even fly over the place."

Their experiences in Tokyo and Manila were a major influence on their decision to stop touring and retreat to their London studio. Even in England, though, The Man harassed them. The *International Times*, an underground newspaper largely financed by McCartney, was busted for its open advocacy of marijuana, homosexuality and nudity, and its editor, John 'Hoppy' Hopkins was sentenced to nine months imprisonment for possessing a tiny amount of pot. As the Beatles were recording *Sergeant Pepper's Lonely Hearts Club Band*,

Mick Jagger, Keith Richards and Paul's good friend, art dealer Robert Frazer were busted at a party, for drug possession. Paul rallied behind the trio, paying 5,000 pounds to run a full-page letter in the London *Times* headed, "The law against marijuana is immoral in principle and unworkable in practice." The letter was signed by John Lennon MBE, Paul McCartney MBE, George Harrison MBE, Richard Starkey MBE, Brian Epstein, novelist Graham Greene, drama critic David Bailey, broadcaster David Dimbleby, physicist (and co-discoverer of DNA) Francis Crick, and many other prominent Britons. The letter likely sent a signal to police forces in Great Britain and abroad that Paul McCartney was someone they should keep their eyes on.

Queen magazine ran an interview with Paul in which he owned up to dropping acid and rhapsodized about its mind-expanding effects. "We only use one-tenth of our brains," he told the debutantes, dukes and duchesses that read the snooty upscale mag. "Just think what we'd accomplish if we could tap that hidden part. It would be a whole new world." (The myth that humans only use one-tenth of their brains is rooted in a misunderstanding of the work of renowned psychologist and philosopher William James.) The establishment, in the argot of the day, freaked out. Home Office Minister Alice Bacon, declaring herself "horrified" by Paul's views, asked "What sort of society are we going to create if everyone wants to escape from reality into a dream world?"

Her Majesty herself got involved in the controversy, dispensing with the usual small talk when hosting a reception attended by Sir Joseph Lockwood, chairman of the band's recording company, EMI. "The Beatles are turning awfully *funny*, aren't they?" asked the Queen.

Still, with their long string of critical and wildly popular hits, culminating in *Sergeant Pepper*, the Beatles were largely immune to criticism and, they thought, police raid. They were enshrined, quite rightly, at least in many quarters, as being as important to Britain's self-esteem as Churchill, the Monarchy, or Shakespeare. When they succeeded, it was British success. When they failed, as they seemed to, dramatically, with Paul's experimental film project *Magical Mystery Tour,* it was perceived almost as a national failure. McCartney was savaged in the vicious British press for the enterprise. It wouldn't be the last time.

It is no wonder the British establishment handed them MBEs and fretted over their successes and failures. At the height of their fame in the mid 60s, the top tier tax rate in the country, which the Beatles, the Stones and other top groups were certainly in, was an astounding 90 percent, so a huge amount of their earnings was flowing straight into the British Exchequer. It is no wonder the bands reacted. Harrison wrote the song *Taxman,* the Beatles registered the earnings of their second film *Help!* in the Bahamas, and the Stones became tax exiles in southern France.

It was not only The Man taking the lion's share of the Beatles' income. When they started, they were seeing only an incredibly chintzy 1 percent royalty from their record label. By the late 60s two parties were moving in to try to sort out the mess of the band's finances. One was a rough and tumble New Jersey schemer named Allan Klein, the other the combined forces of New York lawyers Lee and John Eastman, respectively father and brother of Paul's new inamorata and later wife, Linda Eastman. Perhaps either were better than the late Brian Epstein, who while certainly important in helping the Beatles make their original breakthrough, was no match for the shark-like lawyers and accountants of the music industry once the band moved into the big-time.

Klein, even though he had already stolen vast sums from the Rolling Stones, was supported by Lennon, Harrison and Starr. McCartney was convinced Klein was a crook, and so enlisted the Eastmans to try to fight his control of the band. The rift was only one factor in the break-up of the Beatles. At the same time as they were bickering over money, Yoko Ono was moving into the recording studio with them and destroying the old equilibrium of the quartet. The recording of the White Album was a nightmare. Yoko had a bed set up for herself in the studio, John and Paul were barely speaking, and an exasperated George Martin and Ringo Starr both quit the project—though eventually returned to it. They continued to create brilliant music, but by April of 1970 the party was over, with the announcement in giant front-page headlines like the one on the *Daily Mirror* that screamed PAUL IS LEAVING THE BEATLES.

The Fleet Street newspapers continued their fevered coverage once the legal battle began on February 19, 1971. The eleven-day hearing, held in the Royal Courts of Justice in the Strand before Mr. Justice Stamp was formally titled "McCartney vs Lennon, Harrison, Starkey and Apple Corps", but in reality it was McCartney vs Allan Klein. Both of them (but none of the other Beatles) were in court every day, but neither spoke a word to the other. Paul would later recall as he sat beside his wigged and gowned counsel, David Hirst QC, and behind a three-foot pile of supporting legal documents, that he began having cold feet about taking Klein to court. "Anyone else suing the Beatles would have been immoral," he said, "but for one of the Beatles to sue them. . .it was almost as if I was committing an unholy act."

Judge Stamp did not think it unholy. In the end he totally agreed with the deposition made by McCartney and his lawyers, and condemned Klein for taking a commission "grossly in excess" of what he should have. A bitter Klein (once described as "having all the charm of a broken lavatory seat") later kvetched "the judge got Beatlemania."

With Stamp's decision, it was official—Klein was out, and more importantly, the Beatles were no more. However, it was by no means the end of Paul's career. He almost immediately released a solo album, and then formed a new band, Wings, which released seven albums and toured extensively from 1971 to 1981. He recorded best selling (though drippy) duets with other superstars like Stevie Wonder and Michael Jackson, has written and recorded several albums of classical music, and deep into the twenty-first century has continued to perform solo at the world's largest venues.

Nor was the end of the Beatles the end of McCartney's interactions with The Man. In fact, the biggest and worst incident was still to come.

Most of Paul's issues with The Man stemmed from his fondness for smoking marijuana but in 1972, he strayed into another controversial issue. On January 30, a day known forever after as Bloody Sunday, British soldiers shot dead fourteen Catholic civil rights demonstrators in Londonderry, Northern Ireland. McCartney responded by writing and recording a new song, *Give Ireland Back to the Irish* that called for an end to Britain's three-hundred-year rule and independence for the province. In interviews he appeared to support the Irish Republican Army, a group branded as being terrorists by Great Britain. His song was banned by the BBC but went on to hit Number One both in the Irish Republic, and in (republican) Spain. Still, a shaken McCartney was apparently so dismayed by the whole political controversy he had created that his next Wings release was a sappy sing-along version of possibly the sappiest song ever, the children's ditty *Mary Had a Little Lamb*.

Also that year, he was busted—twice—for marijuana. At a concert in Sweden, the police crashed into the backstage and shut the show down (risking electrocution) by chopping through a 20,000 watt cable, then arrested the band and carted them off to jail, and charged them with trafficking. Ultimately McCartney and his new mates convinced the magistrates that the grass had been given to them as a gift by fans, and they got off with a collective $2,000 fine. They also had to sign a written promise to never use pot again while in Sweden, although according to the Wings drummer Denny Seiwell, the forced affidavit meant little to them, as the very next day "a guy from Holland gave us some and we shared it from a paper plate inside the bus with all the press and the fans right outside."

In September, a policeman, possibly acting on a tip from a neighbor uninfected by the Love Paul virus, possibly reacting to a story in the London *Daily Mail* headed WHY I SMOKE POT—BY PAUL, raided the singer's Scottish farm and found five marijuana plants growing in his greenhouse. He was charged with three counts of growing and possessing cannabis, a charge usually punished with jail time.

Weeks before the trial his new song *Hi, Hi, Hi*, with primitive lyrics about a proposed seduction of a "funky little mama" with whom he proposes getting "high, high, high" hit Number Five in the UK, even though it was banned by the BBC. It was probably not an ideal soundtrack for his court date, but somehow, once again, the future Sir Paul got off lightly. His solicitor claimed that the marijuana seeds had been sent to him by some fans, and got a derisive laugh from the journalists in the courtroom when he argued that McCartney had had "an interest in horticulture for many years." McCartney received a fine of 100 pounds, which he no doubt paid from his potted plant and seed budget.

Even though the Scottish trial was attended by dozens of reporters and TV crews, McCartney was saved much coverage, since the verdict came down on the same day as a much bigger story, the deadly bombing of London's Old Bailey law courts by the IRA that seriously injured 125 people, and killed one. McCartney did have an exchange with a BBC reporter that would be unfortunately prophetic of an experience seven years in his future, much less pleasant than this one:

Paul: "Well, I'm glad to have got off like this y'know. I'm glad it wasn't jail."

BBC Reporter: "Did you think it might have been?"

Paul: "I thought it might have been, but it would have been okay as long as I could have taken me guitar with me."

Paul's next album, *Band on the Run* seemed to reference either being a prisoner or an escapee, especially with the title track's lines about being *Stuck inside these four walls. . .sent inside forever.* He wanted to get away from the U.K. to record it, but because of his recent Scottish drug conviction he was banned from the U.S., so instead recorded it in Lagos, Nigeria. There, he was hassled, not by The Man—as the repressive military regime of President Yakubu Jack Gowan had other matters on its hands at the time, such as killing two million people in the would-be breakaway state of Biafra, but by local musicians including rock drummer Ginger Baker (Cream, Blind Faith) who had started a studio in Lagos in competition with the one McCartney was using and by local thieves who nearly killed him.

The biggest name in Nigerian music was Fela Ransome Kuti, who was leading yet another breakaway state called Kalakuta, entirely populated by musicians (!). Kuti, until the ever-diplomatic Paul McCartney persuaded him otherwise, thought the British interlopers were ripping off Nigeria's music. The always-volatile Ginger Baker thought his empty studio was being ripped off, until Paul agreed to record one song for the album there, *Picasso's Last Words*. As for the thieves, they did rip off Paul and Linda, stealing money and demo tapes from them at knifepoint and ignoring Linda's screams "Leave him alone! He's a *musician!*" Locals, expats and studio personnel thought the pair were lucky to get away with their lives. Since robbery carried the death sentence in the country, thieves frequently killed their victims to avoid later being identified. McCartney's famous charm saved his ass once again.

They did avoid getting busted for smoking dope in Nigeria but weren't so lucky while mixing the album in Los Angeles. Linda and Paul were stopped by traffic cops for running a red light and caught with seventeen grams of grass in Linda's purse and a still-glowing joint hidden under a passenger seat. Linda took the rap, was charged with possession and "contributing to the delinquency of a minor" because their daughters Heather, Stella, and Mary were in the car with them. Eventually, both charges were dropped but it was only the prelude to a much, much, more serious incident that followed.

Paul McCartney had only played in Japan once before—at the disastrous Budokan Hall event back in 1966. Since then, attempts to get visas for the new band were always turned down due to Paul's Scottish drug bust. However, a new manager of McCartney Productions worked hard to get the ban lifted and in 1979 the Japanese government finally agreed to let McCartney and Wings play 11 concerts across the country.

On January 16, 1980, two flights, one from London, one from New York, arrived at Tokyo's Narita Airport, carrying Paul, Linda, their children, the band and a large road crew and entourage. Inexplicably, since they had been specifically warned not to carry any drugs with them, a customs agent opened Paul's suitcase to find a large bag containing 7.7 ounces of marijuana. McCartney was detained and alarm bells began going across the customs hall. No one else was stopped, and the rest of the large party continued by bus to the elegant Hotel Okura where the Presidential Suite was booked for the McCartney's. Instead of being able to check into the Presidential Suite, Paul was taken to a Tokyo jail to face five hours of interrogation by a group of drug squad officers, few of whom spoke English. He learned that he faced charges of smuggling, or even peddling, and a potential seven-year jail term with hard labor. He was then put into general custody for the night where he claims he did not sleep for a moment, instead sitting on the floor with his back to the wall, convinced he might be raped.

The next day the McCartney management team discovered that Japanese authorities had cancelled all the tour dates. The dozens of giant posters for the Tokyo concert they had passed on the bus ride from the airport to the hotel were now already down. All Wings music, played non-stop on radio the day before, had completely disappeared.

Paul was transported to the Tokyo Police Narcotics Control Department, handcuffed, and with a rope around his neck "like a dog" as he later described it. There he was interrogated for another six hours by the tough chief investigator, Koyoshi Kobayashi. A sea of media besieged Linda and the band at the hotel. A huge mob of hysterical young women crying his name, "Paur! Paur!" surrounded the jail. His lawyer flew in from New York, his manager from London to try to help. Everyone had seen enough movies set in World War II Japanese Prisoner of War camps to be extremely worried for Paul's welfare.

The following day McCartney was taken to a courtroom where District Judge Haruo Matsumoto granted the prosecutor's application to keep him behind bars for ten days of further questioning. Paul was transferred directly to Tokyo's forbidding Kosuge Prison where he was placed with a group of Japan's most hardened criminals.

The case got attention around the world. Johnny Carson joked that after Paul landed at Narita, his suitcase remained in a holding pattern for another four hours. Senator Edward Kennedy phoned the judge from Washington. A deranged Beatles fan named Kenneth Lambert showed up at Miami Airport and announced, even though he had neither ticket nor money, that he wanted to be flown to Japan so he could spring Paul from jail. In an altercation with the gate staff he pulled out a toy gun, and a police officer shot him dead.

McCartney later described conditions inside the prison as "barbaric." The food—mostly seaweed and onion soup, was poor, and the tiny cell only outfitted with a thin sleeping mat. He did, however, gradually lose his fear of prison rape and began to take communal baths with the other prisoners. "By the end, I was like, 'Come on! In for a penny. I'm going in with the boys,'" he said. "So we all went in there and it was fun, y'know, being in the tub with all these Japanese guys."

The only communication he was able to have with his fellow Japanese inmates was shouted brand names—'Kawasaki!' 'Toyota!' 'John Player Special' and everyone's favorite, 'Johnny Walker!' One of his inmates on the range, a rough heavily tattooed yakuza gangster in on a charge of murder, demanded he sing *Yesterday*. Even though there was officially a rule of silence, McCartney had to oblige, following it with three more familiar tunes, sung a cappella, without benefit of accompaniment of his traditional mates John, George or Ringo.

After nine days, the Japanese authorities, citing his full confession and "repentance", and the fact he had by now suffered "social punishment" released and immediately deported him. There were severe financial repercussions. The Japanese promoters had to be reimbursed about $250,000 U.S. for the cancelled tour. The long pointless stay in the snazzy hotel by his family and retinue cost another $130,000. The Wings band basically fell apart and he never did get to perform in Japan.

He has never really explained why he had ignored all the warnings he had been given about travelling to Japan and had openly carried nearly eight ounces of hemp into the country. "There are times in your life when you think to yourself, 'Okay, you're an idiot' and that's one of them. I was an idiot".

There is another theory about the bust, which is that Yoko Ono orchestrated it all. Writer Fred Seaman, author of the controversial book *The Last Days of John Lennon,* described on the Canadian TV talk show *The Shirley Show* the visit by Paul to see John Lennon at his Dakota apartment the day before he was to fly to Tokyo. According to Seaman, Yoko Ono made sure that Paul did not get to see Lennon, but instead interrogated him about his plans for the visit to her home country. He told her about the "dynamite" marijuana he had for the trip and that he would be staying in the Presidential Suite of the Okura Hotel. According to Seaman she was infuriated that McCartney would be spoiling the "hotel karma" of her favorite Tokyo Hotel, and so once McCartney left the Dakota she conspired, either with authorities in Japan, or by putting a spell on Paul with one of her psychic astrologer advisors, to make sure he was busted before he could get to the Presidential Suite. Did Yoko Ono conceivably have the power in Japan to make that happen? She does come from one the very richest families in the country. Her grandfather was private personal banker to the Emperor. As a child, her servants had to enter and leave her room and attend to her on their bended knees. And she certainly held a grudge against McCartney, although arguably it had been resolved by 1980. In any case, that's the blame-Yoko Ono story. Paul McCartney has stated he doesn't believe it.

Tokyo was still not his last pot bust. In 1984, while vacationing in Barbados, he and Linda were snitched on by a domestic, and arrested by the local police—even though grass was openly sold on the beaches of the island. Fined, and with their holiday ruined, they returned to England, where one of Linda's bags was found to contain a tiny amount of weed—a fraction of an ounce. She was found guilty but escaped with another fine of just 75 pounds.

Did all these drug busts destroy McCartney's career? On the contrary. In fact like Frank Sinatra years earlier, McCartney's career in his 50s, 60s and now 70s was in some ways even more spectacular than his career as a Beatle. In 1997, he was back in Buckingham Palace being knighted by the Queen. Flanked by his daughters (one of them, Stella McCartney, now a wildly successful fashion designer), he knelt, as Her Majesty touched him on both shoulders with the sword of King Edward the Confessor. The self-titled "Japanese Jailbird" became Sir Paul McCartney.

By the turn of the millennium he had become one of the most revered musical figures in the world. While certainly not leaving rock and roll behind, he also branched into classical composition with *Liverpool Oratorio,* the ballet score *Ocean's Kingdom* and three other full-length classical pieces. He even wrote and recorded the song *Mull of Kintyre* for guitar and bagpipes, now considered a sort of contemporary new Scottish National Anthem.

Almost every major British star, and some American ones, was enlisted to sing at the Queen's Golden Jubilee at Buckingham Palace in 2012—Elton John, Phil Collins, Eric Clapton, Tony Bennett, Brian Wilson, and, natch, Queen. There was no question, though, who the headliner would be—Sir Paul. He again headlined at the Live 8 concert raising money to fight African famine, opening the star-studded show with *Sergeant Pepper* and ending it, hours later, with *Hey Jude*. He followed that by playing halftime at the Super Bowl, and then headlining the massive opening ceremonies of the London Olympics, broadcast to millions around the world.

He may have been busted a few times by The Man, but he has also been honored by Him—not just with an MBE and a knighthood, but with the French Légion d'Honneur, the Peruvian Grand Cross of the Order of the Sun, eighteen Grammys, an Academy Award, an asteroid named 4148 McCartney, a couple of honorary doctorates, one from them from Yale, and the Gershwin Prize, presented to him at the White House by President Obama.

Perhaps his wildest accomplishment is his claim that he has heard birds chirping the chorus of the old Beatles' standard *From Me to You*. For an animal rights activist like McCartney, it must be a supreme pleasure to know that in the words of the old pop song (née Coke commercial) that pushed his music out of the Top Ten for a few brief weeks, he has taught the world to sing (in perfect harmony), and that world apparently includes birds as well as people.

Fans, Groupies and the Death of a Blues Brother

Police may not feel much affinity with musicians, but even the most hard-nosed among them likely has some minimal grudging respect for their talent and power over their audience. This attitude is rarely extended to the fans of the music. Watch the footage of The Doors' infamous Miami concert, or of numerous other rock concerts since the 1960s, and you see dozens of examples of what appears to be police glee in hurling fans off stages, pushing them around, and arresting them.

It is perhaps little wonder. The word "fan" is simply a short form of the word "fanatic", and the most extreme of fans do exhibit behavior that is zealously extreme, far outside the norms of acceptable levels of enthusiasm. Music can make people a bit crazy.

Self-described Super Groupie Pamela Des Barres remembers her first attempts to scale into the fortress of Rock and Roll during the Beatles 1964 North American tour. Hearing that for their Los Angeles concerts the band would be staying at a rented Bel Air mansion, Des Barres and a then equally ditsy teenager named Pam Miller persuaded the son of comic Jerry Lewis to help them climb over the wall of the Lewis residence to the temporary Beatles' abode. There, in the bushes, they spent a chilly night trying to spy on the Fab Four through the curtains. In the morning, they were spotted by the Beatles' aide-de-camp Neil Aspinall, who called the police. Then, says Des Barres, "a few minutes later we were hauled off by unamused boys in blue, shoved into police cars, driven promptly out of Bel Air, and asked very impolitely never to return."

Des Barres like many others unfaithfully shifted her attention to the Rolling Stones. She recalls a Long Beach Arena Stones concert in which "one half-nude girl climbed down the drapes and hung on to Mick's corduroy-clad leg until two guards pried her off and tossed her back into the wailing crowd." Following the concert Des Barres laid siege the Stones' hotel, along with dozens of other crazed fans, where she witnessed two tennybops banging on the door of Brian Jones' room, begging for an autograph, until he finally came out with a broom in hand, shouting at them, "If you don't get the hell out of here, I'll drag you in here and *fuck* you!!!"

Des Barres took part in the infamous Sunset Strip riots of 1966 (later immortalized in *For What It's Worth* by the Buffalo Springfield). She says, "The LAPD arrived in full force, clubs swinging and sirens blaring," and recalls, "I knew we were in trouble at that moment because I looked straight into the red eyes of a stern-faced Strip cop who was standing on the corner waiting for the likes of me to come along." She remembers "I made a dash across the street and into the Union 76 ladies' room. As I careened, bug-eyed, across the Sunset on a red light, I heard Rodney Bingenheimer [also a groupie of sorts, later a DJ, known as "The Mayor of Sunset Strip."] cheering for me to outrun the two enraged cops. My heart was pounding but I felt safe on top of the commode, knowing that MEN would never enter a LADIES' room, much less the door to a stall!! I was outraged and appalled when they forcibly removed me from my secure hiding place and *dared* to handcuff me! I heard one of them say to the other, "We can add resisting arrest to the drunk and disorderly."

Des Barres continues, "The charming police officers ignored us all the way down to the Beverly Hills police station...where a police woman removed the gold-plated cross from around my neck. I called them all blasphemous motherfuckers who would burn in hell for wrenching Jesus away from me in my time of need." Following a night in jail, "We were led to a kindly old judge who put us on three years' probation and gave us a curfew of 11 o'clock for six months." After a tearful display of histrionics from the two musically crazed teens, the judge reduced the sentence to six months probation and two weeks of curfew.

After making sexual conquests of everyone from Mick Jagger to Gram Parsons to Waylon Jennings to Woody Allen and Don Johnson, she became a musician herself, performing under the tutelage of Frank Zappa as part of the all-girl groupie musical group The GTOs. The group quickly fell apart after several of its members were arrested and detained for drug possession. Does The Man have no sense of humor?

On the other side of the country, Joanne "Jo Jo" LaPatrie took up the mantle where Des Barres left off, losing her virginity to Jimi Hendrix at the Woodstock Festival, then moving on to Jim Morrison and Rod Stewart, who wrote *You Wear It Well* for her. Her real goal was Paul McCartney, so she moved to England, seduced several of his roadies and began shadowing his Wings' tours. One of the queens of rock groupies, Linda Eastman, now ensconced as Paul's wife, put an end to LaPatrie's pursuit, so Jo Jo settled for Denny Laine, founder of the Moody Blues and now McCartney's lead guitarist. She was commemorated in several rock biographies—Ginger Baker affectionately said that "no sane man would go near her," and the lyrics of the Lennon-McCartney hit *Get Back* includes the line *Get back Jo Jo, go home*

Jo Jo did not *get back* and did not *go home* but instead ended up living on the grounds of Alexander Thynn, the 7th Marquess of Bath, who certainly himself sounds like The Man. A member of the

House of Lords until the Labour Party reforms of 1999 got rid of most of the hereditary peers, Thynn had open sexual relations with more than seventy women (whom he called "wifelets") including LaPatrie, some of whom he installed in cottages around his rambling Wiltshire estate.

The most original groupie was Cynthia "Plaster Caster" Albitton, who gained fame in the 60s by enshrining the erect members of her musical heroes—Jimi Hendrix, Anthony Newley and Zal Yanofsky being among the best known—by casting them first in alginate, then plaster. She began in Chicago, but after Frank Zappa became a patron of her offbeat "art" (though never himself the subject of it), she moved to Los Angeles, which she found to be a "veritable groupie heaven", with no lack of willing assistants eager to prepare the subjects for casting. By the twenty-first century she began referring to herself as an artist and a "recovering groupie", and in the spirit of sexual equality began also casting the breasts of female musicians. In 2010 she unsuccessfully ran for mayor of Chicago on the "Hard Party" ticket.

By far the most notorious groupie, and the one with the most serious interactions with The Man, was Cathy Evelyn Smith, born in Hamilton, Ontario in 1947 to an unwed mother and adopted by a couple living down the road in St. Catherines. Her adoptive mother was an ex-Ringling Brothers circus performer. By sixteen, Cathy had dropped out of high school. She was young, pretty, and obsessed with music, in particular with drums and drummers. In the early 60s, the hottest drummer in Ontario was Levon Helm. His band, Levon and the Hawks, was then backing up Ronnie Hawkins. It would become Bob Dylan's band, and then go on to become The Band. They were possibly the most practiced band in the world, playing behind Hawkins for four hours a night, five days a week, for years on end. When Robbie Robertson joined the band in 1960 he was famously told by Hawkins, "You won't make much money, but you'll get more pussy than Frank Sinatra."

Hawkins and the Hawks began their career in bars in Arkansas—bars that according to Hawkins were so tough "you had to puke twice and show your knife just to get in." In 1961, they moved permanently to Ontario, from where all but Hawkins and Helms hailed, and played primarily at three bars—the Coq d'Or in Toronto, the "Ceeps" CPR Hotel in London, and the Grange in Hamilton. Cathy Smith, dolled up to try to look the drinking age of twenty-one, met Levon and the others at the Grange. On her first night at the bar, she experienced the combination of attraction and lack of respect she would get from all the performers she became involved with: The Band, Gordon Lightfoot, Hoyt Axton, Ron Wood, Keith Richards, Robert de Niro and John Belushi. Helm announced that he was dedicating the next song to his new friend Cathy, which of course thrilled her until she heard him add, "and the name of the song is *Short Fat Fanny.*"

The band lived in the seedy motels along the west end of Toronto's lakeshore. The motels are all now gone, replaced by giant modern lakeside condos (in one of which, full disclosure, this book was written). Their favorite was the *Seahorse,* an unprepossessing motor inn that also has another claim to counter culture fame, as it once hosted another 60s icon, Peter Fonda, who holed up in it to write the script of his movie *Easy Rider.* Five years before that, one night at the *Seahorse* the band partied late into the night with their new friend Cathy and then bassist Rick Danko took her to bed, until he found out she was not on the pill, at which point, as she says, "things ground to a halt, and he got out of bed and wandered off down the hall." He was soon replaced by Levon Helm, who apparently had different standards, and she happily made love to him and sometimes to other members of the band over the next few months.

The band also performed in the nearby city of Buffalo. Returning across the Peace Bridge, border officers found marijuana on one of them. The band were released so they could play a gig in the town of Kitchener, but had to return to meet the arresting officer so he could lay the charges that could very possibly have sent them to jail, and ended their careers. Instead, they concocted a plan—they would get Cathy Smith to have sex with the officer, then tell him she was only fourteen and would report him unless he dropped the charges against the Hawks.

"At first I couldn't believe that they would ask me to do something like that," remembers Smith, "But I was their friend and I wanted to help them out. So I went on my mission of mercy. I really didn't expect a policeman to accept such a proposition, but that was naive of me too. The deed was done at the Westpoint Motel on the Lakeshore, and the less said about it, the better. For days afterward I felt unclean. But it worked; they got off. And it didn't change my feelings about the Hawks. I was right there in the audience, wherever they played."

Only a few weeks later, Cathy discovered she was pregnant. She was convinced that Levon was the father, but got little support from him. Luckily she got more from both Rick Danko and pianist Richard Manuel, and the unwanted child became known to them all as the "band baby". She considered an abortion, but they were illegal, dangerous and difficult to access in Canada in the 60s. She also considered forcing Helm to take care of her by threatening them she would get the band busted if he didn't. In the end she did give birth to the baby girl and at the age of seventeen began bringing her up herself, though after six months realized she couldn't do it on her own and so gave the girl up for adoption.

Smith began supporting herself by working as a waitress at the Riverboat, the biggest of the many coffee houses in Toronto's new folk-music/hippie scene in the bohemian part of the city called Yorkville. Many of the major folk performers of the era performed at the club—Kris Kristofferson, Ian & Sylvia, Odetta, Neil Young and Gordon Lightfoot. Cathy befriended many of the singers, including another young woman carrying an unplanned child who would soon also be put up for adoption—Joni Mitchell. Mitchell wrote her famous hit *Both Sides Now* in the cramped backstage of the Riverboat, while Smith made espressos for the customers. Phil Ochs wrote his, *Changes,* one afternoon in the back room, and sang it that night, with Smith one of the first to hear it.

Smith began her affair with Gordon Lightfoot during her Riverboat waitressing stint, but before it got truly underway, she was distracted by a local rogue named Paul Donnelly. This writer spent some time hanging with Donnelly in the 1980s in Nassau, by which time he was a high-rolling international smuggler—and so can attest to his raffish, charismatic charm. It is no surprise that Cathy Smith fell for him in the mid 60s. Always trying to help out guys in need, Cathy, as she had with The Band and would again with Ronnie Wood and then John Belushi, bailed Donnelly out of a major jam—this time, by marrying him.

There weren't a lot of drug dealers in Toronto in that era, but there were a lot of narcs. They were on to Donnelly, and following one sale of a mere matchbox of grass, they pounced on him. Sentenced to a three-year term in prison, he managed to convince the judge to reduce his term as he had a good job in advertising and a girlfriend he was about to marry. Cathy went along with it, and the pair were married for thirteen months, until Smith, feeling that though, "she had been an idiot to marry him, but having got him out of jail had done her duty", finally sickened of his shenanigans and left him.

Within months she was involved in what she calls the greatest romance of her life, reconnecting with Gordon Lightfoot. Her timing, for once, was good. Lightfoot had just come out of a fallow period in which he had been managed by Dylan-manager Albert Grossman and recorded by United Artists, and was about to enter the most productive years of his long career, working with producer Lenny Waronker and Warner Brothers, writing dozens of new hits, one of the biggest ones about his relationship with Cathy Smith.

She lived a life of music royalty with him, dining out at the fanciest steak houses in town, drinking so many $300 bottles of

Châteauneuf-du-Pape "that we should have bought an interest in the vineyard," attending Maple Leaf hockey games with him, smoking marijuana from his specially built spring-loaded stash in his downtown bachelor pad. He would often work there, she recalls, songwriting from dusk to dawn, while she adoringly sat nearby, "embroidering his jackets or adding various beads and baubles to the clothes he wore onstage."

The honeymoon wouldn't last forever. After a year, she recalls, "our relationship had become a complete farce, but amazingly enough we still loved each other and didn't know how to get out of it." He went off on long solo sailing trips on Georgian Bay and wilderness canoeing trips through Northern Canada and threatened that he was going to return to his Swedish wife, while she had flings with Jack Nicholson (shooting *The Last Detail* in Toronto) and with Gordon's friend Brian Good, leader of the country band The Good Brothers. At one point the pair went off on a reconciliatory holiday to Hawaii, but got into such a row over some illegal amphetamines that he dangled her off their twentieth story hotel balcony, attracting the attention of security guards who charged up the elevator and pounded on their door in an attempt to save her.

The pair were as close as Canada came to producing show biz royalty, and so ended up at official Ottawa events with real royalty, but even those fancy nights led to rows and misunderstandings. At a formal dance on a royal visit, Prince Charles turned beet red after he was caught staring at Smith's nicely displayed ample bosom, and she almost had a very public contretemps, first with Margaret Trudeau, then with Lightfoot, after he implied that he might be having an affair with the Prime Minister's wife.

During one of their fights Lightfoot socked her and broke her cheekbone. The combative relationship, though, gave Lightfoot his biggest hit. One night Smith, sick of what she called his jealous rages, went off on her own to party with friends. Lightfoot, fueled as usual by prodigious amounts of coffee, Canadian Club whiskey and cigarettes, sat up through the night writing a song about her.

Sundown hit Number One on both the *Billboard* and *Cashbox* album charts, and the title track topped the singles chart, doing something Lightfoot had always dreamed of—knocking one of the Beatles (Paul McCartney, with *Band on the Run)* out of the top spot. In the words of Lightfoot's biographer Nicholas Jennings, "it was a rare double-pinnacle feat, one that catapulted Lightfoot into superstardom, boosting every aspect of his career, from record and ticket sales to media coverage and venue size—even the number of groupies waiting for him backstage."

Lightfoot allowed Cathy to come on tour with him to sing backup on a few of his songs, but to the disappointment of some members of the audience kept her on a very short leash. At a big show at West Point Military Academy, Lightfoot recalls, "We were playing in a big concert hall to a roomful of cadets, all in uniform. I brought her out to sing harmony on *High and Dry* and when she left the stage all the guys in front were yelling, 'Bring back the girl.'"

Lightfoot didn't like being upstaged, and he got even more upset when Cathy began singing backup for another major Toronto folksinger, Murray McLauchlan. "What the hell are you doing?" he shouted at her. "Living in my house and working for the competition?"

"There was a lot of jealousy, a lot of drinking," remembers McLauchlan. "They weren't a good match. Gord's not that complicated; he's very down-to-earth. Cathy was extremely complicated, smart and ambitious. I suspect she probably saw Gordon as a means to an end, an opportunity. Not a gold digger, that wasn't her game. But she was attracted to fame. She wanted to be around famous people, maybe perceiving that as a shortcut to being famous. Gord was in love with her, but she was looking to fly the coop."

She did, leaving Lightfoot to return for a short time with her Band-mates Levon Helm and Richard Manuel, while they were touring with Bob Dylan. This was the crazy period when Dylan fans would snap up the tickets to his show, then spend all their time booing him. Perhaps it was the constant, violently antagonistic reception to the Band's electric back up of Dylan that led the virtuoso musicians to respond badly. Levon Helm treated Cathy poorly, then temporarily abandoned the band and the tour, and returned to Arkansas. Richard Manuel abused himself with alcohol so much that Smith remembers "you could see his liver—literally see his liver—bulging out of his belly. And his skin was incredible; his skin was so saturated with alcohol that it drooped over his muscles. I had the feeling that if I pressed my thumb against it, it would leave an impression forever."

Levon and the Hawks would soon transform itself into The Band and create some of the most unique and acclaimed music of the era. Their most famous song, *The Weight,* has some of the best loved, most convoluted and most scrutinized lyrics in classic rock. One of the many theories about what the lyrics are all about is that it references the band's favorite girlfriend and biggest fan, Cathy Smith. Levon Helm referred to her as "Short Fat Fanny". For the record, she was neither short nor fat. Do the references in the song to *"Fanny"* obliquely refer to Cathy Smith? Some say they do. There are other theories, some sacred, some secular. One of the wilder ones has it that all the names in the song are references to the films of Spanish filmmaker Luis Bunuel.

Cathy wasn't analyzing song lyrics. She'd had enough, and she had other options. She moved on from The Band, from Lightfoot and from Toronto, and headed to Los Angeles, where she began a two year affair with country/folk singer Hoyt Axton—driving his tour bus, singing back up, being his mistress, and on at least one occasion, writing songs with him. She then moved on to a bigger catch—probably the biggest catch of all—the Rolling Stones. Through 1978 she became part of the Stones' entourage, travelling with them to Paradise Island, Paris, New York and Colorado. She was primarily involved with Keith Richards, and began to develop her interest in heroin through him. She remembers seeing Richards go for nine days and nights without sleep, and says five was very common with him. However, she admonishes, "Like everyone else associated with the Stones I began to find out that you can admire them, but it's a disaster to emulate them. No one, but *no one* can keep up with the Rolling Stones' fast-paced way of life."

Working as major domo for Ron Woods' L.A. house that served as the Stones HQ, she eventually ran afoul of the drug-crazed mob over a fairly minor financial issue and was fired. She was out on the street on her own again, this time with a heroin addiction habit to support. She became a dealer of the dangerous drug—first going to Thailand to oversee a shipment of a kilo of China White heroin for an American dealer. She was shafted, never paid the $10,000 she had been promised. It is reported she made an attempt to have the dealer killed, but eventually did not go through with it.

The following year she became involved with another drug dealer, Paul Azari, who under thirteen aliases helped wealthy people escape Iran following the fall of the Shah. Their ticket into the United States was usually large amounts of heroin, smuggled out with their heirlooms. Azari delivered nineteen kilos of Persian Brown heroin, with a street value of about $13 million, to Cathy's apartment at the corner of Sunset Boulevard and La Cienega Drive. Cathy sold the drug to a wide variety of customers, and for her troubles got to use some of it herself. She would later become adept with needles, but at this point was still, like most people, scared of them. Instead of shooting the drug she adopted a technique that she called "Chasing the Dragon" (later the title of her memoir) that required melting the heroin on a tilted piece of tinfoil, then inhaling ("chasing") the fumes with a rolled Benjamin or an improvised tinfoil straw. It was basically a precursor of the method developed a few years later of using an empty pop or beer can with holes pricked in a corner of it to make a pipe to smoke crack cocaine.

By 1982, the Persian Brown was long gone, and Cathy was living day-to-day, still wired on heroin, still dealing from a clapped-out 1964 Plymouth that she used to get around the hard streets of West Hollywood. In February, she got a call from another small time dealer and showbiz wannabe named Leslie Marks, telling her that John Belushi was in town, and was "looking for some stuff." She went on the hunt on his behalf. She knew him—they had met on the set of *Saturday Night Live*, when The Band had been the musical guests, and also on the set of Steven Spielberg's only comedy, *1941*, in which Belushi had starred. She had also likely met his partner Dan Ackroyd during the early 70s, when Ackroyd was running an after-hours illegal "Booze Can" speakeasy in Toronto. Who knows—as the saying goes, if you can remember the 70s, you weren't really there.

Belushi is remembered today primarily as a comic actor, but in the early 80s, he and Ackroyd were equally serious about music. They created their alter-egos The Blues Brothers on *SNL*, but then moved on to turn it into a real band. They enlisted Dave Letterman's bandleader Paul Schaffer to help them assemble skilled saxophonists "Blue" Lou Marini and Tom Malone, plus two graduates of Booker T and the M.G.'s—guitarist Steve Cropper and bassist Donald "Duck" Dunn, and some other expert R&B sidemen. With Belushi and Ackroyd providing the lead vocals, the band released their debut album, *Briefcase Full of Blues*, which reached Number One on the *Billboard 200* chart, and went double platinum.

By 1982, though, the Blues Brothers act was considered to have worn out its welcome, and Belushi hadn't had a major hit movie since 1978's *Animal House*. He was living in decadent squalor in a bungalow of Hollywood's Chateau Marmont Hotel, handed a weekly allowance of $2500 by Paramount Pictures to come up with a new picture, most of which he used to buy cocaine, but now, increasingly, he wanted to use to buy heroin. His wife, Judy, and his partner Ackroyd were back in New York, both worried about Belushi spiraling out of control in Los Angeles. Ackroyd was working hard on the script of what was meant to be their next picture, *Ghostbusters*, while Belushi was trying to turn an idea of his titled *Noble Rot* into a comedy about the California wine industry, while trying to deflect Paramount President Michael Eisner's entreaties that he star in a filmed version of the bestseller, *The Joy of Sex*. "They want to put me in a diaper!!" complained Belushi, the man who had virtually invented the toga-clad, gross-out, frat boy humor of the era. And so now he needed some heroin.

Cathy Smith did not have enough money of her own to buy Belushi the smack he needed, but after getting cash advances from him she would head out into the winter nights and bring him back the dope in fairly small amounts worth $200 or $300. He was not enough of a user to know how to shoot himself up, nor did he have the physical dexterity to do it. Cathy, on the other hand, now considered herself an expert, not just in using, but in the dangers of using. Had she actually been there for the moment of Belushi's death, Nurse Cathy, as she called herself, likely could have prevented it.

For now, the party continued. Smith set Belushi up with speedballs—two-for-one combinations of cocaine and heroin, and the pair of them, plus various other hangers-on, went off to entertain themselves in the showbiz capital. One of Belushi's favorite haunts was The Guitar Center, where he bought himself new drumsticks, a new amplifier, and noodled with the idea of buying himself a new, expensive guitar. While he whiled away the hours with Cathy Smith, his minders at Paramount, his agent Bernie Brillstein and his partner Dan Ackroyd desperately tried to find him. When Ackroyd finally connected, Belushi angrily defended his right to do his own thing, demanding of Ackroyd, "How is it you can disappear in Canada for two goddamn weeks and everybody doesn't go crazy? Why me?"

The night of his death, both Robin Williams and Robert de Niro came to hang out with Belushi at his Chateau Marmont bungalow. Even with the party atmosphere going, neither got on well with Smith. De Niro says he found her "trashy." She says she found him "utterly frightening" and had to shoot herself up with some more heroin just to deal with him. Williams used the same word—frightening—to describe

Smith and told Belushi biographer and famed Watergate journalist Bob Woodward, "He had never seen John with such a crusty woman." Williams left the party, drove home to Topanga Canyon, and told his wife Valerie that he had been with Belushi and, "God, man, he was with this lady—she was tough, scary."

With the movie stars gone, Cathy asked Belushi if he wanted her to leave as well, but he demurred. Even though he'd been up for days, he wanted her to stay and feed him more drugs. She says she could not believe the amount of cocaine Belushi used. "Even the Stones had never done anything near that quantity. He was a big man, of course, but I found it hard to believe that even his body could accommodate so much of the drug." She also, in a rather nice turn of phrase, described him as, "one of those people who feel they have to do personal battle with the night in order to make the sun come up."

After testing a speedball on herself, she injected Belushi with one. He then decided he needed to take a shower, so she washed his back for him, but was terrified he might slip and fall, knowing if he did she'd never be able to get him back up. She then took a shower herself, and Belushi offered her the fancy new jogging suit that Ovitz had sent him as yet another perk of working for Paramount. Smith made a sexual advance on him, but unsurprisingly, he was not interested. Heroin is no aphrodisiac. Belushi lay down on one of the bungalow's beds, and finally fell asleep. As he snored, Cathy not knowing what to do with him, or with herself, sat down with one of the many yellow legal pads that were sprinkled through the rooms, ready to be used for scriptwriting, and began writing a letter to her old boss Bernie Fiedler, the owner of the Riverboat club back in Toronto:

> *My Dearest Bernie*
>
> *I'm not too long in writing, huh? Sorry about that! How on earth are you? How I miss you! There's not a man on this planet with a sense of humor like yours...and I'm dying on the vine because of it!...Paul Donnelly offered to fly me up there if I wanted to visit, but he wanted me to stay with him and somehow I got the impression that he was seeing the whole experience through his dick! I mean excu-u-use me!...I was considered coming back to Toronto and see what's shaking there for a while. I sure wish I had the money to lease a store, and pay somebody a percentage to run it, secure an import-export license and go around the world doing all the shopping for it. What do you think? I love to travel, not to mention shop!*
>
> *Whatever, I must get out of LA soon. It's driving me to an early death, what with all my self-abuse. I'm such a sucker for a good time! Ho-ho-ho.*
>
> *Speaking of ho-ho-ho's I've heard some very funny, I think, jokes lately...*

At that point she was interrupted by noises from Belushi's bedroom, and went to attend to him. As he was suddenly wheezing loudly, she woke him up, and asked him what the matter was. He told her his lungs were congested, so she got him a glass of water and then told her she was going to get herself something to eat. "Don't leave," he whimpered, then fell back asleep. They were his last words.

Cathy ordered herself some toast and coffee from room service, then cleaned up the syringes and other drug paraphernalia so they wouldn't be found by the hotel maid, checked once more on John, then split. She left her half-finished letter to Bernie Fiedler behind, to be later found by the police, then headed to a bar on Santa Monica, had a brandy, placed a bet on a racehorse, and went home to bed.

Later that morning, Belushi's bodyguard/trainer Bill Wallace came by to deliver a typewriter to his boss, and found him, lying on the bed, dead. Paramedics were called, then police, then all the agents, studio executives, wife, friends and others who had been part of his complicated life. Everyone, that is, except for Cathy Smith, who blithely woke up around two and decided to return Belushi's Mercedes-Benz. The hotel was a sea of crime tape and cops, and very shortly she found herself in handcuffs and whisked off to the Hollywood police station.

Homicide Detective Richard D. Iddings began interrogating her, putting the session down on tape.

"To begin with," said Iddings, "Be very candid with me. Don't hold anything back."

"No, I—," said Smith. "I have nothing to hold back. What happened? Did something happen to John?"

"Well, he's dead, to start with," replied the detective. He continued to ask her about her connection with Belushi, and about heroin. He searched her arms with a magnifying glass, looking for track marks, and he searched her purse and found the syringe and spoon she had taken from the apartment the night before. However, the detective never asked her about the source of the heroin, and did not push the fact when she told him she had been arrested and held for possessing narcotics paraphernalia two months earlier. She was released, feeling she had just got the luckiest break in her life. She could easily have been charged with violation of the conditions of her parole for the previous arrest. She almost felt it was as if the police didn't want to know, didn't want to become involved with drugs or with the details of what had happened to Belushi.

The coroner, though, did do an autopsy and found in Belushi's blood, bile, and urine vast quantities of cocaine and morphine. (Heroin metastasizes into morphine immediately upon injection into the bloodstream). In a 100 ml sample of his urine, for instance, there was nearly 56 milligrams of cocaine—a huge accumulation. The autopsy report was simple—"John Belushi, a 33 year-old white male, died of acute toxicity from cocaine and heroin."

Cathy Smith ran. First to St. Louis, then, under a pseudonym, to Toronto. After a few weeks two *National Enquirer* reporters, Tony Brenna and Larry Haley, found her there and after feeding her a considerable amount of alcohol got a confession out of her that ran as a banner headline in the next edition of the supermarket rag—I KILLED JOHN BELUSHI—I DIDN'T MEAN TO BUT I AM RESPONSIBLE. The story caused a huge stir, especially in Los Angeles, where the *Herald Examiner* ran a series of stories accusing the police of bungling the case by not arresting Cathy Smith, not doing a body search or a blood test of her, and not questioning Robert de Niro or Robin Williams. The LAPD has been accused since the very earliest silent movie days of covering up the sometimes-sordid activities of the town's most valuable human assets, and the *Examiner* was suggesting it was now happening again.

Deputy Police Chief Dan Sullivan dismissed the charges as being "a bunch of baloney" and stated that the time and money needed to continue investigating Belushi, whom he described as "this creep", could be better used for high-school drug prevention programs. Nonetheless, the police force put out a warrant for first-degree murder for Smith's arrest. Cathy hired one of the best-known criminal lawyers in Canada, Brian Greenspan, to fight extradition to the US. She was neither the first nor last high-profile client for him. Others have included Justin Bieber, Alan Eagleson, Naomi Campbell, Omar Khadr and Kevin O'Leary.

Eventually, in June 1986 she did return to the US and accepted a plea bargain, pleading guilty to involuntary manslaughter and several drug charges. She served fifteen months at the California Institution for Women for the death of John Belushi, and was deported to Canada after her release. She moved back to Toronto to work as a legal secretary. Three years later she was arrested again, in Vancouver, with two grams of heroin in her purse, for which she received a $2000 fine and twelve months' probation. She died in 2020, two weeks prior to the publication of this book.

Charlie Manson

The inclusion of Charles Manson in this chronicle may come as a surprise. Manson is not primarily remembered as a musician, just as Adolf Hitler is not primarily remembered as an artist, but the truth is, he was one. Not a great musician, not even a good one, but a person whose intense relationship with music, and with The Man, had a profound effect on not just his life and criminal behaviour but the lives of people around him and ultimately on the zeitgeist of his times, and the culture of California, America and the world.

Manson was born in 1934 to 16-year-old Kathleen Maddox, described by many, including Charlie, as being a teen prostitute, though there is no positive proof this was the case. She was certainly a spunky, wild teen who met Charlie's father, Colonel Scott, in an Ohio bar, and soon, impressed by his smooth-talking ways and his fancy name (though it was in fact just his Christian name, not a military rank) found herself pregnant by him. As soon as he learned there was a child on the way, Scott disappeared. Kathleen found herself another man, William Manson, probably also in Ritzy Ray's, the same bar where she had met Scott, and convinced him to marry her.

Kathleen seemed to prefer dancing and drinking in bars to staying with either her son or husband. In 1937, Manson divorced her, leaving her with nothing and leaving Charlie with nothing but a surname that, thirty years later would become synonymous with evil. She then filed what was then known as a "bastardy suit" against Scott. In the courtroom, the first of many he would see in his lifetime, Charlie, aged three, met his biological father for the first time. The judge decreed that Scott was to pay $5 a month child support, but he never paid it.

Two years later Kathleen and a girlfriend enticed a stranger into the idea of a threesome, and then with the help of her brother, rolled the man, knocked him out and stole $27 from him. Thirty years later, it would take the police more than three months to pin the blame on Manson and his gang for the Tate/Labianca murders, but it took the West Virginia police only hours to find and arrest these bumbling robbers. Within a scant seven weeks, Charlie's mom Kathleen was convicted of the assault and robbery and sentenced to five years in the Moundsville State Prison.

In order that her son could occasionally visit his mother in jail, he was sent to live with his uncle and aunt who lived in a mining town just five miles from the prison. They did not want the boy, who had already developed a reputation as being a disagreeable troublemaker. As his cousin Jo Ann said, "There was never anything happy about him. He never did anything that was good."

If the kid weren't traumatized by the lack of a father, or the fact that his mother was now serving five years in jail, he was certainly traumatized by his first—and second—day at school. He was assigned to Mrs. Varner's class. The woman was remembered long after her retirement, according to one of the administrators of the school for "how awful she was to her students." In the press hysteria that surrounded the Manson trial, a reporter found a contemporary of Manson's who simply said the martinet teacher "scared the shit out of me." On Manson's arrival in her classroom, Mrs. Varner decided she would initiate the newcomer with a day of berating him about his scrawny frame, inept skills, and jailbird mother. The boy ran home, crying. Uncle Bill responded by accusing the boy of being a sissy, weepy little girl, and the next morning punished him by dressing him in one of cousin Jo Ann's dresses, and then marching him back to the classroom, where he was forced for the rest of the day to endure the taunts of the other children, and Mrs. Varner. If that wouldn't scar a five-year-old for life, nothing would.

The boy grew moody, rebellious, and violent. There were only three things that interested him—guns, knives, and music. He taught himself to play the piano, and although he hated being dragged to church, he developed a good singing voice and so was warily welcomed into the choir. As for a family, though, he basically didn't have one, and wouldn't, until his created his own out of the runaway hippy girls of California, twenty-five years later.

He was branded as incorrigible. In 1947, his mother, now out of jail but at her wits' end, shipped him off to a school for delinquents called The Gibault School for Boys. Neither his grades nor his behavior improved, and Manson's main memory of the school was being regularly beaten by the priests "with paddles as big as ball bats." Within ten months he ran away from the school and went to Indianapolis, where he supported himself by robbing stores. Eventually, he was caught and sent to Boys Town, the juvenile facility in Nebraska made famous by the hit film of that name starring Spencer Tracy and Mickey Rooney.

Within four days he escaped from it, found a gun and an accomplice named Blackie Nielsen and robbed a casino and a grocery store. Two weeks later he was caught and soon packed off to a reform school in Plainfield, Indiana. It seems to have been quite a hellhole. Charlie was whipped on numerous occasions and raped by other inmates. He tried to run away six times. After stealing a car on his last escape and making it as far west as Utah, he was caught, and sent to the National Training School in Washington, D.C. He was almost eligible for parole by 1952, but then was caught sodomizing another inmate while holding a razor blade to the boy's neck.

Prison psychiatrists, used to dealing with the worst delinquents in the country, were convinced Charles Manson had been irreparably damaged by the experiences of his childhood, and was beyond rehabilitating. Somehow, though, using the jailhouse skills he would later use to con rock stars, record producers and runaways, he managed to get himself released. After seven years in reform school, he returned to McMechen, West Virginia in May 1954 and got a job mucking out stalls at a race track, found a girl, got her pregnant, and married her. He also got his hands on a guitar, learned some basic chords and became obsessed with playing and singing the songs of the day, particularly those of MOR crooner Frankie Laine.

He loved playing guitar, but he was not keen on working, so he returned to one of his old tricks—stealing cars. He drove one of them to Florida and another to California where he was captured and received his first sentence to adult jail—three years in San Pedro's Terminal Island Penitentiary. While in Terminal Island he received an education that would serve him well in the future. First, he picked the brains of all the pimps in the joint to find out how to recruit, run, and profit from a string of girls. Second, he took correspondence courses while in prison from one of the leading pop psychology gurus of the 1950s, Dale Carnegie. The lessons learned from the jailhouse pimps and from Carnegie's best seller, *How To Win Friends and Influence People* would serve Manson very well in his future career as a pimp, con man and cult leader.

He got out of Terminal Island on parole but was soon back in prison with a ten-year sentence for Treasury Check forgery. He continued his jailhouse education at the McNeil Island Penitentiary on Washington State's Puget Sound. Learning about scientology gave him a lot of the spiritual blather he would put to good use convincing his future followers that he was the reincarnated Son of God. To further his musical skills, he approached McNeil's most notorious prisoner, Alvin "Creepy" Karpis, for steel guitar lessons. Karpis, once the FBI's Public Enemy Number One, had in the 30s run the so-called Karpis-Barker Gang along with "Ma" Barker, and had the longest record of any inmate at Alcatraz Prison—twenty-six years. While in prison he had become an accomplished steel guitar player. In the memoir he wrote after being released and deported to Canada in 1969, Karpis remembered:

"This kid approaches me to request music lessons. He wants to learn guitar and become a music star. 'Little Charlie' is so lazy and shiftless, I doubt if he'll put in the time required to learn. The youngster has been in institutions all his life—four orphanages, then reformatories, and finally federal prison. His mother, a prostitute, was never around to look after him. I decide it's time someone did something for him, and to my surprise, he learns quickly. He has a pleasant voice and a pleasing personality, although he's unusually meek for a convict. He never has a harsh word to say and is never involved in even an argument."

Karpis was likely the first person (of many) to hear Charlie's new musical goal—he had now decided that one day he would bigger than The Beatles. He began practicing non-stop, writing songs, playing both guitar and drums in a prison band, and even convincing the parole board that if released he could support himself as a musician. He learned how to ignore the mockery of his musical efforts by other prisoners and guards. "Hey, Manson, when you're all alone in your cell with your guitar, do you fuck it?" was one of the gibes often thrown at him by his jailers.

While in McNeil, Charlie befriended an ex-Hollywood extra imprisoned on marijuana charges named Phil Kaufman. Manson, a firm believer in the adage that "it's not what you know, it's who you know" got something he felt was invaluable from Kaufman—his first music industry contact, who Kaufman encouraged Manson to look up upon release—a Universal Studios executive named Gary Stromberg. After Kaufman was later released, he became something of a player in the music business himself, "executive nanny" to Mick Jagger, and tour manager for The Flying Burrito Brothers. He also would hang out extensively with the girls in Manson's freewheeling "family" at the Spahn Ranch, later joking that he "had sex with more serial killers than anyone else in show business."

After seven years in McNeil, Manson was released in March 1967, and ended up drifting to Berkeley, California, epicenter of the drug-fueled musical revolution of the 1960s. Charlie in his mind was now a great artist and singer-songwriter, and so would no longer stoop to the menial labor jobs or even the petty crime that had sustained him in the past. He did try pimping, but in the Summer of (Free) Love there wasn't much call for paid sex. He did a little busking, and played in a few coffee shops and clubs, but there was a lot of competition from the hundreds of wannabe hippy folksingers in the Bay Area.

Instead Charlie put Dale Carnegie's and scientology founder Ron Hubbard's lessons to good use. He assembled a group of female acolytes around him who provided him with food, shelter, sex and wheels, listened to his wisdom and praised his music. He picked his disciples carefully, finding girls, and later guys, who had severe father issues, and providing them with an alternative father figure—himself. One of his favorite seduction techniques, in fact, was to tell prospective partners they had to abandon all inhibitions and imagine, as Charlie made love to them, that it was <u>their own father</u> making love to them. Of course, his guitar helped as well. Charlie was smart about it— he didn't carry on to his followers about just wanting to become rich and famous. Instead, he told them his goal and his mission was to teach the world a better way to live through his music. Who in 1967 could resist that?

By the end of the year Charlie felt he had practiced enough, and it was time to get to Los Angeles and become a star. Taking four of his new hippy girlfriends along, he managed to get down to the City of Angels and into Universal to meet the contact Phil Kaufman had provided him—Gary Stromberg. The producer was intrigued enough to give him a three-hour studio session, but it ended up a disaster. Manson was overwhelmed by the technical complications of recording and produced nothing Stromberg felt was worthwhile.

Disappointed but undeterred, Manson continued to seek out other industry contacts in his quest for musical stardom. At one point he got an opportunity to play his songs for Cass Elliot, of The Mama and Papas. Demos of his songs were also presented to Paul Rothchild, the producer of The Doors, and to Frank Zappa, avant-garde leader of the Mothers of Invention. They took the time to listen, but they all passed. But then Charlie got a break, connecting with his two biggest contacts in the record business—Dennis Wilson and Terry Melcher.

Dennis Wilson was the drummer, sometimes singer, and in-house wild man of The Beach Boys. He was also the only actual surfer in the group that invented surfing music. Like his brother Brian, he harbored deep anger over the childhood abuse by their father Murry, but unlike Brian he was not traumatized by it, and instead lived a hedonistic devil-may-care life in a giant old hunting lodge on Sunset Boulevard that had been built in the 20s by cowboy comedian Will Rogers. He invited all manner of musical mooches to his pad, especially if there was potential for some 60s-style free love, so it was no surprise that Manson and his gang of girls showed up, and for weeks on end never left.

Wilson introduced the wannabe rock star to his friends, including some genuine rock stars, like Neil Young. Young remembers Manson singing to him "off-the-cuff things he made up as he went along, and they were never the same twice in a row. Kind of like Dylan, but different because it was hard to glimpse a true message in them, but the songs were fascinating. He was quite good. I asked him if he had a recording contract. He told me he didn't yet, but he wanted to make records. I told Mo Ostin at Reprise about him and recommended that Reprise check him out." The studio chief, like almost everyone else, eventually passed on Manson.

The Beach Boy host, when not dallying with the Manson chicks, was also praising and promoting the talents of their leader. He told the British music magazine *Rave* that his new pal, who he called "the Wizard" was both "God and the Devil. He sings, plays and writes poetry and may be another artist for [the Beach Boys' company] Brother Records." The management team at Brother Records were not so sure about the scruffy, smelly hippie, especially after they ran a police check on him. They urged Dennis to get rid of Manson, and he eventually did, but not before introducing the singer to one of the most powerful figures in pop music, Terry Melcher, who would unwittingly play a major role in the tragedies to come.

Melcher, the only son of peaches-and-cream movie star Doris Day, was Hollywood royalty. He had become one of the major producers of the L.A. sound of the late 60s, producing hit records with The Byrds, The Beach Boys, Van Dyke Parks and Paul Revere and the Raiders. Manson met Melcher at 10050 Cielo Drive in the house the producer shared with his girlfriend, actress Candice Bergen. Manson badgered the well-connected producer to come up to the Spahn Western Movie Ranch, where he and his "family" were now ensconced, so that he could audition for him. Melcher was a no-show for several appointments, but he finally did make his way up to Chatsworth and listened, without much enthusiasm, to a performance of Charlie, backed up by his gals. Melcher was trying to make an exit from the creepy scene when Charlie, probably well aware that his big audition had failed, took his anger out with a savage beating of a visiting movie stuntman. Fifty years later, a variation on the scene would be re-enacted by Brad Pitt playing a stuntman visiting the Manson Family at the Spahn Ranch in Quentin Tarantino's re-imagination of the Manson story, *Once Upon a Time in Hollywood*. The real beating was a sufficient turn-off for Melcher that he vowed never to have anything more to do with Manson, but that was not to be.

Wilson, though, was still sufficiently intrigued by the jailbird songwriter that he decided to include one of Manson's songs, *Cease to Exist,* on the next Beach Boys' album. While it wasn't quite the Beatles-style mega-success he had planned for himself, Manson was still ecstatic, convinced the writing credit would put him on the fast-track to super-stardom. It would not quite work out that way. The band re-wrote much of the song and changed the title of it to *Never Learn Not to Love.* After one of the Manson tribe totaled Wilson's Ferrari and others stole one of his gold records and many of his clothes from his Sunset Boulevard home, he decided he owed nothing to Charles Manson. He removed Manson's name from the song and took sole writing credit for it. When he found out, Manson went ballistic.

By 1969 much of the world—and certainly the corner of it inhabited by the Manson Family—was descending into madness. On the other side of the planet the Beatles were squabbling and about to break up. They did hang together long enough to record their brilliant but often very strange penultimate album, officially called *The Beatles,* but referred to by everyone as the *White Album.* Charlie became obsessed with it, in particular with the heavy metal nonsense song penned by Paul McCartney, inspired by Pete Townsend's over-wrought *I Can See For Miles* and named after a British seaside carnival ride, *Helter Skelter.* Manson was convinced the song had hidden meanings and messages heralding a giant race war in America between blacks and whites that he was destined to initiate. He sent dozens of letters and telegrams to the Beatles about it, all of which naturally went unanswered, and he forced his followers to listen to the record endlessly.

Convinced now that his musical career had been thwarted, that he had been rejected by Melcher, betrayed by Wilson, ignored by The Beatles, and of course pilloried by The Man, Manson vowed revenge. He began by having his gang "creepy-crawl" homes of musical celebrities like the Mamas and the Papas' John and Michelle Phillips, breaking into their houses at night, not to steal anything but just to quietly rearrange their furniture and then sneak away in order to freak them out. The Family moved on to brutally murder a music teacher and part-time drug dealer named Gary Hinman. They decorated his apartment using his blood with the cats paw symbol of the Black Panthers in an unsuccessful attempt to try to get Charlie's predicted race war going, then stole his musical instruments, including a set of bagpipes.

On August 9, 1969, a night that will be forever etched in infamy in the history of Los Angeles, Manson sent a group of his followers to 10050 Cielo Drive, the home of producer Terry Melcher, to murder everyone there, and then, in his words, "do something witchy" with their remains. Melcher, however, no longer lived in the house. At the end of 1968 he and Candice Bergen had moved away. Shortly thereafter the owner, showbiz agent Rudi Altobelli rented it the hottest film director in Hollywood, Roman Polanski, and his wife, movie star Sharon Tate.

The killers didn't know who the victims were and didn't care. They had been given their orders to kill everyone in the house, and that's what they did. Roman Polanski was away in England, prepping a film. In the house that night were Sharon Tate (very pregnant, with what would be her first child), and her friends Abigail Folger, heir to the coffee fortune, celebrity hairdresser Jay Sebring and Polanski associate Voytek Frykowski, along with a young visitor, Steve Parent. All six were brutally shot or stabbed to death. Then one of the killers, Susan Atkins, smeared the word "PIG" across the front door in Sharon Tate's blood, a reference to another song (this one *Piggies*, written by George Harrison) from the *White Album*. The group, drenched in blood, returned to the ranch. After learning the details of the murder, Manson himself returned to Cielo Drive to view the carnage and re-arrange some of the bodies and the furniture like a deranged puppeteer.

The following night, Manson entertained his family with his guitar, then sent them out again, this time to the Los Feliz area of Los Angeles that Charlie had been introduced to by his jailhouse friend Phil Kauffman. There, they somewhat arbitrarily picked on the home of Leno and Rosemary LaBianca, and killed the couple in cold blood. Again, they made the murders as gruesome as possible, sticking a carving fork into Leno's belly, carving the word "WAR" on his abdomen, and writing the words "Death to Pigs" and "Healter Skelter" on the walls in blood, misspelling the word "Helter."

The violent murders set the city, and the country, on fire. They did not have the planned result of igniting a race war, but they did create a firestorm of fear and paranoia, with sales of guns, guard dogs, and security systems exploding across California over the following months. Civic authorities and the press went on a rampage demanding action from the police, but Manson had covered his tracks well. It was not until December 1 that LAPD Police Chief Ed Davis announced that the force had cracked the cases (mainly through confessions by some of the girls). They had suspects in jail, and they had a motive for the Tate murder—revenge on Terry Melcher. The *L. A. Times* headline proclaimed, "Grudge Against Doris Day's Son Linking to Tate Slayings." Eight days later, on December 9, *Charles Milles Manson, Address: Transient, Occupation: Musician* was formally charged with the murders of seven people and jailed at downtown Los Angeles' Hall of Justice.

The murders vied with the moon landing, the My Lai Massacre, Woodstock, and Altamont as one of the seminal events and biggest news stories of the final years of the 60s. Manson's macabre fixation on The Beatles certainly made people question their faith in the value and power of the new music. As British music writer Barney Hoskins wrote, Charlie and Altamont between them "managed to undo the whole notion that rock music was a positive force for change."

John Lennon would have none of it. Asked by *Rolling Stone* founder Jann Wenner what he thought of Charlie Manson and the whole *Helter Skelter* business, he simply replied that he thought Manson was "barmy" for reading messages into the song, and said the lyrics were just gibberish, just meaningless noise.

The trial of Charles Manson and his family vies with the trials of O. J. Simpson, Patty Hearst, and Michael Jackson as being one of the great legal circuses of the last fifty years. On the opening day of the trial Manson arrived from his holding cell with a giant X cut into his forehead, later modified into a swastika. He distributed a printed diatribe stating that he had "X'ed" himself from the world. His three co-defendants, Susan Atkins, Pat Krenwinkel and Leslie Van Houten promptly carved X's into their own foreheads. Other girls from the Manson Family showed solidarity with Charlie by appearing every day outside the courthouse, with X's burnt into their foreheads with a soldering gun.

District Attorney Vincent Bugliosi prosecuted the trial, and Judge Charles Older attempted to keep it under control, but it was not an easy task. There were wild outbursts from Manson and his three female co-defendants, leaks to the press, and several mistrial motions, one of them caused by the President of the United States. Richard Nixon, in a tub-thumping law and order speech, described Manson in the midst of the trial as being "guilty of eight murders without reason." Defense attorney promptly made a motion for a mistrial, as the President's comments would obviously affect the jurors, but the judge did not allow it since the jury was sequestered, with no access to the news. Charlie, though, secretly got a copy of the *L. A. Times*, with a blazing headline reading "MANSON GUILTY, NIXON DECLARES", and boldly held it up in the courtroom so that the jury could read it. More chaos ensued, but ultimately the long trial continued, running from June 15, 1970 to April 19, 1971, when the Judge finally pronounced the sentence.

There were thousands of articles written about Manson and his "family", and hours of television coverage. Every day, hundreds of letters and packages arrived at the jail for Manson with requests to join the Manson Family, offers of marriage, and other proposals too weird to recount. While Manson had not quite attained his goal of becoming "bigger than the Beatles", he had certainly become more famous, or at least more notorious, than 99 percent of the world's musicians. His music, however, was still not released. Charlie still yearned to be a rock star, and he came up with a plan to try to make it happen. From jail, he enlisted his still-loyal disciple Lynette "Squeaky" Fromme (who would go on five years later to attempt to assassinate President Gerald Ford) to persuade Dennis Wilson and Manson's old jailhouse pal Phil Kaufman to try to do something with the audition tapes Charlie had made in 1968. Wilson would have nothing to do with her, claiming that he had turned over all the tapes he had to the District Attorney. However, Kaufman found some other demos Manson had made in a Van Nuys studio. He decided to spend his own money to have 2000 copies pressed of a record he titled *LIE*. Included on the album were Charlie's songs *Cease to Exist, People Say I'm No Good,* and *Don't Do Anything Illegal*. The front cover was the wild-eyed portrait of Manson that had been the cover of a recent issue of *LIFE* magazine. The back-liner notes were words from Charlie about his childhood: "No mother, no father. In and out of orphanages and foster homes. . .I can't tell anybody nothing that they don't already know. But I can sing for them, and I got some music that says what I like to say if I ever had anything to say."

Unfortunately for Charlie's ego and Kaufman's investment, neither mainstream record stores nor even small head shops would stock the record. No one would risk accusations of endorsing a mass-murderer by offering his album for sale. Kaufman ended up with a garage-full of unsold albums, and received visits by angry Manson Family girls brandishing knives and demanding Charlie's share of the (non-existent) sales, and also a court order garnisheeing any proceeds of the record to the son of Voytek Frykowski, killed on Cielo Drive in August 1969. Some of the songs are now available on YouTube. The lead comment under Manson's version of *Cease to Exist*, by one Isak Larsson, is telling: "It creeps me out that this is so good."

Years later Manson did see his goal of having his songs professionally released. In 1988, the Lemonheads recorded his *Home Is Where You're Happy,* and in 1993 Guns N' Roses followed with his *Look At Your Game, Girl.* Performing Manson's music fit with the band's reputation as "The Most Dangerous Band in the World". At one of their shows, just for instance, singer Axl Rose was held backstage by police after physically assaulting a security guard, while a roadie sang the rest of the concert. In 1989, oddball actor/singer Crispin Glover recorded Manson's *Never Say 'Never' to Always* (in a falsetto) for his album *The Big Problem#The Solution / The Solution=Let it be.*

In the early 90s singer Brian Hugh Walker took Charlie's last name (and Marilyn Monroe's first) to become Marilyn Manson, a highly controversial Goth singer, actor, and visual artist.

At the end of his long trial, Manson was allowed to speak. In his defense, he blamed both his rotten childhood, and music, for his actions. Speaking for more than an hour, he proclaimed, ""My father is the jailhouse. My father is your system. . .I am only what you made me. . .you want to kill me? Ha! I am already dead," and then continued, "the music is telling the youth to rise up against the establishment. Why blame it on me? I didn't write the music."

On April 19, 1971, Judge Older sentenced Charlie, Susan, Leslie and Pat to die in the gas chamber. It was not to be. A year later the California Supreme Court voted to abolish the death penalty. Manson spent the rest of his life behind bars. He died on November 19, 2017. After Older pronounced the 1971 sentence, Manson, his voice shaking, meekly told the judge, "I accept this court as my father. . .I accept my father's judgement."

It is curious that few questioned the fact that Manson was found guilty of the murders when he was not even present for them. He was not present at the Sharon Tate murders at all, and although he was in the LaBianca house, he left before the murders were committed. Of course, he not only was a terrible defendant in court, but he had a dreadful attorney—himself. Nonetheless, one wonders about the motivation of the prosecution in hanging the murder rap on him. One wonders whether male chauvinism, and music, had anything to do with it. Imagine if Manson had been the leader of a male gang. Would the leader of a male gang who was not present for murders be found guilty of them? Did the fact that Manson's followers were female mean that the prosecution, the jury and the public could not imagine that the women could act on their own, without mystical control by their leader? More relevant to our thesis, did Charlie's image as a long-haired musician contribute to the need to convict him along with the women who actually performed the murders? Was The Man, to a greater or lesser degree, taking revenge on all the long-haired singers and musicians leading the world's youth away from convention, goodness and normality?

The Twenty-Seven Club

The Twenty-Seven Club is a club to which no-one wants to belong. Its membership requirement is rockstar death at age twenty-seven. Its members include the late Brian Jones, Jim Morrison, Janis Joplin, Jimi Hendrix, Ron "Pigpen" McKernan, Alan "Blind Owl" Wilson, Kurt Cobain, and Amy Winehouse.

Though their deaths were largely by self-inflicted misadventure, they all had considerable interaction with The Man throughout their twenty-seven-year long lives. Keith Richards, someone people thought would flame out by twenty-seven, but who has somehow instead made it well past seventy-two, reports, "The life of a musician is fraught with danger. It's a pretty dark road at times, and it's no wonder some of the best go far too early."

We can go right back to the nineteenth century, to find charismatic Brazilian folk pianist Alexandre Levy, who died in 1892 at twenty-seven, but the founding member of the club is the bluesman who sold his soul to the devil, **Robert Johnson**. For most of the musicians chronicled in this book, "The Man" means a figure of authority, often in uniform—a cop, a border guard, a mayor, a drug czar, an FBI chief, maybe even a President. In the case of Robert Johnson, considered by some the greatest blues guitarist of all time, his struggles with The Man transcend all these petty mere mortals. For The Man he fought was Lucifer—The Devil Himself.

Or so the story goes.

Born in the deepest, darkest end of the American South, the Mississippi Delta, Johnson vowed not to become tied to the plow like all his sharecropper family and neighbors, so instead went on the road as an untrained, itinerant musician, trying to eke out a living on street corners and juke joints. As contemporary blues artist Taj Mahal reminds us, it was a dangerous life for "walking bluesmen" of those days. They had a good chance of being robbed, lynched, or run down by the white trash of the south. Bluesmen were in equally as much danger from their own race, since southern black preachers would vehemently condemn what Christians then called "the devil's music".

Increasingly by the 1920s, only women and children were found in Southern black churches. Their menfolk were instead rocking inside local juke joints. The Baptist preachers, no longer making any real money on their collection plates, would try to bring their congregations back by railing that people would go to hell for listening to this new "devil's music".

Johnson was caught between his passion for the blues and the demands of the straight world. Very early in his career he married fifteen-year old Virginia Travis, but when she died in childbirth, and he and his music were blamed for the death, he angrily abandoned the straight and narrow and went on the road, dedicating himself instead to the goal of becoming a great musician.

He sought out skilled local blues artists like Son House, who was back playing the juke joints after spending two years of a fifteen-year sentence at the Mississippi State Penitentiary. However House, and others like Willy Brown, and their audiences scorned Johnson for his lack of skill, and he soon disappeared. When he mysteriously reappeared a year later, he was transformed—suddenly by far the best guitarist in the south, with a weirdly seven-stringed guitar, and amazing fingers flying over the frets.

The mystery of how he turned from a guitar bum to a guitar hero was solved by myth. The only possibility, it was thought, was that Johnson had "been to the crossroads" where he had sold his soul to the devil, who in return had given him devilish skills with his guitar. (Various locations in the deep south claim to be the famous crossroads—perhaps the most likely is the intersection of Highways 61 and 49 near Clarksdale, Mississippi.)

The songs he wrote and sang reflected both the hellbound myth, and the cruel realities of the south. His tune *Hellhounds On My Trail* tells the true story of his own stepfather, chased by a lynch mob, sprinkling hot pepper behind him so the bloodhounds could not catch him.

Robert Johnson's life was cut short in August of 1938 when he was poisoned by strychnine-laced whiskey in the Three Forks juke joint in Greenwood, Mississippi. A man was charged with the murder, but was released by the police. The reason, it is claimed, is because everyone thought Johnson played the devil's music, and so deserved to die.

Johnson's music was mostly forgotten until the 1960's, when **Brian Jones**, founder of the Rolling Stones discovered it and convinced bandmates Keith Richards and Mick Jagger to cover and record the 35-year-old blues tunes. Like Johnson, Jones would live a troubled life. Like Johnson, Jones would die at twenty-seven.

Although Brian Jones started and named the Stones, and was the original leader of the band, the power dynamic shifted away from him towards Jagger, Richards and manager Andrew Loog Oldham. Jones' drug use, arrests and subsequent passport and visa issues with the authorities eventually led to his being thrown out of the group. For Jones, The Man was not just the London Vice Squad and Scotland Yard. It was also Mick Jagger.

Described by many as being highly intelligent, Jones nevertheless had a troubled, messy adolescence – twice suspended from school, fathering not one, not two, not three, but four children by four different girls.

When he created the Stones, he was probably the best musician and most important and visible member of the group. But as the band evolved from doing covers of Robert Johnson and Muddy Waters songs to playing their own material, the power naturally evolved away from the blues purist and towards the writers—Jagger and Richards. He tried, but failed. "To be honest", says Jagger, "Brian had no talent for writing songs. None. I've never known a guy with less talent for songwriting."

Producing no original material, with his bandmates ignoring him, with his exotic girlfriend, Anita Pallenberg, leaving him to take up with Richards, and with his drug busts, the world was coming unravelled for Brian Jones. He was arrested for drug possession on May 10, 1967, and again on May 21, 1968. The Stones wanted to tour the United States for the first time in three years, and Jones' busts led to problems getting him an American work visa. He was also crashing motorcycles, losing cars and ending up in hospitals. On June 8, 1969 Jagger, Richards and drummer Charlie Watts visited him at his house (a country cottage, originally owned by A. A. Milne, writer of *Winnie The Pooh*) and asked him to leave the band.

Less than three weeks later, on July 3, Jones was found unconscious at the bottom of his swimming pool. He was pulled from the pool by his Swedish girlfriend, Anna Wohlin. She felt he was still alive and tried to call the authorities, but she spoke little English, and it took them some time for them to understand her, and to send assistance. By the time paramedics arrived, he was dead, aged twenty-seven.

The Stones presented a concert in tribute to him two days later in London's Hyde Park, with Jagger reciting a poem by Percy Bysshe Shelley about the death (at twenty-five) of his friend John

Keats—"He is not dead, he doth not sleep/He hath awakened from the dream of life", and releasing thousands of white butterflies above the huge crowd in his memory.

Some blamed the Stones for his death. When asked whether he felt guilty about it, Mick Jagger told *Rolling Stone* magazine: "No, I don't, really. I do feel that I behaved in a very childish way, but we were very young, and in some ways we picked on him. But, unfortunately, he made himself a target for it; he was very, very jealous, very difficult, very manipulative, and if you do that in this kind of a group of people you get back as good as you give. To be honest, I wasn't understanding enough about his drug addiction. No one seemed to know much about drug addiction. Things like LSD were all new. No one knew the harm. People thought cocaine was good for you."

The investigating police and coroner described what had happened to him as "death by misadventure" but associates of the Stones claimed they had information that he had been murdered. The primary suspect was Frank Thorogood, a carpenter who had been working on Jones' house. Rumors swirled in the music world for forty years about his death, and in 2009 the British newspaper *The Mail on Sunday* argued that new evidence uncovered by writer Scott Jones showed that Thorogood killed Jones in a fight, and that senior police officers had covered up the true cause of Brian Jones' death.

Following the sensational newspaper report, the Sussex Police's Crime Policy and Review Branch re-opened the case, but ultimately decided that there was no new evidence to prove that the coroner's verdict of "death by misadventure" was incorrect.

If Brian Jones was the gorgeous chick-magnet Adonis of British music, **Jim Morrison** cut a very similar Byronic romantic swath across America. He would have even more public battles with The Man than the Rolling Stones founder, most famously remembered for being the first rock star to be arrested and beaten up by the police while in the middle of a concert.

While there were tens of thousands of conflicts between the generation that came of age in the Sixties and their parents, few were as high profile as Morrison's. There has probably never been a more intimate example of the struggle between Music and The Man than the one between Morrison and his own father.

The generational battles began as Morrison grew up as a military brat, moving from one naval base to another across the United States. His naval officer father levied family punishment in the military manner known as "dressing down"—yelling at and berating his children until they were reduced to tearful admissions of their failings. In 1964, by now an Admiral, Morrison was the Commander of the US Naval Fleet during the Gulf of Tonkin incident, in which the US Navy provoked North Vietnam into aggression, thus providing a trumped up cause for the US to attack North Vietnam, and start what the Vietnamese call The American War. Admiral Morrison found time while commanding the fleet of aircraft carriers and destroyers cruising the coast of Vietnam to virtually disown his son. His last communication with Jim was in 1966, when he wrote a letter, telling his son he had a complete lack of talent as a singer, and that he should give up on his goal of being a musician. His offspring reciprocated with the line in his epic song *The End* – "Father? Yes, son? I want to kill you."

Ironically, while neither Admiral Morrison nor likely any other top military brass were fans of The Doors, the band was the favorite group of the American GI's slogging through the jungles of Vietnam.

The Doors were one of the most unique bands to come out of the sixties. They were spare—they had no bass player, and no real lead guitar player—simply Robbie Kreiger, who doubled as both lead and rhythm guitarist, drummer John Densmore, the distinctive sounds of Ray Manzarek on electric organ, and Morrison, who fronted and sang, but played no instruments. Neither Morrison nor Manzarek had musical training, and unlike many of the British bands of the day, they had not even a long-standing passion to become rock stars.

Both really wanted to become filmmakers, and met while at UCLA film school. Nonetheless, their band became highly successful, their music made a huge impact, and more than any other band of the sixties except for the Beatles and Stones, their music is still being bought and loved today, decades after Morrison's death.

"Erotic politicians, that's what we are," said Morrison. "We're interested in anything about revolt, disorder, and chaos." The Doors induced more bacchanalian frenzy than almost any other, and also got what today seems an extraordinary amount of attention from the police. It seems odd now to see footage of the band's outdoor concerts, with more uniformed cops than musicians, violently hurling female fans off the stage or dragging them to the sides of it, sometimes ducking around Morrison as he sings the song, treating him with kid gloves. Their body language makes it clear that while they realize they can't treat him with the authoritarian contempt they can his frenzied female fans, they wish they could. Eventually, they did.

Before a concert in New Haven Connecticut, a cop, walking around backstage, came upon Morrison and a girl in a dressing room shower stall. According to the police report, they were "making out". According to Morrison's report, they were merely talking. Not recognizing Jim as the headliner of the concert, he ordered the pair to get out. Jim told him to go fuck himself. The cop maced him.

Twenty minutes later, his face streaming with tears from the mace, Jim took to the stage but stopped the concert half way through the first song and told the audience what had happened to him, describing the cop as a "little man in a little blue suit with a little blue cap."

In response, the cops showed up on the stage. Jim offered them a chance to say their thing. They deferred, instead <u>doing</u> their thing: grabbing the mike away from him and hauling him offstage, punching him in the face, and kicking him after he fell down the stairs. They then charged him with obscenity and resisting arrest. As *The New York Times* would note, in a long story about the aborted concert, it was the first time ever that a rock musician had been arrested onstage.

At the height of their fame and success, in the summer of 1968, the *Village Voice* awarded Morrison the title Vocalist of the Year; Ray Manzarek, ahead of runners up Ravi Shankar and Eric Clapton, Musician of the Year; and The Doors as the best band.

However, the concert pandemonium continued. During a March 1, 1969 show in Coconut Grove, Florida, a woman rushed the stage and poured a bottle of champagne over Morrison, ostensibly to cool him off on the very hot night. As the cops dragged her away, he good-naturedly pulled his shirt off, suggested he might pull his pants down, and urged the crowd to do the same. They responded by pulling their clothes off and hurling blouses, pants, bras and underwear at him. They then began to jump on the stage, and soon a phalanx of police and security guards were hurling fans back to the auditorium floor. One of them grabbed Morrison and threw him into the audience.

As the craziness continued, Kreiger and Densmore bailed, leaving only Manzarek pumping his electric organ onstage. The concert ended after less than an hour, in a complete shambles but with no arrests, no busting of heads, no riots. In fact, a few of the hundred police that were present came back and drank beers with the band following the show.

However, a *Miami Herald* reporter managed to get the local elected authorities in a lather with a claim that Morrison had exposed himself on stage and tried to incite a riot. A local television station found a few evangelical Christians to put on air to bemoan his behavior.

Did Morrison actually pull it out on stage? He certainly considered it. He was a major fan of the Living Theater, the avant-garde theater group that was appearing nightly in Los Angeles, stark naked. Even in the more staid Miami, the pseudo-hippie musical *Hair* was currently running, with its climatic scenes of full frontal nudity.

He threatened to do it, but did he actually do it? Not according to Robby Kreiger. "No, he didn't", he told *Rolling Stone* reporter Ben Fong-Torres. "If he did, believe me, somebody would have snapped a shot of that. It wasn't that easy to miss."

Nonetheless, four days later Miami police, egged on by the local press and legislators, issued warrants, charging Morrison with one felony charge: "Lewd and lascivious behavior in public by exposing his private parts and simulating masturbation and oral copulation" and three misdemeanors—two counts of indecent exposure, two counts of open profanity, and one count of public drunkenness during the performance. The combined maximum prison sentence on the six charges would be for three years, 150 days in Raiford State Prison.

The charges claimed that "Mr. Morrison did lewdly and lasciviously expose his penis." The District Attorney's office delayed charging Morrison for several days as they searched in vain through hundreds of pictures taken of the event for a single one showing Morrison exposing himself. The best they could come up with was a photo of Morrison on his knees, staring closely at Robby Kreiger's fingers as they flew across the neck of his Stratocaster guitar, which they offered as proof of oral copulation. Then, to try to increase their likelihood of throwing something at Morrison, since the band had flown from Miami following the concert for a vacation in Guadalupe and Jamaica, the FBI charged them as well with "unlawful flight."

Regardless of how little evidence they had, the charges were very serious. The jeopardy increased when homophobic singer and Florida citrus fruit spokeswoman Anita Bryant got into the fray, leading "decency rallies" in Dade County to rail against rock, and particularly The Doors, and especially Jim Morrison. Radio stations stopped playing The Doors music, and one by one, every remaining city on what was The Doors first major tour cancelled the upcoming concerts. Tour manager Bill Siddons estimated the cancellations cost the band "at least half a million dollars," and said they "really destroyed (the band's) morale, and almost caused it to break up."

On April 4, 1969, Morrison surrendered to the FBI. Well over a year later, in August 1970, the trial began. All three officials—the police chief Bernard Garmire, the prosecutor Terence McWilliams and the Judge Murray Goodman—were running for re-election at the time, so were trying to score political points by coming down hard on Morrison.

All three of his band members testified that he did not expose himself at the concert, and the defense attorneys argued that nothing that had happened exceeded local community standards, but on September 30, 1970 the jury found Morrison guilty of profanity and indecent exposure. Judge Murray Goodman sentenced him to four months of hard labor in the Dade County jail. The Doors' attorney filed for appeal, and with Morrison still bound by a $50,000 surety, the band flew to England, to appear at the largest festival in history.

The massive Isle of Wight festival ended in another shambles, with music fans, declaring that the concert should be free, battling security guards as they tried to rip down the corrugated steel fences around the massive venue. Morrison's mesmerizing, desperate performance of the band's apocalyptic song *The End* seemed to be appropriate for the closing of both the festival and the violent, deadly decade.

In late 1970 Morrison collapsed on stage at a concert in New Orleans. On April 17, 1971 he abandoned the band and left to live in Paris with his girlfriend Pamela Courson, with the claim that he would try to stop drinking. He spent his last months writing poetry, wandering the streets alone, and frequently visiting the Père Lachaise Cemetery where Frédéric Chopin, Oscar Wilde, Edith Piaf and other artists are buried.

On July 3, 1971, after a day of heavy drinking, he was found dead in his bathtub. It was exactly two years to the day after Brian Jones had died in his swimming pool. There was some mystery about his death, as an autopsy was never performed, but the French authorities listed the cause of his death as heart failure. He was buried at the Père Lachaise Cemetery. Just as he used to visit the graves of dead singers and poets in the necropolis, so has his grave become a macabre shrine, still visited by the thousands who worship this young Adonis of rock, dead at twenty-seven.

A year younger than Janis Joplin, Jimi Hendrix and Canned Heat founder Alan "Blind Owl" Wilson, Morrison entered the Twenty-Seven Club nine months after Joplin, Hendrix and Wilson had died, all between September 3 and October 4, 1970. In 2010 Florida Governor Charlie Crist announced a posthumous pardon for Morrison for the charges laid at the Miami concert.

Canned Heat was a was a major boogie/rock band of the late sixties, named appropriately after a 1928 blues song about an alcoholic who killed himself by drinking Sterno "Canned Heat" fuel. They became known as the "bad boys of rock" (are there any "good boys" of rock?) after a police informant fingered them and Denver police jailed them for drug possession. They were forced to raise bail by selling off the publishing rights to their songs at fire-sale rates to Al Bennett, the president of their label, Liberty Records.

"Blind Owl" Wilson, the co-founder, leader, singer and songwriter of the group died of a barbiturate overdose—possibly a suicide—on September 3, 1970. Following his death the group fell on hard times, and according to their drummer Adolfo de la Parra resorted to importing marijuana from Mexico to make ends meet. The other founding member, Bob Hite collapsed from a heroin overdose on stage at the famed Palomino Club in Los Angeles, and died later at his home.

Somehow the band stayed together and still performs today, although with only de la Parra and bassist Larry Taylor surviving from the original lineup that headlined the Woodstock Festival in 1969.

Sharing the bill with them at Woodstock was **Janis Joplin**. The most famous female rock singer of the psychedelic era, Joplin transformed herself from being a shunned outsider into a celebrated insider by becoming a musical superstar. In high school, she was overweight, ostracized and bullied, called names like "pig", "freak" and "nigger-lover". At the University of Texas, a fraternity named her the "Ugliest Man on Campus".

She escaped to California, where she became addicted to methamphetamine, had a run-in with the law over shoplifting and began her life-long bottle a day consumption of Southern Comfort alcohol. She created an extremely energetic love-life, claiming that she had gotten it on with "a couple of thousand cats" in her life, "and a few hundred chicks". One of her longer affairs was with Ron "Pigpen" McKernan, co-founder of the (also perhaps appropriately named) Grateful Dead, who is also, with his death on March 3, 1973, a card-carrying member of the Twenty-Seven Club.

Her distinctively powerful, raspy voice first got attention when she sang with the Haight-Ashbury group Big Brother and the Holding Company. By 1967, she was one of the biggest stars of the new rock, performing in '68 and '69 at the Hollywood Bowl, the Monterey Pop Festival, and at Woodstock. In the summer of 1969, while performing in Tampa, Florida, she was busted for using "vulgar and indecent language." She was handcuffed backstage, charged and booked by the Tampa police.

In the early summer of 1970, she was one of the headliners of the Festival Express, a train that was to cross Canada from Montreal to Vancouver carrying a gang of A-list rock stars who were to perform in various cities along the way. However, before it started the mayors and city councils of both the opening and closing cities forced the cancellation of the event in Montreal and Vancouver, so instead the tour began in Toronto and ended in Calgary.

In Toronto, a protest by fans that the $14 ticket price was too high nearly stopped the tour before it began. The crisis was averted by Jerry Garcia of the Grateful Dead calming the unruly crowd with a free concert in a nearby park.

The same "Music Should be Free" mantra was repeated in Calgary, with the mayor of the city, Rod Sykes, getting into the action, calling the concert promoter, Ken Walker "eastern scum" who was "trying to skim" the young people of Alberta. Walker claims that he responded by punching the mayor in the mouth, and boasted he had a scar on his hand to prove it. The ongoing battle between music and The Man was starting to get violent.

Janis Joplin knew which side of the fight she was on. In appreciation of what she described as a "fantastic event," Joplin at the start of her set at the Calgary concert presented Walker with a case of tequila, which the promoter then carted offstage with his scarred hand.

The much-loved singer only played a very few more concerts that summer, but in September booked into the Landmark Motor Hotel in Hollywood while she recorded what would be her final album, *Pearl*. She began shooting heroin again. Her habit cost her $200 a day—multiply that times ten to get a rough equivalent of the cost today. On October 4, 1970, she was found dead in the motel, the victim of a heroin overdose.

Only three days earlier, her contemporary **Jimi Hendrix** had been buried in Seattle, also from a drug-related death, also aged twenty-seven.

Hendrix is the only member of the Twenty-Seven Club who had himself served in uniform as "The Man"—a paratrooper, member of the 101st Airborne division of the United States Army. After getting out of the army, Hendrix moved to Nashville to try to become a musician. He remembered what weekend entertainment was available in the sixties in the Tennessee town. "On Sunday afternoons we'd go down to watch the race riots," he recalled. "We'd take a picnic lunch because they wouldn't serve us in the restaurants. One group would stand on one side of the street and the rest on the other side. They'd shout names and talk about each other's mothers and every once in a while, stab each other. Sometimes if there was a good movie on that Sunday, there wouldn't be any race riots."

The violence was nothing new to him; his childhood had been mercifully somewhat free of racial strife, but not of the problems of a broken family. Shuttled back and forth between Seattle and Vancouver, he even at one point was sexually abused—by a man in uniform.

From Nashville, Hendrix began touring as a backup musician with Wilson Pickett, Little Richard, Sam Cooke and Ike and Tina Turner. In 1966 he met up with Chas Chandler, ex-bassist of The Animals, who took him to London and created a group around him called The Jimi Hendrix Experience. Within a year he had the number two album (second only to *Sergeant Pepper*) on the charts and was touring Europe and North America. He was soon the highest paid rock musician in the world, and the headliner at the Monterey Pop Festival in 1968 and at Woodstock the following summer.

Both were iconic performances, with Hendrix burning his guitar at the climax of his Monterey set, and playing a psychedelic version of *The Star-Spangled Banner* at Woodstock, full of virtuoso guitar, feedback, sustain and distortion to simulate the sounds of warfare. Whether it was anti-American or rah-rah pro-American is up for debate, but conservative America certainly found it shocking.

Along with his new-found wealth and fame came a spiral into arrests and violence. In January 1968 he was arrested and received a large fine for a drunken, violent escapade in Gothenburg, Sweden. Soon after, he was involved in two more violent encounters while living in Benedict Canyon, California.

Then, on May 3, 1969, he had his most serious confrontation with The Man. Entering Canada through Toronto's Malton (now Pearson) Airport, he was stopped by customs who found what they suspected to be heroin and hashish in his luggage. He was held at the airport and in police custody for some time, and eventually charged with drug possession.

Hendrix and his road manager Gary Stickells were anxious they get out in time to make the 8 PM gig at Maple Leaf Gardens, but the booking detective told them he would "get it done as quickly as possible" because he knew his own teenaged kids had tickets and "they'll kill me if I don't get (Hendrix) out." There were often subtle complexities like this in the battles between music and The Man. The cops were further pressured by the management at the hockey arena venue, who told them that the sell-out crowd of eighteen thousand might riot if they had to cancel the show. The police released Hendrix on $10,000 bail, then escorted him to the Gardens, and remained in the arena to watch his performance.

The possible twenty-year sentence weighed heavily on Hendrix for the next six months. In December, he returned for his court date. Again, he was searched as he entered the country, and again, he was arrested—for a single mystery tablet in his guitar case, and spent the night in jail. This time, though, the pill was determined to be a legal medication, and he was released.

His bandmates Noel Redding and Mitch Mitchell stated they believed the drugs in the original bust had been planted on Hendrix, either by cops, fans or a jilted lover. After a three-day trial and eight hours of jury deliberations, Hendrix was acquitted on all charges. The courtroom, filled with young fans, exploded with applause, and Hendrix, flashing a peace sign, said that Canada had given him "the best Christmas present I ever had." However, the bust and trial took a serious toll on Hendrix. The FBI opened a file on him that included not just the Toronto bust but charges going back to joyriding in stolen cars as a teenager. Paranoia ran deep in the rock community, starting with the apprehension in May of Hendrix, the twin events on May 16 of John Lennon's passport being revoked and the marijuana bust of Jefferson Airplane bassist Jack Casady, and the arrests on May 28 in London of Mick Jagger and Marianne Faithful. It really seemed that spring that the establishment was at war with rock and roll.

Hendrix continued to record and tour. In the summer of 1970, he made a series of festival performances culminating with the Isle of Wight Festival, believed at the time to be the largest collection of humans—650,000—in the history of the world. This writer was on the stage, just a few feet away from Hendrix, filming him for a documentary ultimately released in 1997 as *Message to Love*, and witnessed Hendrix' dangerous lifestyle, slapping his arm against a Marshall amp and out of the spotlight between songs so his roadie could shoot him up before he returned to playing. Everyone thought they were invincible in those days, but Hendrix was not. He died three weeks later in London, on September 18, 1970. The coroner's inquest concluded he died after aspirating his vomit from asphyxia while intoxicated by barbiturates—eighteen times the recommended dose of sleeping tablets. He was twenty-seven.

Fourteen years later, **Kurt Cobain**, founder and lead singer of Seattle grunge band Nirvana, would join the infamous club. The product of a dysfunctional family with divorced parents and two uncles who had committed suicide, Cobain had his first drink at thirteen, his first guitar at fourteen, and his first mugshot at nineteen, after being arrested for trespassing and malicious mischief for climbing on an abandoned warehouse. He was also arrested for spraying graffiti with provocative slogans such as "God is Gay" around Seattle.

Although his band Nirvana began very much as an alternative, grunge/punk effort, it became one of the most successful groups of the 1980s, selling over eighty million albums. His music and his stance were highly political, mostly on the subjects of LGBTQ rights and abortion, and he had a hard time with fans who responded to his music but not to the meaning of his lyrics. He was harassed by anti-abortion activists, one of whom threatened to kill him if he returned to the stage. Cobain had great problems dealing with the fame and attention that came his way, and the sense that he was somehow supposed to be a spokesman for his generation.

In January of 1990 Cobain met punk rocker Courtney Love. It was not exactly love at first sight, but by 1992 she was pregnant and they were married on Waikiki Beach in Hawaii—Cobain wearing pajamas because he was "too lazy to put on the tux."

Their relationship was exceedingly stormy. On March 18, 1994 Love called Seattle police, telling them Cobain was talking about suicide and had locked himself in a room. When police arrived, they confiscated several guns and a bottle of pills from Cobain, who told them he was not suicidal, but had locked himself in the room to protect himself from Love.

Later that month Love, friends and record company executives forced him to undergo a detox program at a Los Angeles rehab center, but after a day there he escaped by climbing over a high fence, and returned to Seattle. Love hired a private detective to track him down, but he never reappeared. He was discovered dead from a three-day-old shotgun blast to his head.

Ever since, the Seattle Police Department has been receiving at least one request a week to re-open the investigation into Cobain's death. In 2014, on the twentieth anniversary, the Seattle police did finally develop film of Cobain's body that had gone unprocessed for twenty years. However, after re-examining this new evidence, cold-case detective Mike Ciesynski announced that as far as the Seattle police were concerned, Cobain's death remained a suicide.

And although Cobain's death is officially described by Washington state authorities as a suicide, many people, including Courtney Love's own father, hint that she was involved.

Tom Grant, the private detective originally hired by Courtney to search for her missing husband, believes he was being set up as part of a plot, and that Courtney Love was involved in Cobain's death, and he stated as much in the BBC documentary *Kurt and Courtney*. He accuses her of encouraging the suicide, and notes that the pair were actively talking about divorce. With a divorce, Courtney would have gotten at best 50 percent of Cobain's fortune, but with his death, 100 percent.

Courtney Love made it past twenty-seven and is still performing today. As Amy Phillips of the *Village Voice* wrote, she is "willing to act out the dream of every teenage brat who ever wanted to have a glamorous, high-profile hissy fit, and she turns those egocentric nervous breakdowns into art. Sure, the art becomes less compelling when you've been pulling the same stunts for a decade. But honestly, is there anybody out there who fucks up better?"

She has been involved with The Man throughout her life; arrested numerous times for disrupting airline flights, striking audience members and violating parole. She has also been in and out of lockdown rehab a number of times, just as has the final member of this edition of the Twenty-Seven Club, **Amy Winehouse**.

Very much the psychic heir to the punk excesses of Kurt Cobain and Courtney Love, Amy burst onto the scene with her albums *Frank* and *Back to Black,* and what became her signature song, *Rehab*. The press gushed over her rebellious punk persona. The *Daily Telegraph* praised her for "strutting into gloriously ballsy, bell-ringing, bottle-swigging, doo-wop territory." London's *Jewish Chronicle* breathlessly described her as a woman "with tattoos" (indeed, by then she had twelve), who "swears like a docker" and "smokes weed", and claimed that "her rafter-shaking vocals belie her age, postcode, everything." *Time Magazine* called her "mouthy, funny, sultry, and quite possibly crazy" and then called her *Rehab* the Best Song of the Year.

Like a lot of artists, she made the mistake of reading her own notices, and then, in her case, trying to live up to them. She was addicted to bad behavior from an early age, cutting herself at nine, and drinking to excess in her teens. By 2005 she was alcoholic, a heavy drug user, and allegedly both anorexic and bulimic. In 2007 she was hospitalized with an overdose of heroin, ecstasy, cocaine, ketamine and alcohol. Also that year, the London *Sun* posted a video of a woman alleged to be Winehouse apparently smoking crack cocaine and speaking of having taken ecstasy and valium. London's Metropolitan Police, after viewing the video, questioned her, but did not lay charges, much to the disapproval of some Members of Parliament, who complained about it in the House of Commons.

Both her father and her record company attempted to have her detained under Britain's Mental Health Act. Of course, the world knows about her reaction to this idea, from the lines in her famous song: "They tried to make me go to Rehab / But I said, 'No, no, no.'"

At the same time, she was increasingly getting into trouble with the law. Inspired by her role model Lisa "Left Eye" Lopes, lead singer of the R&B trio TLC, who had set fire to the two million dollar mansion of her boyfriend, Atlanta Falcons player Andre Rison, after an argument, and received a $10,000 fine and five years probation, Amy set out on her own path of bad relationships and bad behavior.

Her relationship with her boyfriend and husband Blake Fielder-Civil was contentious in the extreme. On one infamous night the pair had a long knockdown fight in their suite at London's luxury Sanderson Hotel. The *Daily Star* ran front page pictures the next day of the pair, Blake with criss-cross slash marks on his face and neck, Amy with a bloodshot eye, scratches on her brow, eye makeup running hopelessly down her face, her wrist and arm in bandages, and her feet in tattered blood-stained ballet slippers.

The pair of them also ended up in court together. Fielder-Civil was imprisoned for six months after pleading guilty to an incident with a pub landlord. The prosecution alleged that 200,000 British pounds of Amy Winehouse's money had been given to the landlord to "throw the court case and not show up." The British press again made front page news out of the sensational arrest, as the police had used a battering ram to break down the couple's door, and a distraught Amy was photographed in tears, kissing her spouse goodbye as he was led off in handcuffs.

She was again photographed despondent outside Pentonville Prison, forbidden access to see her man. Many disapproved of her choice of spouse. She admitted to punching a female fan in the face for criticizing her for having taken Fielder-Civil as a husband. Winehouse then kneed her husband in the crotch as he attempted to calm her down.

While on tour in Norway, police stormed her room in the SAS Hotel Norge in Bergen. She and Fielder-Civil were charged with drug possession, held overnight in jail and fined 3850 kroner.

In March 2009, Winehouse was arrested and charged with common assault after dancer Sharene Flash claimed she had been punched in the eye at the 2008 Prince's Trust charity ball. The arrests, court appearances, and stints in rehab wrecked havoc with Winehouse's touring schedule. Numerous tours and performances had to be cancelled. When she was invited to perform at the Grammys in Los Angeles, the U.S. State Department refused to issue her a visa. They eventually rescinded their decision, but too late, so in similar way to the methods Paul Robeson had used fifty years earlier, the embattled singer had to perform by satellite link from a London studio.

Her problems with the law continued. She pled guilty to a charge of assaulting the manager of the Milton Keynes Theatre after he asked her to move her seat and was given a conditional discharge. Later, after a six-hour pub crawl through her London neighborhood of Camden, she was alleged to have head-butted a passer-by who hailed her a taxi, and then to have punched Moroccan musician Mustapha el Mounmi in the face because he would not give up a pool table in Camden's Bar Tok. She was held overnight in the Holborn Police Station for the incidents but was released without charge the next day.

Her inappropriate, not to say idiotic actions at British music events would cause more sullying of her reputation than her interactions with the law. At a Hyde Park concert for Nelson Mandela's ninetieth birthday, she changed a line of the song *Free Nelson Mandela* to "Free Blakey, my Fella"—an ill-advised way of drawing attention to her then incarcerated husband. At *Q* magazine's annual awards ceremony, she heckled Bono, in the midst of his politically charged acceptance speech for the Band of Bands award, shouting out "Shut up! I don't give a fuck!" It was just about the ultimate rock and roll faux pas, and was not received well by many of the attendees, although *Rolling Stone* magazine did admit that with anarchic actions like these, "Amy is bringing a rebellious rock 'n roll spirit back to popular music."

Her life continued as a blur of stomach-pumping drug overdoses, cancelled concerts, police interactions and drinking binges. On July 23, 2011, she was found by her minder in her house in Camden, not breathing. Police, two ambulances, and a paramedic on a bicycle arrived, but she could not be revived, and was declared dead at the scene. The official cause of her death was declared to be alcohol poisoning. She was, of course, twenty-seven— the final member, as of this writing, of the club no-one wants to join.

Songs About The Man

Considering the many musicians, songwriters and singers who have had interactions with The Man, and the rich potential of the material, there are surprisingly few songs in this genre. However, there are some good tunes about The Man, so let us wrap up this book with a look at some particularly interesting ones.

One of the best cloaks its deadly subject matter in such a mellow melody that many listeners have probably never realized what the song is all about. With the singer praising *The Green Green Grass of Home*, it sounds like the sort of saccharine tune that John Denver or the Osmonds would have written, or one from a very middle-of-the-road Broadway musical. Instead, it is poignant and tough-minded, and presents the last words of a jailed man on death row, who is about to be electrocuted.

The song has a unique structure—the first two verses describe a man returning by train to his country home after many years away. At the station, he is met by his parents and his old sweetheart, Mary. They are glad to see him, and he is glad to be back, glad to be able to touch *the green, green grass of home*.

In the third verse, the tone shifts abruptly. It seems the earlier verses were just a dream—the man has now awakened from it to the reality that he is currently surrounded by four grey walls and that this is his last day on earth. He is about to be executed. Once dead, he'll be shipped home, to be buried and become nothing but fertilizer for *the green, green grass of home*.

The beautiful song was written by Curly Putman in 1964. It was his biggest hit, though another bitter ballad *D.I.V.O.R.C.E.* comes a close second. It was first sung by Johnny Darrell, then hit Number Four on the country charts in a version by Porter Wagoner. Two years later Welsh singer Tom Jones had a worldwide Number One hit with the song. It has since been covered by many people, including Elvis, Stompin' Tom Connors and Merle Haggard. Dean Martin, or at least his arranger, butchers it with a chorus of saccharine backup singers joining in behind him. Possibly the best version is by Joan Baez, though she is arguably the wrong gender to be touting Mary's *lips like cherries*. It is a great song, subtle to the point of having its meaning masked invisible. Unlike *I Shot the Sheriff*, which flaunts its meaning boldly in its title.

I shot the sheriff, sang Bob Marley, in this most famous of reggae songs, *but I did not shoot the deputy*. Why the admission of guilt in the killing of the sheriff is at all mitigated by the denial of guilt regarding the deputy is never really made clear. The song claims that he killed the sheriff in self-defense, and that the sheriff always hated him, although for what he did not know.

Marley was himself no stranger to violence. He was the target of one of the most dramatic and politically charged assassination attempts on a musician in history.

Michael Manley was elected Prime Minister of Jamaica in 1972. He embarked on democratic-socialist reforms regarding land ownership, public free education and nationalization of major industries that endeared him to many, including reggae musicians like Bob Marley, but also made him hated by the Jamaican business establishment, and more importantly, by the US government and CIA. US Secretary of State Henry Kissinger attempted to force Manley to change his policies, but only a day after Kissinger's state visit to Jamaica Manley instead announced that his country was recognizing the Cuban government of Fidel Castro, and supporting Castro's involvement in fighting the apartheid regime of South Africa by sending troops to Angola. The now infuriated US determined to use the CIA to bring Manley down. Over the next four years, according to reports from CIA defector Phillip Agee, investigative journalist Gary Webb and Manley himself, the CIA used bombings, assassinations, propaganda, infiltration of agents such as Bay of Pigs veteran Luis Posada Carriles and covert financial support of opposition parties to attempt to destroy Manley's People's National Party.

The campaign climaxed just before the 1976 election, in which Manley was opposed by Edward Seaga of the Jamaica Labour Party. Seaga's JLP was supported by the US, and by the powerful Shower Posse, a Jamaican gang known to have smuggled guns and drugs into both Jamaica and the US with the help of the CIA. Only a few days before the election, Bob Marley and the Wailers decided to headline a giant concert, dubbed "Smile Jamaica" in Kingston, that was perceived to be an endorsement of their friend Michael Manley.

Two days before the concert, seven gunman invaded Marley's home/studio, and shot Marley, his wife, his manager and a studio worker, then fled and headed for the area of Tivoli Gardens, home turf for the Shower Posse. Astonishingly, although Marley's group were all seriously wounded, none were killed. Though the gunmen were never brought to justice, many suspected, in the words of US Ambassador Sumner Gerrard, that the incident was "an attempt by JLP gunmen to halt the concert, which would feature the 'politically progressive' music of Marley and other reggae stars."

The authorities never charged anyone with the shooting, but Don Taylor, the star's wounded manager, claimed that both he and Marley were present at a ghetto court in which the gunmen were tried and executed, after one of them confessed that the job was done for the CIA in return for cocaine and guns.

There was little pushback against either Marley's *I Shot the Sheriff* or against Eric Clapton's cover of the song, a fact that was used in an attempted defense of a rougher song about The Man, *Cop Killer*, that triggered intense pushback by the highest levels of US police and government.

Cop Killer was inspired by the constant police brutality against blacks, especially the beating of Rodney King by members of the L.A.P.D. It was written by Ice-T and Ernie C and performed by their band Body Count. It has extremely raw lyrics, rapped from the perspective of an angry cop killer.

Released by Warner Brothers just days after the acquittal of the officers involved in the 1991 Rodney King beating led to massive protests and riots across Los Angeles, the song was widely condemned by the authorities. Tipper Gore, at the time wife of Tennessee Congressman Al Gore (and later the US Second Lady), began the assault on the song in her role as co-founder of the Parents Music Resource Center, a Washington-based group that would ultimately be successful in forcing record companies to put warning labels on records with what they considered violent or sexually explicit lyrics.

The charges against it were continued by Dennis R. Martin, President of the National Association of Chiefs of Police, who claimed that "the *Cop Killer* song has been implicated in at least two shooting incidents and has inflamed racial tensions in cities across the country," and continued, "It is an affront to the officers—144 in 1992 alone—who have been killed in the line of duty while the police were upholding the laws of our society and protecting all of its citizens."

Ice-T defended his song, saying, "I'm singing in the first person as a character who is fed up with police brutality. I ain't never killed no cop. I felt like it a lot of times, but I never did it. If you believe that I'm a cop killer, you believe that David Bowie is an astronaut," referring to Bowie's song *Space Oddity*. Professors Mark S. Hamm and Jeff Ferrell argued that the cop-killer theme had been heard many times before, such as in the old songs written in admiration of gangster Pretty Boy Floyd, or others by acclaimed fiddler Tommy Jarrell like *Policeman* that included the line, *Policeman come and I didn't want to go this morning, so I shot him in the head with my 44.* They concluded their brief by saying "Perhaps the best-known case is Eric Clapton's cover version of Bob Marley and the Wailers' *I Shot the Sheriff*, which reached the top of the US music charts in the mid-1970s (a feat not approached by Ice-T). *I Shot the Sheriff*, though, never suffered the sort of moral and political attacks that *Cop Killer* did. How do we account for this difference?" They were of course implying there was one standard for white rock stars, another for black rappers.

The professors' arguments did not sway the government. Vice-President Dan Quayle branded the song "obscene", and President George H. W. Bush publicly denounced "any record company that would release such a product." Police organizations across the United States called for a boycott of all products owned by Time-Warner. Death threats were sent to Warner Brothers Records executives, and shareholders threatened to pull out of the company. When Ice-T planned a concert in Auckland, the New Zealand Police Commissioner attempted to ban him, saying, "Anyone who comes to this country preaching in obscene terms the killing of police, should not be welcome here."

Ultimately *Cop Killer* was removed from the album *Body Count*, and Ice-T left Warner Brothers Records. Warner president Mo Ostin said he understood the rapper's decision to leave, and praised him as "a terrific artist who spoke the truth."

Fifty years earlier the fabled songwriting team of Jerrry Leiber and Mike Stoller wrote a pair of songs about crime and punishment that managed to slip into the mainstream with much less controversy.

Riot in Cell Block Number Nine is a rhythm and blues song—sometimes hard-edged, sometimes humorous—originally performed by the Robins, later covered by the Coasters, sung from the perspective of a man serving time for armed robbery who witnesses a jailhouse riot that is eventually shut down by the tommy-gun-toting warden.

The song was pretty heady stuff for 1954. CBS found the lyrics too provocative and banned it from Peter Potter's "Juke Box Jury" radio show and KNXT's Los Angeles TV shows. But in general it got radio play and made it into the all-important Top 40.

Leiber and Stoller went back to their Brill Building drawing board and came up with another one—*Jailhouse Rock*, which Elvis Presley released in 1957 both on record and as a movie of the same name. Both song and film contributed to the perception of rock and roll in general, and Elvis in particular, as being symbols of teenage anti-establishment rebellion. The song, with its very original and amusing lyrics, sits at position 67 on *Rolling Stone*'s list of the 500 Greatest Songs of All Time.

Juvenile Delinquency was the subject of much brow-beating analysis in the 1950s, with the common refrain that it was caused, or at least encouraged, by pop culture products like rock and roll music and comic books. It was even the subject of the straightest form of pop music—the Broadway musical. In Stephen Sondheim and Leonard Bernstein's *West Side Story,* the song *Gee, Officer Krupke* is sung by the street gang The Jets to a New York police officer, light-heartedly trying to excuse their anti-social behavior by claiming their mothers are all junkies and their fathers are all drunks.

Sondheim and Bernstein wanted to break a Broadway taboo by ending the song with the line, "Gee Officer Krupke, Fuck You!" but Columbia Records, who owned the rights to the soundtrack, put the kibosh on that idea. Sondheim eventually changed the ending of the line to "Krup You!"—and later claimed he thought the change to be the best lyric in the musical.

Gee, Officer Krupke was written for the very middle-class sensibilities of the 1959 Broadway audience. Many other Songs about The Man were much more serious—some deadly serious.

Joe Hill was a Swedish-American labor activist, songwriter and member of the Industrial Workers of the World (the 'Wobblies'). In 1914, he was accused of the murder of a shopkeeper and even though there was no evidence, found guilty. Many people spoke out about the political, rigged nature of the trial, and many prominent, international figures called for clemency, to no avail. Hill was executed by firing squad in 1915.

Some of Hill's many protest and union songs are remembered today, but none as much as the powerful song commemorating him written by Alfred Hayes and Earl Robinson in the 1930s, and sung by Paul Robeson and Pete Seeger, then by Phil Ochs and Joan Baez (her version sung most famously at the Woodstock Festival), also by Bruce Springsteen.

> *I dreamed, I saw Joe Hill last night*
> *Alive as you and me*
> *Says I "But Joe, you're ten years dead"*
> *"I never died" says he*
> *"I never died" says he*
> *"The copper bosses killed you, Joe"*
> *"They shot you Joe" says I*
> *"Takes more than guns to kill a man"*
> *Says Joe "I didn't die"*
> *Says Joe "I didn't die"*

I Fought The Law was written by Sonny Curtis of Buddy Holly's band, The Crickets, and was first popularized by the Bobby Fuller Four. It is a powerful, but incredibly simplistic song, with only one line about the singer's crimes (*Robbin' people with a six-gun*) and only one about his punishment (*Breaking rocks in the hot sun*), and then not one, not two, but <u>twenty</u> repeats of the line, *I fought the law and the law won.* Nonetheless, it works. It was a big hit—top ten in 1966, and #175 on Rolling Stone's list of The Greatest Songs of All Time.

Bobby Fuller was found asphyxiated in his car six months after the release of the song. The Los Angeles Police Department declared it an apparent suicide "by inhalation of gasoline", but since he was also drenched in gasoline, and his finger had been broken, there were many unanswered questions about his death, with some believing he had been murdered. The NPR radio show *All Things Considered*, the book *I Fought the Law: The Life and Strange Death of Bobby Fuller* and the TV series *Unsolved Mysteries* all explored accusations that Fuller was in fact killed, either by Charles Manson (very doubtful, since Manson was behind bars in 1966) or by the LAPD, because of Fuller's connection with a Mafia-linked woman and with the rock and roll counter-culture, or by the Mafia itself.

The Clash recorded a cover of the song that was released on their 1979 album *The Cost of Living* and used in the film *Rude Boy*. The band later disapproved and disowned the film, saying they felt it wrongly portrayed all black people as muggers and thieves.

Their version had a second life in 1989 when The Man used it to try to secure the surrender of Panamanian dictator Manuel Noriega. Noriega was a Panamanian soldier trained by the American CIA in spycraft who after a number of intrigues—one of them, ironically, known as the "Singing Sergeants" incident, became the strongman dictator of Panama in 1983. Although supported by the US for many years and providing them bases for their fight against Daniel Ortega in Nicaragua, the U.S. eventually grew weary of his authoritarian excesses and more particularly with his involvement in Colombian cocaine smuggling.

In 1989 the US invaded Panama, a move the United Nations condemned as a "flagrant violation of international law." After the country fell to the U.S. invaders, Noriega took refuge in the Apostolic Nunciature—the official Papal headquarters in the country. Unable to invade it because of the US treaty with the Vatican, the army brought in Psychological Warfare experts, who set up a giant sound system outside the building and blasted The Clash's *I Fought The Law* at intense volume 24 hours a day. After ten days the noisy punk rock finally got to him, and Noriega surrendered. He fought the law—and the law won. He spent the next 17 years in a Miami prison, then the next seven at La Senté prison in Paris, then the next five in El Ranacer prison in Panama. He was released to a hospital in 2017 and died of a brain hemorrhage on May 29 of that year. I guess, as the song says, his race was run.

The battles over Civil Rights and the Vietnam War and the outlandishly racist behavior of American authorities in the deep south brought numerous responses from musicians. Jazz artists like John Coltrane and Oscar Peterson wrote highly regarded instrumental pieces about the turmoil, such as Coltrane's *Alabama* and Peterson's powerful *Hymn to Freedom*. Peterson's Canadian compatriot Neil Young was involved in probably the two most successful songs reacting to the struggles of the late 60s and early 70s. As part of the Buffalo Springfield, he and songwriter Stephen Stills sang *For What it's Worth*, a song inspired by the police response to the Sunset Strip riots of 1966.

Stills and Young met in Thunder Bay, Ontario, while both were touring with different bands, but would not combine forces until after Young's band, The Mynah Byrds, was broken up by The Man. The Mynah Byrds' leader singer, Rick James, had deserted from the U.S. Navy to avoid deployment to Vietnam, but in early 1966 the Navy tracked him down in Toronto and charged him with being AWOL. James faced a possible five years hard labor, but his attorney eventually brought the punishment down to five months, which he served in the notorious Portsmouth Naval Prison in Kittery, Maine. He then returned to Toronto, where he received further detention, and then eventually headed south to the mecca of Los Angeles. There, he befriended hairdresser Jay Sebring, and only by dint of a severe hangover missed the party at Sharon Tate's house that ended with the Manson murders. He survived Charles Manson but had many more troubles with the law. After a string of records including his gold hit *Super Freak*, James was involved in two serious incidents, which led to charges of assault with a deadly weapon, aggravated mayhem, torture, forcible oral copulation, false imprisonment, and most seriously, the kidnapping of music executive Mary Sauger. He was lucky not to have gotten life, but he did spend five years behind bars in Folsom Prison.

Meanwhile, with James gone, Young and bassist Bruce Palmer sold the band's equipment in order to buy an old hearse. They drove it from Toronto to Los Angeles where they fortuitously linked up with Stills, and started the new band. Astonishingly, within days they were playing at The Troubadour on the Strip, and within a few months had their Top Ten Gold Record hit in radio play on the convertibles cruising the Strip and around the world. *For What It's Worth* was an intelligent, measured and very tuneful look at the battles going on between the new generation and The Man. But it was their only hit. The band broke up soon after, as Palmer was arrested for marijuana possession and deported back to Canada, and Young and two other band members were arrested for disturbing the peace after a noisy party with Eric Clapton. Three years later, though, Young reunited with Stills and joined the band that would become Crosby, Stills, Nash and Young.

On May 4, 1970, members of the Ohio National Guard killed four and wounded nine peacefully protesting students on the campus of Kent State University. Young responded to the incident by turning it into a song, *Ohio* that the quartet recorded and released within weeks of the deadly incident. Lyrically, it doesn't compare with *For What It's Worth* (the bridge consists of four repeats of *Na, na, na, na, na, na, na* and the outro ten repeats of the line *Four dead in Ohio*) but it captured the sorrow and zeitgeist of the anxious times. Due to the specific naming of Nixon in the lyrics, it was banned by many AM radio stations, but nonetheless became one of the anthems of the counter culture and anti-war movement, and the fight against The Man.

Johnny Cash wrote two songs about the US prison system, and performed them in the mid 60s inside the maximum-security penitentiaries. *Folsom Prison Blues* contains the two most chilling, gruesome lines ever put to paper—*I shot a man in Reno / Just to watch him die* (his artistic license on full display, since if he committed murder in Nevada, it is never explained why he would be serving time in a California state prison.) His *San Quentin* is even tougher, with Cash singing he wants the prison to rot and burn in hell. "The Man in Black" as he was billed, is probably the singer most associated with themes of crime and punishment, which is a little ironic, since his own single run-in with the law was laughably wimpy—a few hours in jail in Starkville, Mississippi for picking flowers late at night on private property.

Randy Newman's *Jolly Coppers on Parade* is an uneasy mix of paradox and mordant irony. Newman is one of the most brilliant of all songwriters, but as so frequently happens with him his irony seems to get so far ahead of him that his message and meaning can get lost. Unlike his most successful songs, *Sail Away*, which brilliantly skewers slavery, *Burn On*, which attacks pollution with wit and gusto, and *Political Science*, which acidly dices American imperialism, it can't be said that *Jolly Coppers* is anywhere near as precise in its dissection of American police. The tune certainly draws the listener in, and makes one wonder where he is going with it. Ultimately though, the answer is—nowhere very interesting or profound.

Songs about The Man are not usually known for their infectious melodies, but stream the 1978 hit *Rasputin* by the German disco group Boney M, and just try to keep your feet from tapping. The lunatic dance tune tells the lurid story, of all the crazy subjects for a disco song, of Grigori Rasputin, the notorious mystical advisor to the Russian Czar Nicholas II. The song clicked—almost everywhere. It was either Number One or Number Two in almost all countries, except for two. In the US, for some reason, it failed to even chart. In the USSR, it was banned.

If there ever was someone who could rightfully be titled The Man, Rasputin was it. *Ra Ra Rasputin, lover of the Russian Queen, there was a cat that really was gone.* He was, according to the song, *Russia's greatest love machine. Most people looked at him with terror and with fear / But to Moscow chicks he was such a lovely dear.* According to Boney M's version of history, *he ruled the Russian land and never mind the Czar / But the kazachok he danced really wonderbar.* The crazy musical history lesson goes on to describe the Russian court intrigue that led to the poisoning and then shooting of *Ra Ra Rasputin, Russia's greatest love machine,* then ends with a sardonic voice intoning *Oh, those Russians.* Nutty musical fun.

At the complete other end of the musical spectrum is *Strange Fruit*—a bitter and angry song, the pivotal vehicle of Billie Holiday's *oeuvre*, a moving tirade against lynching, still a common occurrence in the American South when the song was first recorded in 1939. While lynching was outlaw vigilante "justice", usually organized by the Ku Klux Klan, it is common knowledge that many Southern sheriffs, hidden by white robes and hoods, participated in Klan activities, and almost no lynchings were ever investigated by the police or prosecuted by the law.

The song was written first as a poem by Lewis Allan, who also wrote the anti-intolerance song *The House I Live In* for Frank Sinatra, and would later adopt the two sons of Julius and Ethel Rosenberg, executed for spying in the Red Scare hysteria of the early 1950's. Holiday, Sonny White and arranger Danny Mendlesohn got to work on it, and turned it into a song.

It was a controversial sensation from the start. Billie added elements of the story of her own father's death, not by lynching in his case, but by being turned away at several Dallas hospitals because of the color of his skin. She sang it with trepidation over the reaction it might create. She only performed it as the final, closing song of the night, and usually with tears in her eyes and in those of most of the audience.

It became such news that *Time* magazine ran a story on the shocking song – with a picture of Billie – thought to be the first time ever that either *Time* or its sister magazine *Life* had ever run a photo of a black person.

Not every one quite got it, of course. Years later, Billie recalled that it had "a way of separating the straight people from the squares and cripples. One night in Los Angeles, a bitch stood up in the club where I was singing and said, 'Billie, why don't you sing that sexy song you're so famous for? You know, the one about the naked bodies swinging in the trees'" She added, "Needless to say, I didn't."

Her producer, John Hammond, whatever his liberal sensibilities, wouldn't record it, and so she had to record it not at Columbia but at the smaller Commodore Records label, on April 20, 1939. Nonetheless it became Holiday's best selling and most famous record. However it got little airplay, as the radio networks of the day were frightened of the possible backlash to the song by authorities in the deep south.

Billie knew that the strong words of the song were likely one of the reasons she was being so actively harassed by the police and the drug department, and so it was difficult and gut-wrenching for her to deal with it. The renowned black poet and author Maya Angelou met Holiday in 1958, in the company of Angelou's inquisitive 12-year-old son Guy. When the boy asked her, "What's a pastoral scene, Miss Holiday?" Angelou remembers, "Billie looked up slowly and studied Guy for a second. Her face became cruel, and when she spoke her voice was scornful. 'It means when the crackers are killing the niggers. It means when they take a little nigger like you and snatch off his nuts and shove them down his goddam throat. That's what it means.'" Yikes.

The song was dubbed, "a declaration of war—the beginning of the Civil Rights Movement," and later "the song of the century."

Samuel Grafton of the *New York Post* wrote, "If the anger of the exploited ever mounts high enough in the south, it now has its *Marseillaise*."

The *Marseillaise*, not a pop song but instead a national anthem, is for my money the most powerful and stirring song ever written about this subject. The song was born in blood—written by a young Frenchman, Claude-Joseph Rouget de Lisle, about the invasion of France by the armies of Prussia and Austria. It became known as *La Marseillaise* because volunteers from Marseilles, in the capitol to assist the Parisians, were the first to take to the song, and marched through the streets of Paris singing it. It was officially named the new National anthem of France in 1795, and quickly became the rallying cry of the French Revolution. Just one of its many violent bloody verses goes like this:

> *Allons enfants de la Patrie,*
> *Le jour de gloire est arrivé !*
> *Contre nous de la tyrannie*
> *L'étendard sanglant est levé,*
> *Entendez-vous dans les campagnes*
> *Mugir ces féroces soldats ?*
> *Ils viennent jusque dans vos bras*
> *Égorger vos fils, vos compagnes !*
> *Aux armes, citoyens,*
> *Formez vos bataillons,*
> *Marchons, marchons !*
> *Qu'un sang impur*
> *Abreuve nos sillons !*
>
> *En anglais:*
> *Arise, children of the Motherland,*
> *The day of glory has arrived!*
> *Against us, tyranny's bloody standard is raised,*

The bloody flag is raised
Do you hear, in the countryside,
The roar of those ferocious soldiers?
They're coming right into your arms
To cut the throats of your sons, your women!
To arms, citizens. Form your battalions,
Let's march, let's march!
That their impure blood
Should water our fields!

It is an exceedingly provocative piece of music, and so it is little wonder The Man didn't like it. From 1804 to 1830, it was banned by Napoleon Bonaparte, Louis XVIII, and Charles X. It was not reinstated as the national anthem until 1879. By the twentieth century it became the anthem not just of France but of revolutionary, anti-authoritarian movements worldwide. It even became the semi-official anthem of another country—following the October Revolution, the lyrics were translated into Russian and it became for many years the Soviet Union's co-national anthem, along with the *Internationale*.

One of the most iconic uses of the song is in the classic World War II drama *Casablanca*, when Nazi German officers, drinking in Rick's Café, bellow out the German patriotic song *Die Wacht am Rhein*, but are drowned out by the anti-Nazi freedom fighter Victor Laszlo (played by Paul Henreid) bravely leading the rest of the nightclub's patrons in singing *La Marseillaise*, to the bemusement of the worldly and cynical Rick (Humphrey Bogart), the wary eyes of both Laszlo's and Rick's lover Ilsa Lund (Ingrid Bergman) and the thrill of the audience. It is a wildly stirring cinematic moment, ending as the German Major Heinrich Strasser (Conrad Veidt) imperiously demands that the amusingly corrupt Police Prefect Louis Renault (Claude Rains) immediately shut down the club. The scene brings tears to the eyes of the audience, and apparently brought tears to the eyes of the extras and bit players in the film, many of them themselves Jewish refugees from Germany and Eastern Europe, as they performed it for director Michael Curtiz.

La Marseillaise has been referenced in dozens of other pieces of pop and classical culture, from the music of Shostakovich, Verdi, Wagner and Rossini, to the opening bars of another "anthem" of sorts—Lennon and McCartney's *All You Need is Love*.

Recently there has been a movement by prominent French politicians to tone down the bloody anti-German rhetoric of the lyrics in the light of the very close current friendship between France and Germany, but that movement has failed. The French love the song. As British historian Simon Schama said, in the aftermath of the 2015 ISIS terrorist attack on the Eagles of Death Metal concert at the Bataclan Theater in Paris, the song is "the great example of courage and solidarity when facing danger; that's why it is so invigorating, that's why it really is the greatest national anthem in the world, ever. Most national anthems are pompous, brassy, ceremonious, but this is genuinely thrilling. Very important in the song...is the line 'before us is tyranny, the bloody standard of tyranny has risen'. There is no more ferocious tyranny right now than ISIS terrorism, so it's extremely easy for the tragically and desperately grieving French to identify with that."

La Marseillaise is a good example of how and why music is the most powerful of all the arts. Music attracts the most passionate and controversial of artists to create and perform it. It creates the most extreme reactions from its fans and followers. And it creates the strongest reaction and the greatest pushback from The Man.

Back in 1956, Elvis Presley was berated with criticism and condemnation. As city councils debated whether to shut down his concerts, Frances Melrose in the Denver *Rocky Mountain News* wrote, "It's a toss-up which is worse. Elvis or his fans. I'd say the edge goes to Elvis." A frightened Patsy Dinan in the Amerillo *Daily News* fretted "he worked himself into an orgiastic rhythm, losing himself to the savage beat. The air raid siren screams of the crowd heightened as Presley's bumps and grinds grew more frantic."

It wasn't just Elvis who got the old fogies upset. Bill Haley, who with his little spit-curl and his suit and tie seems today about as dangerous as Lawrence Welk, got newspaper writers tied in a knot back in 1956. Under the hysterical headline 13,000 ALMOST BERZERK IN GARDENS ROCK 'N' ROLL ORGY, *Toronto Star* reviewer Stan Rentin wrote, with the usual near-racist allusions, "Like natives at a voodoo ritual, the crowd writhed and reeled until their pent-up emotions burst the dam of reason and they clambered onto the stage and into the aisles to dance."

Rock and roll, and jazz before it, were just the first waves of music to terrify the press, the establishment and the authorities. By 1963 Joan Baez was leading Martin Luther King Jr. and a crowd of hundreds of thousands in singing *We Shall Overcome* in Washington. It would soon become the powerful anthem of the Civil Rights Movement and would even, to the surprise of many, be referenced in an important speech by President Lyndon Johnson. We have seen how the folk songs of Victor Jara so upset the Chilean military junta that they killed him. Years later, N.W.A. and Public Enemy would be penning rap songs that would give a voice to the Black Lives Matter movement. Whether songs are sung from the stage or the streets or from a jail cell filled with arrested protestors, music is a powerful tool in the hands of the oppressed or the powerless.

The battle between Music and The Man is not over.

Endnotes

1. The Clash

The Roots of the Conflict

Source material for this introductory chapter includes *Music: A Subversive History* by Ted Gioia (New York: Basic Books, 2019) and *Music & Politics* by John Street (Cambridge, UK: Polity Press, 2012). Also useful was uber-intellect Marshall McLuhan's *Understanding Media: The Extensions of Man* (Cambridge, MA: MIT Press, 1994).

The early use of language and singing was researched in *Now You're Talking—The Story of Human Conversation from the Neanderthals to Artificial Intelligence* by Trevor Cox (London: Vintage / The Bodley Head, 2018)

Darwin's perceptions about music, as discussed in this opening chapter, are found in his groundbreaking *The Descent of Man* (Amherst, NY: Prometheus Books, 1998). References in this chapter to the slave trade between Africa and the Americas are from Alexander Falconbridge's *An Account of the Slave Trade on the Coast of Africa* (London: J. Phillips, 1788). The Paganini story is mostly sourced from the excellent biography of the violinist on Wikipedia. Insights into the creation of gospel, jazz and rock and roll were found in *Devil's Music, Holy Rollers and Hillbillies* by James A. Cosby (McFarland and Company, 2016). The brilliant historian Jon Meacham linked forces with country singer Tim McGraw to create *Songs of America* (New York: Random House, 2019), a great overview of the history of music in America that was also useful. Insights and data regarding the revolutionary nature of music are from *1965: The Most Revolutionary Year in Music* by Andrew Grant Jackson (New York: Thomas Dunne Books, 2015). Primary source for the material on Elvis Presley was *The Elvis Atlas—A Journey Through Elvis Presley's America* by Michael Gray and Roger Osbourne (New York; Henry Holt, 1996).

2. You Say You Want a Revolution

John Lennon

There is possibly more writing about John Lennon than about any other musician. The source material used for this chapter were *The Lives of John Lennon* by Albert Goldman (New York: William Morrow, 1988), *Gimme Some Truth – The John Lennon FBI Files* by Jon Wiener (Berkeley: University of California Press, 1999), *The Beatles* by Bob Spitz (New York: Little Brown, 2005), *Lennon Legend: An Illustrated life of John Lennon* by James Henke (San Francisco: Chronicle Books, 2003), *John Lennon—The Illustrated Biography* by Garth Thomas (Croxley Green: Transatlantic Press, 2008) and *The Mourning of John Lennon* by Anthony Elliott (Berkeley, CA: University of California Press, 1999).

Clapton by Eric Clapton (New York: Three Rivers Press, 2007) was used as reference for Eric Clapton's role in the 1969 Toronto Rock and Roll Revival.

For an analysis of the music of John and Paul, I used *Revolution in the Head* by Ian Macdonald (Chicago: Chicago Review Press, 2007)

Victor Jara

Source material for the Victor Jara chapter included articles *Former Chilean Military Officers Charged in 1973 Murder of Singer Victor Jara* (*The Guardian*, July 23, 2015), *They Couldn't Kill His Songs* (*BBC News*, SEPTEMBER 5, 1998) and *Murdered Chilean Folk Singer Laid to Rest After 36 Years* by Gideon Long (*The Guardian*, December 8, 2015). Also very useful were the Wikipedia biographies on Victor Jara, Salvadore Allende, Joan Jara, and Colonel Augusto Pinochet.

The Rolling Stones

There are dozens of books about the Rolling Stones. The five most useful for this chapter were *Mick – The Wild Life and Mad Genius of Jagger* by Christopher Anderson (Gallery Books, 2012), *Keith Richards* by Victor Bockris (Poseidon Press, 1992) *Up and Down With the Rolling Stones* by Keith Richards' dealer, Tony Sanchez (John Blake Publishing, 2010), *Altamont – The Rolling Stones, The Hells Angels, and the Inside Story of Rock's Darkest Day* by Joel Selvin (Dey St/Harper Collins Publishers, 2016) and *Life* by Keith Richards and James Fox (Little, Brown and Company, 2010). All five are entertaining, informative and original.

Also useful was Nik Cohn's important look at the first fifteen years of rock and roll, *Awopbopaloobop Alopbamboom* (Weidenfeld & Nicholson, 1969), *The Mammoth Book of the Rolling Stones* by Sean Egan (London: Constable & Robinson, 2013) and *S.T.P— A Journey Through America with the Rolling Stones* by Robert Greenfield (Cambridge, MA: Da Capo Press, 1974). The story of the Toronto bust was written from my personal perspective attempting (but unfortunately failing) to get in to the El Mocambo concert, and from many books including *Before They Made Me Run: Keith Richards and the Bust That Saved the Rolling Stones* by Jason Schneider (Toronto: Electric Books, 2015). The leading female character in the drama tells her story in *Beyond Reason* by Margaret Trudeau (Toronto: Grosset & Dunlap, 1979). The book received one of the most scathing left-handed compliments of all time from her ex-husband: "Not bad for someone who has written more books than she has ever read."

The Plastic People and the Velvet Revolution

Though primarily about the music scene in the USSR, *How the Beatles Rocked the Kremlin* devotes several pages to the rock revolution in Czechoslovakia that were useful for the writing of this chapter. Other sources were *How a Revolutionary Czech Rock Band Inspired Vaclav Havel* by James Sullivan (*Rolling Stone,* December 19, 2011), *1998 And All That: Plastic People of the Universe and the Velvet Revolution* by Ed Vulliamy (*The Observer,* September 6, 2009), *Paul Wilson—The Impact of the Plastic People on a Communist Universe* by Jan Velinger (*Radio Prague International-* "Czechs in Toronto", May 31, 2005), *The Plastic People of the Universe* by Joseph Yanosik (*Perfect Sound Forever* online music magazine, March, 1996), *When Vaclav Havel Allied Himself With the Hairy Musicians* by Chris Johnstone (*Radio Prague International,* July 12, 2017), and *The Plastic People of the Universe* by Richie Unterberger (richieunterberger.com). Information about the *Zlatni Struni* is from *Rock 'n' Roll to Rack-and-Pinion* by Joe Fiorito (*Toronto Star,* January 5, 2005)

Dead on Arrival

Most of the information in the chapter is from Joe Keithley's two colorfully written and illustrated books about the history of his band - *I, Shithead* (Vancouver: Arsenal Pulp Press, 2003) and *Talk-Action=Zero* (Vancouver: Arsenal Pulp Press, 2011). Also useful were radio interviews with Keithley including *Punk and Politics: a conversation with D.O.A.'s Joe Keithley* with Carolina de Ryk (CBC Radio "Daybreak North", July 9, 2019). There is also very useful information in the newspaper articles *From D.O.A. to MLA? Only in B.C.* by Alexandra Gill (*Globe and Mail*, April 11, 2018) and *What the Hell Happened to Joey Sh*thead?* by Kelvin Gawley (Burnaby *Now*, September 28, 2019). The author also conducted an interview with Keithley, which assisted in the writing of the chapter. Thanks to Joe Keithley for permission to quote the lyrics of his songs *Fucked Up Ronnie* and *Police Brutality*.

3. Up From Slavery

Josephine Baker

Primary source for the chapter on Josephine Baker is the excellent biography of her, *Josephine Baker: The Hungry Heart* by her adopted son Jean Claude Baker and Chris Chase (New York: Cooper Square Press, 1993). There is a very good biography of Baker on Wikipedia and a film biography called *Josephine Baker's Banana Dance* that can be seen on YouTube. *When Paris Sizzled* by Mary McAuliffe (Lanham, MD: Rowman & Littlefield, 2016) is a good overview of life in Paris in the 1920s.

Paul Robeson

The material in this chapter was sourced from three biographies of Paul Robeson: *The Whole World in His Hands—a Pictorial Biography of Paul Robeson* by Susan Robeson (Secaucus, NJ: Citadel Press, 1985), *Paul Robeson—The Man and His Mission* by Ron Ramdin (London: Peter Owen Publishers, 1992) and *Paul Robeson—Biography of a Proud Man* by Joseph Nazel (New York: Holloway House Publishing, 1980). All three are long out of print. I am grateful to the University of Toronto Music Library where I was able to access these materials.

Also very useful was *Paul Robeson's Legendary Border-Straddling Concert* by Alexandra Gill (*The Globe and Mail*, May 18, 2002 (updated April 17, 2018).

Leadbelly

I was introduced to the story of Leadbelly through the wonderfully profane, jive-talking biography of him on the website badassoftheweek.com. Highly recommended. The definitive full biography is the very detailed and well-written *The Life and Legend of Leadbelly* by Charles Wolfe and Kip Lornell (New York: Da Capo Press / Harper Collins, 1992). Gordon Parks' 1976 feature film *Leadbelly* is a well-made and entertaining look at the life of the singer.

Billie Holiday

I used both *Lady Sings The Blues* by Billie Holiday and William Duffy (New York: Doubleday, 1956) and *Billie Holiday—Wishing on the Moon* by Donald Clarke (Cambridge, MA: Da Capo Press, 2000) as source material for the chapter on the life of Billie Holiday. Clarke claims that *Lady Sings The Blues* is "hopelessly inaccurate", but I have chosen, when there are discrepancies between her version of the story and his, (written in England forty years after her death) to go with her version of events. However, others may disagree with my choice. Indeed, Billie Holiday herself once claimed, perhaps in jest, that she had not only not written her autobiography, but had not even read it.

Background on Harry Anslinger and the War on Drugs is from *Chasing the Scream—The First and Last Days of the Drug War* by Johann Hari (New York: Bloomsbury Publishing, 2015) and *The Hunting of Billie Holiday* by Johann Hari (*Politico*, January 17, 2015). Also most useful was *Cannabis—The Illegalization of Weed in America* by Box Brown (New York: First Second Books, 2019)

Chuck Berry

The two best accounts of Chuck Berry's tumultuous life are his own *The Autobigraphy* (New York: Harmony Books, 1987), written in the Lompoc Federal Correctional Institute and the self-proclaimed unauthorized (but very comprehensive) biography *Brown Eyed Handsome Man: The Life and Hard Times of Chuck Berry* by Bruce Pegg (New York / London: Routledge, 2002).

Nina Simone

Nina Simone's sad life and difficult career is told in the documentary film *What Happened, Miss Simone?* (Radical Media, Netflix, directed by Liz Garbus, produced by Liza Simone). There is an excellent biography of Nina Simone on Wikipedia. Her own autobiography is *I Put a Spell on You* by Nina Simone with Stephen Cleary (New York: Da Capo Press, 2003). Also useful when writing this chapter was the extraordinary historian Jon Meacham's *Songs of America: Patriotism, Protest and the Music That Made a Nation* (Random House, 2019).

4. Music and Power

Music vs The Kremlin

The Rest is Noise—Listening to the Twentieth Century by Alex Ross (New York: Farrar, Strauss and Giroux, 2007) is a very good source for information about the relationship between classical composers such as Dmitri Shostakovich and the Kremlin.

How The Beatles Rocked the Kremlin by Leslie Woodhead (New York: Bloomsbury, 2013) is an excellent account not only of the influence of "the Bitles" on the USSR, but also of response of the Kremlin to jazz and other popular music.

Reference material for the story of Pussy Riot and Vladimir Putin is primarily newspaper articles such as *How Pussy Riot Boosted Putin* by Rosie Dimanno (*Toronto Star,* December 5, 2012), *Six Songs That Shook Russia* by Mansur Mirovalev (*Toronto Star,* December 10, 2012), *Pussy Riot Gets Crowds—and Jail* by Olivia Ward (*Toronto Star, August 18,* 2012), *Jailed Punk Rocker Soaked up T.O.Scene* by Khristina Narizhnaya (*Toronto Star,* August 20, 2012), and *One Free, Two Face Siberia: Pussy Riot Court Shocker* (Metro/AP, October 11, 2012). Also very useful is the very detailed 44 page biography of the band in Wikipedia, and the documentary feature film *Pussy Riot: A Punk Prayer,* produced and directed by Mike Lerner and Maxim Pozdorovkin (KinoSmith, 2014, available on ITunes).

Miriam Makeba

There is no better source material for the story of Miriam Makeba than her own excellent and engrossing *Makeba—My Story* by Miriam Makeba with James Hall (New York: Plume/New American Library, 1987).

Singing for a Cause

The primary overview source material for this chapter was *Talkin' 'Bout a Revolution—Music and Social Change in America* by Dick Weissman (Milwaukee: Backbeat Books, 2010).

The story of Woody Guthrie and his most famous song is told in *This Land is Your Land—Woody Guthrie and the Journey of an American Folksong* by Robert Santelli (Philadelphia: Running Press Book Publishers, 2012). Source material for the story of *We Shall Overcome* and Pete Seeger was *Sing It—A Biography of Pete Seeger* by Meryl Danziger (New York/Oakland: Seven Stories Press, 2016) and *Pete Seeger vs The Un-Americans—A Tale of the Blacklist* by Edward Renehan (Wickford, RI: New Street Communications, 2014). The travails of singing the American national anthem was referenced from *Why is 'The Star Spangled Banner' So Hard To Sing?* By Lauren Effron and Sheila Marikar (ABC News, July 11, 2012).

Source material for Bernice Johnson Reagon included *Bernice Johnson Reagon on Freedom Fighting* by Fred Bouchard (berklee.edu, April 10, 2009), *www.bernicejohnson reagon.com/about*, *Bernice Johnson Reagon* (thehistorymakers.org, November 21, 2003) and *Bernice Johnson Reagon On Leading Freedom Songs During The Civil Rights Movement* (NPR-Fresh Air with Terry Gross and David Bianculli, June 19, 2020).

Source material for Joan Baez's involvement in the civil rights movement was her memoir *And a Voice to Sing With* by Joan Baez (New York: Penguin Books, 1987). Tales of Bob Dylan in the 60s are from *Another Side of Bob Dylan* by Victor Maymudes (New York: St. Martin's Press, 2014).

Source material for Buffy Sainte-Marie was *Buffy Sainte-Marie—The Authorized Biography* by Andrea Warner (Vancouver/Berkeley: Greystone Books, 2018).

Narcocorridos

The definitive study of the drug ballads of Mexico and the people who sing them is the excellent *Narcocorrido: A Journey into the Music of Drugs, Guns and Guerrillas* by Elijah Wald (Rayo/Harper Collins, 2001). Other source materials for this chapter were *The Savage Silencing of Mexico's Musicians* by Manuel Roig-Franzia (*Washington Post*, December 26, 2007), *Mexican Cartels Take Aim at Musicians* by Myles Estey (*Toronto Star*, January 25, 2013) and *Death in the Midday Sun* by Martin Hodgson (*The Guardian,* September 19, 2004).

Music vs Donald Trump

Source material for the story of Donald Trump's unauthorized use of music includes the articles *The Rolling Stones Demand Trump Stop Using its Music at Rallies, But Can The Band Actually Stop Him?* by Travis M. Andrews (*Washington Post,* May 6, 2016), *Get Off of My Song! Stones to Trump* by Deena Zuru and Jim Acosta (*CNN,* August 16, 2017), *Donald Trump Allegedly Wanted to Sue the Rolling Stones in the 1980s* by Alex Shephard (*The New Republic,* 2016), *Can't Always Get What You Want: Why Artists Struggle to Stop Politicians Using Their Songs* (*The Guardian,* October 30, 2018), *How You Can't Always Get What You Want Became Donald Trump's Bizarre Theme Song* (*The Guardian,* November 9, 2016) and the book *Trumped!- The Inside Story of the Real Donald Trump—His Cunning Rise and Spectacular Fall* by John R. O'Donnell with James Rutherford (New York: Crossroad Press, 2016)

The most comprehensive story of the many musical artists who have been co-opted by politicians is *Stop Using My Song: 35 Artists Who Fought Politicians Over Their Music* by Eveline Chao (*Rolling Stone,* July 8, 2015).

Source material for the battle between Bruce Springsteen and Ronald Reagan was found in two excellent books: *Songs of America: Patriotism, Protest and the Music That Made a Nation* by Jon Meacham and Tim McGraw (Random House, 2019) and *All Shook Up – How Rock and Roll Changed America* by Glenn C. Altschuler (Oxford: Oxford University Press, 2003)

5. Only in America

Frank Sinatra

Three major books provided the source material for this chapter. Sinatra tried to prevent the publication of *His Way—The Unauthorized Biography of Frank Sinatra* by Kitty Kelley (New York: Random House, 1986), and fortunately his lawsuit failed, as it is one of the most revealing and lively showbiz biographies ever written. Equally thick, and equally revealing, is *Sinatra—The Chairman* by James Kaplan (New York: Doubleday, 2015). Kaplan writes well about Sinatra's life, and also explores in detail his music. Information in this chapter also was gleaned from *Frank Sinatra* by Chris Rojek (Cambridge, UK: Polity Press, 2004), a cerebral look not just at Sinatra's life but also his larger cultural significance.

On a much smaller scale, but also useful was the e-book *Frank Sinatra: The Dark Story of His Mafia Connections* by James Bankes (Amazon Kindle, 2015).

Rock and Roll

A great source for the story of Jerry Lee Lewis' life was Nick Tosches' biography, *Hellfire* (New York, Dell Publishing, 1982). It is a written in a wonderfully baroque and florid style befitting its subject. Also useful is the Arena/BBC documentary film *The Jerry Lee Lewis Story*, which includes the full religious rant that preceeded the recording of *Great Balls of Fire*, as quoted in the chapter. Not always accurate (nor intended to be) but always entertaining is the 1989 feature film co-written and directed by Jim McBride, *Great Balls of Fire*. It is based on the book of the same name by Lewis' teen bride Myra Gale Brown.

The best account of the life of Alan Freed is *Big Beat Heat* by John A. Jackson (New York, Schirmer Books/Macmillan, 1991). Also useful was Glenn C. Altchuler's *All Shook Up – How Rock and Roll Changed America* (New York, Oxford University Press, 2003). The Elton John quote is from his *Me* (Henry Holt and Company, 2019). David Halberstam's *The Fifties* (New York/Toronto, Random House, 1993) contains an excellent account of the payola scandals and is a terrific history of the politics and culture of the decade. Further information on Dj's and the politics of payola was found in Arnold Passman's *The Deejays* (New York, Macmillan, 1971).

Louie Louie and the FBI

There is a pop cultural treasure trove of material about *Louie Louie*. The definitive work on the song is *Louie Louie – The History and Mythology of the World's Most Famous Rock 'n Roll Song* by Dave Marsh ((New York, Hyperion 1993). 255 pages of elegant and amusing prose dedicated to *Louie Louie.* If your preference is for an extensive website dedicated to all things *Louie Louie,* go to The Louie Report (www.louielouie.net) where there are dozens of stories about the history and relevance of the song, including, of course, the investigation of it by the FBI. The blogmaster, Eric Predoehl, hosts "International *Louie* Day", and has also been in production on a documentary film about the song for many years, but although extensive credits rivaling those of *Star Wars* are listed on the website, the film, as of this writing still does not appear to have been completed or released.

Taboo Tunes—A History of Banned Bands and Censored Songs by Peter Bletcha (San Francisco: Backbeat Books, 2004) tells the sordid tale of *Louie Louie. The FBI Investigated the Song 'Louie Louie' for Two Years* by Rose Eveleth examines the song in the erudite *Smithsonian* Magazine (May 23, 2013) as does the less erudite but more amusing Dave Berry in numerous articles in the Miami *Herald* including *The Birth of Wail* (April 29, 2007).

Van Halen

Source material for the early Pasadena years of the Van Halen story was the definitive *Van Halen Rising* by Greg Renoff (Toronto: ECW Press, 2015). Noel E. Monk picks up the story once he became road manager and then manager of the group in his excellent memoir *Running' With the Devil* (New York: Dey Street/Harper Collins, 2017). David Lee Roth tells the story from his point of view in *Crazy From the Heat* (New York: Hyperion, 1997)

Also useful was a long interview with Edward Van Halen titled *Is Rock 'n Roll about Reinvention?* produced by the Smithsonian Natural History Museum of American History and Zocalo Public Square. It can be found online.

Michael Jackson

Source material for the chapter on the woes of Michael Jackson is primarily from *The Final Years of Michael Jackson* by Ian Halperin (Montreal: Transit Publishing, 2009). Also useful to the story were *Michael Jackson—Did He Do It?* By Susan Schindehette and others (*People* Magazine, December 8, 2003), *Troubled Times in Neverland* by Christian Cotroneo (*Toronto Star,* November 23, 2003), *Singer's Grip on Reality Was Relinquished a Long Time Ago* by Ben Rayner (*Toronto Star,* November 20, 2003) , and *The Man in the Mirror: Peter Pan* by Alexandra Gill (*The Globe and Mail,* April 20, 2004)

6. But Wait – There's More

Sir Paul McCartney

There are hundreds of books about the Beatles, fewer about McCartney's life as an ex-Beatle. One of the most comprehensive and useful books about the history of the fab four is the massive, beautifully illustrated *The Beatles Anthology* by John Lennon, Paul McCartney, George Harrison, Ringo Starr, Neil Aspinall, Sir George Martin and Derek Taylor (San Francisco: Chronicle Books LLC, 2000).

By far the most useful source material for this chapter was the excellent *Paul McCartney—The Life* by Philip Norman (New York: Back Bay Books, 2016). Information about the purported connection between Yoko Ono and Paul's bust in Japan is from the website rec.music.beatles. Also useful was *A Primer on Paul McCartney's Complicated History With—and Triumphant Return to—Japan* by Joshua Mellin (*Flood* Magazine, November 14, 2018).

Philip Norman reports that Paul McCartney has written a memoir of his incarceration in Kosuge Prison in Japan, but to date it has not been publicly released.

Fans, Groupies and the Death of a Blues Brother

Pamela Des Barres tells the story of her colorful career as a rock groupie in *I'm With the Band: Confessions of a Groupie* (Chicago: Chicago Review Press, 1987) and chronicles the lives of other celebrated groupies in *Let's Spend the Night Together* (Chicago Review Press, 2007). If you want more Des Barres, she voraciously posts tales of her career on Instagram.

The definitive book on the death of John Belushi is Bob Woodward's *Wired – The Short Life and Fast Times of John Belushi* (New York: Simon & Schuster, 1984). It was surprising subject matter for this most famous of Washington political reporters, and though he seems somewhat out of his element, it is a very well-researched and well-written book.

Cathy Evelyn Smith tells her own story in her honest and very readable memoir *Chasing the Dragon* (Toronto: Key Porter Books, 1984). Information about the years she spent with Gordon Lightfoot are sourced from *Lightfoot* by Nicholas Jennings (Toronto: Viking – Penguin Random House, 2017). Robbie Robertson describes the years she spent with The Band (né Levon and the Hawks) in his excellent *Testimony* (Toronto: Alfred A. Knoff, 2016). Also useful was the article *The Investigation Centers on a Burnt-Out Case, Cathy 'Silverbag' Smith* by Michael Small (*People* Magazine, July 19, 1982). *Outlaw Blues: Adventures in the Counter-Culture Wars* by Jonathon Taplin (Los Angeles: Annenberg Press Innovation Lab Series, 2011) is a very unusual and interesting electronic book/multi-media project that was useful for this and other chapters of the book.

Charlie Manson

Charles Manson's sordid life is described in detail in the brilliant biography, *Manson—The Life and Times of Charles Manson* by Jeff Guinn (New York: Simon & Schuster, 2013).

The Twenty-Seven Club

Source material for Robert Johnson was *Remastered: Devil at the Crossroads* written by Jeff and Michael Zimbalist, directed by Brian Oakes (2019: Netflix) and *The Search for Robert Johnson* produced and directed by Chris Hunt *(1991*: Iambic Productions, Channel 4).

The many sources listed for the chapter on the Rolling Stones were also used as source material for the death of Brian Jones. Most useful of these were *Up and Down With the Rolling Stones* by Tony

Sanchez (John Blake Publishing, 2010) and *Life in Pictures—The Rolling Stones* by Susan Hill (Bath, UK: Parragon, 2012)

Source material for the story of Jim Morrison came from three books: *The Doors* by The Doors with Ben Fong-Torres (New York: Hyperion Books, 2006), *The Doors Unhinged* by John Densmore (North Charleston, SC: Percussive Press, 2013) and *No One Here Gets Out Alive* by Jerry Hopkins and Danny Sugarman (New York: Plexus Publishing/Grand Central Publishing, 1980). Essential viewing for another perspective on Morrison is the feature film *The Doors*, written by J.Randal Johnson and Oliver Stone, directed by Oliver Stone, produced by Bill Graham, Sasha Hatari and A. Kitman Ho and released by Tri-Star Pictures (1991).

The story of Janis Joplin's last days is found in the film of her last tour, *Festival Express* produced by Gavin and Willem Poolman and John Trapman, directed by Frank Citanovitch and Bob Smeaton, THINKFilm, 2003) and in *Piece of My Heart: A Portrait of Janis Joplin* by David Dalton (New York: Da Capo Press, 1991). Also useful is the 1974 Canadian-made, Golden Globe-nominated feature documentary *Janis* written by Howard Alk and Seaton Findlay, directed by Howard Alk, produced by Budge Crawley, released by Universal Pictures (1974).

The main source for the the story of Kurt Cobain and Courtney Love is the documentary film *Kurt & Courtney* written, directed, narrated and produced by Nick Broomfield (1998: Capitol Films, BBC, available on Netflix). Also useful were *Strange Love: The Story of Kurt Cobain and Courtney Love* by Lynn Hirschberg (*Vanity Fair*, September, 1992) and *A Big Juicy Fuckup for Hissyfit-Having Little Girls Who Hate Being Little Girls* by Amy Phillips (*Village Voice*, February 17, 2004)

The complete, definitive chronicle of Amy Winehouse's short life is *The Amy Winehouse Story* by Nick Johnstone (London: Omnibus Press, 2011).

Songs About The Man

33 Revolutions Per Minute by Dorian Lynsky (New York: Harper Collins e-books, 2018) provided information for some of the songs celebrated in this final chapter.

Information on *Cop Killer* and Body Count is from *Original Gangstas - The Untold Story of Dr. Dre, Eazy-E, Ice Cube, Tupac Shakur and the Birth of West Coast Rap* by Ben Westhoff (Hachette, 2017)

Part of the story of *Jailhouse Rock* was researched in *The Elvis Atlas—A Journey Through Elvis Presley's America* by Michael Gray and Roger Osbourne (New York; Henry Holt, 1996).

The story of Joe Hill, the political activist, and *I Dreamed I Saw Joe Hill*, the song, are told in *Talkin' Bout a Revolution—Music and Social Change in America* by Dick Weissman (New York: Backbeat Books, 2010) Joe Hill's life is also told in much greater detail in *The Man Who Never Died – The Life, Times and Legacy of Joe Hill, American Labor Icon* by William M. Adler (New York: Bloomsbury, 2011)

The story of *I Fought the Law* is told in *I Fought the Law—The Life and Strange Death of Bobby Fuller* by Miriam Linna and Randell Fuller (New York: Kicks Books, 2014).

The creation of Neil Young's two songs about The Man are chronicled in *For What It's Worth: Inside Buffalo Springfield's Classic Protest Song* by David Browne (*Rolling Stone,* November 11, 2016) and *Neil Young's Ohio—The Greatest Protest Record* by Dorian Lynsky (*The Guardian,* May 6, 2010)

The background of Randy Newman's *Jolly Coppers on Parade* and the use of the song in the musical *The Education of Randy Newman* is described in *Randy Newman's American Dreams* by Kevin Courrier (Toronto: ECW Press, 2005).

Finally, the story of *La Marseillaise* was researched from *Story of La Marseillaise* by Benjamin Stevens (Boston: The Musical Record, 1896 (retrieved 2012) and *What are the Lyrics to the French National*

Anthem, La Marseillaise—And What Do They Mean? by Maddy Shaw Roberts (*classicfm.com*, February 1, 2019). The description of the feelings of the French about the song following the ISIS attack on the Eagles of Death Metal concert is from *Simon Schama Explains La Marseillaise* (*BBC News*, November 17, 2015).

Bibliography

1965: The Most Revolutionary Year in Music by Andrew Grant Jackson (New York: Thomas Dunne Books, 2015)

All Shook Up – How Rock and Roll Changed America by Glenn C.Altschuler (Oxford: Oxford University Press, 2003)

Altamont – The Rolling Stones, The Hells Angels, and the Inside Story of Rock's Darkest Day by Joel Selvin (Dey St/Harper Collins Publishers, 2016)

And a Voice to Sing With by Joan Baez (New York: Penguin Books, 1987)

Another Side of Bob Dylan by Victor Maymudes (New York: St. Martin's Press, 2014)

Awopbopaloobop Alopbamboom by Nik Cohn (London:Weidenfeld & Nicholson, 1969)

Before They Made Me Run: Keith Richards and the Bust That Saved the Rolling Stones by Jason Schneider (Toronto: Electric Books, 2015)

Beyond Reason by Margaret Trudeau (Toronto: Grosset & Dunlap, 1979)

Big Beat Heat by John A. Jackson (New York:Schirmer Books, 1991)

Billie Holiday—Wishing on the Moon by Donald Clarke (Cambridge, MA: Da Capo Press, 2000)

Bing Crosby—A Pocketful of Dreams by Gary Giddins (Boston: Back Bay Books, 2001)

Bound for Glory by Woody Guthrie (New York: Plume/Penguin Books, 1943)

Brown Eyed Handsome Man—The Life and Hard Times of Chuck Berry by Bruce Pegg (New York: Routledge, 2002)

Buffy Sainte-Marie—The Authorized Biography by Andrea Warner (Vancouver/Berkeley: Greystone Books, 2018)

Cannabis—The Illegalization of Weed in America by Box Brown (New York: First Second Books, 2019)

Chasing the Dragon by Cathy Smith (Toronto: Key Porter Books, 1984)

Chasing the Scream—The First and Last Days of the Drug War by Johann Hari (New York: Bloomsbury Publishing, 2015)

Chronicles Volume One by Bob Dylan (London: Simon & Schuster, 2004)

Clapton by Eric Clapton (New York: Three Rivers Press, 2007)

Crazy From the Heat by David Lee Roth (New York: Hyperion, 1997)

Devil's Music, Holy Rollers and Hillbillies by James A. Cosby (Jefferson, NC: McFarland and Company, 2016)

Frank Sinatra by Chris Rojek (Cambridge, UK: Polity Press, 2004)

Frank Sinatra: The Dark Story of His Mafia Connections by James Bankes (Amazon Kindle, 2015)

Gimme Some Truth – The John Lennon FBI Files by Jon Wiener (Berkeley: University of California Press, 1999)

Hellfire by Nick Tosches (New York: Dell Publishing, 1982)

His Way—The Unauthorized Biography of Frank Sinatra by Kitty Kelley (New York: Random House, 1986)

How Music Works by David Byrne (San Francisco: McSweeney's, 2012)

How The Beatles Rocked the Kremlin by Leslie Woodhead (New York: Bloomsbury, 2013)

I am Brian Wilson by Brian Wilson with Ben Greenman (New York: Random House, 2016)

I Fought the Law—The Life and Strange Death of Bobby Fuller by Miriam Linna and Randell Fuller (New York: Kicks Books, 2014)

I, Shithead by Joe Keithley (Vancouver: Arsenal Pulp Press, 2003)

I'm With the Band: Confessions of a Groupie by Pamela Des Barres (Chicago: Chicago Review Press, 1987)

I'm Your Man—The Life of Leonard Cohen by Sylvie Simmons (Toronto: McClelland & Stewart, 2012)

I Put a Spell on You by Nina Simone (New York: Da Capo Press, 2003)

John Lennon – The Illustrated Biography by Garth Thomas (Croxley Green, UK: Transatlantic Press, 2008)

Josephine Baker: The Hungry Heart by Jean Claude Baker and Chris Chase (New York: Cooper Square Press, 1993)

Keith Richards by Victor Bockris (Poseidon Press, 1992)

Lady Sings The Blues by Billie Holiday and William Duffy (New York: Doubleday, 1956)

Lennon Legend: An Illustrated life of John Lennon by James Henke (San Francisco: Chronicle Books, 2003)

Let's Spend the Night Together by Pamela Des Barres (Chicago: Chicago Review Press, 2007)

Life by Keith Richards and James Fox (New York: Little, Brown and Company, 2010)

Life in Pictures—The Rolling Stones by Susan Hill (Bath, UK: Parragon, 2012)

Lightfoot by Nicholas Jennings (Toronto: Penguin Canada, 2017)

Louie Louie – The History and Mythology of the World's Most Famous Rock 'n Roll Song by Dave Marsh (New York: Hyperion 1993)

Makeba—My Story by Miriam Makeba with James Hall (New York: Plume/New American Library, 1987)

Manson—The Life and Times of Charles Manson by Jeff Guinn (New York: Simon & Schuster, 2013)

Me by Elton John (New York: Henry Holt and Company, 2019)

Mick – The Wild Life and Mad Genius of Jagger by Christopher Anderson (New York: Gallery Books, 2012)

Miles—The Autobiography by Miles Davis with Quincy Troupe (New York: Simon & Schuster, 1989)

Moanin' at Midnight by James Segrest and Mark Hoffman (New York: Pantheon Books, 2004)

Music & Politics by John Street (Cambridge, UK: Polity Press, 2012)

Music: A Subversive History by Ted Gioia (New York: Basic Books, 2019)

My House of Memories by Merle Haggard (New York: Harper Collins, 1999)

Mystery Train by Greil Marcus (Plume/Penguin, 1975)

Narcocorrido: A Journey into the Music of Drugs, Guns and Guerrillas by Elijah Wald (Rayo/Harper Collins, 2001)

No One Here Gets Out Alive by Jerry Hopkins and Danny Sugarman (New York: Plexus Publishing/Grand Central Publishing, 1980)

Now You're Talking—The Story of Human Conversation from the Neanderthals to Artificial Intelligence by Trevor Cox (London: Vintage / The Bodley Head, 2018)

Original Gangstas - The Untold Story of Dr. Dre, Eazy-E, Ice Cube, Tupac Shakur and the Birth of West Coast Rap by Ben Westhoff (Hachette, 2017)

Outlaw Blues: Adventures in the Counter-Culture Wars by Jonathon Taplin (Los Angeles: Annenberg Press Innovation Lab Series, 2011)

Paul McCartney—The Life by Philip Norman (New York: Back Bay Books, 2016)

Paul Robeson—Biography of a Proud Man by Joseph Nazel (New York: Holloway House Publishing, 1980)

Paul Robeson—The Man and His Mission by Ron Ramdin (London: Peter Owen Publishers, 1992)

Pete Seeger vs The Un-Americans—A Tale of the Blacklist by Edward Renehan (Wickford, RI: New Street Communications, 2014)

Phil Spector—Out of His Head by Richard Williams (London: Omnibus Press, 2003

Positively 4th Street by David Hajdu (New York: Picador, 2001)

Revolution in the Head by Ian Macdonald (Chicago: Chicago Review Press, 2007)

Running' With the Devil by Noel E. Monk with Joe Layden (New York: Dey Street/Harper Collins, 2017)

Sinatra—The Chairman by James Kaplan (New York: Doubleday, 2015)

Sing It—A Biography of Pete Seeger by Meryl Danziger (New York/Oakland: Seven Stories Press, 2016)

Songs of America: Patriotism, Protest and the Music That Made a Nation by Jon Meacham and Tim McGraw (Random House, 2019)

Story of La Marseillaise by Benjamin Stevens (Boston: The Musical Record, 1896 (retrieved 2012)

S.T.P— A Journey Through America with the Rolling Stones by Robert Greenfield (Cambridge, MA: Da Capo Press, 1974)

Taboo Tunes—A History of Banned Bands and Censored Songs by Peter Bletcha (San Francisco: Backbeat Books, 2004)

Tales From Beyond the Tap by Randy Bachman (Toronto: Viking/Penguin Canada Books, 2014

Talk-Action=Zero by Joe Keithley (Vancouver: Arsenal Pulp Press, 2011)

Talkin' 'Bout a Revolution—Music and Social Change in America by Dick Weissman (Milwaukee: Backbeat Books, 2010)

Testimony by Robbie Robertson (Toronto: Alfred A. Knoff, 2016)

The Amy Winehouse Story by Nick Johnstone (London: Omnibus Press, 2011)

The Beatles by Bob Spitz (New York: Little Brown, 2005

The Beatles Anthology by John Lennon, Paul McCartney, George Harrison, Ringo Starr, Neil Aspinall, Sir George Martin and Derek Taylor (San Francisco: Chronicle Books LLC, 2000)

The Dirt: Confessions of the World's Most Notorious Rock Band by Mötley Crüe (Tommy Lee, Neil Strauss, Nikki Stix, Mick Mars, Vince Neil) (New York: Dey Street Books, 2002)

The Doors by The Doors with Ben Fong-Torres (New York: Hyperion Books, 2006)

The Doors Unhinged by John Densmore (North Charleston, SC: Percussive Press, 2013)

The Elvis Atlas—A Journey Through Elvis Presley's America by Michael Gray and Roger Osbourne (New York; Henry Holt, 1996)

The Final Years of Michael Jackson by Ian Halperin (Montreal: Transit Publishing, 2009)

The FBI War on Tupac Shakur and Black Leaders by John Potash (Baltimore: Progressive Left Press, 2007)

The Life and Legend of Leadbelly by Charles Wolfe and Kip Lornell (New York: Da Capo Press / Harper Collins, 1992)

The Lives of John Lennon by Albert Goldman (New York: William Morrow, 1988)

The Man Who Never Died – The Life, Times and Legacy of Joe Hill, American Labor Icon by William M. Adler (New York: Bloomsbury, 2011)

The Mammoth Book of the Rolling Stones by Sean Egan (London: Constable & Robinson, 2013)

The Mourning of John Lennon by Anthony Elliott (Berkeley, CA: University of California Press, 1999)

The Pop, Rock and Soul Reader by David Brackett (Oxford: Oxford University Press, 2005

The Rock and Roll Hall of Fame – The First 25 Years Edited by Holly George-Warren (Collins Design 2009)

The Rest is Noise—Listening to the Twentieth Century by Alex Ross (New York: Farrar, Strauss and Giroux, 2007)

The Sixties—Years of Hope/Days of Rage by Todd Gitlin (New York: Bantam Books, 1987)

The Whole World in His Hands—a Pictorial Biography of Paul Robeson by Susan Robeson (Secaucus, NJ: Citadel Press, 1985)

This Land is Your Land—Woody Guthrie and the Journey of an American Folksong by Robert Santelli (Philadelphia: Running Press Book Publishers, 2012)

Trumped!-The Inside Story of the Real Donald Trump—His Cunning Rise and Spectacular Fall by John R. O'Donnell with James Rutherford (New York: Crossroad Press, 2016)

Unbelievable—The Life, Death and Afterlife of The Notorious B.I.G. by Cheo Hodari Coker (New York: VIBE Books, 2003)

Understanding Media: The Extensions of Man by Marshall McLuhan (Cambridge, MA: MIT Press, 1994)

Up and Down With the Rolling Stones by Tony Sanchez (John Blake Publishing, 2010)

Van Halen Rising by Greg Renoff (Toronto: ECW Press, 2015)

Waging Heavy Peace by Neil Young (Blue Rider Press, 2012)

When Paris Sizzled by Mary McAuliffe (Lanham, MD: Rowman & Littlefield, 2016)

Who I Am by Pete Townsend (HarperCollins Publishers, 2012)

Wired – The Short Life and Fast Times of John Belushi by Bob Woodward (New York: Simon & Schuster, 1984)

Why Bob Dylan Matters by Richard F. Thomas (New York: Dey Street Books, 2017)

Why The Monkees Matter by Rosanne Welch (Jefferson, NC: McFarland & Company, 2016)

Acknowledgments

First, my thanks to my agent, Maryann Karinch, who has supported and championed the book from the beginning and shepherded it through to publication.

Phillippa Baran was my most diligent and enthusiastic beta-reader, taking time out of the creation of her own book to carefully highlight for me all the misused present participles and misplaced commas of my prose, and providing very valuable advice.

I received early assistance from fellow non-fiction writers Ken McGoogan, Jason Schoonover and William J. Mann. All three were helpful in the process of getting an agent and a publisher, and enthusiastically encouraged the project.

Will O'Hara, Aaron Fenton and Ashley Rowe were three beta-readers who provided very useful notes and advice during the writing of the book.

Barry Pearson, Tom Barlow, Carolyn Rowe, Travis Steffens and Brianna Rowe provided helpful advice on the writing and publication of the book.

I am grateful to Councillor Joe Keithley of the City of Burnaby, aka Joey Shithead of the band D.O.A., for the interview he gave me about his life in punk rock and politics.

Also most helpful were the librarians at the University of Toronto Music Library and the Toronto Public Library who helped me dig out valuable information about the history of music.

Finally, my sincere thanks to Judith Bailey and her colleagues at Armin Lear Press for publishing and promoting the book.

Index

Abtey, Jacques, 107-109, 111-112

Ackroyd, Dan, 72, 397-398

Agnew, Spiro, 268, 289-291

Allen, Steve, 220-221, 305,

Allende, Salvadore, 41, 43, 224, 458

Altamont Speedway Free Festival, 12, 57-63, 225, 340, 413, 458, 474

Anka, Paul, 165

Anslinger, Harry, 149-158

Apollo, 2, 11, 323

Apollo Theater, 138

A$AP, 262-264

Auschwitz, 215

Baez, Joan, 5, 233-235, 440, 445, 455, 464, 474

Bach, Johann Sebastian, 16-17, 177, 188

Baker, Josephine, 100-119, 122, 460

Baker, Susan, 84

Balin, Marty, 60-61

Bankhead, Tallulah, 148-149, 155

Barrientos, Lieutenant Pedro, 42-43

Beach Boys, 165, 334, 409-411

Beatles, 3, 8, 21, 26-39, 44-45, 48, 50, 52, 130, 184, 192, 199-206, 236, 276, 326, 369-387, 394, 407, 411, 413-414, 424, 457, 459, 462, 469, 476, 479

Beck, Jeff, 19
Bèdard, Rita, 72-73
Bee Gees, 16
Beethoven, Ludvig van, 16-18, 188, 214, 216
Belli, Melvin, 58
Belushi, John, 390, 392, 397-402
Berry, Chuck, 18, 27, 33, 45, 159-175, 263, 307-310, 321, 323, 327, 462
Berry, Richard, 327-336
Black, Shirley Temple, 83
Blackbird, 236-237
Blair, Tony, 74-75
Blues Brothers, 397
Bogart, Humphrey, 276-277, 291, 453
Bonaparte, Napoleon 18, 119, 453
Bono, 268, 437
Bono, Sonny, 86-87
Brezhnev, Leonid, 201
Buffalo, 294, 321, 390
Burgess, Anthony, 18
Bush, George W., 257
Caravaggio, Michelangelo, 3
Carey, Mariah, 21
Carmichael, Stokeley, 222-223
Carter, Bill, 66
Casablanca, 104, 453
Casanova, Giacomo, 17
Cash, Johnny, 19, 95, 136, 304, 449
Castrati, 16
Castro, Fidel, 69, 116, 129, 223, 282, 441
Cellini, Benvenuto, 13-14
Chapman, Mark David, 39
Clark, Dick, 159

Cobain, Kurt, 418, 433-434

Cohen, Leonard, 145, 159, 240, 476, 496

Cohn, Roy, 231

Cole, Nat King, 167,

Copland, Aaron, 190-191

Coppola, Francis Ford, 216-217

Christgau, Robert, 56, 367

Darwin, Charles 5-6, 456

Davis, Miles, 177, 179, 221, 477

De Gaulle, Charles, 100, 108, 112

Dionysus, 2-3

Disco Demolition Night, 4

Dixie Chicks, 258

D.O.A., 85-98, 459, 483

Domino, Fats, 27, 33, 300

Dorsey, Tommy, 268-269

Driberg, Tom, 51-54

Dylan, Bob, 131, 145, 226, 232-236, 240, 247, 312, 389, 392-395, 409, 464, 475

Eagles, 64, 260, 345

Eagles of Death, 5

Eisenhower, Dwight, 191, 263, 304, 317

El Mocambo Tavern, 67-73, 458

Epstein, Brian, 30, 45, 375-376

Escalante, Janice, 168-170

Faithful, Marianne, 50, 55, 77, 432

Falconbridge, Alexander, 21, 456

FBI, 24, 27, 36-39, 49-50, 114, 117, 122-123, 139, 169-170, 191, 223, 230, 235, 240-241,266, 268, 270, 274-275, 279, 285-286, 291, 311-312, 319, 325-336, 407,418, 426-427, 432, 457, 475

Fleetwood Mac, 345

Freed, Alan, 3, 165, 293-321

Gardner, Ava, 275-276

Garrett, Peter, 86-87

Gesualdo, Carlo, 14
Giancana, Sam, 277-286
Gillespie, Dizzy, Frontispiece, 226
Ginsberg, Allan, 33, 52, 83
Goebbels, Joseph, 213-214, 216,
Graham, Bill, 57-58, 471
Grande, Ariana, 5
Grateful Dead, 50, 57, 59-61, 429
Grayburn, Judge Lloyd, 71-72
Guthrie, Arlo, 94,
Guthrie, Woody, 94, 139, 229-230
Harvest Music Festival, 5
Haley, Bill, 27, 455
Harrison, George, 28, 31, 50, 130, 204, 370-371, 375-377, 412
Havel, Václav, 79-84
Hawkins, Ronnie, 34, 389-390
Haydn, Joseph, 16
Hemingway, Ernest, 104, 107,
Hendrix, Jimi, 2, 17, 388-389, 418, 428, 430-433, 496
Hill, Joe, 126, 193, 445, 472
Hitler, Adolf, 2, 29, 106, 188, 210-217, 270, 371, 404
Hlavsa, Milan, 80, 83
Holiday, Billie, 2, 71, 142-158, 450-451
Holly, Buddy, 307, 315, 326, 445
Hoover, J. Edgar, 2, 24, 26, 36, 49, 114, 127, 145, 149, 223, 267, 279, 286, 332-333
Hope, Bob, 148
Houston, Whitney, 21
Howlin' Wolf 13, 45
Humphrey, Hubert, 268, 288-289
I Fought The Law, 445-447
Jackson, Janet, 21,
Jackson, Michael, 21, 353-367, 468

Jagger, Mick, 44-78, 118, 211, 241, 255, 375, 388, 408, 420-422, 432, 458,

Japan, 32, 108, 115, 121, 204, 355, 373-374, 381-384, 469

Jara, Victor, 3, 40-43, 224, 283, 455,458

Jirous, Ivan, 80, 83

Jefferson Airplane, 50, 60-61, 432, 496

John, Elton, 75, 92-93, 203, 226, 305, 320, 384, 467

Johnson, Frank, 22

Johnson, Robert, 20, 418-421, 470

Johnson, Lyndon Baines, 277, 279, 288-289, 455

Jones, Brian, 3, 50, 52-53, 56, 69, 387, 418, 470

Joplin, Janis, 418, 428-430, 471,

Keithley, Joe, 85-98, 459, 483

Kennedy, Joe, 278-279

Kennedy, John F., 13, 66, 116, 199, 221, 268, 277, 278-289, 290-291,

Kennedy, Robert, 117, 266, 278-283, 331

King, Dr. Martin Luther, 40, 115-116, 127, 179-180, 235, 283, 332, 455

King Henry V, 15

King Pentheus, 3

Klein, Allan, 58, 376-377,

Krasner, Lee, 3

Kremlin 184-209, 459, 462

Kubrick, Stanley, 18

Kweskin, Jim, 5, 136

La Marseillaise, 104, 110-112, 452-454, 472-473

Lang, Michael 58-59

Leadbelly, 13, 130-141, 230, 461

Lennon, John, 2, 26-39, 44, 57, 159, 202, 208, 268, 283, 369-377, 383, 388, 413, 432, 454, 457, 469

Lennon, Julia, 26-27

Lennon, Julian, 38

Lewis, Jerry Lee, 167, 292-326, 466

Lincoln, Abraham, 147, 191, 257,

Little Richard, 33,-34, 296, 305, 323, 431,
Lomax, John, 136-140
Los Tigres del Norte, 245-246
Louie Louie, 326-336, 467
Love, Courtney, 433-435, 471
LSD, 31, 33, 48-50, 60, 128, 422
Lucas, George, 60
Luciano, Lucky, 273-274
Maillard, Carol, 238
Malcolm X, 127, 180, 283
Maltz, Albert, 271, 280-281
Manchester, William, 13
Mandela, Nelson, 94, 221, 225-226, 437
Makeba, Miriam, 181, 218-227, 463
Manley, Michael, 440-441
Manson, Charles, 328, 403-417, 446, 448, 470
Marley, Bob, 440-443
Martin, Dean, 277, 285-287
Martin, George, 30, 377, 469,
McCarthy, Senator Joe, 114, 126, 231
McCartney, Paul, 28, 32, 38, 69, 75, 205-206, 226, 236, 369-385
McLuhan, Marshall, 35, 456
Memphis, 22-23, 65, 165, 298, 304-305, 312, 314, 322, 325
Merkel, Angela, 18
Miami, 113, 280, 320, 382, 386, 425-428, 447, 467
Mitchell, John, 37
Monk, Noel, 347-352
Monroe, Marilyn, 222, 277, 282-283, 416
Morrison, Jim, 2, 17, 34, 388, 418, 422-428, 471
Mozart, Wolfgang Amadeus, 16-17, 19
Narcocorridos, 443-453, 464
Nero, 12
Newman, Randy, 449

Newport Folk/Jazz Festival, 5, 177, 233
Nitzsche, Jack, 241
Noriega, Manuel, 446-447
Nuwās, Abū, 10
Ochs, Phil, 3, 43, 392, 445,
Oldham, Andrew Loog, 45, 420
Ono, Yoko, 32-39, 208, 376, 383-384, 469
Osbourne, Ozzy, 16, 346
Paderewski, Ignacy Jan, 86-87
Paganini, Niccolò, 19-20
Pallenberg, Anita, 63, 68-72, 241, 421
Palin, Sarah, 257, 259
Patton, General George, 110-111
Paul Revere and the Raiders, 328, 332, 410
Payola, 303, 317-321, 326, 467
Peace Arch Park Concert, 96, 126-127
Peekskill Riots, 123-126, 230
Pelyushonok, Yuri, 202
Phillips, Sam, 22-23, 298, 304-306, 312-313,
Pied Piper of Hamelin, 13, 310
Pinochet, General Augusto, 41-43
Pitt, Brad, 410
Plastic People, 79-84, 459
Plato, 10
Plow My Vulva, 7-8
Pollock, Jackson, 3
Pope John XXII, 14
Pope Gregory I, 15
Pope Gregory XVI, 20
Presley, Elvis, 23-24, 240, 294, 298, 312, 315, 370, 444, 454-455
Prince Charles, 76-77
Princess Diana, 76
Princess Margaret, 52, 55, 75

Pussy Riot, 2, 184, 206-209, 463

Putin, Vladimir, 2, 18, 184, 206-209, 463

Queen Elizabeth II, 32, 52, 75,

Rasputin, 193, 449-450

Reagan, Ronald, 256-257, 268, 289, 291, 465

Reagon, Bernice Johnson, 237-239

Reed, Lou, 2, 83

Richards, Keith, 17, 44-78, 160, 375, 390, 395, 418, 420-421, 458

Richards, Marlon, 64, 68, 70

Robertson, Robbie, 234

Robeson, Paul, 3, 4, 96, 120-129, 189, 223, 230, 437, 445, 460

Rogosin, Lionel, 220-221

Rolling Stones, 4, 44-78, 225, 238, 254-264, 340, 347, 376, 387, 395-396, 399, 420-422, 458

Roosevelt, Franklin D., 216, 268, 271

Rose, Axl, 16, 416

Roselli, Johnny, 267

Rosner, Eddie, 197-199

Rossini, Gioachino, 16, 19, 454

Roth, David Lee, 337-352

Rush, 260-261

Sainte-Marie, Buffy, 239-242

Sánchez, Rosalino "Chalino", 248-250

Sanchez, "Spanish Tony", 51, 54, 64, 458

Santana, Carlos, 19, 61

Seeger, Pete, 43, 94, 138-139, 145, 230-232, 445, 463

Shostakovich, Dmitri, 184-192, 454, 462

Siegel, Bugsy, 273-274

Simon, Paul, 225, 240

Simone, Nina, 176-182, 221, 225-226, 462

Sinatra, Dolly, 266-267, 269

Sinatra, Frank, 2, 4, 14, 127, 142, 199, 212, 221-223, 256, 266-291, 298, 300, 384, 389, 450, 466

Slick, Grace, 60

Smith Cathy Evelyn, 68, 389-402

Sneiderman, David, 49-50, 53

Socrates, 10

Sondheim, Stephen, 444,

Spector, Phil, 13, 38, 45, 86, 238, 241

Springsteen, Bruce, 43, 145, 256-257, 445, 465

Squamish Five, 91

Stalin, Joseph, 123, 184-199, 207,

Starr, Ringo, 30, 201, 237, 372, 374, 377, 383, 469

Stilyagi, 199

St.Louis, 101-102, 160-161, 163-164, 166, 168-169, 172, 402

Strauss, Richard, 213-216

Swaggart, Jimmy Lee, 295, 306-307, 324

Tharpe, Sister Rosetta, 292, 294

The $64,000 Question, 316

Thoreau, Henry David, 8

Toronto, 33-35, 47, 67-74, 82-83, 91, 127, 148, 208, 240, 323, 361, 390-395, 397, 399-400, 402, 429, 431-432, 447-448, 455

Toscanini, Arturo, 187

Touré, Skou, 222-225

Townsend, Pete, 411

Tromboncino, Bartolomeo, 14

Trudeau, Justin, 69, 262

Trudeau, Margaret, 69-71, 73, 393, 459

Trudeau, Pierre, 35, 69-71, 73, 459

Trump, Donald, 18, 209, 230-231, 254-264, 359, 465

Twenty-One, 316-317

Twenty-Seven Club, 418-438

Van Halen, 259, 337-352, 468

Vicious, Sid, 67

Wagner, Richard, 210-217

Van Doren, Charles, 316-317

War on Drugs, 3, 150-158, 461
Waters, Roger, 217
We Are The Champions, 8, 261
We Shall Overcome, 33, 229, 238, 455
Welles, Orson, 148,
White, Colonel George, 156-157
Wilder, Billy, 195, 286
Wilson, Paul, 80-82, 459
Winchell, Walter 114
Winehouse, Amy, 128, 418, 435-438, 471
Woods, Ronnie, 64-67, 396
Wonder, Stevie, 21, 159, 377
Wycliffe, John, 14
Wyman, Bill, 47, 63
Young, Neil, 204, 240, 261, 264, 391, 409, 447-449, 472
Xi, Zhu, 15
Zappa, Frank, 80, 83-84, 334, 388-389, 409

The Author

    Peter Rowe has been involved with music since the 1960s, when he was filming events like the Isle of Wight Festival, the Toronto Rock and Roll Revival, and concerts by the Jefferson Airplane and the Mothers of Invention. Performers he filmed in that era include John Lennon, Jimi Hendrix, Miles Davis, Leonard Cohen and Joni Mitchell. He also directed documentary profiles of the psychedelic soul band The Chambers Brothers and of famed New York disc jockey Cousin Brucie. Stories of his documentary and dramatic filming are described in his first book, Adventures in Filmmaking.

    Rowe has made over 190 films as a director, writer, or producer. His ten features include Treasure Island, starring Jack Palance, and The Best Bad Thing, starring George Takei. He filmed his best-known recent TV series, Angry Planet, in thirty different countries on all seven continents.

    Rowe also developed an interest in songwriting and singing, but that career had to be aborted after he lost one of his vocal chords after ingesting sulphuric acid while filming on top of a volcano in Vanuatu. Following the accident, Rowe has returned to other pursuits such as writing and painting. He can be found on Instagram and Facebook or at peter@peterrowe.tv.

www.ingramcontent.com/pod-product-compliance
Lightning Source LLC
Chambersburg PA
CBHW020046170426
43199CB00009B/191